A Theory of Legal Punishment

This book argues for a mixed theory of legal punishment that treats both crime reduction and retribution as important aims of the state.

A central question in the philosophy of law is why the state's punishment of its own citizens is justified. Traditionally, two theories of punishment have dominated the field: consequentialism and retributivism. According to consequentialism, punishment is justified when it maximizes positive outcomes. According to retributivism, criminals should be punished because they deserve it. This book recognizes the strength of both positions. According to the two-tiered model, the institution of punishment and statutory penalties, as set by the legislature, are justified based on their costs and benefits, in terms of deterrence and rehabilitation. The law exists to preserve the public order. Criminal courts, by contrast, determine who is punished and how much based on what offenders deserve. The courts express the community's collective sense of resentment at being wronged.

This book supports the two-tiered model by showing that it accords with our moral intuitions, commonly held (compatibilist) theories of freedom, and assumptions about how the extent of our knowledge affects our obligations. It engages classic and contemporary work in the philosophy of law and explains the theory's advantages over competing approaches from retributivists and other mixed theorists. The book also defends consequentialism against a longstanding objection that the social sciences give us little guidance regarding which policies to adopt. Drawing on recent criminological research, the two-tiered model can help us to address some of our most pressing social issues, including the death penalty, drug policy, and mass incarceration. This book will be of interest to philosophers, legal scholars, policymakers, and social scientists, especially criminologists, economists, and political scientists.

Matthew C. Altman is Professor of Philosophy at Central Washington University, USA. He is the author of *A Companion to Kant's "Critique of Pure Reason"* (2008) and *Kant and Applied Ethics* (2011), coauthor of *The Fractured Self in Freud and German Philosophy* (2013), editor of *The Palgrave Handbook of German Idealism* (2014) and *The Palgrave Kant Handbook* (2017), and series editor of *Palgrave Handbooks in German Idealism* and *Palgrave Handbooks in the Philosophy of Law*. He has also published numerous articles on applied ethics, philosophy of law, and the history of philosophy.

Routledge Research in Legal Philosophy

Procedural Justice and Relational Theory
Empirical, Philosophical, and Legal Perspectives
Edited by Denise Meyerson, Catriona Mackenzie, and Therese MacDermott

A Theory of Legal Punishment

Deterrence, Retribution, and the Aims of the State

Matthew C. Altman

Routledge
Taylor & Francis Group
LONDON AND NEW YORK

First published 2021
by Routledge
2 Park Square, Milton Park, Abingdon, Oxon OX14 4RN

and by Routledge
52 Vanderbilt Avenue, New York, NY 10017

Routledge is an imprint of the Taylor & Francis Group, an informa business

British Library Cataloguing-in-Publication Data
A catalogue record for this book is available from the British Library

Library of Congress Cataloging-in-Publication Data
Names: Altman, Matthew C., author.
Title: A theory of legal punishment: deterrence, retribution, and the aims of the state / Matthew C. Altman.
Description: Milton Park, Abingdon, Oxon; New York, NY: Routledge, 2021. | Series: Routledge research in legal philosophy |
Includes bibliographical references and index.
Identifiers: LCCN 2020049904 (print) | LCCN 2020049905 (ebook) | ISBN 9780367698102 (hardback) | ISBN 9781003143352 (ebook)
Subjects: LCSH: Punishment–Philosophy. | Criminal law–Philosophy. | Punishment in crime deterrence. | Lex talionis.
Classification: LCC K5103 .A477 2021 (print) | LCC K5103 (ebook) | DDC 364.601–dc23
LC record available at https://lccn.loc.gov/2020049904
LC ebook record available at https://lccn.loc.gov/2020049905

ISBN: 978-0-367-69810-2 (hbk)
ISBN: 978-0-367-69816-4 (pbk)
ISBN: 978-1-003-14335-2 (ebk)

Typeset in Galliard
by Deanta Global Publishing Services, Chennai, India

Contents

Preface

Punishment, like slavery, is a peculiar institution. We as a society deprive people of their freedom, have them perform forced labor, and sometimes even kill them,[1] yet we seldom give it a second thought. One big difference is that we punish people who are responsible for crimes rather than enslaving people because of their race. Following the American Civil War, with the country thinking about when we are justified in taking away people's freedom, the Thirteenth Amendment was enshrined in the U.S. Constitution: "Neither slavery nor involuntary servitude, except as a punishment for crime whereof the party shall have been duly convicted, shall exist within the United States, or any place subject to their jurisdiction." Slavery violates people's rights unless it is used as a form of legal punishment. There are different possible reasons for exempting criminals specifically from this prohibition, including the belief that they deserve hard treatment for their past acts or that the threat of hard treatment will deter potential criminals in the future. Historically, these two different lines of argument – retributivism and consequentialism – have dominated the philosophical conversation.

Recent developments, especially in the United States, are prompting us to reexamine the purpose and value of punishment. A punitive approach to criminality and exaggerated worries about public safety have led to a huge increase in the U.S. prison population since 1970, far outpacing population growth, changes in the crime rate, and incarceration rates in other countries. Prisoners are subjected to brutal conditions, including sexual violence, torture, and death, due to prison overcrowding, lack of funding, and lack of oversight. And the effectiveness and cost of capital punishment has come under scrutiny, with declining executions, recent abolitions and moratoriums, and near-record low levels of public support.

Historians can explain how these things have happened and social scientists can measure the effects on offenders and the community, but it is up to philosophers to determine whether a penal system is justified. Philosophers of law, in particular, investigate the normative foundations of law and reasons to punish. At its most useful, this sort of inquiry can give us moral standards to evaluate existing policies and guide reform efforts, if necessary. For example, because mass

1 … especially people of color in the American South. See Garland (2010).

incarceration is due in part to punitive practices such as increased sentences for drug possession and three-strikes laws, we ought to evaluate the theoretical justification of legal punishment in order to decide whether such practices further the cause of justice and the consequences are worth it.

This book adds to a growing body of philosophical research on punishment. Although a lot of excellent work has been done recently, many theorists fail to appreciate the implications of distinguishing punishment as an institution from the distribution of individual punishments, do not adequately take social scientific research into account, make overly general claims about people's supposed lack of responsiveness to incentives, and do not explicitly relate theories of punishment to the political institutions that would apply them. By identifying separate roles for the legislature and the criminal judiciary, I incorporate both consequentialism and retributivism into a mixed theory. Although there are key differences, the resulting two-tiered model of punishment echoes theories that were developed about seventy years ago. Many philosophers abandoned consequentialism in the 1970s, primarily because of concerns about the social sciences' lack of predictive power. However, with recent advances in criminology and a recognition that our current approach to punishment is failing, it is time to revive this tradition.

Acknowledgments

I have benefited greatly from conversations with scholars who have engaged my work at professional conferences. I presented shorter, early versions of chapters and parts of chapters at meetings of the Association for Practical and Professional Ethics, the Northwest Philosophy Conference, the International Kant Congress, and the World Congress of Philosophy.

Many people read and provided feedback on the manuscript. Cynthia Coe is the best philosopher I know, and her extensive help on this book throughout the process, both writing and revising, has been invaluable. Several other people made helpful suggestions on specific chapters relevant to their areas of expertise and their interests, and assisted me in refining my ideas: Reid Dale, Phillip Downes, Chad Flanders, Casie Grevé, Lowell Murphree, Roger Schaefer, Terrence Schwartz, Julia Stringfellow, Benjamin Vilhauer, and Wendy Williams.

Erin Bledsoe at the James E. Brooks Library at Central Washington University provided crucial research assistance in tracking down numerous books and articles, for this and other projects, over many years. Victoria Green also helped with information gathering.

Central Washington University gave me time off from teaching in the form of a sabbatical during fall 2019 and winter 2020. CWU's School of Graduate Studies and Research funded Faculty Research Appointments in winter 2019 and spring 2020.

My children, Lucy and Sam, are sources of daily inspiration. I am also grateful to my parents, Doug and Sheryl, and my sister, Lisa, for their continuing encouragement.

Finally, I would like to thank the three anonymous reviewers at Routledge for their comments, as well as senior editor Alison Kirk for her support of the project.

There is a stereotype of the isolated philosopher who, cloistered in his room, thinks great thoughts and writes them down so that others can partake of his wisdom. That has not been the case with me. A supportive group of professional colleagues, friends, and family members have been generous with their time and have helped make this book better than it otherwise would be. The errors in this book are mine, any insights of value are largely plagiarized – and so they should be since that is how knowledge grows, if it grows at all.[1]

1 I plagiarized this sentence, word for word, from N. Morris (1982, ix).

Introduction

Punishment, it seems, has always been with us. Gods have visited divine retribution on humanity and parents have corrected their children ever since there have been gods and parents. Legal punishment exists throughout the world. If a nation were to do away with punishment entirely, we would think it is at best a dangerous social experiment and at worst a devolution into anarchy. In *Brave New World*, Aldous Huxley imagines a world without punishment, where people are controlled by genetic engineering, drugs, propaganda, and social reinforcement. The cure is worse than the disease. History, literature, and common sense, as misguided as it sometimes is, all seem to be telling us that punishment is necessary if we want to have both individual freedom and social order.

The ubiquity of punishment makes it seem natural and hardly in need of justification. However, the things that we do to criminals would be wrong in just about any other context: forcibly taking their property (fines), putting them in cages (prison), and killing them when they pose no immediate threat (execution). Punishment also involves a number of normative claims that are not settled: about the wrongness of criminals' behavior, the value of society, the necessity of hard treatment, and the justice of enforcement. Practical philosophy can help to address these questions, not only because it includes the study of ethics and the foundation of law, but also because of philosophy's interdisciplinarity and the fact that several intersecting fields of research converge on the study of punishment. This book is an attempt to bring philosophical thinking to bear on punishment: to propose and defend a mixed theory, and to explain its real-world implications.

Two major theories

Although legal punishment had been addressed by prior philosophers, it only became a distinct object of philosophical scrutiny in the eighteenth century. Since then, two theories have dominated the conversation: consequentialism and retributivism. According to consequentialism, the state reduces crime by threatening potential criminals with punishment if they break the law (general deterrence). The actual imposition of punishment not only makes the threat credible, in general and in the minds of those who are punished (specific deterrence), but it also keeps criminals from committing other crimes (incapacitation) and improves their characters so they are less likely to reoffend upon release (rehabilitation).[1] Historically, the main proponents of consequentialism are Cesare Beccaria (1738–1794) and Jeremy Bentham (1747–1832), both of whom appeal to the principle of utility to justify the institution of punishment as a mechanism for maximizing overall happiness. As Beccaria puts it, punishment is justified only insofar as it is necessary for "defending the repository of the public well-being from the usurpations of individuals" (1995, 10). Although they defend the law as an incentive system to reduce crime, they also criticize contemporary penological practices, with Beccaria focused on the overuse of the death penalty (1995, 66–72) and Bentham focused on prison reform (1970, esp. ch. XII–XV [pp. 143–86]). If the same social aims can be achieved more effectively and with less suffering – with imprisonment instead of the death penalty and a more humane prison system that encourages moral improvement – then we ought to change the system.

Consequentialists evaluate a punishment or policy by comparing its consequences to the consequences of other options. We ought to do what produces the best outcomes. In this way, consequentialism is forward-looking. Different versions of consequentialism are distinguished by which ends they say we ought to achieve. According to utilitarianism, for example, any rule or action ought to maximize happiness and minimize suffering (Bentham 1970, ch. I, §§2–5 [pp. 11–12]; Mill 2001, 7). Punishment can be justified if the burden imposed on criminals efficiently reduces the greater harm caused by criminal activity.

By contrast, retributivism is backward-looking in the sense that we ought to punish offenders because they deserve it for their past conduct. Even if nothing else is accomplished as a result, on this view punishment is intrinsically valuable. Criminals may deserve to be punished because they incurred a debt to society (repayment theory) or took unfair advantage of the system (fair-play theory), such that punishment would annul the wrong (annulment theory) or publicly denounce it (denunciation theory) – there are different ways of understanding the basis of that desert claim (Cottingham 1979; Walker 1999).[2] On any of these variations, retributivism refers to people's guilt in determining both who ought

1 Bentham writes:

> The immediate principal end of punishment is to control action. This action is either that of the offender, or of others: that of the offender it controls by its influence, either on his will, in which case it is said to operate in the way of *reformation*; or on his physical power, in which case it is said to operate by ***disablement***: that of others it can influence otherwise than by its influence over their wills, in which ease it is said to operate in the way of *example*. (1970, ch. XIII, §2n [p. 158n])

2 Michael Davis says that desert theory is only one kind of conceptual theory among others. However, he also says that "desert theories seem to be the direct descendants of traditional retributivism" (2009, 90–91). Like Davis, Cottingham (1979) and Walker (1999) claim that desert theory is only one retributivist position, and that other versions of retributivism such as fair-play theory are alternatives to desert theory rather than kinds of desert theory. When I refer to retributivism, however, I mean it in the classical sense that I have defined here, as a synonym for desert theory. Thus, I agree with Honderich, who writes:

to be punished and how much. On the latter issue, retributivists disagree about whether a punishment ought to be equivalent or only proportionate to the crime (equality retributivism versus proportional retributivism). Retributivists also disagree about what desert claims entail regarding punishment, whether

1) guilt is necessary and sufficient to justify punishment (positive or bold retributivism), and punishment is morally obligatory (extreme or maximalist retributivism);
2) guilt is necessary and sufficient to justify punishment (positive or bold retributivism), and punishment is morally permissible (moderate or minimalist retributivism); or
3) guilt is only necessary for punishment, and there must be some other positive (usually consequentialist) reason to punish, such as promoting the common good (negative, weak, or modest retributivism; or side-constrained consequentialism).[3]

Having desert as a positive reason to punish does not necessarily, by itself, establish that one has a duty to punish. It could mean either (1) that one has a duty to punish (that the reason *is* overriding) or (2) that one would be justified in punishing even if there is no other reason to do so (that the reason *may be* overriding).

> It is or becomes pretty clear that all of these claims about desert, desert claims, are ways of saying one main thing, whatever it is. That some have slightly different implications does not much affect the fact. They are all ways of saying that a certain penalty or punishment stands in a certain relation to a past offence or something about a past offence, which relation makes the punishment right – morally obligatory or at least permissible. The relation is what is crucial and fundamental to retribution. (2006, 22)

Duff also says that the different varieties of retributivism set out by Cottingham are "different attempts to articulate and explain" the claim that "punishment is justified if and only if it is deserved in virtue of a past crime" (1996, 7). At some point, this becomes a verbal quibble, since both sides recognize that there are different varieties of retributivism.

3 Dolinko identifies two views: "bold" (positive) retributivism and "modest" (negative) retributivism (1991, 541–44). Golding calls negative retributivism a "*minimalist* position" (1975, 85). L. Alexander (1980) distinguishes among "weak retributivism" (desert as a necessary condition), "moderate retributivism" (desert as necessary and sufficient), and "extreme retributivism" (we *must* punish the deserving). *Black's Law Dictionary* distinguishes "maximalist retributivism," "minimalist retributivism," and "negative retributivism" (Garner 2019, 1575). The maximalist position requires punishment for the guilty, the minimalist position allows it, and the negative position is explicitly consequentialist and uses retribution only as a side constraint ("side-constrained consequentialism"). Mackie defines negative retributivism as the view that someone who is innocent may not be punished, and separates this position from permissive retributivism, which says that the guilty may be punished (1982, 4; 1991, 678–79). I cannot think of a form of negative retributivism that would not hold *both* that the guilty may be punished *and* that the innocent may not be punished, so I conflate negative retributivism and permissive retributivism. Zaibert rejects these labels and claims instead that retributivism provides a *prima facie* reason to punish that may be outweighed by "other factors," including "the sorts of considerations typically associated with utilitarianism" (2006, 213–24).

Those two positions differ regarding the weight of the desert claim. So, talking only about positive (1 and 2) and negative (3) retributivism, as many philosophers do, elides an important distinction between the extreme positive position (1) and the moderate positive position (2).

Historically, the main proponents of retributivism are Immanuel Kant (1724–1804) and G. W. F. Hegel (1770–1831). Kant claims that we have a positive moral duty to punish the guilty and that failing to give people what they deserve implicates us in their crimes (1996b, 6:331–35).[4] Hegel claims that criminals upset the relation of right in a law-governed state. By punishing them, the state negates, annuls, or cancels (*aufzuheben*) the wrong (or negates the negation of right), thus reestablishing a just social arrangement (1991, §§99–100 [pp. 124–27]).[5] For both Kant and Hegel, giving criminals what they deserve acknowledges that they are responsible for their actions and, by holding them accountable, treats them with a kind of respect. Kant says that basing punishment decisions on what will be produced as a result demeans offenders by treating them "merely as means," or as instruments of social engineering (1996b, 6:331–32). And Hegel says that people have a right to be punished because they have a right to be treated as responsible agents (1991, §§99–100 [pp. 124–27]).

One way of understanding the differences between consequentialist and retributivist theories of punishment is to adapt the classic distinction between consequentialist and deontological (duty-based) theories of ethics. Actions can be right or wrong, but experiences, states of affairs, and people can be good or bad. Ethical theories are distinguished by how they define and relate the right and the good. Value-based theories, including consequentialism, define the right in terms of the good. According to utilitarianism, for example, happiness is good, and the right thing to do is maximize happiness. Similarly, the utilitarian theory of punishment says that happiness is good, and the right thing to do is maximize happiness by preventing

4 As is customary in Kant scholarship, references to Kant's writings throughout the book give the volume and page number(s) of the Royal Prussian Academy edition (*Kants gesammelte Schriften*), which are included in the margins of the translations.

5 Neither Kant's nor Hegel's theory of punishment is as clear as we are often led to believe. Kant was a proponent, in various parts of his writing, of retributivism (1996b, 6:331–35) and consequentialism (1997, 27:286–88). And Hegel writes:

> Punishment … has a variety of determinations: that it is retribution; and also a deterrent example, a deterring threat made by the law; and also a contribution to the self-awareness and betterment of the culprit. Each of these different determinations has been regarded as the ground of punishment, on the ground that it is the essential determination, and by default the others, since they are different from it, have been regarded as only accidental. But the one determination which is assumed as ground does not amount to the whole punishment; the latter, as something concrete, also contains all of the rest, and in it these are only linked to the first without having their ground in it. (2010, 405–6)

Although Kant and Hegel are usually considered retributivists – proponents of desert theory and annulment theory, respectively – it is a matter of scholarly debate how to interpret their positions.

crimes through general and specific deterrence, restraint, and rehabilitation. Duty-based moral theories, by contrast, define the rightness of actions independently of the good. According to Kant's ethics, we ought to do our duty regardless of the consequences; it is valuable in itself. Happiness is defined separately from duty and is only conditionally good, depending on whether someone also has a good will (Kant 1996a, esp. 4:393–401). Similarly, the retributivist theory of punishment says that giving guilty people what they deserve is intrinsically good, regardless of the consequences. Punishment is justified because of what offenders did, without considering whether it deters potential criminals in the future.[6]

There are other theories of punishment, including expressivism, moral education theory, societal safety-valve theory, restitutive theory, and self-defense theory, to name a few. Often, however, these theories are more about specific methods to use rather than different kinds of justification, distinct from retributivism and consequentialism. According to expressivism, for example, punishment serves the symbolic function of expressing the community's attitudes of resentment and indignation at being wronged, and to signify a judgment of disapproval. On one interpretation, this is primarily forward-looking: it signals to potential and actual criminals that the behavior is wrong and will not be tolerated, so it has a deterrent effect on future crimes. On another interpretation, the hard treatment that criminals get in prison is itself symbolic because it is a kind of secular penance that they owe to the state. This is right in itself, regardless of whether criminals are reformed as a result.

6 The distinction between retributivism and consequentialism has been challenged by Michael Davis (2009), who claims that even traditional retributivist positions such as Kant's and Hegel's are consequentialist in some senses of the term. For one thing, they rely on arguments in which a conclusion follows from the premises, making them consequentialist in a logical sense. Retributivists also claim that punishment should be inflicted in order to achieve some aim, such as justice, as a consequence of the punishment. Furthermore, Davis says, it is misleading to distinguish the two theories based on whether they are backward-looking or forward-looking. After all, consequentialists must believe there is some relationship between the crime and the punishment (lest they risk unjust punishment), and retributivists believe that the institution of punishment is there to ensure justice in the future, such as restoring a relation of equality between offender and victim, annulling the crime, or negating the offender's advantage. As an alternative to the consequentialist/retributivist distinction, Davis suggests that we distinguish theories based on whether the rightness of a punishment depends on facts in the world (e.g., whether punishment has a deterrent effect) or on some conceptual relationship between crime and punishment (e.g., that a wrongdoer deserves hard treatment). The former are what he calls empirical or externalist theories, and the latter are conceptual or internalist theories.

Davis is right that theories of punishment are more varied and complicated than the traditional distinction between consequentialism and retributivism seems to allow. However, I wonder whether his clarification is more illuminating. In the logical sense of "consequentialist," nearly every philosophical position is consequentialist. And defining the "aim" of retributivist punishment as justice in the future obscures what defines justice for the retributivist: giving people what they deserve based on past actions. In short, although Davis is correct, his distinction does not seem more useful than the more common distinction between consequentialism and retributivism, especially since the latter distinction also tracks a common distinction in ethical theory.

Like John Stuart Mill's utilitarianism and Kant's deontological theory in ethics, we keep returning to consequentialism and retributivism in our moral, legal, and political discourse on punishment. For example, debates about the death penalty usually focus on a cost-benefit analysis about deterrence and whether the money could be better spent on other crime-prevention efforts; whether death is the only appropriate, deserved punishment for murderers; and whether it is worth it given the inevitable execution of some innocents, who do not deserve it. According to the U.S. Supreme Court, "the death penalty is said to serve two principal social purposes: retribution and deterrence of capital crimes by prospective offenders" (*Gregg v. Georgia*, 428 U.S. 153 [1976], 183; see also *Enmund v. Florida*, 458 U.S. 782 [1982], 798; *Atkins v. Virginia*, 536 U.S. 304 [2002], 318–19; *Roper v. Simmons*, 543 U.S. 551 [2005], 571; and *Kennedy v. Louisiana*, 554 U.S. 407 [2008], 441).[7] It is unclear, however, whether these two contrary positions can be maintained within the same system, given that they often have different practical implications. If the death penalty does not deter but murderers deserve to die, where should we put our limited resources? Without any rule-governed way to apply these (sometimes) competing principles, they provide little guidance for policymakers. Indeed, adopting both principles encourages arbitrary decision-making because public officials can pick and choose which theory to use depending on which position they want to take, resulting in a kind of moral subjectivism. It seems that we need to prioritize one of the two theories so that we know what is justified in cases where consequentialism and retributivism come into conflict.

The contest between these two theories defined the field until Paul Johann Anselm Feuerbach (1775–1833) introduced an important distinction. Feuerbach (1801, 2014) distinguishes the function of the legislature from the function of the criminal judiciary. Legislators write penal laws to discourage potential criminals and preserve the public order (on his view, to prevent rights violations), and judges apply the law as written in condemning and punishing the guilty.

7 Dolinko notes that retributivism has been in the ascendency in U.S. appeals courts since the mid-twentieth century, while utilitarianism is on the wane (1991, 537). With regard to the death penalty at least, U.S. courts want to hold both theories. As for rehabilitation, the U.S. Supreme Court has both flatly rejected it as a reason to extend an offender's prison term (*Tapia v. United States*, 564 U.S. 319 [2011]) and endorsed is as a goal of juvenile imprisonment (*Graham v. Florida*, 560 U.S. 48 [2010], 74, 79). The Court also has permitted civil confinement solely for the purpose of incapacitation, when, as is the case with some sex offenders, they are likely to reoffend and not be deterred (*Kansas v. Hendricks*, 521 U.S. 346 [1997], 372–74). Like the U.S., most countries do not explicitly commit themselves to one theory of punishment or another and, when punishment rationales are given, they are often inconsistent. According to Bagaric, Australia and the United Kingdom have both utilitarian and retributive objectives (1999, 543–44). Fox and Freiberg claim that governments have appealed to a number of different principles to justify criminal sentencing, often at the same time: deterrence, rehabilitation, denunciation, incapacitation, education, and community protection (1985, 444). For his part, Duff believes that trying to classify existing systems according to philosophical theories is bound to fail: "It would clearly be absurd to try to explain any existing penal system, whose historical development reflects an unsystematic diversity of competing influences, in terms of some unitary set of coherent values and purposes" (1986, 5).

Thus, punishment serves a social purpose insofar as it is a threat, and the threat is carried out by judges. This is a mixed theory that justifies legislative action on consequentialist grounds and judicial action on retributivist grounds, specifically legalistic retributivism (i.e., criminals deserve to be punished because they break the law).

This distinction was refined by H. L. A. Hart (1907–1992) in the twentieth century. When we try to justify punishment, we could be talking about different things: we could be talking about why we should adopt an institution of punishment, or we could be talking about why and how much we should punish particular criminals. Hart posed these as three separate questions: "What justifies the general principle of punishment? To whom may punishment be applied? How severely may we punish?" The first question concerns punishment's "*General Justifying Aim*," while the second and third questions concern its "*Distribution*," both its "*Title*" and its "*Amount*" (2008, 3–4). So long as these different topics are distinguished, Hart says, one does not have to choose either consequentialism or retributivism. They could function together but at different levels, with regard to either punishment policies or judgments of specific offenders.

Early proponents of mixed theories included such philosophers as Anthony Quinton, Stanley Benn, and John Rawls. In the 1950s, all of them proposed utilitarian justifications of the practice of punishment while also claiming that we should punish individual criminals because they deserve it. However, these mixed approaches have different conceptions of how the general justifying aim of punishment is related to its distribution. Quinton (1954) and Benn (1958) both argue that the answer to the question of whom specifically to punish follows logically from the meaning of the concept "punishment." Retributivism is thus a logical, conceptual, or definitional claim rather than a normative philosophy: only the guilty are able to be punished, lest we contradict the meaning of the term. According to Rawls (1955), on one conception of rules (as practices), we can think of legislators as establishing the laws and assessing their consequences, since their purpose is to protect the community. Judges then follow the rules by applying the laws in particular cases and giving people what they deserve. If they do not give people what they deserve – by, say, purposely imprisoning innocents – then they are not acting as judges anymore and they are not punishing people, since they would be violating the practice as defined by the rule.

Because these mixed theories incorporate both utilitarianism and retributivism, inevitably there is the possibility that they will have conflicting implications. If utilitarianism is overriding – we should punish individual offenders if and only if it maximizes utility – then it would seem to constrain retributivism to the point where the theory collapses into utilitarianism, which is not a mixed theory. For example, if a murderer escaped to an isolated desert island, and they posed no additional threat and punishing them would not deter other murderers, then they should not be punished, even though they deserve to be. And if utilitarianism is not overriding – we should punish the guilty regardless of the consequences – then non-utilitarian considerations could also shape the institution of punishment, in which case it becomes a disguised form of retributivism. For example, the death penalty would remain in place, as a deserved punishment, even if it had no deterrent effect and siphoned funding from more effective methods of crime control. To avoid both horns of this dilemma, some mixed theorists try to maintain a strict distinction between the general justifying aim of punishment and its distribution. But that can be difficult. For example, what should we do if utilitarianism dictates that we punish a class of criminals in a way that is disproportionate (either too much or too little) to the guilt of individual criminals who fall under that class? If neither theory is overriding, we are at an impasse.

As a theory of punishment, consequentialism became less popular in the 1970s mostly as a result of sustained critiques and perceived failures of the social sciences.[8] Prior to that time, legislators, criminologists, and the public generally believed that imprisonment and the threat of imprisonment were supposed to deter potential criminals and rehabilitate convicted criminals. However, if we cannot tell what kinds or degrees of punishments affect the crime rate, and if we are unable to measure the impact of rehabilitative programs on recidivism, then consequentialism gives us no guidance about which policies and practices to adopt. There are so many psychological, social, economic, political, and legal factors that affect the crime rate that we cannot isolate punishment, let alone its kind or degree, as one cause among many. And without being able to measure the effects of punishment, we cannot do a utilitarian calculus to determine the best of the available options. If we can be morally obligated to do only what we are able to

8 Histories of the rise and fall of rehabilitation as an ideal, and of consequentialism more generally, can be found in Tonry and Morris (1978), Bottoms and Preston (1980, ch. 1–3), Allen (1981), Galligan (1981), Radzinowicz and Hood (1981), von Hirsch (1985, 3–18), Duff and Garland (1994, 8–16), Ryberg (2004, 3–5), M. Davis (2009, 84–85), and V. Bailey (2019). In addition to concerns about the predictive power of the social sciences, political opposition to rehabilitation came from both the left and the right. People on the left objected to the unfairness of indeterminate sentencing, since judges and parole boards tended disproportionately to punish Black offenders. People on the right objected that rehabilitation programs were too lenient and that victims deserve justice. See Bushway and Paternoster (2009, 121–23). The general population supported more punitive policies such as mandatory minimums and imprisonment for drug offenders because of their fear of crime and anger at criminals. However, philosophers may have different reasons for their shift toward retributivism, as Cederblom points out:

> The resurgence of the idea of just deserts among the general public might be interpreted simply as a reaction to the increase in crime. To a public which feels threatened by and angry toward lawbreakers, the idea of "giving them what they deserve" is undoubtedly satisfying. But among scholars, the renewed interest in retributivism is surely not the result of anger over crime. One suspects rather that it results from a confluence of factors such as the growing documentation of the failure and abuse of rehabilitation programs, the general decline in respectability of utilitarianism (the chief rival of retributivism among philosophic theories of punishment), and the rise of contractarian and natural rights theories which might serve as an underpinning for a retributivist approach to punishment. (1977, 2)

Since this is a philosophy book and not a history book – about justifications and reasons rather than causes of events – I will relegate these historical musings to a footnote.

do ("ought implies can"), then our inability to calculate the consequences means that we should not be consequentialists when it comes to punishment.

The apparent failure of utilitarian theories, and indeed of all forward-looking deterrence theories, paved the way for the ascent of retributivism, which, in different forms, remains the dominant theory of punishment. Although most philosophers are willing to grant that punishment has some impact on reducing crime and thus that consequentialism is true in this general sense, we should decide which actions to punish and how much based on what criminals deserve. On this view, the severity of the punishment should match the seriousness of the offense.

The two-tiered model of punishment

In this book, I defend a mixed theory that I call the two-tiered model of punishment. My view is not entirely original. It has its roots in the views of Feuerbach, Hart, and Rawls. But there are significant differences, in part because of developments in philosophy and criminology in recent decades, that make the two-tiered model stronger as a theoretical alternative to either utilitarianism or retributivism considered on its own.

Although the position I defend is a mixed theory of punishment, I usually refer to it as the two-tiered *model* rather than the two-tiered *theory* because two theories – consequentialism and retributivism – are plugged into it as a kind of organizing structure. On my view, the institution of punishment as well as designated offenses and statutory penalties, as set by the legislature, are justified based on their costs and benefits, in terms of deterrence and rehabilitation. The law exists to preserve the public order. Criminal courts, by contrast, use retributivist claims to determine who is punished and how much, based on what offenders deserve. David Wood calls this a form of "split-level dualism" (2002, 304–6). Distinguishing the two roles makes sure that criminals are not punished beyond what advances the general welfare (because individual judgments are constrained by legislation), and it precludes punishing the innocent because judges and juries consider only the guilt of the accused and not the consequences of a given judgment (so that they do not consider, for example, whether framing an innocent defendant would maximize the good).

The two-tiered model of punishment avoids the two biggest criticisms of mixed theories. First, it is not a disguised form of either consequentialism or retributivism. Unlike the mixed theories of the 1950s, the two-tiered model does not merely make a conceptual distinction between practices and specific decisions within a practice. Instead, both consequentialism and retributivism are independently justified, meaning that one cannot simply be absorbed into the other without losing something of moral significance. Although the consequentialist concerns of the legislature constrain the retributivist aims of the criminal courts, that constraint is not absolute. When a prescribed range of punishments is unreasonably excessive or inadequate, there is a deliberative process to determine what is appropriate. A second reason why a mixed theory is now more defensible than it was seventy years ago is because there has been significant progress in the social sciences, such that they can more clearly and justifiably guide public policy. We can now make reliable (or reliable enough) generalizations regarding punishment to comparatively assess more and less effective punishments or alternatives to punishment, and more and less effective rehabilitation methods. Therefore, we can choose among the available options on consequentialist grounds.

Outline of parts and chapters

The book is divided into five parts. In Part I, I define what punishment is (Chapter 1). Although I largely follow the standard definition set out by Antony Flew, Benn, and Hart, I do not focus exclusively on legal punishment. Seeing how legal punishment is different from other kinds of punishment will help to illuminate its distinctive function in advancing the aims of the state. Because there seems to be no way to define punishment without begging the question in favor of one theory or another, however, I propose a few different stipulative definitions that will help to guide the evaluative discussions in the rest of the book.

In Part II, I defend consequentialism and retributivism. Punishment helps to maintain the social order, and the rightness of a given set of punitive policies depends on how well it accomplishes its aim and whether the social order itself is justified (Chapters 2–3). Yet there is also value in the state's expressing the community's resentment at being wronged (Chapter 4). Drawing on Hart's distinction between the general justifying aim of punishment and its distribution, I propose the two-tiered model as a way that we can simultaneously be committed to consequentialism and retributivism in, respectively, the legislature and the criminal judiciary (Chapter 5).

I give three arguments in Part III for why the two-tiered model is the right way of organizing these theories. Legislators and criminal court judges are in different positions, epistemically, with regard to the social effects of punishment in general and the guilt or innocence of particular defendants. Their different frames of reference entail that the legislature is more bound by consequentialist concerns and the courts are more bound by retributivist concerns (Chapter 6). Following that, I argue that the two-tiered model can accommodate a compatibilist theory of freedom. Under compatibilism, people can be held responsible, even if determinism is true, so long as they are determined in the right way. The legislature and the judiciary take two different perspectives on a person's action, as determined or free (Chapter 7). Finally, I show how the implications of the two-tiered model accord with our moral intuitions regarding, for example, the punishment of innocents and the prohibition on cruel punishments (Chapter 8). One shortcoming of previous mixed theories is that they often sound like mere proposals or suggestions, with little argument about why the system *should* be organized in this way. I correct that oversight in Part III.

Having established the reasons behind consequentialism and retributivism, and the reasons why they should be combined in a two-tiered model, in Part IV I explain how to make punishment decisions at both the policy level and the level of individual judgments. I begin by explaining how consequentialist reasoning regarding deterrence can be validated by the empirical social sciences (Chapter 9). We need not adopt a retributivist system, which faces problems of its own, in order to devise a punishment schedule (Chapter 10). A recurring challenge to mixed theories is that combining two opposing positions leaves us with the choice of either prioritizing one over the other or following one or the other arbitrarily when they conflict. I explain the two-tiered model's decision procedure in Chapter 11: conflicts between the legislature and the courts are solved not by subsuming one to the other, but through a public process of deliberation by which the community achieves reflective equilibrium.

In Part V of the book, I demonstrate the value of the two-tiered model by applying it to two controversial topics regarding punishment. First, I make the case that the death penalty should be abolished because of its lack of deterrent effect. Assessing its effectiveness is crucial for formulating public policy (Chapter 12). Second, I show how restorative justice practices can be used instead of or in addition to traditional punitive measures in ways that reinforce the law's retributive function (Chapter 13). These two examples illustrate how the two-tiered model can be action-guiding as we consider penological reform.

Conclusion

With legal punishment, the state intentionally and systematically inflicts harm on its own people. It is incumbent on us to examine the practice, to evaluate its supposed justifications, and, if necessary, to reform our policies. Because philosophers are trained in analyzing concepts, investigating values, and assessing arguments, we are uniquely situated to perform this task. My (admittedly lofty) hope is that this book will not only add to the body of existing research on punishment, but that it will raise the quality of discussion about issues of pressing public importance.

Part I

Defining punishment

> The beginning of wisdom is the definition of terms.
>
> – Attributed to Socrates

A methodical treatment of any subject begins with explaining what exactly is being discussed. With punishment in particular, there are mistakes that people make because of how they define the term, or because they equivocate among different definitions at different points in their arguments. It is easy to define punishment in a way that begs the question in favor of a particular theory. Additionally, defining only legal punishment narrows the scope of one's inquiry, but it also obscures what makes legal punishment like and unlike other kinds of punishment. Definition does not amount to justification, but it does begin a process by which one can focus on what is distinctive about legal punishment and can justify it without circularity.

1 Crimes and burdens

Many philosophers of law attempt to define legal punishment specifically as the "standard or central case" of punishment, and they set aside a consideration of how punishment functions in families, clubs, and schools (e.g., Flew 1954, 292; Benn 1958; Hart 2008, 5; Scheid 1980, 453–54; Philips 1986, 393–94). However, there is no reason for legal punishment to be the template for what punishment is in general. We learn the concept of punishment in our homes and schools before we are aware of how the law is enforced. One could just as easily claim that legal punishment is a variation on how we respond to moral offenses, rather than vice versa.[1] There is no "central case" of punishment, because different applications of the term are relevant in different situations. In fact, delineating the different contexts in which people are punished – who is punished and by what authority – helps to reveal how punishment is justified under the law, as opposed to other contexts. As Thomas McPherson says, to define punishment in exclusively legal terms

> is to discourage at the outset the raising of what may be substantial issues. It is to relegate to the realm of the "sub-standard" what are surely quite common uses of "punishment," examination of which might throw light on the general concept of punishment, if there is one. (1967, 22)

To understand legal punishment, it is important to identify what it shares with other forms of punishment as well as the special aim or aims that make it distinct.

Philosophers since H. L. A. Hart have been careful to distinguish the definition of punishment from its justification (2008, 4). If we define punishment in terms of what it accomplishes, we risk begging the question in favor of one theory or another. For example, Herbert Packer follows Hart (2008, 4–5) in defining legal punishment using five characteristics (Packer 1968, 21), but then he adds a

1 Even *Ballentine's Legal Dictionary* includes two definitions of punishment, only one of which is specifically legal: (1) "the penalty for violating the law … imposed by a judge, either as a sentence in a criminal case or as a civil penalty in a civil action" and (2) "the treatment of a person who breaks the rules, most commonly a child, by a parent or teacher" (Lynton 1995, 541).

sixth in his "revised definition": "It must be imposed for the dominant purpose of preventing offenses against legal rules or of exacting retribution from offenders, or both" (Packer 1968, 31). This definition begs the question in favor of deterrence theory or retributivism, or both, and it automatically rules out other theories.

Unfortunately, a definition of punishment that does not beg the question is elusive. Therefore, I will propose several stipulative definitions that reveal general patterns of reasoning. These stipulative definitions significantly overlap with one another but are distinguished in terms of their epistemic requirements and the reasons for punishing. The necessary and jointly sufficient conditions that each definition picks out are not true of all punishments, but they can be assumed for the sake of argument so that I can distinguish between definition and justification, highlight the different justifications of punishment, and identify similarities and differences among the different theories.

Imposing burdens

Defining punishment in general is difficult because there are two demands pulling in opposite directions. First, there is pressure to expand the definition to include the many contexts in which people can be punished, including in a family setting, in school, in the workplace, in criminal court, in the afterlife, and so on; as well as the many kinds of punishments that someone can receive, including scolding, withholding privileges, fines, isolation, physical harm, and more. Yet the definition must also be limited so it does not include the indiscriminate infliction of pain by anyone. It will help to proceed step by step, being pulled by these opposing forces until we settle on one or more working definitions of punishment.

The most basic element of punishment is the fact that it involves some kind of imposition, inconvenience, distress, sanction, harm, suffering, evil, or burden. I will use the language of burdens, which I mean in a broad sense, to include pain (e.g., spanking), deprivation (e.g., imprisonment), shame (e.g., stocks), and other punitive treatments, with the idea that no one kind of burden (e.g., suffering per se) is a necessary condition for something to be a punishment. A reward is the opposite of a punishment, and what distinguishes them is that the former is a benefit and the latter is a burden. Parents who "punish" their children with candy and television probably do not understand what punishment is. Punishment is supposed to be unpleasant. Being imprisoned deprives people of their freedom and being executed deprives people of their lives, so they both take away something that people value. Thus, we begin to define punishment by noting its negative character:

D1: Punishment is the imposition of burdens.

Although the imposition of burdens is necessary, clearly it is insufficient because not every imposition of burdens is a punishment; the definition is too broad. Hart includes it as only the first characteristic of legal punishment: it "must involve pain or other consequences normally considered unpleasant" (2008, 4). Being hurt by a mugger and being struck by lightning are both painful, but neither is a punishment.

Recognized authority

Perhaps being struck by lightning could be a punishment, depending on the meaning attached to it or whether it is an intentional act. The bolt of divine retribution is a common trope in both Eastern and Western culture. Zeus hurled a thunderbolt at Capaneus when he said that not even the gods could stop him from invading Thebes (Aeschylus 1961, 100–101 [ll. 423–56]; Sophocles 1984, 65–66 [ll. 140–55]; Euripides 2005, 15, 41 [ll. 177–83, 1172–88]). The prophet Elijah called down God's wrath on his enemies in the form of fire from heaven (2 Kings 1:10, 12). And during the Qing dynasty in China, children who did not show filial piety were said to be struck by thunderbolts as punishment (Hammond 1992). If lightning is nothing but a naturally occurring electrostatic discharge – if there is no conscious entity inflicting it on someone – then there is no reason for it, only a cause. What distinguishes lightning as divine retribution from being struck by lightning as a random event is that, in the aforementioned examples, the harm is imposed by an authority against someone because they did something wrong: Capaneus for his hubris, Elijah's enemies for their resistance, and Chinese children for their lack of respect.

Suffering can also occur in ways that depend on people's actions but that still does not amount to punishment. Smokers who develop lung cancer may not expect it, but it is not random like a lightning strike. The cancer is the result of their smoking. But since no one is imposing the cancer on them as a response to their smoking – there is no intention behind the event – then it is not a punishment. By contrast, parents who catch a child smoking may ground the kid as a punishment to achieve some end, such as discouraging the habit.

In the cases of Zeus and Capaneus, and the parents of the smoking child, someone is inflicting harm on someone else. So, unlike random events, punishment is an intentional act. As Stanley Benn puts it, punishment "must be the work of personal agencies (i.e. not merely the natural consequences of an action)" (1958, 325). Furthermore, although just about anyone can hurt another person – muggers and victims, dogs and mail carriers, gods and humans – only some people (or entities) can inflict punishment. In the paradigm cases of punishment – parents punishing children, teachers punishing students, bosses punishing employees, or states punishing their citizens – punishment seems to involve holders of power or authority and others who are bound by or subject to that authority.[2] This is the source of the law's obligatoriness. Even very powerful people can be punished if

2 Hobbes writes: "*A Punishment, is an Evill inflicted by publique Authority, on him that hath done, or omitted that which is Judged by the same Authority to be a Transgression of the Law*" (1996, 214).

there is some sovereign to which they answer – for example, a president being impeached by the people's representatives in the legislature. Only certain people can punish:

> **D2: Punishment is the imposition of burdens by a recognized authority (i.e., the authorized imposition of burdens).**

Arguably, parents have a kind of natural authority over their children, an authority that is reinforced by the law, which sets out their rights over their children and parental responsibilities. When focusing on legal punishment, Hart says that the authority must be "constituted by a legal system against which the offense is committed" (2008, 5). Authority is lost when people no longer recognize the authority, in either a legal or a moral sense. Former U.S. presidents can no longer command the armed forces, and parents lose some formal authority when their children turn eighteen. One could make the case that being an authority assumes some kind of recognition, that an unrecognized authority is no authority at all. I will risk the redundancy ("recognized authority") to emphasize the special status that a punisher must have.

How we understand authority and the grounds on which it is conferred will impact our beliefs about who can punish. A king can punish his subjects, but can the subjects punish their king? It would seem that they cannot, since they have no authority over him. But that may construe authority too narrowly. The execution of Louis XVI during the French Revolution could be considered a punishment inasmuch as the people were asserting their sovereignty over the king, as rights-bearers who were protecting their natural rights (or giving the king what he deserved for violating their rights). There are cases of abused children who kill their abusive parents, which may be not only acts of self-defense but also acts of punishment, insofar as the children have moral standing to give them their just deserts. One reason why vigilantism is such a fraught moral issue is that there is widespread disagreement about whether vigilantes have a kind of authority (moral or otherwise), who is to evaluate their claims to authority, whether their authority is undermined by their violent methods and the fact that they act outside of the established legal process, and so on.[3] These marginal cases generate interesting conversations, but it is unnecessary to settle them in order to establish a working definition of punishment. The concept of authority is vague, but not perniciously so.

Although there has to be some sort of general acceptance of the legitimacy of the harm, that is derivative, at least in part, from the recognition of the punisher's authority. The Judeo-Christian God metes out divine punishment because God is an all-good and all-powerful creator, which gives God authority over us. A

3 Scheid claims that vigilantes do punish people, although he says that the punishment may be "unauthorized" (1980, 457).

mugger has no such authority. The concept of authority includes some measure of legitimacy, warrant, right, or recognition. One gains power by having a gun, but not authority, and certainly not the right to punish. One is a normative concept, and the other is merely descriptive. People who are stronger than I am can harm me, but they have no authority to punish me simply by virtue of their strength.

In trying to rule out such cases, however, we have to be careful not to confuse a definition of punishment with its justification. A government that does not have the support of its people may, in some sense, be illegitimate, depending on how we conceive of justified legal authority, but, as the government, it still punishes people. It is a recognized authority in the sense that people realize that it controls the police and enforces the law. Similarly, rules are often enforced with punishment regardless of whether they are good or bad rules. In the United States prior to the Civil War, fugitive slave laws established penalties (usually steep fines) for people who assisted runaway slaves. Such laws may be unconstitutional and morally wrong, but when the laws were in place, punishing people for violating the laws amounted to punishment, even if the punishment was unjustified.

Violating a rule

Defining punishment as the imposition of burdens by a recognized authority (D2) will not suffice either, because not every case of harm, even by an established authority, is a case of punishment. For example, a state's decision to reduce taxes may inadvertently lower funding for public schools, but the negative consequences for children are not acts of punishment. If the harm is imposed accidentally, unintentionally, or as a side effect of unrelated decisions, then it is not a punishment.

Even intentional harms need not be punishments if they are merely expressions of anger or are otherwise arbitrary. If I, as a college professor, were to lower the grades of students who wear white shoes to class, then I would be harming them but not punishing them. For it to be punishment, I must be acting on a particular kind of reason. Specifically, students who are punished must have done something wrong or something that is broadly accepted as wrong, such as cheating on a test or plagiarizing a paper. Capaneus offended the gods with his arrogance; murderers disregard the value of human life. In short, someone who is harmed must have violated a rule, and the authority must take that violation as a reason to punish them. David Boonin calls this the "retributive requirement" (2008, 17–21), and Ambrose Lee calls it the "response requirement" (2019, 372–81). Every definition of punishment includes a justificatory burden for the authority – to prove a defendant's guilt beyond a reasonable doubt, for example – that overcomes the *prima facie* wrongness of harm. Something must make particular offenders culpable and proper targets of punishment. That is, offenders are punished *because* of their offenses:

D3: Punishment is the imposition of burdens by a recognized authority because someone has violated a rule.

An established law is one kind of rule that people may be punished for violating. There are also moral obligations, social expectations, filial duties, and many other kinds of rules for which someone could be punished. Not every transgression listed in Dante's *Inferno* is an illegal act. And communities often ostracize people who violate social conventions. If someone shows up drunk and belligerent to too many parties, that person is likely not to be invited in the future. This may not only be an act of self-protection on the part of the hosts but also a rebuke of the partygoer, who is expected to change their behavior before being invited back.

The variety of obligations we have complicates what it means to violate a rule. I may have a rule that students in my class are not supposed to wear white shoes – even though I never tell them about it. If I were to drop students' grades because I am holding them to a rule that only I know, it imposes burdens, to be sure, but calling it punishment stretches the term too much. The students would not plead to my department chair that they are being wrongly punished, as if they are being falsely accused of something they did not do. Rather, they would say that the grade changes are undeserved acts of malice because there is no generally acknowledged standard against which I am judging their actions.

Consider a more extreme case. In 2014, Elliott Rodgers killed six people and injured fourteen others in what he called "the day of retribution." He vowed to "punish" women who were not attracted to him and to kill men and women with active sex lives, saying that they "deserve it just for the crime of living a better life than me" (M. Garvey 2014). His use of the word "punishment" is misplaced here. He inflicted pain on people because they frustrated his desires and because their lives were more fulfilling than his. Not only did he lack the authority to punish them, but he also justified his actions with reference to an expectation that only he had, a sense of entitlement to sex that was not recognized or accepted by others. If we harm someone without there being a "breach of law," then "it degenerates into an arbitrary act of violence that can produce nothing but bad social effects" (Williams 1961, 575). Rodgers's rampage was an act of vindictiveness rather than punishment.

Acknowledged rules

Another way to limit the application of the term "punishment" is to focus on the kinds of rules that people can be punished for violating. People are punished for breaking rules that are established somehow. Philosophers disagree about what establishes rules as laws. Hart, for example, says that primary rules must be established by a process governed by secondary rules, or rules that set out how properly to make rules (such as those outlined in the U.S. Constitution) (2012, esp. 91–99). But when we are talking about rules in a broader context, covering parental and social expectations as well as the law and morality (among other things), there must be a different way of specifying the rule provision.

In order to constrain us, any enforceable rule must at least be promulgated. It must be established by the authority and known or knowable by the public –

ignorance of the law is no excuse for violating the law – so that the offender did something wrong and was aware (or should have been aware) that it was wrong:

> **D4: Punishment is the imposition of burdens by a recognized authority because someone has violated a rule that was acknowledged or should have been acknowledged as a rule.**

Punishment is possible when the authority and the violator stand in a certain kind of relationship, not only of differential power, but of shared or mutually recognized standards.[4] Adulterers cannot complain that they ended up in Dante's hell when the rule is clearly spelled out as the Seventh Commandment. If a late penalty is described in a syllabus, students who submit late assignments recognize that the rule is there and that they will be punished if it is broken, even if they do not agree with the rule. Of course, as Glanville Williams says, it is not enough that a rule is technically a law but unknown or undiscoverable by nearly everyone, like the Star Chamber. Rather, "opinions about what people are obliged legally to do should be capable of being ascertained by legal research" (1961, 576). To have *mens rea*, criminals must be aware that what they are doing is wrong or illegal.

The added clause ("was acknowledged or should have been acknowledged") allows those who are or claim to be ignorant of the law also to be punished. The M'Naghten Rules, which established a common law position regarding criminal liability for mentally disordered defendants, anticipate this problem. Prosecutors do not need to establish that accused criminals are familiar with the specific statutes that they are accused of violating, let alone the precise penalties. Few people are intimately familiar with specifics of the laws to which they are being held, and few people actually do "legal research." Instead, it is enough that people under the law know that some acts are wrong and that they should not do them. Unless people are legally insane or otherwise impaired, they should know not to steal from people even if they are not familiar with the statutes regarding theft. That recognition, coupled with the fact that the act is legally prohibited, is enough for criminals to be punishable.[5]

4 There is some overlap between *recognized* authority and *acknowledged* rules, but, again, I will risk redundancy for the purpose of clarity.

5 "If the question were to be put as to the knowledge of the accused solely and exclusively with reference to the law of the land, it might tend to confound the jury, by inducing them to believe that an actual knowledge of the law of the land was essential in order to lead to a conviction; whereas the law is administered upon the principle that every one must be taken conclusively to know it, without proof that he does know it. If the accused was conscious that the act was one which he ought not to do, and if that act was at the same time contrary to the law of the land, he is punishable; and the usual course therefore has been to leave the question to the jury, whether the party accused had a sufficient degree of reason to know that he was doing an act that was wrong: and this course we think is correct, accompanied with such observations and explanations as the circumstances of each particular case may require" (*M'Naghten's Case*, UKHL J16, 8 ER 718 [1843]).

The acknowledgment requirement can get complicated when rules are implied or otherwise unspoken. Parents may tell their children not to eat cookies between meals. If they have candy between meals and are punished for it, the kids cannot claim to have been unaware of the rule. It turns out that the rule was not to eat sweets between meals rather than a narrow prohibition on cookies specifically. Other rules are unspoken but assumed to be known by both the authority figure and the subordinates. Siblings cannot claim to be wrongfully punished for punching each other in the face just because their parents did not tell them not to do it. They should have known that it was wrong and that they were liable to be punished for it. And people generally expect not to be accosted by drunk and belligerent guests when they go to parties, even if that expectation is not written on the invitations.

The acknowledgment clause also goes in the other direction. Not only does the rule have to be promulgated, but people who break the rule must be capable of acknowledging it. Defendants who are found not guilty by reason of mental disease or defect are often sentenced to be treated in psychiatric facilities for indeterminate periods. Such involuntary commitments are not punishments because the purpose of the burdens – the lack of freedom, the mandatory treatment, and so on – is not to make them suffer, and it is not done because they broke the law. In these cases, the defendants could not comprehend the wrongness of their actions, so they were not legally obligated to know that they were acting wrongly ("ought implies can"). They undergo psychiatric care so that they can be restrained while they are dangerous and, when they are found competent, they can reenter society. It is treatment, not punishment.

Although D4 is not as precise as it could be, it will suffice as a working definition to guide the discussion that follows. It includes, at a more general level, the five elements of legal punishment that Hart (2008, 4–5) sets out, following both Antony Flew (1954) and Benn (1958): pain ("imposition of burdens"), offense against rules ("violated a rule"), targeted at an offender ("someone"), intentionally administered by someone other than the offender, and administered by someone with authority ("recognized authority").[6] This so-called standard definition (or Flew–Benn–Hart definition) of punishment includes several different elements: the fact that some harm is being inflicted, who is inflicting the harm, on whom, and for what reason. I have attempted to remain neutral regarding the reason why the punishment is inflicted in order to avoid begging the question in favor of any particular justification of punishment such as deterrence or retribution – but I will say more about this later.

The only thing I add to the standard definition is the claim that the rule must be acknowledged or able to be acknowledged. Although this may be assumed in

6 Since Hart considers legal punishment as "the standard or central case," he restricts these elements accordingly: punishment is the result of "an offense against legal rules," "administered by human beings," and "imposed and administered by an authority constituted by a legal system" (2008, 4–5).

Hart's definition of what makes something a legal rule, it is important to make this explicit, lest people be held to standards that do not exist for them. I already mentioned the unspoken prohibition on white shoes in class; the rule is not publicized. Other examples would be if a government created laws that are incomprehensible, contradictory, retroactive, or that change so frequently that people cannot follow them. As Lon Fuller notes, these would not be bad laws; they would fail to be laws at all (1969, 39–40). Similarly, imposing burdens on people who violated a law before it was law would not be a bad punishment; it would not be a punishment at all (*nulla poena sine lege*). In cases like these, the unknown or *post hoc* rule would be a mere prevarication and an excuse to harm those who are not legally or morally culpable. There is neither *mens rea* nor strict liability if the action was not a crime when it was performed.

Punishments and penalties

Two major criticisms of the standard definition have persisted. One objection is that the definition is too broad. Joel Feinberg claims that punishment serves a symbolic social purpose. Among other things, punishment is an expression of disapproval, and any imposed burdens by the state that do not include this expressive function, such as parking tickets, are better classified as penalties rather than punishments (1970, 95–118). The definition should be revised to exclude mere penalties. A second objection is that the definition is too narrow. The standard definition, including D4, assumes that people who are punished must have violated a rule. On this view, innocent people cannot be punished, by definition. If innocent people can be punished, even if they are punished wrongly or unjustly, then the definition would have to be broadened to include that possibility.

The first question is whether an expressive function should be included as part of the definition of punishment rather than or in addition to being a potential justification of the practice. As Feinberg puts it, "punishment is a conventional device for the expression of attitudes of resentment and indignation, and of judgments of disapproval and reprobation, on the part either of the punishing authority himself or of those 'in whose name' the punishment is inflicted" (1970, 98). By expressing these attitudes, punishment serves "such symbolic functions as disavowal, nonacquiescence, vindication, and absolution" – that is, a public distancing from the act, refusing to condone an injustice, reaffirming the authority of the law, and relieving others of suspicion (115; see also 101–5). Punishments such as prison or execution are powerful symbols of public denunciation – prisoners are temporarily ostracized or permanently removed from society – while penalties such as simple scolding, fines, suspending drivers' licenses, and the like do not have the full force of society's condemnation behind them. On the expressivist view, because both penalties and punishments fit the standard definition, the definition must be wrong, or at least incomplete. Any definition must include an expressive function that would exclude penalties and capture this essential element of punishment.

I argue in Chapter 4 that legal punishments ought to express our collective sense of resentment toward criminals. The question is whether social condemnation should be included in the definition of punishment or whether it is a characteristic that most punishments, especially justified, legal punishments, tend to have. One way to challenge Feinberg's claim would be to discover a punishment that does not also include condemnation or denunciation. Psychological behaviorists, for example, understand punishment to include any consequences of an action – either removing something that the person desires or introducing something that the person does not want – that decrease the frequency of that action in the future (Holth 2005). When a local sheriff gives someone a speeding ticket and the driver has to pay a fine, the county is removing something (negative punishment) that the person wants, namely money (positive reinforcer). When parents scold their child for talking back, the parents are doing something (positive punishment) that the child does not want to endure (negative reinforcer). Sending people to prison is a combination of both. Not only are prisoners deprived of their freedom (positive reinforcer, negative punishment), but they also have to endure harsh living conditions that they want to avoid (negative reinforcer, positive punishment).[7] This is why philosophers of punishment often use the imposition of suffering, deprivations, or burdens interchangeably. On this interpretation, a speeding ticket, spanking, and prison time would all be punishments. Indeed, they all deter future bad behavior, which, according to consequentialism, is the primary aim of punishment.

In the philosophical context, this behaviorist characterization is too broad, since it would be present in nearly every case of operant conditioning. Withholding a treat from my dog until she sits down, while I am training her to sit on my command, is not a punishment. One common objection to Feinberg's expressivist theory is that it considers all sorts of unpleasant things done to people, anything that attempts to motivate them to change, including mere criticism, as forms of punishment (Hanna 2008). Because criticism is an act of condemnation but not a punishment, expression is not sufficient for punishment.

Feinberg himself says that he is not proposing an alternative theory of punishment. That is, he is not saying that punishment is *only* a matter of conveying society's condemnation of crimes, but rather that punishment *also* serves an expressivist function that is overlooked by other definitions and justifications of punishment. So, a counterexample to Feinberg would have to fulfill the elements of my definition – imposition of burdens, recognized authority, because someone

7 Admittedly, this explanation of positive and negative punishment is somewhat oversimplified because it assumes that consequences are either reinforcing or punishing. In reality, positive and negative punishment and positive and negative reinforcement contingencies are not mutually exclusive and often work in tandem. Furthermore, consequences that appear to be punitive at face value can be reinforcing for some individuals. For example, one child may hate timeouts, while another one may appreciate the time to calm down and rest. One potential criminal may hate the idea of prison, while another one wants prison time to improve their reputation among their criminal peers.

violated a rule, acknowledged or should have acknowledged as a rule – but not include an expressive element, thus showing that expression is not necessary.

Consider the case of the title character from Herman Melville's novel *Billy Budd*. Facing a false and slanderous charge from the ship's master-at-arms, the innocent Billy Budd, in a moment of exasperation, strikes and kills his accuser. Everyone believes that the accuser's allegations are false, that the killing was unintentional, and that Billy is morally guiltless, so they feel pity for him. Yet the captain and the other officers try him, convict him, and sentence him to be hanged, despite their belief in his moral innocence (Melville 2016). This is clearly a punishment, but in this case, what is being expressed? Billy himself is not being condemned or denounced. Feinberg defines condemnation as a fusing of resentment ("the various vengeful attitudes") and reprobation ("the stern judgment of disapproval"), but neither seems applicable here (1970, 101). There are no "attitudes of resentment and indignation" (98); this is not "a symbolic way of getting back at the criminal" (100). The captain punishes Billy because the law defines the act as a capital crime, and he must act decisively and strongly to deter other potential mutineers. Not Billy himself but Billy's action is being "denounced" by the British navy, and only in a general sense of being marked as prohibited.

Drained of its overtly emotive elements, the idea that a punishment denounces the crime amounts to little more than the claim that criminals should be punished because they break the law. Billy is punished because the British navy prohibits mutinous acts. The standard definition includes an element of condemnation in this less expressive sense. Condemning such acts would then have to be justified, with the two prime candidates for justification being consequentialism and retributivism. In the case of Billy Budd, one could make the case that he is being punished because he committed a crime, and anyone who commits that crime, whether intentionally or unintentionally, deserves to be punished (retribution); or that he is being punished in order to disincentivize other potential mutineers from doing the same thing (deterrence). Both are expressive in this broader sense of considering the act to be unjust or wanting it not to happen again, but these are justifications rather than definitions.

Narrowing the definition of punishment in the way that Feinberg suggests would beg the question in favor of the expressive theory. A strict utilitarian would determine whether associating social condemnation with a given punishment would support its deterrent effect. If it does not – that is, if the disapproval does not increase positive consequences – then expressing disapproval would not be included as part of the punishment because it would inflict unnecessary distress. Similarly, a dispassionate judge, representing a dispassionate society, could act on retributivist principles and give defendants precisely what they deserve without a hint of moral outrage and without aiming at some social purpose. For an equality retributivist, the goal would be to establish an equivalence of crime and punishment. Indeed, if the crime and punishment are equivalent (say, murder and execution), then expressing disapproval would upset the equivalence by imposing an additional burden. Of course, either of these possible approaches may yield unjustified punishments, but whether they are as justified as alternatives to expressive condemnation is a separate question from whether they are punishments at all. In other words, legal punishment may be justified insofar as it serves an expressive purpose – indeed, I argue for a version of expressive retributivism in Chapter 4 – but that is not what defines it as punishment.

Punishing innocents

According to D4, for burdens to be punishments, they must be imposed on people who violate rules. A second common objection is that, under this definition, innocent people cannot be punished, because they have not done anything wrong. That contradicts our common use of the term, since, for example, we often talk about exonerees as having been wrongly or unjustly punished. The question is how to handle the punishing of innocents without begging the question or otherwise favoring one theory or another.

For many future-oriented, consequentialist theories, the guilt of the accused seems to be incidental. People can be punished to achieve some social aim even if they are innocent. That seems morally problematic. In defense of their positions, then, some consequentialists embrace the standard definition and claim that innocents cannot be punished – in a conceptual sense rather than as a moral injunction. If, by definition, we cannot punish innocents, then consequentialism does not need to defend itself, either to convince us that punishing innocents is sometimes justified or to explain why we should never punish innocents on consequentialist grounds. Benn uses this tactic to defend his own utilitarian theory of punishment:

> "Punishment" implies, in its primary sense, inflicting suffering only under specified conditions, of which one is that it must be for a breach of a rule. Now if we insist on this criterion for the word, "punishment of the innocent" is a logical impossibility, for by definition, suffering inflicted on the innocent, or in anticipation of a breach of the rule, cannot be "punishment." It is not a question of what is morally justified, but of what is logically possible. (1958, 331)[8]

An innocent person who is framed would be harmed to accomplish some social end, not because of a rule violation, and punishment (per the addition in D3) must be imposed because someone violated a rule. This is what Hart calls the "definitional stop," and it would foreclose debates in the philosophy of law about whether the punishment of innocents is morally justified (2008, 5–6). We would not be able to debate the preference for a system in which only the guilty are punished over a system in which innocents may be punished, because the latter is logically impossible – a contradiction in terms.

8 Similarly, Hobbes says: "Punishment is only for Transgression of the Law, and therefore there can be no Punishment of the Innocent" (1996, 219). See also Quinton (1954); Armstrong (1961, 480–81); Bradley (1988, 26–27); and Dimock (1997, 42).

The problem is that this distinction has no moral force behind it. Judges could accept that it is not punishment, strictly speaking, and still think that they are justified in framing the innocent if it would, say, pacify a threatening mob. And if a judge refuses to frame someone and sparks a riot for no other reason than because of a desire for conceptual purity, so to speak, that seems like the wrong reason not to do it. Because, on this view, the innocence of the defendant limits what we can do to maximize utility, Whitley Kaufman characterizes this as "the conceptual version of the mixed theory" (2008, 40), and he claims that its method is "to bypass the substantive moral debate about the merits of the utilitarian and retributive theories of punishment in favor of an analysis of the logic of the concept of punishment" (41). If punishing innocents is wrong, surely it is because it is unfair to the accused or detrimental to society in the long run, not because it is an oxymoron.

According to H. J. McCloskey, proponents of the definitional stop confuse the concepts of "punishment" and "deserved punishment." An innocent person can be punished – there is nothing incoherent about that – but they cannot, by definition, be deservedly punished, because they are innocent (1962, 319–25).[9] We have to separate these ideas. Consider the following three scenarios:

1) A Black man is convicted of murdering a white woman and is sentenced to death. Statistically, he was more likely to get the death penalty because of his race and the race of his victim (Gross and Mauro 1984). Although there is strong evidence of his guilt, his sentence is in part the result of racial prejudice.
2) A Black man is wrongly thought to be involved in some local burglaries, so some white men confront him and kill him on the street.
3) A physician's implicit bias against his Black patient leads to lower quality of care and results in an earlier death than he would have had if he had been given the treatment that white patients tend to receive (Hall et al. 2015).

Case #1 is a case of punishment because it follows the standard definition: ostensibly, the murderer faces execution because of his guilt. However, it is unclear whether the defendant is punished because he violated a rule or because he is Black, or both. The criminal justice process has as its stated goal to punish the guilty, not to execute Black men. Did the jury meet that standard? This is a question of whether the evidence was sufficient to warrant the judgment – that is, whether it is justified – not whether it is a punishment at all. If it is discovered

9 Duff elides this distinction between a punishment and a deserved punishment:

> Punishment must … be justified by reference to the guilt of the person punished; and if that person is not in fact guilty he may insist that he is, by mistake or by design, being victimised, *not* punished. … The punishment of the innocent is inconsistent with the justificatory criteria of punishment: to deny that the innocent victim is punished is to insist on the impropriety of what is done to him under the guise of punishment. (1986, 152)

later that he is innocent, it would be odd to say that he was actually not being punished the whole time he was on death row. Case #3 is not a case of punishment because, despite the authority of the doctor and the imposition of burdens, the patient did not violate a rule. The treatment of the Black patient should be evaluated on separate moral grounds. Case #2 is a marginal case: the white men claim to have the authority to make a citizen's arrest, and the Black man (Ahmaud Arbery) is thought to have broken a law. Whether the white men really had any authority, whether the Black man actually violated a rule, and whether this is the appropriate punishment – these questions help us identify what is wrong with the killing. Most likely, the real violation is jogging through a white neighborhood within sight of angry racists, which is not a rule that should be acknowledged, and the harm is inflicted by a group with force but no authority. The definition of punishment should not be used to avoid moral questions but to help us to articulate the different kinds of moral questions to ask. Ultimately, we should condemn the killing, not argue about whether it is a punishment.

In order to subject the punishment of innocents to moral scrutiny – that is, to make it a proper subject of debate within the philosophy of law and a potential objection to consequentialist theories of punishment – the definition of punishment must not rule it out as conceptually incoherent. The problem is that the version of the standard definition that I proposed earlier seems to assume that the person must be guilty:[10]

> **D4: Punishment is the imposition of burdens by a recognized authority because someone *has* violated a rule that was acknowledged or should have been acknowledged as a rule.**

D4 seems to imply that innocents, whether they are known to be innocent or incorrectly believed to be guilty, cannot be punished – the definitional stop. It makes material guilt the basis of punishment rather than probative guilt, the latter of which is based on the evidence presented at trial. However, if the actual guilt of the accused is a condition of their being punished – they must have violated rules *in fact* – then any wrongful conviction, no matter how justified by the evidence, would not result in a punishment but something else. Yet, as I already mentioned, we say that people who are eventually exonerated and released from prison were wrongly punished, not that they were not punished at all.

To accommodate this, D4 could be revised to include an epistemic qualifier:

> **D4′: Punishment is the imposition of burdens by a recognized authority because someone *is believed to have* violated a rule that was acknowledged or should have been acknowledged as a rule.**[11]

10 Duff also seems to make this assumption when he defines punishment as "the infliction of suffering on a member of the community who has broken its laws" (1986, 267; see also 151).

11 Hart and Flew both include this qualification: Hart says that a punishment "must be of an actual *or supposed* offender for his offense" (2008, 5; emphasis added), and Flew says

This covers erroneous convictions made in good faith – that is, defendants who are probatively guilty but not materially guilty. However, that is only one class of innocents. Under D4′, an innocent person who is purposely framed and punished in order to pacify an angry mob is not punished because the person violated a rule or is believed to have violated a rule (at least not by the people who are doing the framing), but because doing so will (or may) maximize overall happiness. Nonetheless, to all appearances, this seems to be a case of punishment, since it involves the same legal apparatus (laws, courts, prisons, etc.) as other punishments. The only question is whether it is right or wrong to do it (Scheid 1980, 459).[12]

This discussion reveals that, although the "because" clause is necessary, it also complicates things by introducing a reason for why burdens are imposed on someone. Thus, it blurs the distinction between the definition of punishment and its justification. As a proposed definition, D4 includes an assumption about when punishment is appropriate, and, in doing so, it begs the question in favor of legalistic retributivism. It is backward-looking in the sense that punishment is a result of what criminals actually did or are believed to have done – they broke the law – rather than what will be accomplished by means of the punishment.[13]

Martin Perlmutter (2014) uses this kind of strategy in defense of retributivism. He reasons that consequentialists cannot really provide a theory of punishment at all, since punishment must be backward-looking, assigning burdens based on people's past behavior rather than future benefits.[14] On his view, punishment is defined as harming criminals because they are guilty, a retributivist aim.[15] The

---

that punishment "must (*at least be supposed to*) be of the offender" (1954, 293; emphasis added). Similarly, D. Locke says that "What is logically necessary for punishment is not that the person *be* guilty, but that he be *believed to be* guilty" (1963, 569); H. Morris says that "punishment is the imposition upon a person who is *believed to be* at fault of something commonly believed to be a deprivation where that deprivation is justified by the person's guilty behavior" (1968, 482–83; emphasis added); and von Hirsch says that "punishing someone consists of doing something painful or unpleasant to him, because he has *purportedly* committed a wrong, under circumstances and in a manner that conveys disapprobation of the offender for his wrong" (1985, 35; emphasis added). Zaibert restricts his own account of punishment to "the first-person perspective": "the punisher could be entirely wrong as to the blameworthiness of what she seeks to punish, and still engage in punishment" (2006, 29).

12 Scheid also says that qualifying the definition by referring to what is reasonably believed does not accurately characterize punishment as a system or institution. The purpose of the system is to punish actual offenders, not supposed offenders (1980, 458–59).

13 Glover accuses Mabbott of begging the question in this way: "The logical point seems to be that the very definition of law involves punishment for its infringement, so that once you have law instead of advice or request, punishment is logically entailed" (Glover 1939, 498).

14 Feinberg makes a similar claim when he says that deterrence could be accomplished without public denunciation, but that would not achieve the aims of punishment (1970, 103).

15 Zaibert defines punishment as doing something to an offender whom we blame for something, because we blame them (2006, 3). Although he says that this does not by itself justify anything, it does entail that punishing someone who is not blameworthy is "logically

resulting argument is simple: Consequentialism allows for the punishing of innocents. Since people can only be punished if they do something wrong, innocents cannot be punished. Therefore, consequentialism is false as a theory of punishment, and retributivism is true.

In order to avoid begging the question in favor of retributivism, one could remove material or probative guilt as a condition of punishment and replace it with merely the claim of wrongdoing. Framing an innocent person is punishment because the supposed criminal is said to have committed a crime, even if the person did not (material innocence) and even if there is no incriminating evidence that justifies the authority's actions (probative innocence). In that case, the authority may base its decision on the circumstances (e.g., the potential cost to society of not pacifying an angry mob) rather than the person's guilt:

> **D4″: Punishment is the imposition of burdens by a recognized authority because *the authority claims that* someone has violated a rule that was acknowledged or should have been acknowledged as a rule.**[16]

This definition allows for the intentional or accidental punishment of innocents. However, in doing so it creates the opposite problem: it begs the question against the retributivist and in favor of the consequentialist. For retributivists such as Perlmutter, the backward-looking nature of punishment is what essentially distinguishes it from other imposed harms. Punishment is a response to what the person did, not what someone says the person did. Since merely stating that someone has violated a rule is not essentially tied to the person's material or probative guilt, the elements in D4″ are not jointly sufficient for the retributivist. On that view, the person must have actually violated the rule.

Of course, Perlmutter may be wrong. Not every retributivist has to define punishment as he does, in explicitly retributivist terms. The definition may function well as a definition, provided that the claim that someone is guilty is subject to evaluation. In other words, the retributivist could accept D4″ as a definition but say that there are good and bad reasons for saying that someone has violated a rule: a good reason is that the person actually did it or is thought to have done it, and a bad reason is that we are trying to pacify an angry mob, deter others, or derive other benefits.

The real problem here seems to be that D4″ begs the question in favor of legal justifications and against moral justifications of punishment. According to D4″, the authority makes it a punishment simply by saying it is. The government

absurd" (27) – a kind of definitional stop (24–37). In defending the response requirement, Lee also defends the definitional stop. He says that knowingly punishing an innocent person on consequentialist grounds may be justified, but it is not punishment (2019, 373–75).

16 Honderich seems to prefer this formulation: punishment is "an authority's infliction of a penalty, something intended to cause distress or deprivation, on an offender or someone else *found to have* committed an offence, an action of the kind prohibited by the law" (2006, 15; emphasis added).

can punish so long as they have the power to punish – that is, if they control the criminal justice apparatus. However, if the power was taken illegitimately, then one could question whether what they do amounts to punishment rather than mere threats and intimidation. D4″ thus elides an important distinction between justified and unjustified authority and the justified and unjustified imposition of burdens.

Any definition of punishment is supposed to be value-neutral, but if the concept of punishment itself is value-laden, then a value-neutral definition is bound to miss something (McPherson 1967). For example, parents who spank their children for fighting are punishing them (corporal punishment). But abusive parents who hurt their children at every apparent slight – not doing well in school, perceived arrogance, tying their shoes the wrong way, and so on – are not punishing the children but abusing them. What distinguishes the punishment is that, even if we think that the parents should not spank their children in the first case, the justification and the proportionality of the harm are, unlike abuse, within the realm of what is reasonable.[17] The challenge for any definition of punishment is not to rule out as unreasonable any of the plausible theories of punishment or any specific punishments, even those with which we disagree.

The appeal to vagueness, and my alternative

All the definitions that I have proposed so far either seem too narrow because they rule out the punishing of innocents, or they beg the question for or against some theories of punishment. To correct this and allow for marginal cases that do not seem to fit the standard definition, Flew's and Hart's strategy is to reconceive what a definition is. Flew claims that "punishment" is vague enough that any definition, including the standard definition, should not be construed as a set of necessary and jointly sufficient conditions (1954, 291–92, 303).[18] Instead, as Hart puts it, he sets out the "standard or central case of punishment," with non-standard or secondary cases that do not meet all the conditions but share enough family resemblances to the standard case that we would still classify them

17 Brooks says that the difference between legal punishment and parental punishment is that parental punishment is private and may be done for "largely arbitrary" reasons, whereas legal punishment is public and done "because a person has performed a crime" (2012, 2–3). However, there are better and worse reasons for parents to punish. If the harm is inflicted arbitrarily and indiscriminately, then it is abuse rather than punishment. Furthermore, by making material guilt rather than probative guilt the reason for legal punishment, Brooks seems to rule out the punishment of innocents by definition – the definitional stop.

18 Mabbott concedes this point to Flew:

> The word "punishment" is used in a variety of ways and one cannot lay down rules to determine where its use becomes appropriate. Thus it is impossible to give a precise definition of the word as ordinarily used. This is the "vagueness" point. It is also true that there are various different criteria for its use, and not all of these need be satisfied for the use to be natural and legitimate. This is the point about "open texture." (Mabbott 1955, 256)

as punishment (2008, 5; see also Ten 1987, 2). Conceiving of the proposed definition of punishment as picking out standard cases rather than listing a set of necessary and jointly sufficient conditions allows for specific instances of punishment that do not meet one or more of these conditions. As Flew says, "there is no *contradiction* involved in saying that you accept a system but propose nevertheless to allow an occasional exception" (1954, 302). For example, punishing innocents is similar enough to punishing the guilty that both are construed as punishments, even though punishing innocents does not meet one of the conditions under the standard definition (i.e., that the person is punished because they committed a crime). The retributivist punishes people because they are guilty and in proportion to their degree of guilt, but innocent people can be wrongly convicted and still be punished, and, possibly, innocent people could be punished as part of a general practice of punishment whose aim is deterrence.

The tendency of some theorists, then, is to leave the definition purposely flexible and to allow for exceptions. But the idea that a definition picks out only the central case of punishment also poses problems. A definition is usually construed as specifying the necessary and jointly sufficient conditions for applying a term. If we define bachelors as unmarried males, then any unmarried male is a bachelor, and someone who is either married or not male is not a bachelor. To say that there are exceptions to this introduces uncertainty and does not accomplish what a definition is supposed to accomplish. For example, what would it mean to say that Lucy is an unmarried woman who shares enough "family resemblances" with bachelors that we will call her a bachelor? What standard are we using to include her and not others, and, if that standard is not contained in the definition, what work is the definition really doing? With punishment in particular, the definition is supposed to be neutral with regard to possible justifications of punishment. However, if it defines only the standard case and allows for non-standard cases of punishment, then, without criteria for what to include, it invites circular reasoning. We would allow or not allow exceptions based on our implicit assumptions about what *just* punishments are.

Don Scheid's proposed solution is no better. He says that we should treat punishment as a "reducible concept," meaning that, in different circumstances, we simply "subtract" one or more of the necessary criteria. The criteria that remain cover the marginal cases that are ruled out under the full (non-reduced) definition (1980, 461–62). This approach renders definitions virtually useless, especially without any standard for when it is appropriate to remove criteria and when it is not. How would it clarify things to say that Lucy is a bachelor once we "subtract" the male criterion from the definition? The "reducible concept" idea entails that there are different necessary and sufficient conditions for the same term. And if "punishment" is a reducible concept but "bachelor" is not, Scheid needs to explain why.

Rule-breaking in sports will help to illustrate how difficult it is to define punishment without begging the question. Committing a foul in basketball is a penalty, and the player who is fouled may get one or two free throws. But if a basketball player takes a bribe to throw the game, they are suspended or even banned from the league. Both actions meet the standard definition: an authority (a referee or the league) imposes some burden on the player or their team because they did something wrong. But Feinberg seems right to claim that only the bribed player is punished while the player who commits a foul is given a mere penalty.

Flew and Hart would say that the responses to fouls and bribery are similar – they share family resemblances – but that penalties on the court diverge enough from the standard case that they do not count as punishments. The problem with this approach is that, if we leave the definition vague and fluid like this, assumptions can creep in that beg the question. In the case of rule-breaking in sports, what criteria are used to distinguish punishments from penalties? The difference seems to be that one is generally accepted as part of the game, while the other is not. In basketball, players are jostling for control of the ball, so fouls are bound to happen. Sometimes fouls are intentionally committed toward the end of the game to stop the clock and force free throws that will change possession of the ball and give the trailing team a chance to score. This is an accepted strategy. By contrast, taking bribes corrupts the game so that it does not do what it claims to be doing: having top-level athletes compete to see which team is better. Basketball fans and the league accept fouls but condemn bribery.[19]

What this shows is that, if the definition of punishment is only supposed to pick out central cases, such that there are exceptions, then it allows one to assume the rightness of a given theory, without argument. In the basketball example, we include suspensions but not on-the-court penalties because we assume that expressivism is true: the former is condemned and the latter is not. This does not really keep the definition neutral. Instead, it obscures its lack of neutrality by providing for exceptions that we judge based on our own theoretical assumptions. In other words, if we say about punishment, as Justice Potter Stewart said of obscenity, "I know it when I see it," then the judgments we make regarding possible exceptions are likely to beg the question in favor of our chosen theory (*Jacobellis v. Ohio*, 378 U.S. 184 [1964], 197). I know punishment when I see it because I know what punishment ought to be.

If we weaken the notion of definition in the way that Flew, Hart, and Scheid suggest, then reasoning about punishment becomes very difficult. Something that meets the conditions that are specified by the definition may not be a punishment, and something that does not meet those conditions may be. It would be extensionally false to say that something is a punishment if and only if it is the imposition of burdens by a recognized authority because someone has violated a rule that was acknowledged or should have been acknowledged as a rule.

A preferred strategy, and the one I will adopt, is to use some of the proposed definitions in order to advance the analysis of punishment and its justification, but in full awareness of the limitations of those definitions. Each justificatory theory presupposes a slightly different definition of punishment, with some common features and some key differences. D4 and its derivatives (D4′ and D4″) will thus serve as stipulative definitions. Each one will be construed as setting out the

19 McCloskey makes a similar distinction (1962, 313–14).

necessary and jointly sufficient conditions for punishment, which is the traditional sense of what it means to define something. However, I make no claims about their truth. Indeed, the provisional qualities are false – they pick out necessary and sufficient conditions, but not the right ones – because each definition is open to the charge of circularity: for example, D4 favors legalistic retributivism and D4″ favors consequentialism. Nonetheless, stipulating conditions for the sake of argument will allow us to proceed without begging the question, consciously or unconsciously. The standard definition and its variants provide provisional qualities that will illuminate the similarities and differences among the different proposed justifications. In other words, by adopting provisional semantic criteria in the form of a stipulative definition, we are better able to probe the inferential patterns involved in discussions of the goodness/justness of a rule while keeping them formally distinct. They are heuristically useful in evaluating theories of punishment. Such definitions carve out precise semantic constraints and render questions of inference tractable by virtue of their finitistic and definite form.

Definition and justification

Leo Zaibert argues that mixed justifications are bound to fail because they rest on a narrow definition of punishment. If punishment is defined in legal terms only, then mixed approaches, even if they could justify legal punishment, could not justify punishment per se, which is also justified in other contexts (2006, 7–37). Although I agree that philosophers ought to provide a definition that covers both legal and non-legal punishments – indeed, I do so in this chapter – this does not preclude different kinds of justifications. Zaibert assumes that the definition of punishment includes a reason for punishment, specifically as a response to blame (3), and he further claims that punishing someone because they are blameworthy (retributivism) is an intrinsic good (181–216). If, like Zaibert, I distinguish what he calls the theory of punishment from its justification (7–37), I can both define punishment in general and provide a mixed justification of legal punishment in particular.

The working definitions that I have proposed (D4, D4′, and D4″) are useful, among other reasons, because of their plasticity. While some theorists focus only on legal punishment as the standard case, my stipulative definitions are broad enough to identify commonalities among punishments in different contexts, yet they also provide the tools for specifying how the different kinds of punishment are distinct. Namely, they can be tailored to different kinds of punishments in different circumstances by clarifying the nature of the authority and the kind of rule that the offender should have acknowledged. Parents have parental authority over their children, and because punishment is used in that context to correct behavior such as lying, being mean to siblings, not doing their chores, and so on, the rules that they should acknowledge are moral standards rather than legal standards. God has divine authority over people, and the people should obey divine law and legitimate religious authority. The state has legal authority over its citizens and people in its territory, and it enforces the law that has been created formally through the legislative process, as defined by secondary law.

As noted earlier, the factual question of what defines punishment ought to be distinguished from the evaluative question of what justifies punishment. Whether something is a punishment is a different question than whether something is a bad or unjust punishment. Still, as we saw, it can be difficult to separate these issues, much as it is difficult in aesthetics to distinguish stuff that is bad art from stuff that is not art at all. One advantage of the definitions of punishment provisionally proposed in this chapter is that they help us to identify the different elements that are subject to evaluation, or the different ways that punishing someone can be wrong. That is, the definitions, while not themselves evaluative, give us ways to focus an evaluation and explain which feature or features of a given punishment make it justified or unjustified.

One stipulative definition of punishment that I am using –

> **D4: Punishment is the imposition of burdens by a recognized authority because someone has violated a rule that was acknowledged or should have been acknowledged as a rule.**

– can be broken down into its constituent parts:

a) "imposition of burdens,"
b) "recognized authority,"
c) "because someone has violated a rule," and
d) "was acknowledged or should have been acknowledged as a rule."

Specifying these conditions allows us to articulate the reasons behind our moral judgments. A given act of punishment may be justified or unjustified with regard to one or more of the elements of the proposed definition. In other words, this definition serves two purposes: not only does it distinguish punishments from non-punishments, but, when coupled with a theory of punishment, it also provides the means to evaluate whether and in what ways a punishment is unjust. I will consider each of the elements in turn, with examples that are not punishments and examples that are unjust punishments, to show how this works.

Because this chapter is about defining punishment rather than defending a specific justification of legal punishment, I will try to avoid controversial cases. Hopefully, the following examples are intuitively just or unjust, and there would be general agreement about their appropriateness regardless of which of the prominent theories we adopt.[20] The following scenario describes, I believe, an uncontroversial case of justified punishment:

> Without provocation, Sam punches someone in a bar in Michigan. He is arrested for battery, put on trial in a criminal court, and convicted. As a result

20 I set aside abolitionism for the moment. It is not so much a theory of how punishment is justified as it is a refusal that punishment can be justified.

> of this crime and in light of his prior convictions, the judge sentences him to two years in prison.

This fits the definition of punishment because (a) there is an imposition of burdens (incarceration), (b) the burdens are imposed by a recognized authority (a criminal court established by the state of Michigan), (c) Sam is sentenced because he has violated a rule (he is convicted of battery), and (d) the rule was acknowledged or should have been acknowledged (the law against battery is a public statute that was promulgated by the state).

We can use the definition (D4) to identify the different elements of the punishment that are open to evaluation. At this point, it is not a matter of identifying whether the prison sentence is a punishment (an "is" question) but establishing whether the punishment is justified (an "ought" question). The heuristic that I explained above reflects the following valid deontic modal inference:

> **Given a definition D of punishment stipulated by criteria D(a), D(b), D(c), and D(d), the provisional sufficiency of this definition entails that punishment P is just whenever D(a) is satisfied justly, D(b) is satisfied justly, D(c) is satisfied justly, and D(d) is satisfied justly.**

In other words, for a punishment to be justified, it must be positively evaluated under each of the four different elements (a–d) that define punishment. Setting the evaluative terms in italics, in this case:

a) The burden is *not wrong in itself*, since the harm (two years in prison) does not seem *inhumane* or otherwise beyond the range of *acceptable* penalties.
b) The criminal justice system in Michigan is *legitimate* and *authoritative* because it is empowered by the people and by the state's governing documents to enforce the law.
c) Sam was charged with violating a *just* law (against battery), and his sentence was *appropriately* given to him upon his conviction, which was arrived at as a result of a *fair* trial.
d) Sam *should* have known that battery is illegal or that it is *wrong* to hurt someone for *no good reason*.

If one of these elements were corrupted – e.g., Sam acted in self-defense, or he was sentenced to be executed – then it would still be a punishment, but it would be an unjust punishment – e.g., undeserved or disproportionate.

History provides many examples of unjust punishments, and the different elements of the definition (D4) help to identify what about each case makes it unjust. For example:

a) "imposition of burdens": Islamic states such as Iran, which follow strict interpretations of Sharia law, sometimes cut off the hands of thieves when they are convicted of stealing (Amnesty International 2018). This is a punishment, but it is wrong because it is cruel and excessive, even if the person knew about the rule and it was imposed by an established government.

b) "recognized authority": Augusto Pinochet's military dictatorship in Chile was recognized as the governing authority by the United States and others, and it had the power to enforce the law. However, it established itself as the result of a coup, thus ignoring the political process laid out in the Chilean constitution. Because its authority was illegitimate, the punishments it handed down were unjust, even when it tried to administer the laws that were in place prior to the coup.

c) "because someone has violated a rule": A court refused to allow Martin Luther King Jr. to lead a protest in Birmingham in 1963, and he was later arrested and jailed for holding a public demonstration without a permit. He violated an established rule. The punishment was wrong because enforcing the violation was an effort to suppress King's free speech rights and maintain segregation.

d) "was acknowledged or should have been acknowledged as a rule": In 1998, a Michigan man was convicted under an 1897 law of shouting profanities within earshot of women and children. He was fined $75 and ordered to perform community service. One could say that he should have acknowledged the rule – ignorance of the law is no excuse, and the law was available to him and everyone else. However, it was a little-known, archaic law that remained on the books for years without being enforced, so the punishment was unjust. (The law was also later ruled unconstitutional.) ("Anti-Swearing Law Unconstitutional" 2002)

The point of this exercise is to indirectly validate the usefulness of the proposed definition(s) of punishment (D4 and its derivatives, D4′ and D4″). Not only does it provide the conditions under which an action can be classified as a punishment or not a punishment. It also provides an evaluative taxonomy that can be used to judge the rightness or wrongness of particular punishments, and to identify the specific element or elements of the punishment that make it unjust. There are different ways that something can fail to be a punishment, and different ways that something can fail to be a justified punishment.

Part II

Normative foundations

Any mixed theorist worth the label has to believe that deterrence theory and retribution are both right in some sense. If we believe that we can give offenders a proportional punishment if and only if it maximizes happiness and only to the extent that it does so, then we are consequentialists. If we believe that deterring criminals is only a beneficial but incidental side effect of punishing the guilty because of what they did, then we are retributivists. A mixed theorist believes both that punishment is instrumentally good to accomplish some valued aim (consequentialism) *and* that punishment is intrinsically good because offenders deserve it (retributivism).

To begin to make my case for the two-tiered model of punishment, the following chapters present separate justifications of consequentialism and retributivism – respectively, in terms of the function of punishment in preserving the public order and in expressing the community's resentment toward offenders. I then suggest a way that these two contrary justifications can be jointly maintained in a two-tiered system, where we distinguish between the consequentialist aims of the legislature and the retributivist aims of the criminal judiciary. The institution of punishment in general as well as statutory penalties are justified on consequentialist grounds, while the distribution of punishments to particular offenders is based on what they deserve.

2 Preserving the public order

A defense of consequentialism

Even though punishment is so commonly accepted, it should strike us as odd and in need of justification. It is *prima facie* wrong to intentionally inflict pain or deprivation on people, so if punishment is justified in some cases, there must be a compelling reason why the harms are worth it, or are better than not harming them. Punishment may bring about better consequences than not punishing, by incapacitating criminals and deterring people from committing crimes (consequentialism), or it may accomplish something that is good in itself, such as giving criminals what they deserve because they deserve it (retributivism). Regardless of what we identify as the proper justification, there need to be reasons to punish that would make something good out of what is normally bad.

There are some justifications that can be dismissed at the outset. The fact that it is a cultural commonplace, that it has been around for a long time, that it is "natural," or that we really want to do it carry little weight in favor of purposely harming people, which, all things being equal, ought to be avoided. A dentist who pokes at your gums in an effort to improve your oral health is a good doctor. A dentist who does it only to carry on a long and venerable tradition is a slave to the past, and one who does it for fun is a sadist.

In the legal context, punishment serves a social purpose: the reason why a state punishes its citizens is to enforce the law, or more generally to preserve the public order. This is accomplished by separating criminals from the general population (incapacitation), rehabilitating or depriving them so they are less likely to reoffend (specific deterrence), and using punishment as a threat to disincentivize criminal activity by others (general deterrence). State policies regarding punishment are justified only if they accomplish these aims better than less harmful alternatives. Thus, legal punishment as an institution is justified on consequentialist grounds.

Different authorities, different aims

As I said in Chapter 1, defining punishment is not the same thing as justifying punishment. Thus, although there is a definition of punishment in general and we can identify what different kinds of punishment have in common, that does not entail that there is one common justification of all kinds of punishment. In fact, punishments in different contexts are and ought to be justified differently, by appealing to distinct normative principles. The justification of punishment depends on the aim of punishment, which varies by context. To illustrate this, imagine the following case:

> Person A refrains from doing something that has been expressly prohibited but admits that they would do it if they thought that they could get away with it.[1]

Assuming that the prohibition itself is justified and that the prohibited act is wrong, then person A has a bad character and bad intentions, but they have not acted wrongly. Are we justified in punishing person A? It depends. There is no right answer to this question until one has specified who person A is, the circumstances, and the kind of authority that the punisher has over them.

In the following case, punishment would be justified:

1) Two parents instruct their children not to burn down the house, and none of them do. But one of the children says that they really want to, that they have no concern for the family's well-being or property, and that the only thing holding them back is the prospect of being punished.

The parents would be doing nothing wrong if they were to ground the child or confiscate their cell phone (undoubtedly the kid's most prized possession) in an attempt to discourage such an attitude (specific deterrence). The parents may also enlist a psychiatrist to help the child work through their hostility and develop concern for others (rehabilitation). One can imagine the parents watching the kid more closely and not leaving them alone in the house (incapacitation). And hopefully this would send a strong message to the other children that they disapprove and that similar feelings in them will not be tolerated (general deterrence). In short, the child's character in this case, even without an overt act, would justify punishment for the purposes of improving them morally, restraining the budding psychopath, and deterring the other children. The offensive "act" in this case, which violated a standing rule, was the having of a bad character.

The parents do not have a concern for their house primarily, but a concern for the child's character (and the characters of their other children). So, at least in principle, their response would be justified on consequentialist grounds, as a means to accomplish a valuable end. In this case, they are trying to change the kid so that, when they grow up, they will be an upstanding citizen and a good person – that is, someone who does not have these urges, which, if acted upon, would have to be checked by the law. Ultimately, the parents want their offspring to internalize a standard of rightness rather than being motivated by the threat of punishment. Reforming the child's character, as the goal of the parents' actions, is enough to justify the punishment regardless of whether the kid has in fact

1 I use "they" here and elsewhere as a gender-neutral singular pronoun. See Baron (2020, ch. 5).

committed arson. Having a good character is good in itself, not only as a means of protecting lives and property in the future.

The appropriate justification of punishment (and whether it is justified at all) changes if person A is not a child confessing to their parents. Assuming (hypothetically and for the sake of illustration) a traditional Judeo-Christian conception of the afterlife, we can imagine an adult who, after dying, faces divine judgment:

2) The soul of a recently deceased person stands before Saint Peter, outside the pearly gates. The person lived a fairly normal and law-abiding life, but they would have burned families to death on earth had they lived in different circumstances – if, for example, there were no laws against arson, incompetent police, or bribable judges.

The consequentialist argument in this case would be irrelevant. Heaven does not need to be protected from the person; their pyromania does not need to be restrained. They do not need to be made better through rehabilitation because there is no future person for them to be. The souls of others do not need to learn from their example. Rather, the person would not get to heaven because they do not deserve endless bliss. They deserve to be punished – hell, separation from God, or whatever – not because they committed a wrong or illegal act, but because they have a bad character and acted rightly only as a result of circumstantial moral luck. This is irrelevant to and unknowable by the state, but it is relevant to God: as J. D. Mabbott says, "For a moral offence, God alone has the *status* necessary to punish the offender" (1939, 154).[2] If there is such a thing as divine judgment, God is a retributivist.

By contrast, in the case of legal permissibility and whether punishment by the state is justified, it does not matter why someone follows the law. The law is concerned with people's characters only insofar as they can be reliably inferred from their behavior and determinative of the kind of crimes they actually committed – for example, murder versus involuntary manslaughter. It is not illegal to have an immoral character unless one acts on it and breaks the law: "a 'criminal' means a man who has broken a law, not a bad man" (Mabbott 1939, 154). This is so because the state does not have the same purpose as a family or God. Imagine a judge who says that a defendant does not have the right attitude and needs to go to jail as a kind of "timeout," even though no crime was committed or even attempted (i.e., there is no *actus reus*). Legal punishment would not be justified in the following case, even though it is the same action (or inaction) as cases #1 and #2:

3) A citizen follows the law against arson but informs the police that they really want to burn down people's houses, that they have no concern for their

2 Mabbott echoes Montesquieu, who says that magistrates have no right to punish sins against God unless they result in actions "that disturb the tranquility or security of the state." When it is purely a matter of character, the punishment ought to be "ruled by his infinity and not by the weakness, ignorance, and caprice of human nature" (Montesquieu 1989, Bk. XI, ch. 4 [p. 190]).

> fellow citizens' rights, and that the only thing holding them back is the prospect of being sent to prison.

The police would have no basis on which to detain the person or charge them with a crime, and the courts cannot sentence them to prison, since they have neither done something nor even threatened to do something. To be sure, someone with such a character is more prone to committing arson than someone who cares about other people and is not fascinated by burning buildings, but merely having a bad character is not illegal so long as one does not act on that character: "The state is not an agent of cosmic justice; it punishes only such acts as are contrary to legal rules, conformity to which, even from unworthy motives like fear, is considered of public importance" (Benn 1958, 327).[3] The law is succeeding in deterring this would-be arsonist from acting on their desires. The threat of legal punishment is justified in this case because it is useful, but carrying out the threat would be unnecessary and unjustified because they have *not* acted on them. Bad intentions are not enough.[4]

Similarly, we can imagine a convicted arsonist who, after serving their prison term, still wants to burn down buildings. If they refrain from doing so because they hate prison and want to avoid it, the criminal justice system will have done its job. In terms of punishment's general justifying aim, we want to produce law-abiding citizens, not angels. This is one reason why moral education theory is wrong. Society as a whole, especially parents and teachers, may have failed the arsonist by not instilling in them a healthy regard for other people and their property. But the success of specific deterrence or rehabilitation programs is measured in terms of recidivism, not by how many ex-cons send cards to their moms on Mother's Day.

The justification of legal punishment thus becomes clearer when contrasted with other cases of punishment. The following three kinds of punishment correspond to the above scenarios:

1) A child is given a timeout by their parents.
2) A person is sentenced to eternal damnation by God in the afterlife.
3) A criminal is sent to prison by the state.

All three are cases of punishment – that is, all three involve the imposition of burdens by a recognized authority in response to a rule-violation – yet their

3 Oliver Wendell Holmes Jr. wrote something similar in one of his decisions: "As the aim of the law is not to punish sins, but is to prevent certain external results, the act done must come pretty near to accomplishing that result before the law will notice it" (*Commonwealth v. Kennedy*, 170 Mass. 18 [1897], 20). Elsewhere, Holmes says that criminal law only concerns offenders' observable conduct. When intent matters, it is with regard to what a reasonable person could have foreseen, not the offender's actual state of mind (2009, 37–70).

4 Montesquieu says that "where there is no public action, there is no criminal matter" (1989, Bk. XI, ch. 4 [p. 190]); and Beccaria says that "the one true measure of criminality is the damage done to the nation and …, therefore, those who believe the true measure of criminality lies in the malefactor's intention are mistaken" (1995, 22).

justifications are very different because of the aim that each authority wants to accomplish.

As noted earlier, the purpose of punishing children is to encourage a better character. One of the responsibilities of parents is to punish their children when appropriate if doing so will teach them important lessons about right and wrong. Except in the most extreme cases, parents do not punish their children to protect others, but to protect children from their own worst impulses, or to influence them at this formative point in their life so that they become morally good. Immanuel Kant (2007) struggled with the problem of how to make children into adults who are willing to do what is right because it is right, when the tools that we have to motivate them depend on their trying to further their own self-interest (i.e., trying to avoid punishment). He recommended the use of a catechism, with moral questions and answers that children would memorize, so that they would slowly be habituated to act rightly, and eventually for the right reasons (Kant 2007, 9:490). Children would not be merely trying to avoid pain, as they do when threatened with a spanking. Punishments such as timeouts have become more common, and we now discourage corporal punishment precisely because we are trying to improve children's characters rather than inflicting punitive harm. Ideally, timeouts allow children to calm down, reflect on what they did, realize the error of their ways, and resolve not to do it again.

By contrast, punishment by the Judeo-Christian God is not intended to correct people's characters, since it is too late by the time of divine judgment. It is not done to protect others or to preserve a lawful system, since God's infinite power is enough to keep the kingdom of heaven functioning:

> Divine punishment … is not institutional in any usual sense of "institutional," and it is not directed – or primarily directed – at maintaining an institution, for it is usually conceived of as deferred punishment. If God were asked why He punished individuals, He need not reply "To uphold the institution constructed of moral rules and divine commands." … we do not need to, and perhaps cannot properly, speak of the point of divine punishment, except in terms of its justice. (McCloskey 1962, 309)

Such punishment is purely retributive, in the sense that a person's punishment is proportionate to how good or bad they are. For example, wicked souls are assigned to specific levels of Dante's hell depending on the crimes the people committed when they were alive. Putting one's deeds on a scale of justice is the perfect metaphor for retributive punishment, where only the guilty are punished and their punishments are equal to their crimes. In the afterlife, people get what they deserve.

The state is neither a parent nor a god. As Paul Johann Anselm Feuerbach writes, the purpose of legal punishment includes neither "*moral retribution* [*moralische Vergeltung*] because this belongs to a moral and not a legal order and is physically impossible[5] … nor ***moral improvement*** [***moralische Besserung***] because this is the purpose of ***discipline*** [***Züchtigung***] but not of punishment" (2014, §18 [p. 386]). So, why does the state punish its own citizens? It is given the authority to enforce the law so that it can maintain itself. This is a Hobbesian point: if the law were not enforced, the state would in effect cease to exist. The law is the codified version of what we as a society are after, and there are different ways of phrasing what it is supposed to do: preserving the public order, promoting the common good, ensuring public safety, or simply reducing crime.[6] State-sanctioned, institutionalized punishment is one of the means that the state uses to enforce the law and achieve our collective ends.

Punishment is crucial for a state's survival because there has to be a reason that conformity to the law is in a person's self-interest. Thomas Hobbes famously wrote that "Covenants, without the Sword, are but Words, and of no strength to secure a man at all," by which he means that the law only constrains people if there are incentives to follow it (1996, 117).[7] It is in their self-interest not to break the law because they would be punished if they did, and the crime is not worth committing if they are punished for it. This is not to say that punishment is necessary to motivate everyone to obey the law; most of us are "acute conformists" who follow the law habitually (Pogarsky 2002). But it is an economic truism that, in most cases and all things being equal, if you increase the cost, you decrease the demand. Increasing the cost of committing a crime reduces the likelihood that it would be worth it for someone to do it, so, in general, people are less prone to violate the law. The institution of punishment is what Ernest van den Haag (1982) calls a "threat system," A. C. Ewing calls "a kind of negative wage" (1970, xi), and Edmund Pincoffs calls "a pricing system in reverse" (1966, 131).[8] The "prices"

5 Feuerbach does not explain what he means by "physically impossible [***physisch unmöglich***]," although an early editor includes this gloss: "so-called *legal retaliation* … is … without any practical utility for the legislator or for the judge, if it is to be used as a yardstick for the relationship of the punishment to the magnitude of the crime" (Feuerbach 2014, §18n [p. 386n]). The idea seems to be that we are not only unable to determine a person's moral guilt, but we also cannot match the punishment to the degree of moral guilt. As I note later in the book, the retributivist's appeal to intuition provides little guidance regarding proportionality.

6 Aquinas says that "Law is nought else than an ordinance of reason for the common good made by the authority who has care of the community and promulgated" (1964–1981, 1a2ae.90,4 [vol. 28, p. 17]); and Locke says that the purpose of the state, and specifically the legislature as the "*supreme power*," "*is the preservation of the society*, and (as far as will consist with the public good) of every person in it" (1980, §134 [p. 69]).

7 Echoing Hobbes, James Fitzjames Stephen says: "Abolish the gaoler and the hangman and your criminal law becomes empty words" (quoted in L. Stephen 1895, 318).

8 Similar views appear in Rawls (1955, 12), Posner (1972, 357–74), Golding (1975, 92–93), van den Haag (1975, 17–18; 1981), M. Davis (1992, 234–53), and Miceli (2019). Hart is an exception to this tradition. He says that punishing a criminal looks like "a price justly extracted because the criminal had a fair opportunity beforehand to avoid liability to pay" (2008, 23). However, elsewhere he cautions against considering punishments to be a kind of tax. Taxes are imposed for the purpose of generating revenue and paying for public goods, while punishments are imposed because criminals violate rules that guide the conduct of citizens (Hart 2012, 39).

are statutory penalties, which are set, in kind and degree, to discourage wrongdoing. Hobbes says that "*a Punishment, is an Evill inflicted by publique Authority… to the end that the will of men may thereby the better be disposed to obedience*" (1996, 214); Locke says that the severity of the punishment must make committing the crime "an ill bargain to the offender" (1980, §12 [p. 12]); Bentham says that "*the value of the punishment must not be less in any case than what is sufficient to outweigh that of the profit of the offence*" (1970, ch. XIV, §8 [p. 166]); and Beccaria says that punishment provides "sufficiently tangible motives to prevent the despotic spirit of every man from resubmerging society's laws into the ancient chaos" (1995, 9). Although none of us are ideal maximizers of utility (criminals especially), the idea is that, in general, people are motivated by a cost-driven calculus where they weigh potential benefits against potential risks, and change their actions accordingly (G. Becker 1968; Kahneman and Tversky 1979). Although individual criminals are often unaware of the specific penalties they are risking – a common challenge to deterrence theory – the threat of punishment reduces criminal activity in the aggregate and helps to maintain a lawful arrangement. Only the latter point is crucial to the justification of punishment as an institution.

Michael Davis includes an appropriate caveat: the law need not ensure "social tranquility" or be so harsh that no one would ever risk breaking the law; "the rules need only forbid the more substantial harms and regulate major conflict" (1992, 72). The mere existence of crime does not make a state untenable, but rampant crime that results in "resubmerging society's laws into the ancient chaos" would (Beccaria 1995, 9). Therefore, insofar as punishment motivates people to follow the law, and the law is what unites us into a community, punishment is "the principle of cohesion" and "society depends on coercion" (L. Stephen 1895, 318).[9]

He also says that punishment is different from the old tariff model (Hart 2008, 167–70). Scheid agrees that the law should be characterized as a threat system but disagrees with the idea that it is a price system. One reason he gives is that criminal law is different from tort or contract law, with the latter more properly concerned with prices. Criminal punishments are designed to prohibit certain conduct, but tort or contract law seeks to correct a maldistribution (Scheid 1997, 466n55). I do not think that such a strict distinction is necessary so long as we see the threat of punishment as the threatened imposition of an especially high cost, or we think of punishment as correcting a maldistribution of advantages as a result of the crime. N. Morris turns this on its head and suggests (half-jokingly) that we use the money we would spend to keep someone in prison and pay them a weekly allowance not to commit crimes, "like a reverse income tax, a reverse crime prevention contribution" (1966, 636).

9 The full quotation, summarizing James Fitzjames Stephen's view in *Liberty, Equality, Fraternity*, is worth including:

> Consider men as a multitude of independent units, and the problem occurs, How can they be bound into wholes? What must be the principle of cohesion? Obviously some motive must be supplied which will operate upon all men alike. Practically that means a threat in the last resort of physical punishment. The bond, then, which keeps us together in any tolerable order is ultimately the fear of force. Resist, and you will be crushed. The existence, therefore, of such a sanction is essential to every society; or, as it may be otherwise phrased, society depends upon coercion. (L. Stephen 1895, 318)

Deterrence

As opposed to non-criminal wrongs, criminal acts cause "social volatility" by creating fear and raising doubts about the state's ability to protect people and their property, among other things (L. Becker 1974). So, preventing those crimes through incentives helps to maintain the social order. First, following through on the punishment of actual criminals makes the threat credible for potential criminals. As Oliver Wendell Holmes Jr. says,

> The law threatens certain pains if you do certain things, intending thereby to give you a new motive for not doing them. If you persist in doing them, it has to inflict the pains in order that its threats may continue to be believed. (2009, 44)[10]

Second, punishing criminals redistributes burdens imposed on the community by their criminal acts. Crime causes people to worry for their safety and perhaps to change their behavior, and these negative effects must be corrected by making them feel safe and incentivizing criminals and potential criminals not to act wrongly in the future. By breaking the law, criminals make themselves available as means to offset the public's losses (Kavka 1994).

Legal punishment is one instrument that the state uses to preserve the public order, and it does so by means of deterrence. Because the aim of punishment is so general, deterrence has to be construed broadly to include different preventive and curative measures.[11] It is a complex concept, and its different meanings often blur together. I use the term to cover any attempt to reduce the likelihood of crimes in the future, including deterring potential criminals and actual criminals by means of threats, incapacitation, and rehabilitation. Traditionally, "deterrence" usually means general deterrence, which is directed at potential (not-yet) criminals to make them less likely to disobey the law. From this perspective, punishments are often construed as threats posed to non-criminals *ex ante* to make committing a crime a bad bet for them. But the criminal law can also serve "as a concrete expression of society's disapproval of an act," which, by

10 Holmes here echoes Feuerbach, who writes:

> I) The purpose of the *threat of punishment* in the statute is the deterrence of all, as possible offenders [*Beleidiger*], from right violations. II) The purpose of its *infliction* is the establishment of the effectiveness of the statutory threat, insofar as without it this threat would be empty (ineffective). (2014, §16 [p. 385])

Bentham also thinks that inflicted punishment is illustrative: "The punishment suffered by the offender presents to every one an example of what he himself will have to suffer if he is guilty of the same offense" (1830, Bk. I, ch. 3 [p. 20]). Cragg holds a similar position: "The function of law is to reduce recourse to the justified use of force in settling disputes. The function of enforcement is to hold or build public confidence in the capacity of the law to fulfil its function" (1992, 204).

11 For this reason, Scheid prefers to talk about "crime control" in a broad sense rather than deterrence in particular (1997, 453–55).

educating people regarding the community's shared expectations, "helps to form and to strengthen the public's moral code and thereby creates conscious and unconscious inhibitions against committing crime" (Andenaes 1974, 8; see also 110–28). For example, Richard Brandt (1958) claims that legal punishment is a formal censure that not only causes discomfort that potential criminals would like to avoid but also reminds them of the wrongness of criminal acts, thus serving a moralizing function (see also Smart 1973, 49–56).[12]

The purpose of legal punishment is to maintain the state, so it works best to accomplish its aim when crimes are successfully prevented. In that case, the state does not have to carry out the threat and impose burdens on its citizens; punishment is unnecessary.[13] Deterring a potential criminal is better than punishing them after the crime because the former minimizes harm to both the victim and the criminal, and it maintains rather than having to reestablish the public order. If the threat of punishment fails to deter, then crimes put the social order at risk: "every instance of the infliction of a punishment is an instance, as far as it goes, of the *failure* of the legislator's design" (Whately 1832, 61; see also Benn 1958, 330). Punishment is inflicted after the fact to produce marginal utility out of something bad. This is very different from God's punishment. When a wicked person goes to hell, that is how divine justice is supposed to work. The sinner has failed, not God and not the system.

Because of the difference between preventive and reactive enforcement mechanisms, some theorists distinguish deterrence of potential criminals from restraint or incapacitation of convicted criminals. However, because no prison is completely secure (escape-proof) and because criminals can commit crimes in prison (despite close supervision), then imprisonment simply makes the commission of additional crimes difficult and less likely than if the offenders were free. This

12 The National Commission on Reform of Federal Criminal Laws (the Brown Commission) states that, in addition to deterrence, incapacitation, and rehabilitation, one objective of the criminal code is "to insure the public safety through ... vindication of public norms by the imposition of merited punishment" (1971, pt. A, ch. 1, §102 [p. 2]). And, in his economic analysis of punishment, Miceli says that, by communicating social values, punishment encourages people to identify the law and thus "functions as a costless supplement to law enforcement as a means of controlling harmful behavior" (2019, 19–20; see also ch. 8).

13 Beccaria writes: "It is better to prevent crimes than to punish them. This is the principal goal of all good legislation, which is the art of guiding men to their greatest happiness" (1995, 103); Kant writes: "Authority punishes, not because a crime has been committed, but so that it shall not be committed" (1997, 27:286); Fichte writes: "Punishment is a means for achieving the state's end, which is public security; and its only purpose is to prevent offenses by threatening to punish them. The end of penal law is to render itself unnecessary" (2000, 228); Bentham writes: "General prevention ought to be the chief end of punishment, as it is its real justification" (1830, Bk. I, ch. 3 [p. 20]); and Mabbott writes: "[The legal] threat of punishment may be so effective as to make punishment unnecessary" (1939, 161). Feuerbach claims that physical constraint (*physischer Zwang*) is not an effective means of maintaining the state, since it is only imposed after a violation of rights has occurred. Psychological constraint (*psychologischer Zwang*) is better because it precedes and prevents the violation (2014, §§10–16 [pp. 384–85]).

reduction in the likelihood of future crimes is therefore a kind of physical deterrence directed at specific criminals (i.e., those who are imprisoned).[14] There is no definitional reason why "deterrence" should be restricted to the effect of psychological incentives only.

In addition, some theorists distinguish what they call specific deterrence, in which the fear of returning to prison makes criminals want to avoid committing additional crimes upon release, from rehabilitation, where criminals become motivated not to recidivate as a result of counseling, drug treatment, or educational and vocational programs. These two approaches involve different kinds of psychological incentives: prison is a negative reinforcer (the prospects of being punished again, and in some cases more harshly, as under three-strikes laws), and success in a legal line of work is a positive reinforcer (the prospects of being reintegrated into society and pursuing a normal, fulfilling life). Although their methods are different (threats and reform), both are forms of specific deterrence in the sense that they make crime by individual criminals ("specific") less likely ("deterrence"). Because the distinction between positive and negative incentives is easily blurred – drug treatment is tough but also holds out the prospects of a better life – I consider rehabilitation to be one kind of specific deterrence.[15] Even incapacitation and rehabilitation are not so different, if one looks through a Foucauldian lens: rehabilitation is a form of internal (psychological) restraint, while prison walls are a form of external (physical) restraint. Bentham says that punishment exerts an "influence" on the offender, "either on his will ... or on his physical power" (1970, ch. XIII, §2n [p. 158]). Therefore, all these measures – incapacitation, rehabilitation, and the fear of future punishments – are forms of specific deterrence, in order "to prevent the offender from doing fresh harm to his fellows"; and they serve a similar purpose as general deterrence, which is "the instilling of terror in other men" (Beccaria 1995, 31, 40).[16]

Retribution

Deterrence is the focus of legal punishment because it motivates people to behave in accordance with the law, thus preserving the public order and furthering our

14 As Levitt and Miles make clear, the distinction between incapacitation and deterrence depends on strictly distinguishing physical constraints and mental incentives:

> Incapacitation, unlike deterrence, is not a behavioral response to incentives, but a restriction of the offender's criminal opportunity set. Incapacitation refers to the inability of an imprisoned offender to commit additional crimes as a result of physical constraints on his movement. (2007, 463)

Foucault, among others, blurs this distinction.

15 Andenaes also includes rehabilitation in his definition of specific deterrence: "By individual prevention we mean the effect of punishment on the punished. At best this results in genuine moral improvement or in the acquisition of pro-social habits" (1974, 9). However, he also distinguishes these at Andenaes (1974, 175–81).

16 For a similar view on the (broad) meaning of deterrence, see Brooks (2012, 37).

collective goals. It is in contrast to retribution, which need not further the aims of the state. Because of this, policies around punishment should not establish statutory penalties in order to give people precisely what they deserve. Not only does the law punish only actions (rather than a person's character or desires, which affect desert), but, as W. D. Ross notes, illegal acts are only a subset of wrong acts. Thus, the general justifying aim of punishment should not be to achieve retribution:

> The offences which the state legislates against are only a small part of the wrong acts which are being done every day, and a system which punishes not all wrong acts, but only those which have been forbidden by law, and does not attempt to reward all good acts – such an occasional and almost haphazard system of intervention does not hold out any good hope of promoting the perfect proportionment of happiness to virtue. (2002, 59)

Ross says that retributivism reflects "an outworn view of the state, one which identifies the state with the whole organization of the community" (59). Although, as I show later, retribution justifies individual criminal sentences, it does not justify the *institution* of punishment. Restraint, specific deterrence, and general deterrence have the same aim: to maintain a system of laws. The purpose of the law will vary – whether it is to protect people's rights, ensure a just distribution of goods, protect the people in power, and so on. But the purpose of punishment is constant across the different purposes that states may have.

Retributivists tend to consider punishment in a vacuum, as if we simply had to equate a harm inflicted by the criminal with a harm inflicted by the state. In doing so, they overlook the context in which punishments are being inflicted and who is inflicting them. The harm of punishment serves a unique function in the legal context that it does not serve in other (e.g., parental or divine) contexts. Don Scheid makes a Hobbesian point when he says that crime control provides a reason to subject ourselves to the constraints of the law, in a way that retribution does not: "it is doubtful that the retributive goal of ensuring that wicked people receive the suffering they deserve would strike many people as a very compelling reason for joining in a social contract" (1997, 452). We have no choice whether to subject ourselves to divine justice (if there is such a thing), but we do choose to engage or continue to engage in a system of laws. As an institution, punishment furthers the interests of the community because, among other things, it furthers the aggregated interests of individual citizens (i.e., the common good). That justifies and motivates a commitment to the social contract.

Another way to understand what gives punishment its value is to imagine a legal system in which punishment fails to achieve its aim. What would an ineffective institution of punishment look like? If criminals were given punishments that were wildly disproportionate to and much less than the seriousness of their offenses, then people would be more likely to commit crimes. For example, if someone who embezzled a million dollars were punished with a week's home confinement, many more people would be willing to risk the punishment because of the incredible gain they could get, even if they were caught. With small fines for theft, more people would steal from their neighbors and shoplift from stores. To be sure, most people have no interest in murder or rape, regardless of the consequences, but that subset of people who are deterred by the prospects of punishment would not be deterred if there were little cost to them. In such a situation, people would have to protect themselves against thieves and predators. Security cameras would not be enough to deter shoplifters, because shoplifters would not worry about being arrested. Instead, shopkeepers would have to make their own threats, increase security, and aggressively defend themselves and their property. Society would become less secure and more anarchic, with people protecting their own families and possessions through violent means, and our lives would be "solitary, poore, nasty, brutish, and short" (Hobbes 1996, 89). In effect, there would be no state, only individuals or clans who protect themselves. The conclusion to draw from this is that, assuming that people are imperfectly rational and liable to commit selfish acts at the expense of others – we can grant this without completely acceding to Hobbes's egoism – punishment is necessary as a deterrent to serve its purpose and preserve society. At the institutional level, punishments that are too lenient to reduce criminal behavior are not intrinsically wrong because they are disproportionate but instrumentally wrong because they are ineffective.

Alternatively, we could imagine a retributivist utopia where all criminals get exactly what they deserve. Police discover every crime and they have no discretion to let anyone off with a warning. No mercy is shown by judges and prosecutors, and every criminal is convicted. If such a system drew funding away from public schools and healthcare, and eventually bankrupted the government, would it have been worth it? Even if there is some intrinsic value in punishing the guilty – something that has yet to be established – we cannot seriously entertain the idea that the consequences for the state's very existence are irrelevant. The state must consider its impact on the public good in order to evaluate whether, even if we ought to give people what they deserve, that is actually the right thing to do. For the state, as opposed to God – the state has limited resources to carry out its obligations – retributivism cannot be action-guiding without at least being supplemented by consequentialism. As a general justifying aim, positive retributivism is wrong. Desert is not, by itself, a compelling reason for a state to punish its criminals.

Circular reasoning?

Before concluding, it is important to note that the argument of this chapter does not beg the question in favor of consequentialism and against retributivism (see Murphy 1973, 227). I am not assuming that, because states have purposes, punishment must be justified by their consequences. It would be possible for states to have nonconsequentialist purposes. Communicating disapproval, instilling moral education, or giving people what they deserve are all possible purposes of punishment, and, if they are not done instrumentally in order to encourage people to act lawfully, then they are alternatives to preserving the public order.[17]

Instead, I have argued that, given our conception of the role played by punishment in a *successful* or *properly governed* state – as opposed to, say, its role for a just God or well-meaning parents – preserving the public order is an appropriate purpose and retribution is not, at least not at the institutional level. Even Kant states in his lectures on ethics that legal punishments have deterrence as their aim: "All the punishments of princes and governments are pragmatic, the purpose being either to correct or to present an example to others. Authority punishes, not because a crime has been committed, but so that it shall not be committed" (1997, 27:286). Assuming (against abolitionism) that punishment is crucial to preserving the public order, a state that did not punish its criminals would not be doing what it ought to do – that is, it would not be achieving its "pragmatic" aims. This is where justification enters, as opposed to question-begging description.

Conclusion

My foundational argument for the institution of punishment identifies only in the broadest terms what the general aim of punishment is: to preserve the public order. Punishment has value in relation to that aim, which is what makes my view a form of consequentialism. In this chapter, I set aside a more specific characterization of the consequences to be achieved, or what an orderly society looks like. In talking about enforcing the law, one could mean maximizing happiness, promoting justice, or protecting rights, among other things. Furthermore, the pursuit of such ends only justifies the institution of punishment as a whole rather than particular instances of punishment (i.e., its distribution). Whether a consequentialist theory regarding punishment's general justifying aim would support the framing of innocents under some circumstances remains an open question.

By contrasting legal punishment with divine and parental forms of punishment, it becomes clear that consequentialism is an appropriate normative theory regarding the legal practice of punishment. Legal punishment is justified because it supports the rule of law, and it supports the rule of law through its consequences: the deterrence of crime and the protection of the public. If legal punishment accomplishes these things, it is sufficient to outweigh the *prima facie* prohibition against intentionally inflicting harm or imposing burdens on people.

17 This is one reason why Michael Davis believes that we should do away with the consequentialist/retributivist distinction: retributivists may value consequences too, such as balancing the scales of justice (2009, 80–82). I discuss Davis's position and his alternative distinction in the Introduction, note 6.

3 The rational and the reasonable

The question of whether efforts to enforce the law are justified is made more difficult by its ambiguity. One may be asking any of at least three different questions. First, there is the question of whether an arrest by the police enforces the law as written ("letter of the law"). But one could also be asking other, more philosophically interesting questions:

1) whether an act of enforcement is an effective way to do what the law, qua law, is intended to do ("spirit of the law"); or
2) whether an act of enforcement that is justified under the law is also morally justified – that is, whether (a) the law itself is morally justified and (b) the method of enforcing it is justified in a derivative sense because it supports the law.

When these questions are not clearly distinguished, it causes confusion and apparent disagreement, even when people actually agree. For example, was it justified for Birmingham police to arrest Martin Luther King Jr. for holding a public demonstration without a permit? He was violating a clearly written statute, so in some sense the arrest was justified. The police did not invent a nonexistent law or plant drugs on him. But the police also enforced that law selectively to stop his protest, something that they could have avoided doing had they used their discretion more judiciously. The law should be a shield, not a sword, and the discriminatory use of the law was an attempt to limit free speech. The value of the law itself is also debatable. There is nothing inherently wrong with requiring a permit for parades and public demonstrations, because a city needs to plan for these things in order to control traffic, among other things. But applying for the permit should not be so difficult that it inhibits the exercise of free speech, and permits should not be refused for people whose message is unwelcome – which is exactly what happened in Birmingham. Indeed, the U.S. Supreme Court later struck down the law as an unconstitutional prior restraint on speech (*Shuttlesworth v. Birmingham*, 394 U.S. 147 [1969]).

These legal and moral issues need to be separated. An action may be legal or illegal (e.g., parading without a permit), but that is a question of legal permissibility (whether the police *can* charge you with something under the law) rather than a question of moral justification (whether they *ought* to charge you with something [1 and 2]). Since the purpose of this book is philosophical rather than legal or historical, the more important questions have to do with the evaluation of the law and its application rather than the mere fact that it is a law and the legal permissibility of enforcing it. As John Austin reminds us, "The existence of law is one thing; its merit or demerit is another. Whether it be or be not is one enquiry; whether it be or be not conformable to an assumed standard, is a different enquiry" (1995, 157). The law can be evaluated in different ways, and there are different standards we can use to assess its enforcement: (1) the law may be effective or ineffective at achieving its intended aim (e.g., crowd control), and (2) it may be morally justified or unjustified, depending on whether its aim is right or wrong (e.g., controlling crowds and facilitating the movement of traffic in theory, but silencing critics of segregation in practice). A theory of punishment should be able to evaluate policies against these two separate standards.

Punishment is one method – historically, one of the tools most commonly used by the state – of preserving the public order. Given this consequentialist understanding of punishment, there are different ways for it to go right or wrong. An institutional arrangement of punishments could be more or less effective in reducing crime. In that case, it would be a better or worse means to an end. But we also have to evaluate the end that is being achieved. If the criminal justice system is maintaining an unjust state, then it is also being used wrongly. In his discussion of social cooperation, John Rawls talks about rational agents as ones who effectively pursue their own self-interest and reasonable agents as ones who engage in fair terms of association, measured against a standard of justice (1980, 528–32). Analogously, one could describe punishment as either rational or reasonable depending on whether it, respectively, effectively advances state interests (i.e., what it takes to be the common good) or advances the cause of justice (i.e., what is in fact right).[1]

Legal justification (1)

If consequentialism is the correct theory for justifying punishment as an institution, then whether legal punishment is justified depends in part on whether it accomplishes the purpose, or can reasonably be expected to accomplish the purpose, that the law is intended to promote. If the threat of punishment does not deter potential criminals (general deterrence) and punishments do not deter actual criminals (specific deterrence), then they are not protecting the public,

1 One drawback of McPherson's claim that the definition of punishment cannot be separated from its justification is that, he says, calling something punishment is already to approve of it (i.e., punishment is "self-justifying"): "If you see someone behind bars and ask why he is there, the answer, 'He is being punished,' itself gives a kind of justification of his treatment. Part of what we mean by 'punishment' is 'justifiable infliction of unpleasantness'" (1967, 26). McPherson is confusing the question of legal permissibility and legal justification with moral justification of the law and its enforcement, or at least he is not distinguishing them.

maintaining the state, and enforcing its laws. The imposed burdens amount to unnecessary harm because they are ineffective, and they are therefore unjustified.

Punishment can be used instrumentally in different ways, which is why I describe the justification of punishment as consequentialist rather than utilitarian. Punishment as a legal institution is supposed to maintain the state and preserve the public order, but, as Antony Duff reminds us, "the idea of 'the common good' sets no very tight constraints on the particular ends or values which the law must claim to serve" (1986, 89). The state's primary aim may not be to maximize happiness. For example, if a state exists in order to protect the rights of its people ("to secure these rights, Governments are instituted among Men"), then their happiness is incidental. They have only the right to live their lives as they want, within boundaries established by other people's rights ("the pursuit of Happiness" rather than happiness itself) (Declaration of Independence, U.S. 1776). On the liberal view, the institution of punishment maximizes freedom by criminalizing threats and harms to persons or property (i.e., "crimes against persons" and "crimes against property"), or actions that destroy the public order under which those rights are respected (i.e., "crimes against society"), and by protecting the rights of the accused. Decisions about government intervention and coercion would, on this view, be based on a kind of rights calculus to assess potential outcomes and to maximize rights protections – a "consequentialism of rights."[2] For example, the legislature restricts people's freedom of movement with trespassing laws because doing so has better consequences for rights – namely, owners' property rights – than doing nothing. And the state has to determine how best to allocate its limited resources in order to fulfill its obligations regarding welfare rights, such as rights to basic education and health care (if there are such things).

Alternatively, Karl Marx claims that punishment can only be justified in a communist system, or else it would be used to reinforce existing social and economic inequalities. Once communism is achieved, then the goal is to remain unalienated from ourselves, the products of our labor, and other people, and to maintain the social cohesion and mutual support to which we have freely consented, without economic coercion (Murphy 1973). Other systems could be designed to promote justice (Plato), to further the natural law (Aquinas), to ensure personal protection (Hobbes), and so on. These are all possible aims. Of course, one could ultimately try to justify any of these legal institutions in

2 Nozick coined the term "utilitarianism of rights," and he rejects that view in favor of his view of rights as side constraints (1974, 28). Sen claims that there can be no utilitarianism of rights. Since only happiness is an end in itself according to utilitarianism, rights are only instrumentally good, so they lose their independent normative force. Sen does conclude, however, that a *consequentialism* of rights is coherent (2000, 499). A similar consequentialist view is defended by Braithwaite and Pettit, who claim that "dominion" ought to be maximized, which they construe as maximizing the liberty of citizens living under the rule of law (1990, esp. ch. 5). For another defense of how a particular version of consequentialism can be made consistent with a rights-based view, see Bentley (2000).

utilitarian terms – in *On Liberty*, John Stuart Mill (1978) tries to justify basic rights as secondary principles derived from the principle of utility, for example – but one need not do so. There are potential political aims other than happiness or rights-protection, and punishment can deter would-be criminals from thwarting those other aims as well.[3]

Cesare Beccaria concludes that, unlike divine justice, which is unchanging, human or political justice "can vary according to how necessary or useful that action is to society" (1995, 5). Montesquieu says something similar when he identifies three kinds of governments (republican, monarchical, and despotic) and their underlying principles, and he says that "the laws given by the legislator should be relative to the principle of the government" (1989, Bk. V [p. 42]). Justification in this sense depends on what the state happens to value. Punishments can be better or worse, justified or not, relative to the state's adopted aims:

1) **State-sponsored punishment is legally justified only if the punishment helps to maintain the state and enforce its laws, or can be reasonably expected to do so.**

In other words, punishment should effectively deter those who would disrupt the social order. A dictator who allows people to vote in free and fair elections, regardless of whether it undermines the government's authority, would be doing the wrong thing. This assessment does not carry a moral charge with it. In a moral sense, it would be a good thing for the regime to be replaced, peacefully (or perhaps not), with a democratically elected ruler. Nonetheless, it is a kind of value judgment. An autocratic leader who allows for such a thing would be a bad autocrat.

To be sure, one can always ask whether an action, including an action taken by the state, is legal. That is a purely factual question or, when the law is ambiguous, an interpretive question for appellate courts. The police who arrested King were enforcing the law as written. This does not answer the question of whether they

3 Flanders argues, because of "the sheer number of conflicting ideas about state punishment that there is a good case to be made for political liberalism *as a political philosophy*, and accordingly, for defending what political liberalism says about the proper function of and limitations upon punishment" (2019, 523). I claim that the justifiability of a given scheme of institutional punishment depends on the justifiability of the political aims, but Flanders claims that "the sheer variety of political-philosophical options when it comes to punishment" entails that we can only commit ourselves collectively to what we can reasonably accept, which is a liberal arrangement (539). This assumes, among other things, that the relative rightness of competing aims of punishment cannot be determined, like our different individual conceptions of the good. Flanders talks about it as a "reasonable pluralism" and "the possibility of differing, yet sensible views about what we should be doing when we punish people" (540). However, if there are more and less just political arrangements – e.g., if a rights-based liberalism is, unlike communism, a form of oppression and self-alienation, or vice versa – then we should not remain agnostic regarding our collective conception of the good. Whether this can be accomplished is the topic for another book.

ought to have arrested him. There is a difference between an action being legal and being legally *justified*. The justificatory question is whether having that law and the accompanying punishment is a good way to further the aims of the state. In many countries, these aims are often spelled out in their founding and governing documents. Regarding the permit to demonstrate, for example, there was a deeper legal question of whether the law as enforced was consistent with the U.S. Constitution as secondary law – namely, whether it violated prohibitions on discriminatory treatment (equal protection) or inhibited free speech. This is not yet a moral question – i.e., it is not a question of whether the aims of the state ought to be promoted – since primary and secondary laws may be unjust (more on this later). But it is an axiological question in a broad (nonmoral) sense, as indicated by the value-laden vocabulary of discovering what is best, most effective, or most consistent with our public values.

In Kantian terms, we are constrained by a hypothetical imperative in assigning specific legal punishments: if we adopt an end (protecting natural rights, supporting communism, maintaining a dictatorship, and so on), it would be irrational of us not also to will the means to that end (Kant 1996a, 4:414–17). As Norval Morris puts it,

> To fail to define our purposes for punishing any human being is to make Pilate's choice; to define our purposes and yet to make no effort to test the capacity of our means to attain them is a similar though a lesser sin against the light. (1966, 634)

Once the aim of punishment is identified, we ought to do what we can to pursue it effectively. A system of punishment is rational if it maintains the state, and in that sense it is justified internally, relative to the aims of the state, rather than being judged against an external, moral standard.

Although this seems like a kind of relativism, a state can get things wrong even by this measure. For example, Germany prohibits Nazi symbols and *Volksverhetzung* (incitement of the people, or hate speech). By contrast, the U.S. allows people to display Confederate flags and swastikas, and it allows white supremacists to express their views openly, with the idea that these are forms of free speech protected under the First Amendment. Both Germany's and the United States' policies are intended to support law and order, and their effectiveness at achieving that end can be evaluated and compared. One could make the case, arguing along with Mill, that such ideas should not be censored in Germany so that their wrongness can be exposed and people holding contrary, morally right ideas can sharpen their arguments, turning their positions into a "living truth" (1978, 32–34). But one could also argue, as Germany does, that forbidding *Volksverhetzung* is necessary, because of its particular history, to support democratic coexistence. Whether Germany's policy of "defensive democracy" is better than the United States' policy, and whether there should be different policies given the countries' different histories, is a contentious issue. We should consider which approach will, under the circumstances, sustain a healthier democracy (since both Germany and the United States are democratic republics). This is a judgment of value or rightness, but it is different from asking whether a state's aims, statutes, and punishments are morally right.

Moral justification (2a): Just system

Talk of maintaining the state may sound authoritarian, and talk of preserving the social order may seem conservative. *Whose* order is being preserved? A state's policies around punishment are usually, perhaps inevitably, shaped by its contingent legal history, including its biases. Consequentialists must be mindful of how easy it is to slide from the idea that a punishment is effective to the idea that it is morally right. Stop-and-frisk may be a useful police tactic, but it may also violate people's rights. The claim that we ought to reduce crime sounds good until being a Black man in a white neighborhood is treated as a crime. Whether a punishment is morally justified, then, is separate from the question of whether the punishment is justified under the law: as Ted Honderich puts it, "*Whenever* a man is punished under a law, however acceptable the law, a moral justification may be dependent upon the rightness of the law but not upon the fact that there *is* a law" (2006, 19). Whether punishment not only effectively achieves the government's aim but is also morally justified depends partly on whether the system being preserved is a just system. Politicians who talk of "law and order" often ignore this question.

Immanuel Kant distinguishes the hypothetical imperative from the categorical imperative, the latter of which amounts to a moral constraint. We are unconditionally required to act rightly regardless of the ends we have (1996a, 4:414–17). Similarly, with regard to punishment, there are two distinct senses of "good": punishments can be effective and rational, given our aims (legal justification), and they can be right and reasonable, given the aims or ideals that we ought to have (moral justification). Rawls makes a similar distinction when he notes that we can evaluate practices or institutions against an independent (moral) standard, but that we can only evaluate particular actions within a practice against the rules of that practice (1955, 27). There is a difference between justice and the rule of law – a difference that Montesquieu, who tends toward relativism, seems not to recognize.

Legal punishment serves a particular function in maintaining the state. However, if we talk about deterrence without identifying what kind of behavior is being discouraged or encouraged, then we do not know whether deterrence is a good thing. The Nuremberg laws effectively made German Jews stateless, and German citizens were legally prohibited from harboring or otherwise protecting them, but the deterrent effect in that case was a bad thing, since it facilitated unjust and inhumane treatment. Some consequentialists believe that utilitarianism is true and thus assume that any punishment that maximizes happiness (by means of general and specific deterrence) is good. But the connection must be made explicit and the goal justified – in this case, happiness as an intrinsic good – if the punishment that supports it is to be justified.[4]

Duff claims that the rightness of retributive punishment depends on whether society has identified the crimes it ought to identify, and more broadly on whether society is decent and the actions it prohibits are, in fact, wrong (2001, 35). This broader normative question about the political and legal system in which standards of behavior are enforced is relevant for consequentialist theories as well. Indeed, a punishment that effectively furthers the aims of the state is morally justified only if the aims of the state are worthy of pursuit:

2a) State-sponsored punishment is morally justified only if the state itself is justified and its laws promote a just arrangement.

Punishment should not only maintain the social order, but a *just* social order. This criterion is about whether the ends (of justice) justify the means (of purposely imposing burdens on offenders). It must be added to ensure that punishment is not, for example, merely propping up an authoritarian regime or serving the personal interests of those in power, even if they are codified in the law and enforced by the government. Although such regimes would have the legal authority to imprison people who criticize the government or to prohibit free and fair elections, it would not be morally justified in doing so.[5] If we relate this to the stipulative definitions in Chapter 1, we are evaluating whether the authority claimed by the governing power is legitimate in a thick, moral sense that goes beyond the mere legality of what it does.

This distinction is similar to the one that John Finnis makes when he talks about the "focal meaning" of law. Breaking with some other natural law theorists such as Aquinas and Augustine, Finnis admits that, although human law ideally ought to reflect natural law, a law that falls short of that ideal may still be a law. Unjust laws are laws, but they are not what is most properly called law (2011, 9–11, 277–80). Similarly, I am claiming that, if a system of punishment effectively maintains the state, it is legally justified punishment. But if the state itself is

4 I have my doubts about the rightness of utilitarianism when it comes to the general justifying aim of punishment. Like Kant, I do not think it is nonsensical to ask whether we ought to maximize happiness, because happiness is only conditionally good. I am more inclined to a rights-based view, which is why I will often illustrate the two-tiered model of punishment with reference to liberalism. I do not have the space to pursue this here. As I mention in the Conclusion of this book, justice and the proper political arrangement are topics for another volume, one on political theory rather than the philosophy of law.

5 Mabbott elides this distinction in defending his version of circular retributivism:

> About the government, whether it is good or bad, I do not enquire. X has broken a law. Concerning the law, whether it is well-devised or not, I have not asked. Yet all these questions are surely relevant before it can be decided whether a particular punishment is just. It is the essence of my position that none of these questions is relevant. Punishment is a corollary of law-breaking by a member of the society whose law is broken. (1939, 160–61)

unjust, then the institution does not have all the characteristics that a justified system of punishment ought to have. One way of putting it is that such punishment is *legal* but not *lawful*. The latter term includes different, more robust normative assumptions – namely, concerning the rightness of the state's aims. An unjust but legal punishment is "aptly referred to by a secondary or non-focal use of the term 'punishment,' a term which in its focal use has a proper role in any satisfactory account of what is required for human well-being" (Finnis 2011, 266).

It seems strange to me that one could try to justify punishment without also talking about the function it serves in furthering the aims of the state. Consider moral education theory. If the purpose of punishment and the threat of punishment is to make criminals and potential criminals better people, then we must identify some standard of what is "better." An authoritarian theocracy that tries to indoctrinate its citizens into a particular religious dogma may, on its view, be making its people better. Whether they are right about that depends on several things, including whether their religious view is correct, whether that method of educating people is morally appropriate, and whether the government should be in the business of proselytizing. Take another example: societal safety-valve theory. If the purpose of punishment is to allow people to express their socially disruptive emotions peacefully and in ways that do not disrupt the social order, one would first have to determine whether the social order is worth preserving. For example, China is very good at making sure that political speech is tightly controlled so that the Communist government is insulated from criticism. That may be an effective means of control, but whether that is a good thing depends on whether the Communist system ought to be preserved, whether there are such things as rights to freedom of speech and the press, and so on. One cannot say, then, that a punishment is good if it assists in people's moral education or if it controls disruptive emotions without answering a series of questions at the institutional level.

Moral justification (2b): Not excessive

A second condition of punishment's reasonableness is that the imposed burden must not be excessive. I have assumed from the outset that intentionally harming someone is *prima facie* wrong. Some philosophers have attempted to justify this claim with various arguments. For example, Mill bases utilitarianism on the claim that "pleasure and freedom from pain are the only things desirable as ends," so actions are "wrong as they tend to produce the reverse of happiness" (2001, 7). The *prima facie* wrongness of harm can be outweighed by some greater benefit, but causing avoidable harm or harm that is not somehow worth it is intrinsically bad. However, there is something peculiar about giving reasons for why we should not intentionally harm other people. If it does not strike us already as wrong, an argument is unlikely to convince us. As Emmanuel Levinas argues, the very attempt to justify suffering presupposes the moral obligations we have to others, in the sense that justifying ourselves before others (even hypothetical others) is a normative moment that testifies to their status as morally considerable persons whose suffering should matter to us. Rather than any propositional argument, that ethical demand to explain our actions presupposes that they have a different moral status than rocks and trees, and that we are obligated not to harm them (Levinas 1997, 115–18; Levinas 1998, 94).

Punishment is intentionally imposing burdens on someone because they violated a rule. The consequences of the punishment support the state, so, when the aims of the state are morally justified, the *prima facie* wrongness of intentional harm is overridden by a more pressing obligation to maintain a just arrangement. If intentionally harming people is *prima facie* wrong, however, then the state can impose only the burdens that are necessary to further the state's aims. Jeremy Bentham puts it simply: "all punishment is mischief: all punishment in itself is evil. ... it ought only to be admitted in as far as it promises to exclude some greater evil" (1970, ch. XIII, §2 [p. 158]). Therefore, the *prima facie* obligation not to cause intentional harm places a side constraint on punishment, even if a more severe punishment would also further the aims of a just state:

2b) State-sponsored punishment is morally justified only if there is no less harmful alternative that would as effectively maintain the state.

Norval Morris refers to this as the principle of parsimony regarding criminal punishment: the least harm should be imposed that will as effectively achieve the social end that we want to accomplish by means of the punishment (N. Morris 1974, 60–62; N. Morris 1977, 171; Tonry and Morris 1978, 445–46, 447; N. Morris 1981, 258, 266; N. Morris 1982, 190–91; Morris and Tonry 1990, 104).[6] The fact that we could deter stealing by cutting off the hands of convicted thieves does not mean that such an extreme punishment is morally justified. Stiff penalties short of mutilation would probably deter all those who are able to be deterred. And even if some marginal increase in deterrence accrued with such extreme penalties, it would also produce other costs, such as lack of respect for a government that would do such a thing to its people. As Montesquieu says, "Every penalty that does not derive from necessity is tyrannical." It treats legal authority as "a pure act of power" rather than a justified attempt to maintain the public order (1989, Bk. XIX, ch. 14 [p. 316]).

The previous two conditions – that punishments should enforce a just system and that they should not be excessive – are each necessary for punishment to be morally justified, and they are jointly sufficient:

2) State-sponsored punishment is morally justified if and only if (a) the state itself is justified, its laws promote a just arrangement, and (b) there is no less harmful alternative that would as effectively maintain the state.

6 Pincoffs seems to have the same idea when he says that inflicting unnecessary suffering is inhumane because it violates "the criterion of humanity" (1966, 123–24).

In short, a system of punishment that effectively maintains a just state with the least amount of harm is morally justified.

Alternatives to punishment

Because the state ought to minimize harm and because punishment is the intentional infliction of harm on its citizens, the state is also obligated to use alternatives to punishment when it is feasible to do so. For example, if we could prevent criminal behavior more effectively and at a lower cost by providing young people with better public education – Beccaria says that "the surest but hardest way to prevent crime is to improve education" – then we ought to do that (1995, 110).[7] Public education serves the positive aim of preparing people to be active citizens and productive members of society, and punishment serves the negative aim of keeping people from being antisocial and disruptive members of society. Like any public policy, consequentialist reasoning would determine the payoff of any potential investment in social services versus punishment.

When responding to wrongdoing, then, the state must consider (1) whether punishment or some other practice, and what degree of punishment or kind of practice, deters more potential criminals from committing crimes; and (2) other social costs and benefits of each, including for the victims. With regard to the first point (1), most theorists assume that people follow the law primarily because of incentives and disincentives. On this instrumental view, all of us are potential criminals, and we would be prone to do bad things if there were no law prohibiting them, accompanied by the threat of punishment. Based on an empirical study of people's attitudes toward and experiences with the law, however, Tom Tyler (1990) shows that most people are not in fact motivated by self-interest when it comes to following the law. Instead, they comply with the law when the legal rules align with their personal values or when the authority that makes the law is thought to be legitimate. In general, people comply voluntarily and crime rates drop when there is a normative commitment to the law (see also Robinson and Darley 1997; Robinson 2000; Robinson 2008b, 175–212; and Robinson, Barton, and Lister 2014, 314–30). This is the "conditional deterrence" theory, according to which legal punishment is only an effective crime deterrent if it is reinforced by other social institutions (Williams

7 When the state educates its citizens and when it punishes the guilty, it is trying to do the same thing: promote the common good. Plato makes the comparison: punishment is inflicted

> for the sake of the future, to prevent either the same man or, by the spectacle of his punishment, someone else, from doing wrong again. But to hold such a view amounts to holding that virtue can be instilled by education; at all events the punishment is inflicted as a deterrent. (1961, 324b [p. 321])

The methods, of course, are different. Punishment is the intentional infliction of suffering in response to wrongdoing. Education is the unintentional infliction of suffering in response to ignorance.

and Hawkins 1986). As I discuss in Chapter 13, restorative justice practices such as shaming and victim offender conferencing may help to strengthen this commitment.

Point two (2), where we consider overall costs and benefits, takes us beyond criminology to broader public policy and the effects of other social programs. For example, a robust public education system produces more engaged and informed citizens who participate in the political process, trains people to enter the workforce and contribute to the economy, and is more likely to sustain supportive family structures, while diverting educational funding into punitive measures such as prisons often has the opposite effects. For those who must be punished, correctional educational, vocational, and drug-treatment programs may produce some of the same benefits. In short, punishment is only one way of achieving crime prevention, so social scientists should consider the variety of institutional settings that affect the crime rate, including legal institutions of criminal justice but also communities, families, schools, and labor markets (Sherman 1997).

Any effort to promote the public good is likely to have both costs and benefits. Constant surveillance and forced behavior modification could achieve a stable social order, and without either allowing victims to be victimized or inflicting the harm of imprisonment on criminals. But, assuming the liberal framework, it would come at the cost of relinquishing most of our basic rights. A system of disincentives (as opposed to preventive interference) deters criminal behavior while also respecting people's freedom to choose. And by punishing only the guilty, we treat people in accordance with their choices rather than treating everyone as a potential criminal who has to be forcibly restrained. Contrary to the therapy model of social control, a liberal system respects criminals' right to be punished – more on this later (H. Morris 1968).

One theme that runs throughout this book is that a merely punitive approach to criminality is not very effective in maintaining the social order. That does not entail that punishment in general ought to be abandoned. Punishment can also serve a symbolic function in, for example, conveying to people that the state condemns those who violate our shared legal constraints. Punishment rebalances the fair system to which we have agreed. It expresses a shared feeling of resentment. All these aims, insofar as they are morally justified, reinforce the legitimacy of the government. I suspect, then, that punishment must be part of any strategy to promote the public good if for no other reason than because of its normative import. The fact that appropriate punishments reinforce the state's legitimacy, in addition to the fact that some people will be motivated not to commit crimes because of the threat of punishment (which demands deterrence) and some criminal activity is inevitable (which demands restraint), means that at least some system of punishment must remain in place.[8]

8 Hanna (2009a) argues that liberal political philosophies could never give a general justification of punishment because punishment aims to impose suffering, and there are always

Still, the more we understand the social conditions that affect rates of criminal activity and nonpunitive strategies for rehabilitating offenders, there is likely to be less and less justified punishment. Some abolitionists claim that punishment is almost completely ineffective, so we ought to adopt other, nonpunitive strategies in every case.[9] My theory of punishment, by justifying the practice on consequentialist grounds, entails that we are obligated to use alternatives to punishment that are more effective than the intentional infliction of harm when such alternatives are available. I doubt that punishment as a whole could be abolished without a net loss to the public good. However, if it could – if abolitionists are correct on this factual issue regarding the greater effectiveness of nonpunitive strategies – then my view would support abolitionism, provided that – and this is an important caveat – it would also allow for the expression of resentment on behalf of the community (see Chapter 4).

Restricted consequentialism

Other caveats are necessary at this point as well. First, the consequentialist reasoning that I have defended pertains only to punishment. I am making no broader claims about consequentialism as a moral theory that would apply to all actions and policies, and to all agents, including individual agents and collective agents such as the state. Punishment as a public institution serves a specific, unique function: namely, enforcing the law. It is different in this sense from other decisions that a person or even the state may make.

Furthermore, the consequentialist justification of punishment is separate from the justification of the state itself, which need not be justified by its consequences. If we assume, for example, that the purpose of the state is to protect people's rights, those rights may be justified on utilitarian grounds (Mill), but they need not be. In fact, they may be justified with reference to a conception of right or justice that is explicitly nonconsequentialist (e.g., Locke, Marx, Rawls, and Nozick). Thus, punishment as an institution is not necessarily justified in terms of how it furthers human happiness Rather, punishment is justified with reference to the aims of the state, and the aims of the state may or may not be justified with reference to consequences.

---

nonpunitive alternatives that would support a liberal social arrangement. There are several problems with this claim. For one thing, his view entails that probation and incarceration are not punishments, because their purpose is restraint and not suffering. Thus, he defines suffering too narrowly, rather than seeing it as one kind of burden that is intended to coerce. Hanna also assumes that the aim of punishment is suffering rather than suffering (or burdens) being the means to achieve some desirable end. By defining punishment as the intentional infliction of suffering on the guilty and claiming that suffering would have to be an end in itself, he begs the question against consequentialism.

9 Boonin (2008) has led the recent abolitionist movement among philosophers. He claims that punishment ought to be replaced with pure restitution. Other abolitionists include Mathiesen (1974), Christie (1981), de Haan (1990), Hulsman (1991), Golash (2005), and Hanna (2008, 2009a, 2009b, 2014).

One may still argue that even this limited kind of consequentialism could lead to immoral punishments. One could imagine a case where a just society would be supported by grossly violating people's rights. Punishing an innocent person to calm a threatening mob is a common example. I will set that aside at this point because it will be addressed in detail in coming chapters. Here I will say only that any *policy* regarding punishment is just if it is instituted by a just government, promotes a just arrangement, and causes less harm than the practical alternatives. The consequentialist justification applies to the institution of punishment and statutory penalties for classes of criminal behavior, not individual accused criminals, whether innocent or not. The distinction between punishment's general justifying aim and its distribution is crucial for the two-tiered model of punishment.

Must I also defend a political philosophy?

On my view, the rightness of the institution of punishment depends on the rightness of the political system that it supports. Thus, I agree with Michael Philips's (1986) claim that the justification of punishment is crucially related to the justification of the state (see also Lacey 1988 and Matravers 2000). In principle, any attempt to develop punishment policies must at some point engage the broader normative question of how we ought to arrange ourselves socially and politically.

I disagree, however, that a *theory* of punishment is impossible without a political philosophy. I develop just such a theory in this book, which, I argue, is true regardless of the form of government that is presupposed. Michael Davis is right to claim, contrary to Philips, that a theory of punishment depends only on broad presuppositions that would be true of any political arrangement, its "deep structure" as opposed to its "surface structure" (1992, 18–41). Davis insists that a theory of punishment need only suppose that people are deterrable (25–27). Such a theory can be explained and defended without specifying the system it supports, with the idea that once a just system is established, the theory shows how coercion is justified under that system, whatever the system turns out to be. Only when one begins to talk more specifically about the kinds of punishments that we ought to have does it become crucial to know what social order is being maintained and to assess its value.

Conclusion

Philosophers too often consider legal punishment as if it were an isolated act rather than an embedded social practice with political ramifications. Once we recognize the function that punishment plays in maintaining a society, then it becomes clear that there are two dimensions to any consequentialist justification of punishment. Punishment policies are rational if they effectively preserve the public order, and they are reasonable if that public order is just. These two conditions, jointly considered, justify the institution of punishment.

4 Expressing resentment

A defense of retributivism

In the previous two chapters, I defended the claim that the institution of punishment is justified by its consequences, specifically in terms of how it maintains the state or furthers the common good. Consequentialism is a normative theory according to which we ought to perform that action, adopt that policy, or create that institution that best maximizes whatever has intrinsic value. Pleasure, perfection, and rights, among other things, may have intrinsic value, and the specific kind of consequentialist theory is defined by what ought to be maximized, or how the public good is defined: hedonistic utilitarianism, perfectionist consequentialism, consequentialism of rights, and so on.

By contrast, according to retributivism, giving someone what they deserve has intrinsic value. Punishment is evaluated independently of whatever good that will be produced. Immanuel Kant, for example, says that criminals ought to be punished because they committed crimes, and that the punishments ought to be equivalent to the crimes, lest we use them merely as means to an end. Punishing criminals for what they did treats them as responsible agents rather than as products of social or instinctive forces (1996b, 6:331–32). On this view, legal punishment is not primarily about how the government relates to the community and promotes its well-being (forward-looking), but about how the public, through the government, relates to individual criminals, who have earned punitive burdens because of the choices they made (backward-looking).

Like Kant, nearly everyone believes that criminals should be punished because they deserve it, even if they do not think that this is the only reason. It is ironic, then, that the law of retribution has been so difficult for philosophers to justify. Arguments for retributivism tend either to beg the question, have no place in broader moral theories, or appeal to morally questionable and irrational impulses. Many of these approaches misconstrue both the feeling at the basis of retributivism and the role of government in responding to that feeling.

In this chapter, I justify a version of retributive punishment by appealing to the feeling of resentment. Looking to resentment in order to explain and justify our intuitive commitment to retributive justice has a long history, going back at least to Adam Smith, and this tradition has been carried on more recently by Jeffrie Murphy. However, those who defend retributivism in this way often claim that resentment includes or is equivalent to anger and the instinctive desire for revenge, and specifically the desire to harm the offender in proportion to the victim's own harm. Because this does nothing to reverse the harm that was done to the victim, however, I claim that we must focus instead on the bare fact of feeling wronged, aside from anger or revenge. Acting on the latter feelings attempts to compensate the victim with more pain, this time suffered by the offender. On my view, by contrast, punishment by the state serves not to "balance the scales of justice," whatever that means, but to express resentment on behalf of the victim and the community as a whole.

The problem of justification

According to retributivism, we are justified in imposing burdens on criminals because they deserve it, because they did something wrong or because of the harm they caused. The "desert base" is some property or some fact about the wrongdoer by virtue of which they (the desert subject) deserve some punishment (the desert object) (Feinberg 1970, 55–94; see also Kleinig 1971). Different retributivist theories have different explanations for why criminals deserve punishment: because they interfered with their victims' autonomy (legal retributivism, e.g., Alan Brudner), because they unfairly took advantage of others (fair-play theory, e.g., Michael Davis), because they denied their victims' equal worth (annulment theory, e.g., Jean Hampton), because they relinquished their rights (rights forfeiture theory, e.g., Christopher Wellman), and so on.

In addition to the different candidates for reasons why offenders deserve to be punished, there are also different ways of understanding what justifying retributivism would entail. It could mean that the state may only punish the guilty (negative retributivism, with guilt as a necessary condition) or that the state must punish the guilty (the extreme version of positive retributivism, with guilt as a sufficient condition), and it could mean that the punishment must be equivalent to the crime (equality retributivism, based on the *lex talionis*)[1] or that it must be proportionate to the crime, which is merely a comparative claim (proportional retributivism). In addition, what the person deserves could be determined by the crime itself, such that all people who shoplift, for example, would receive the same punishment ("grievance retributivism"); or it could be determined by the act plus the criminal's intent or degree of guilt, so that someone who steals for fun would deserve a harsher punishment than someone who steals bread to feed their starving family ("character retributivism" or "deep character retributivism") (Murphy 2003, 43, 106). And of course, this is a porous distinction, since which crime a person commits often depends on intent – for example, whether a person commits murder or involuntary manslaughter, or whether someone is guilty of a hate crime.

1 *Lex talionis* is the law of retaliation, which says that wrongdoers should be harmed (punished) in ways that are equivalent in kind or degree to the harms they caused. The most famous expression of this principle is at Exodus 21:23–25: "If any harm follows, then you shall give life for life, eye for eye, tooth for tooth, hand for hand, foot for foot, burn for burn, wound for wound, stripe for stripe" (New Revised Standard Version).

When it comes to justification, the retributivist faces a challenge that the consequentialist does not. For the consequentialist, we evaluate the infliction of punishment like any other action. According to utilitarianism, for example, we judge all actions against the principle of utility. If we justify the infliction of harm by looking at what it will accomplish, in terms of deterrence or rehabilitation, punishment becomes just another case of maximizing utility. Depriving criminals of freedom or property is worth it because it prevents future crimes, either by others (general deterrence) or by the criminals themselves (specific deterrence). As Jeremy Bentham says, inflicting burdens on offenders is a necessary evil insofar as it minimizes suffering in general (1970, ch. XIII, §2 [p. 158]).

A longstanding objection to consequentialist theories of punishment is that they cannot make sense of what makes punishment distinctive (e.g., Perlmutter 2014). For the consequentialist, punishment is just another way of producing positive outcomes. But this is also an advantage: punishment is clearly entailed by the broader moral theory. Retributivism faces the opposite problem. The retributivist's claim that it is good to intentionally cause criminals to suffer is, so to speak, axiologically homeless. No one defines ethical behavior in terms of annulment, except in the context of punishment. Andrew von Hirsch's claim that "punishment … restores the equilibrium" by "imposing a counterbalancing disadvantage on the violator" sounds more like metaphysics than ethics (1976, 47). And there is a long chain of connections, each requiring its own justification, that gets Kant (1996b) from the categorical imperative to retribution: from the categorical imperative (pure moral philosophy) to the value of outer freedom for finite rational beings (applied moral philosophy), to equal respect for others as free pursuers of ends, to the function of the state in coercing people to respect outer freedom, to the inappropriateness of deterrence, and finally to the law of retribution. Desert as a normative concept applies to people, natural things, and human artifacts. Though it has "moral overtones," "desert is not a specifically moral notion" (Kleinig 1971, 72). Yet it carries so much justificatory weight for retributivists that it is often used as a reason to execute people.

While Bentham can claim that punishment is a necessary evil, retributivists have difficulty explaining why the suffering of the guilty is intrinsically good (Dolinko 1991; Shafer-Landau 1996; Honderich 2006, 23–29). Among other things, it grates against our moral intuition that harm is a bad thing and can only be justified if it is outweighed by some important purpose, such as lessening overall harm. Appealing to a kind of immediate intuition of primitive propositions, not in need of any justification, gets us nowhere. Michael Moore, for example, says that we have "intuitions about desert" (1993, 26), and those intuitions immediately warrant retribution as "a first principle describing an intrinsic value that we each categorically are enjoined to realize in our actions" (25; see also Zaibert 2006, 181–216).[2] And some arguments only seem like

2 Kleinig says that the unpopularity of the concept of desert among philosophers (in 1971) was due to "the unpopularity of intuitionism, with which it is usually associated" (1971, 71).

arguments. Igor Primoratz, for example, supports his retributivism by appealing to justice: "it is justified to requite evil with evil, for it is only just; and it is just because when doing so, we treat another person in the way he has deserved" (1989, 70). If "requit[ing] evil with evil" is giving someone what they deserve, then this begs the question. A punishment is justified because it is just. Hugo Adam Bedau says that retributivists face a choice: either they appeal to nothing beyond desert, in which case it is trivial and question-begging; or they appeal to some end that is accomplished by means of punishment, in which case it collapses into consequentialism (1978, 616).

As I mentioned earlier, retributivists such as Kant claim that punishing offenders treats them with respect because it considers them as rational agents who can be held responsible for what they do, rather than treating them merely as instruments of social improvement (deterrence) or as defective thinkers in need of therapy (rehabilitation). Herbert Morris (1968) concludes that, as persons, criminals have a "right to be punished," so we have a correlative duty to punish them, just as we have a duty to respect their other rights.[3] Respecting people's rights is intrinsically good, regardless of the consequences.

Objections have been raised that this misunderstands the nature of a right. For example, what would it mean for people to have a right that they do not want respected and that they could not voluntarily relinquish (Ross 2002, 63; Quinton 1954, 136)? Furthermore, although such a belief may motivate retributive punishment, it does not justify it, since there are other ways to show respect for those who wrong us, including compassion, forgiveness, and reconciliation. If a governor pardons someone for a crime rather than punishing them, the governor would not be wronging the person or violating their rights, as the view seems to entail (Deigh 1984). Indeed, legal forgiveness may treat the criminal more like a person than putting them in a cage or killing them.

In short, it is easier to talk about wrongdoing (forfeiture of rights, etc.) and the desert base by virtue of which the offender deserves something than it is to make sense of how that desert base actually *justifies* punishment. Nonetheless, this challenge has little effect on the assumptions about desert that are deeply ingrained in the individual psyche and in social practice. J. L. Mackie (1982) calls this the "paradox of retribution." There seems to be no objective justification of retributivism, yet our conception of punishment seems to require that we punish offenders because of their offenses, and that doing so is intrinsically good. Under the circumstances, then, perhaps we ought to admit that retribution is what Friedrich Nietzsche thinks it is: an instinctive impulse to strike back at those who harm us, out of anger or the desire for revenge and

3 Other theorists who talk about a right to be punished include Hegel (1991, §§99–100 [pp. 124–27]), Bosanquet (1965, 201–11), Piper (1978), Murphy (1979, 134–35), Hoekema (1980), Gardner (1981), Duff (1986, 178–86), Moore (1987), Rachels (1991, 144–45), Bennett (2008, pt. II), and Perlmutter (2014).

retaliation (1967, II, 5–6 [pp. 64–67]).[4] If this were the case, it would not be a proper basis for moral behavior, let alone public policy.

Resentment, anger, and the desire for revenge

Because the retributivist impulse is so instinctive, the best place to begin is to examine and evaluate the feelings involved. We quickly realize that it is a complex emotion or set of emotions. Since retribution is aimed only at people who have done wrong, the retributivist impulse includes the feeling of resentment. Thomas Nagel defines resentment as an emotional response that depends on a moral judgment: you resent what someone does to you when "you … think that your plight gave the other person a reason to terminate or modify his contribution to it, and that in failing to do so he was acting contrary to reasons which were plainly available to him" (1970, 83). In other words, the person treated you in a way that is unwarranted, unjustified, or wrong (*actus reus*), and they did it even though they realized that they should not have done it (*mens rea*). P. F. Strawson classifies resentment as one of the "participant reactive attitudes," which "are essentially natural human reactions to the good or ill will or indifference of others towards us, as displayed in *their* attitudes and actions" (2008, 10–11), and he defines resentment specifically as "a reaction to injury or indifference" (15). In other words, in being resentful, you are responding to the fact that someone else is acting in a way that does not treat you with the proper moral regard. Nagel gives the example of someone stealing your umbrella when leaving a restaurant in a rainstorm. You would not only be bothered by it – stubbing your toe is bothersome too – but you would also feel like the thief had been inconsiderate or had not respected your special claim on the umbrella, a claim that they did not rightfully have (1987, 64–66). Both Nagel and Strawson, then, conceive of resentment as a feeling or attitude that someone has toward someone else who is responsible for unjustifiably harming, intending to harm, or failing to help them.

Strawson distinguishes the feeling of resentment that is felt by the victim of a wrongdoing from "the vicarious analogue of resentment" that others in the community feel. They are not resentful, but "indignant or disapproving" (2008, 15). Murphy follows Strawson in distinguishing first-person resentment from third-person indignation (1988a, 18). Strawson's and Murphy's distinction depends on a narrow understanding of what it means to be wronged, however. With regard to criminal acts in particular, there are several ways to understand the nature of the harm that causes the resentment. On an individual level, I could feel that my rights have been violated or that I have not been respected as a person. But, especially under the criminal as opposed to civil law, there is a sense in which society as a whole has been wronged. When an individual is murdered or mugged, other

4 Similarly, Waller says that the foundation of the belief in retribution is the "strike-back desire" that has its roots in animalistic impulses, which were absorbed by early human cultures and passed down to us (2018, 41–52).

members of the immediate community may feel less safe, and thus they may feel that something was taken from them as well. Still others who live under the same law as the criminal and the victim, but who are not directly or indirectly affected by the crime, may feel like the criminal has used an unfair advantage to get ahead, while they play by the rules; they may see it as a violation of the social contract; they may resent having to live in a world where people are victimized; and so on.

According to the *Oxford English Dictionary*, one meaning of indignation is that it is a feeling of contempt, or the sense that someone is unworthy of notice. That does not seem to capture the feelings of a community that holds people to account for breaking its laws. I may feel indignant toward a misguided opinion columnist. Their articles bother me, but, because they are so ill-informed, they do not deserve to be read. By contrast, the idea that criminals have rights that we ought to respect, and the obligation to prove their guilt in criminal trials, shows that we are giving them a kind of recognition or assuming that they are worthy of our attention and efforts at correction. This is at the core of Herbert Morris's (1968) claim that punishing criminals is a way of respecting them: we hold them accountable through a process by which we arrive at and justify the burdens that we impose on them. A second meaning of indignation is anger at what is unworthy or wrongful, and especially the feeling that someone else (not me) has been treated unjustly. On this definition, indignation is simply second- or third-person resentment, so Strawson and Murphy are making a distinction without a difference.

Regardless of what we call it – whether both feelings are resentment (which is my preference) or one is resentment and one is indignation – they amount to the same thing: both individuals and groups of individuals can feel wronged or treated unjustly. These emotions, as opposed to mere sensations, have cognitive content.[5] They are intentional in the sense that they take objects. Specifically, resentment is grounded in or dependent on a normative judgment that someone has acted wrongly and should have avoided it. The judgment is justifiable insofar as the criminal did something wrong, and, in the case of criminal violations, they did it to the victim and to the community as a whole. In other words, resentment is warranted or unwarranted depending on whether it is a proper response to the crime and the criminal, given the facts of the case.

For some philosophers, resentment and retribution are defined by the feeling of anger, and that feeling is irrational. For example, following Aristotle, Martha Nussbaum (2015) equates anger and the desire for retribution, claiming that anger must be directed at someone else, and that it always includes a desire to strike back at the person. Since causing harm to someone does nothing to fix the problem – executing a murderer does not bring back the victim – Nussbaum says that anger and its accompanying retributive principle are unjustifiable: "The

5 Philosophers who develop cognitive theories of emotion include Solomon (1976, 2003), Lyons (1980), de Sousa (1987), Roberts (1988), Neu (2000), and Nussbaum (2001). There is disagreement about what this cognitive content amounts to, whether it is a judgment (Solomon, Neu, and Nussbaum), an evaluation (Lyons), a perception (Roberts), an interpretation (de Sousa), or something else.

fantasy that payback restores is magical thinking, abetted by ideas of cosmic balance that are deeply engrained in many cultures, but not the less irrational for that" (2015, 48).[6] According to H. L. A. Hart, for critics of retribution "it appears to be a mysterious piece of moral alchemy in which the combination of the two evils of moral wickedness and suffering are transmuted into good" (2008, 234–35). The idea that punishing the criminal corrects an injustice or annuls the wrong (à la Hegel) is false. The injustice has been done. The harm inflicted on the victim, the wrongness of the harm, or the guilt of the wrongdoer cannot somehow be erased by harming the criminal.

Murphy often sounds like he is defending just such an untenable position. He claims that resentment involves the feeling that one's status has been lowered, which may be true, and he says that someone who has a healthy sense of self-respect would then desire to lower the status of the wrongdoer in response (Murphy 1988a, 16, 18, 25; Murphy 1988b, 93–94). Murphy (1988b) defends what he calls "retributive hatred," and he condones the state's lashing out on behalf of the people who want criminals to suffer because, he says, such feelings are partly retributive and therefore justified (see also Brudholm 2010). For Murphy, punishment is "the pursuit of revenge under the constraints of law" (2003, 20).[7] This approach is bound to fail, however, both because resentment does not necessarily involve a desire to harm the other – the feeling of having been wronged could as easily be accompanied by despair or forgiveness – and because it engages in the kind of "magical thinking" that Nussbaum criticizes.

Nussbaum's point is well-taken, but it is a mistake to conflate anger, vengeance, and retribution.[8] Conceptually, we can distinguish resentment from the

6 In addition to Aristotle, Nussbaum also echoes Plato: "punishment is not inflicted by a rational man for the sake of the crime that has been committed – after all one cannot undo what is past" (1961, 324b [p. 321]). Similarly, Beccaria says: "the purpose of punishment is not that of tormenting or afflicting any sentient creature, nor of undoing a crime already committed. ... Can the wailings of a wretch, perhaps, undo what has been done and turn back the clock?" (1995, 31).

7 In *Furman v. Georgia* (408 U.S. 238 [1972]), Justice Thurgood Marshall describes the constitutional prohibition on cruel and unusual punishment as just such a constraint against these feelings: "the Eighth Amendment is our insulation from our baser selves. The 'cruel and unusual' language limits the avenues through which vengeance can be channeled" (345).

8 Like Murphy, James Fitzjames Stephen equates the feelings of hated, revenge, and resentment (1967, 152; see also J. F. Stephen 1883, 2:82); and Holmes writes that retribution is "only vengeance in disguise" (2009, 43). Whether all punishment is motivated by vengeance and whether it can be justified by vengeance is a source of longstanding disagreement in the history of philosophy. Plato cautions against retribution, which he identifies as an irrational response to wrongdoing, and says that forward-looking punishment avoids that vengeful attitude:

> In punishing wrongdoers, no one concentrates on the fact that a man has done wrong in the past, or punishes him on that account, unless taking blind vengeance like a beast. No, punishment is not inflicted by a rational man for the sake of the crime that has been committed – after all one cannot undo what is past – but for the sake of the future, to prevent either the same man or, by the spectacle of his punishment, someone else, from doing wrong again. (1961, 324a–b [p. 321])

feeling of anger that someone may have along with it.[9] Anger is a broad and uncomplicated emotion. It has little cognitive content and is most open to the charge that it is merely a heightened, negative feeling of displeasure. One can be angry at other people, angry at animals and things (such as mosquitoes and slow computers), or simply angry in general and prone to overreaction.[10] One can be angry without blaming anyone (e.g., when it rains on my picnic), and someone can assign blame without being angry (e.g., a dispassionate judge reaching a guilty verdict). When I am angry, sometimes I have a good reason and sometimes even I realize that I have no good reason to be angry – as when someone's innocuous habit annoys me. Joseph Butler calls this "hasty" or "sudden" resentment, and he contrasts it with "settled" or "deliberate" resentment (2017, 68–74). Although hasty resentment is not entirely bad – it can further self-preservation – Butler says that we ought to check that feeling and forgive those who anger us in this way. Settled resentment, by contrast, is directed at moral evil or injustice. The object

---

For Aquinas, all punishment is vengeance: "Vengeance is accomplished by some punishment being inflicted upon one who has given offence." However, like Plato, he claims that it is wrong if it is done for its own sake but it is justified if it is promotes some positive end:

> In vengeance … the attitude of the avenger must be considered. Should his intention be centred chiefly upon the evil done to the recipient and is satisfied with that, then the act is entirely unlawful. … Vengenace, however, can be lawful – so long as all proper conditions are safeguarded – if the intention of the avenger is aimed chiefly at a good to be achieved by punishing a wrongdoer; thus, for example, at the correction of the wrongdoer, or at least at restraining him and relieving others; at safeguarding the right and doing honour to God. (1964–81, 2a2ae.108,1 [vol. 41, p. 117])

Hobbes also questions the idea that retributive harm has value in itself and says that vengeance can have a positive aim. Punishment is valuable because of what it accomplishes in helping to preserve the public order:

> A seventh [Law of Nature] is, *That in Revenges*, (that is, retribution of Evil for Evil,) *Men look not at the greatnesse of the evill past, but the greatnesse of the good to follow*. Whereby we are forbidden to inflict punishment with any other designe, than for correction of the offender, or direction of others. … Besides, Revenge without respect to the Example, and profit to come, is a triumph, or glorying in the hurt of another, tending to no end; (for the End is alwayes somewhat to Come;) and glorying to no end, is vain-glory, and contrary to reason; and to hurt without reason, tendeth to the introduction of Warre; which is against the Law of Nature; and is commonly stiled by the name of *Cruelty*. (1996, 106–7)

I distinguish vengeance from retribution based on resentment.

9 Berns says that anger is expressed only when people are held accountable for acting unjustly. As he defines it, anger is necessarily accompanied by "moral indignation" (1979, 153–56). I do not believe that this is how we normally define anger. What he calls anger is what Strawson, Nagel, Murphy, and I call resentment.

10 Because Berns thinks that anger must involve the attribution of blame, he says that "we can become angry with an inanimate object … only by foolishly attributing responsibility to it," and that "we cannot be more than momentarily angry with an animate creature other than man; only a fool or worse would dream of taking revenge on a dog" (1979, 153).

of settled resentment is the (morally or legally) wrong act, and its goal is to inflict appropriate injury rather than mere revenge.[11]

Not all emotions are irrational spasms. Ernest van den Haag wrongly claims that one cannot justify retributivism, as a theory of punishment, by appealing to feelings because feelings cannot serve as evidence for a conclusion: "Clearly retributionism cannot be right or wrong: It is a feeling and feelings just are. Unlike judgments or theories, they are neither right nor wrong" (1983, 29). He uses this as a backhanded defense of retributivism, which he insists is "morally true" precisely because it is based in sentiment rather than facts, as deterrence theory is (29).[12] So, "it is certain, at any rate, that the law must to some extent gratify the retributionist sentiment, the desire to see crime punished – even if it were useless (as it is not) to do so" (29). Van den Haag's appeal to empty emotion is misguided because, once we identify the cognitive content of a reactive attitude, then we can see that the feeling could be mistaken – it may not be a fitting response to its object – either because the accused did not commit the act (no *actus reus*) or because they were not responsible for the act (no *mens rea*). If someone steals my laptop, I can be angry. If I think my friend Cindy did it, I can be resentful toward her. If it turns out that I was wrong and Cindy did not steal it, then I should no longer feel resentment toward her, since she did nothing wrong – but I can still be angry because my laptop is gone, and I can redirect my resentment toward whoever stole it. In such circumstances, I may have to apologize to Cindy. The feeling I had was wrong because the resentment I felt toward her included or was in response to the false belief that she was guilty. Or, if a judge's level of resentment varies depending on the race of a defendant or victim, rather than being based on the seriousness of the crime, then the feeling is unreasonable. Thus, resentment is "open to rational evaluation" (Murphy 2003, 22). The justified attitudes can then be used to allocate punishments on retributivist grounds.

Although anger is one of the most visceral emotions and vengeance is intentional (about doing something to someone), resentment is cognitively rich in that it includes beliefs about standards of morality or legality, claims about accountability, and judgments that apply one to the other.[13] Such beliefs are more or less justified. I resent people, rightly or wrongly, because they are responsible

11 Nozick sets out five differences between revenge and retribution, including the fact that, when acting out of vengeance, one takes pleasure in another person's suffering. By contrast, someone who acts on retributivist grounds may have no emotion or, if anything, may take pleasure in doing justice (1981, 366–70). See also Cragg 1992, 16–17.

12 Van den Haag echoes Bentham here, although Bentham criticizes the appeal feeling. He says that the "principle which approves or disapproves certain actions … merely because a man finds himself disposed to approve or disapprove of them … is not a positive principle of itself, so much as a term employed to signify the negation of all principle." There is no "external consideration," such as utility, "as a means of warranting and guiding the internal sentiments of approbation and disapprobation" (Bentham 1970, ch. II, §§11–12 [p. 25]).

13 To avoid the misguided idea that punishment is nothing but an angry response to being harmed (whether rightly, wrongly, or accidentally), von Hirsch, in his own defense of the backward-looking view, eschews talk of retribution in favor of desert (1976, 45–46).

for wronging me or other members of my community. Whether the feeling of having been wronged is based in truth depends on whether the accused is guilty of the crime. A criminal trial establishes the truth or falsehood of that judgment; or, more precisely, it either proves that the person is guilty or does not prove it, which, given the presumption of innocence, is sufficient under the law. The punishment that follows a guilty verdict or plea expresses the resentment of the victim and of society as a whole, whose general will has not been respected by the criminal.[14] Von Hirsch emphasizes this element of criminal censure: punishment is an acknowledgment that the victim has been wronged, that it is the criminal's fault, and that the community disapproves of it (1976, 48–49; 1993, 10). Similarly, the U.S. Supreme Court calls punishment "an expression of society's moral outrage at particularly offensive conduct" (*Gregg v. Georgia*, 428 U.S. 153 [1976], 183; see also *Spaziano v. Florida*, 468 U.S. 447 [1984], 461, 469). Punishment reduces a wrongdoer's level of well-being because whatever pleasure or gain they got from their crime is undeserved and, collectively, we condemn what they did (Murphy 1988b, 89). The wrong action becomes a desert base – that property or fact by virtue of which the offender deserves the punishment – because I attribute blame for moral or legal wrongdoing to the object of my resentment.

The symbolic function of legal punishment

One problem with expressive retributivism is that its proponents seldom explain the connection between people's reactive attitudes and the state's punitive actions. An appeal to anger or the desire for revenge would not justify legal punishment, since there is no reason why the state should express its citizens' irrational desires. It is not in the business of trying to fulfill their "magical thinking." Similarly, the state would not be justified in punishing criminals just because its citizens think they deserve it. There is a fact/value problem here: the fact that people feel resentment does not, on its own, mean that legal punishment a good thing. So far, the argument that I have given for retributivism looks like this:

1) We feel resentment toward those who wrong us.
2) The feeling of resentment has cognitive content.
3) If the cognitive content is true, then the feeling of resentment is justified.
4) If the feeling of resentment is justified, then the state is justified in punishing offenders based on what they deserve.

Therefore, the state is justified in punishing offenders based on what they deserve (i.e., retributivism is true).

14 "Unlike vengeance, retribution is imposed by courts after a guilty plea, or a trial, in which the accused has been found guilty of committing a crime. Prescribed by the law broken, and proportioned to the gravity of the offense committed, retribution is not inflicted to gratify or compensate anyone who suffered a loss or was harmed by the crime – even if it does so – but to enforce the law and to vindicate the legal order" (van den Haag 1975, 11).

All these premises are true, I believe, but the argument does not justify retributivism because the meaning of 'justified' shifts in premise 4. In the antecedent of premise 4, "justified" means "theoretically validated" or "based in fact," but in the consequent, it means "practically justified" or "morally right." To this point, then, I have not gone much further than van den Haag's appeal to moral feeling or Primoratz's circular retributivism in justifying legal punishment.

The introduction of moral value into the argument comes with the claim that the state ought to express its citizens' feelings of resentment, so long as those feelings are theoretically justified (i.e., based in fact, directed at the right person, and so on):

1) We feel resentment toward those who wrong us.
2) The feeling of resentment has cognitive content.
3) If the cognitive content is true, then the feeling of resentment is justified.
4) If the feeling of resentment is justified, *then the state ought to express its citizens' feeling of resentment.*
5) *If the state ought to express its citizens' feeling of resentment*, then it is justified in punishing offenders based on what they deserve.

   Therefore, the state is justified in punishing offenders based on what they deserve (i.e., retributivism is true).

When the state publicly expresses the community's theoretically justified sense of resentment, it communicates something to both offenders and society as a whole.[15] The state signals to criminals that they have done wrong, that their victims are justified in feeling wronged, and that we will not tolerate the violation of rules that are designed to promote a just social arrangement. According to Jean Hampton, punishment tells criminals that they are not more important than victims, thus reinforcing a commitment to equality under the law (1992b, 5–11; see also Murphy 2003, 104). Joel Feinberg lists several functions of punishment that are accomplished only through legal punishment by the government, including symbolically disavowing the criminal act, reaffirming the force of the law, and absolving other, innocent people of blame (1970, 101–5; see also Wringe 2016, esp. 42–65).[16] Murphy says that "resentment … stands as testimony to our

15 One difference among expressivist theories is whether the audience for the expression is primarily offenders themselves (e.g., Kleinig 1991; Hampton 1992b; Duff 2001; Bennett 2008) or the community in which both offenders and victims are members (e.g., Feinberg 1970, 95–118; Primoratz 1989; Wringe 2016). These are known as "communicative" and "denunciatory" accounts, respectively (Narayan 1993). They are not mutually exclusive, of course. I adopt both positions, as does Tasioulas (2006). There are also "audience-independent" views (e.g., Metz 2000; Glasgow 2015), but, as I discuss in Chapter 13, they depend on a too-broad notion of expression.

16 Hanna (2008) criticizes expressivism because, he says, it entails that any unpleasant response to someone who does something wrong, including mere criticism, is a form of punishment. But this objection overlooks the publicity condition that makes several facets of the

allegiance to the moral order itself" (2003, 20). We are affirming the legitimacy of the law and reinforcing our mutual concern for one another by responding to the wrong with resentment rather than mere anger. The resulting punishment is a collective act with justice as its aim, not mere payback: as Butler puts it, "resentment against vice and wickedness … is one of the common bonds, by which society is held together; a fellow-feeling which each individual has in behalf of the whole species, as well as of himself" (2017, 70). The public expression of resentment, then, is one way of publicly committing ourselves to shared values.[17] If that is a good thing – this is where moral value is introduced into the argument – then retributive punishment is morally justified.

The state is in a privileged position to impose punishment because of the nature of criminal law. Criminal acts threaten the social order, so the offender should be subjected to a public, state-sponsored process:

> unlike torts and contracts, the criminal law involves *public* law. That is, although the direct and immediate victim of a crime typically is a private party (e.g., the person who is robbed, assaulted, or kidnapped), and other individuals are indirectly harmed (e.g., the family members of the direct victim), a crime involves more than a private injury. A crime causes "social harm," in that the injury suffered involves "a breach and violation of the public rights and duties, due to the whole community, considered as a community, in its social aggregate capacity." For this reason, crimes in the United States are prosecuted by public attorneys representing the community as a whole, and not by privately retained counsel. (Dressler 2018, 1; see also Kleinig 1991; Marshall and Duff 1998; and Duff 2001, 58)

Under tort law, the focus is on the loss, and fault only matters in deciding who is responsible for compensating for the loss. Under criminal law, the offender has not only harmed the victim but has also violated the social contract under which we agree to respect one another as persons. The state furthers our collective interest by preserving the common good (through deterrence) but also communicates the value of our legal norms by expressing our collective resentment. These aims are not accomplished by vigilantism or personal vendettas. They are uniquely accomplished by legal punishment.[18] Using Hegelian language, one could say that legal punishment determinately negates resentment: the state both affirms it by validating the cognitive content and expressing it on behalf of the community,

expression possible. Mere criticism does not authoritatively condemn crimes and reaffirm the force of law, for example.

17 Brooks objects to expressivism, in part, because, he says, the community speaks with many voices, with multiple meanings and for different reasons (2012, 109–10). This overlooks the unifying function of the state: *e pluribus unum.* The state adjudicates among the different meanings and reasons, and it communicates a singular set of values (even though they may be pluralistic) that represents the people as a whole.

18 This does not preclude having a role for restorative processes, as I show in Chapter 13.

and it denies it by limiting the community's role through its monopoly on criminal justice.

As John Locke says, the complexity of our feelings and the risk that we will be driven by anger are some of the reasons why the state acts on behalf of the people: if we allow private punishment, "self-love will make men partial to themselves and their friends: and on the other side, ... ill nature, passion and revenge will carry them too far in punishing others" (1980, §13 [p. 12]; see also §125 [p. 66]). Even though people may also feel other, more visceral emotions, the actions of the state are grounded in resentment as a reactive attitude with cognitive content – in this case, the idea of having been unfairly victimized. If we isolate the feeling of resentment, the function of punishment is different from what Murphy thinks it is: not causing harm to criminals in order to satisfy people's desire for revenge – Nietzsche's festival of pain (1967, II, 6 [pp. 65–67]) – but punishing criminals to express people's feelings of resentment. Putting it in this legal context filters out the anger that, according to Adam Smith, makes resentment into a disagreeable sentiment. Resentment becomes "guarded and qualified" by being assessed impartially in court and tempered with mercy (1976, 38).[19] Insofar as the feelings of resentment are theoretically justified, the state's expression of disapproval or condemnation is practically justified in the form of retributive harm.

There are even cases when the victim does not have any clearly defined feeling of resentment, and the state helps to bring that feeling into focus. Naomi Scheman (1993) emphasizes that, for any given emotion, there is no one identifiable feeling, belief, or pattern of behavior that exists to be discovered in either the conscious or unconscious mind. Many of us respond in confused and confusing ways to being wronged, especially if the event is traumatic: a victim may feel shock, anger, or shame; they may blame themselves rather than the perpetrator; and they may not lash out and call for blood as the stereotypical retributivist would. They may not understand what all of this means or why they are acting in this way. An abused child, for example, may have deep attachments to their abuser, rather than resentment. The public feels resentment on their behalf, and the punishment of the abuser is part of an attempt to correct the false belief, resulting from a distorted moral education, that love can be expressed through violence. This does not mean that resentment is "really" present unconsciously. Instead, Scheman claims, society helps to identify and define these feelings as resentment through "conferred similarity of meaning" (31). That is, by recognizing the similarities between this person's feelings, beliefs, and behavior and

19 James Fitzjames Stephen says that "the infliction of punishment by law gives definite expression and a solemn ratification and justification to the hatred which is excited by the commission of the offence" (1883, 2:81), and that "the criminal law stands to the passion of revenge in the same relation as marriage to the sexual appetite" (2014, 99). Although I appeal to resentment rather than hatred and revenge, Stephen and I conceive of the law's function in similar ways.

other cases of resentment, society provides meaning to the emotion by putting it in a social context.

In this way, the community not only expresses the victim's resentment, but in some sense makes it into resentment. It becomes a reactive attitude, not a mere emotional reflex, when we collectively interpret it and approve of it – specifically, by putting an offender on trial, assigning blame, and punishing them accordingly. A victim is likely to feel a sense of abandonment and betrayal, among other things, if a jury of their peers finds the defendant not guilty.

Punishment serves a symbolic social function by expressing social disapproval, and through that process the community affirms its solidarity with victims, a kind of sympathetic resentment (or *resentment with* them about the crime). Any loss of status that they feel is not corrected by lowering the status of offenders (Nusbaum's criticism), but by the community siding with victims: recognizing the harm publicly, agreeing that their resentment is justified, affirming their status as rights-bearing persons who are deserving of protection, asserting that they are part of the community (against any feelings of shame, for example), and demanding that offenders be excluded from it to one degree or another, temporarily or permanently, by means of punishment. This may also help to rehabilitate criminals and deter others from committing crimes in the future, because they want to avoid social disapproval, but the retributive purpose of punishment is distinct.[20]

Feinberg is right, then, that punishment serves an expressive function. According to him, there are two parts to every punishment that are in principle separable: what we do to criminals (putting them in prison, etc.) and the feelings of reproach involved. Although punishment is not *defined* in expressive terms (Chapter 1), it is *justified* by our reactive attitudes. For Feinberg, as for me, punishment is an expression of resentment:

> punishment is a conventional device for the expression of attitudes of resentment and indignation, and of judgments of disapproval and reprobation, on the part either of the punishing authority himself or of those "in whose name" the punishment is inflicted. (1970, 98)

He also recognizes the cognitive content at the basis of the community's feeling of moral disapproval: "punishment expresses the *judgment* (as distinct from any emotion) of the community that what the criminal did was wrong" (100). If the criminal committed the crime, our resentment is justified and we ought to express that resentment by means of punishment. That is what desert amounts to.

20 Duff includes both elements – retribution and deterrence – in his communicative retributivism (see esp. Duff 1986, 233–66; and Duff 2001, 82–98). Moore says that denunciation theorists are utilitarians (or, more properly, consequentialists) because they value social cohesion as an end in itself and want to promote it by means of punishment (1997, 91–92).

Proportionality

An appropriate punishment is proportional to the strength of that feeling, which is correlated with the gravity of the criminal conduct. The cognitive content of resentment includes not only the belief that someone has been wronged but also a belief about the relative weight of that wrong. Philosophers disagree about how to measure the gravity of a crime in order to determine the punishment that is deserved, whether it should be understood in terms of the amount of harm caused, the offender's degree of culpability, or some combination of the two.[21] Although this is an interesting question, it goes beyond the scope of this chapter. For my purposes, it is enough to connect the seriousness of a wrongdoing with the cognitive content and strength of our reactive attitudes. If a friend steps on my foot because they were careless, they owe me an apology. But if my resentment is so intense that I refuse to speak to them ever again, my other friends will try to correct me. Some feelings can be right or wrong because of the beliefs on which they depend; in this case, my negative feelings toward my friend are disproportionate to the offense. My other friends are trying to correct my reactive attitude: carelessly stepping on my foot is not such a despicable act that the person should be ostracized for life. The intensity of the feeling ought to correlate with the wrongness of the act. If it does, then the feeling of resentment is warranted and the resulting punishment is proportional to the degree of the wrong committed. Von Hirsch states it simply: "if censure conveys blame, its amount should reflect the blameworthiness of the conduct" (1993, 15; see also Metz 2000). We usually have stronger feelings of resentment toward violent crimes than financial crimes, for example, which is why murderers get a different kind and degree of punishment than people who are guilty of insider trading. But when the harm caused by financial crimes is particularly devastating, the feeling of resentment must be matched with a harsher penalty, such as Bernie Madoff's 150-year sentence in federal prison. In short, proportionality is justified indirectly by an appeal to our reactive attitudes, and the rightness of our reactive attitudes depends on their cognitive content and the alignment of those attitudes with ethical norms. That cognitive content includes not only the attribution of guilt but the relative wrongness of the offense, or the degree of "moral outrage."

This does not mean that the crime and the punishment need to be equivalent. Punishment is not a matter of righting the wrong, which Nussbaum rightly criticizes. Rapists need not be raped to somehow rebalance the scales of justice. Instead, there should be a direct correlation between the crime and the punishment based on what properly expresses the community's degree of resentment: "it is social disapproval and its appropriate expression that should fit the crime,

21 Hart does a good job of posing the question and setting out the options: "it is not clear what, as between the objective harm caused by a crime and the subjective evil intention inspiring it, is to be the measure of 'seriousness.' Is negligently causing the destruction of a city worse than the intentional wounding of a single policeman? Or are we to pay attention to both objective harm done and subjective wickedness?" (2008, 162).

and not hard treatment (pain) as such" (Feinberg 1970, 118).[22] This is retributivism in a more attenuated form – proportional retributivism rather than equality retributivism. Among other things, it distinguishes the reactive attitude of resentment from mere revenge. Resentment serves as a middle term that, in a sense, disrupts the demand for equivalence, because the crime is not directly related to the punishment. The punishment is proportional to the resentment, which is proportional to the crime.

One frequent objection to expressive retributivism is that there is significant variance in our moral feelings and that there is no common standard to use in determining appropriate punishments (see, e.g., Lippke 2007, 22). This argument rests on a strict distinction between reason and the emotions that, although it has been around for a long time, has been subjected to a Humean critique. Reactive attitudes can be more or less appropriate. By means of a deliberative process, we can subject our feelings of resentment to rational scrutiny to determine what is reasonable, under the circumstances, and what the public response ought to be. Collectively, we can arrive at acceptable punishments.[23]

Conclusion

Although the state may have as an additional aim to punish criminals in order to promote the public good, the feeling of resentment provides a reason for the state to punish the offender even in the absence of beneficial consequences. The state has an obligation to be responsive to its citizens' grievances, provided that they are found to be justified by means of an impartial criminal justice system, which focuses on the cognitive content behind the resentment. Our reactive attitudes are sufficient to justify retribution, and retribution is sufficient to justify legal punishment. This is positive retributivism. But well-founded resentment is also necessary for punishment, in that it makes no sense for society to express its "moral outrage" at an innocent person. That is, were we to frame a criminal as a means to promote some social good, we would be condemning the person's behavior even though that condemnation is unjustified. The judgment underlying the community's feeling of resentment is wrong because the assignment of guilt is misplaced.

When it is justified, the feeling of resentment is approved of by society as a whole and serves as a basis of one of society's most important functions: the punishment of those who violate our shared legal norms. This answers Mackie's

22 This is a significant difference between Feinberg's view and Duff's communication theory. Duff makes the case that hard treatment is necessary to censure the wrongdoer (2001, ch. 3). Feinberg only goes so far as to say that "certain forms of hard treatment have become the conventional symbols of public reprobation" (1970, 100). Duff moderates his position when he considers the merits of restorative justice. This becomes important in Chapter 13.

23 For an evaluation of just how far retributivism can take us on its own, and the process of deliberation that the two-tiered model of punishment uses to arrive at a punishment schedule, see Part IV.

(1982) paradox of retribution by both justifying the practice and doing so in terms of moral feeling, but without devolving into subjectivism or sentimentalism. Justification of the punishment is achieved through a legal process that confirms the cognitive content that underlies the victim's feeling of resentment: the state has found that the victim and the community *were* wronged and that the feeling of resentment is not misdirected. One purpose of punishment, though surely not its only purpose, is to express society's disapproval of criminal actions that contradict the laws that the community has agreed to follow. Resentment is our response to the wrong, and legal punishment is the state's expression of that response.

5 The two-tiered model of punishment

Punishment serves two purposes: preserving the public order through restraint, general and specific deterrence, and rehabilitation (Chapter 2); and expressing the community's reactive attitude of resentment (Chapter 4). These theories of punishment are, respectively, consequentialist and retributivist. The question is how both of them can be true, since, although the theories often arrive at similar punishments, they are opposite theoretical approaches: one is forward-looking, the other backward-looking; one is concerned with outcomes, the other with desert; one focuses primarily on actions, the other primarily on agents; and so on. They also can lead to contradictory conclusions, a prime example of which is the punishment of innocents. Retributivism prohibits punishing someone who does not deserve it, but consequentialism would seem to justify it so long as the balance of costs and benefits is better than the alternatives. There are other examples that reveal the tension between these two views: for example, the death penalty may fail to deter, such that the resources spent on capital cases could be better spent on more effective crime-prevention efforts, yet murderers may still deserve to die; and harsh punishments for minor crimes may be an effective way to maintain the peace even if they are disproportionate to the offenses.

The antinomy of punishment

There are strong arguments for consequentialism and retributivism, so the best or most compelling theory of punishment should incorporate both approaches. As H. L. A. Hart puts it, "any morally tolerable account of this institution [of legal punishment] must exhibit it as a compromise between distinct and partly conflicting principles" (2008, 1). Yet so-called mixed theories of punishment often face a dilemma: either they fail to be action-guiding, since the contrary implications of both views are equally justified, or they prioritize one approach over the other and thus fail to remain mixed theories. For example, *either* they say that we should punish the innocent if the consequences are good enough (consequentialism) and that we should never punish the innocent because they do not deserve it (retributivism), with no way to decide which principle overrides the other in a given case; *or* one concern – desert or the social good – is taken always to override the other, such that it becomes just a roundabout form of consequentialism or retributivism.[1] The supposedly mixed position that John Rawls defends in "Two Concepts of Rules" (1955) is an example of the latter strategy, since it ultimately collapses into a form of rule-utilitarianism. The practice of punishment enjoins judges to give criminals what they deserve, but that practice is justified because it furthers our collective interests.

The former approach, where both principles are adopted without a clear way of prioritizing them, is typified by Thom Brooks (2012). According to his "unified theory of punishment," crime is an infringement of people's rights, and punishment rectifies the wrongs by restoring the rights that were infringed. A punishment should be proportional to the crime, whose seriousness depends on how fundamental the infringed right is. The state should also prevent future rights violations by deterring potential crimes and reducing recidivism. Valuing both proportional, deserved punishments and crime prevention, however, means that there is no guidance in deciding among different policy choices. For example, Brooks recognizes that juveniles are not as responsible as adults, so they typically do not deserve as severe a punishment (175). But he also says that especially dangerous juveniles pose a threat to others' rights, so they should be treated as adults to prevent future rights violations (176–77). The two goals of crime reduction and desert-based proportionality come into conflict, which is exactly what Brooks accuses other mixed theories of doing (Tunick 2016). With no way to resolve issues like these, a mixed view becomes "a shifting patchwork of compromises and arbitrary decisions," with unclear guidance for actual practice (Duff and Garland 1994, 5; see also Tasioulas 2006, 281–82).

Richard Lippke's mixed view seems to fluctuate between the two options. Lippke (2007) says that legal punishment censures offenders in ways that are proportional to the seriousness of their offenses, measured by both the harm to victims and the offenders' degrees of culpability ("censuring equalization retributivism"). Crime reduction plays only a "limited role," and "retributive considerations are accorded priority" (29). So, for example, innocents cannot be framed, regardless of the social benefits. This is "a type of limited moral retributivism" rather than a mixed theory (24). However, Lippke also says that one of the "justifying aims" of punishment is to ensure the equal realization of basic moral

1 Michael Davis describes a similar dilemma, although he does not consider the problem of indeterminacy. For him a mixed theory must prioritize one approach or the other:

> Any theorist adopting (something like) a classic mixed view therefore confronts a dilemma: (1) embrace utilitarian moral theory and risk having the mixed view collapse into a purely utilitarian theory of punishment; or (2) embrace a non-utilitarian moral theory (for example, one recognizing the claims of justice as independent of utility) and risk having non-utilitarian considerations (such as justice) pre-empt utility even when justifying punishment as an institution. (2009, 79)

rights through deterrence, restraint, and rehabilitation (28–29). He concedes that equalization of harms cannot justify punishments for victimless crimes and pure attempts (e.g., attempted murder), so such offenders ought to be punished "simply to discourage their acts" (33–34). If censuring equalization and crime control prescribe different actions for victimless crimes and pure attempts, then the choice of one justification over another in these cases seems arbitrary.

My proposal will avoid both horns of this dilemma. If consequentialism and retributivism are equally plausible or equally justified (as I established in Chapters 2 and 4), and if the resulting mixed theory is to remain a mixed theory and be action-guiding, then there must be a third option other than choosing one theory over the other or simply muddying the waters.

In the *Critique of Pure Reason*, Immanuel Kant faces an analogous problem, albeit epistemological rather than practical, and his reasoning there is instructive. Kant defines an antinomy of pure reason as a contradiction that occurs when two equally good arguments lead to opposite conclusions, thus revealing a conflict of reason with itself. In the Third Antinomy, for example, he confronts two arguments regarding freedom that he thinks lead to an antinomial conflict: one for the existence of a first, uncaused cause (thesis), and one for complete causal determinism (antithesis). Since reason cannot contradict itself, there must be some way to resolve it. Kant shows that, although appearances are determined, things can also be considered as they are in themselves, apart from our forms of knowing. Because the concept of causality does not apply to things in themselves, freedom is possible as an uncaused cause. Under Kant's transcendental idealism, then, the thesis and antithesis are both true, but they are true of different things, or of the same thing considered in different ways (phenomena and noumena) (Kant 1998, A444-52/B472-80, A532-58/B560-86).

Following Kant's lead here and using it as a way forward, I call the conflict between retributivism and consequentialism an antinomy of punishment.[2] Both theories seem right, but they are contradictory.

Thesis	*Antithesis*
The effects of punishment do not matter. People should be punished if and only if, and to the extent that, they deserve it based on their past acts, according to their degrees of guilt.	Only the effects of punishment matter. People should be punished if and only if, and to the extent that, society benefits more than it would from different kinds or degrees of punishments, or from alternatives to punishment.

Prioritizing the thesis over the antithesis, or vice versa, would amount to the claim that one theory is truer or more fundamental than the other. Like Kant, we

2 Ewing also describes the opposition between utilitarianism and retributivism as "the fundamental antinomy in the theory of punishment" (1927, 300); and Quinton calls it "a prevailing antinomy about the philosophical justification of punishment" (1954, 133–34).

need not make that choice, so long as we define our frames of reference. Both consequentialism and retributivism can be true, and they can both be action-guiding, if they function together in a system of criminal justice, but they define and justify the actions of different parts of the system. Analogously, according to my mixed theory of punishment, the legislature identifies crimes and sets statutory penalties based on consequentialist concerns, according to which rules best preserve the public order and accomplish our collective aims; and the criminal judiciary finds people innocent or guilty and assigns penalties based on retributive concerns, according to what they deserve. The *practice* of punishment is justified on consequentialist grounds, and its *distribution* is justified on retributivist grounds. This is the two-tiered model of punishment.[3]

The criminal justice system in the United States

To see what this mixed theory of punishment would look like in practice, it will be informative to map it onto an existing legal system. Since this is only for the purpose of illustration, I will use the system as it exists in the United States. Of course, the U.S. is not monolithic. There is no one criminal justice system, but rather a federal government, fifty states, and over three thousand counties, all with their own laws and law enforcement agencies. In this section, what is important is what the federal and state governments have in common: legislative, executive, and judicial branches with separate powers that check and balance one another.

As opposed to civil law, which covers tort claims between individuals, criminal law pertains to actions that violate the basic rules that allow society to function. So, offenders are prosecuted by federal and state governments – public prosecutors acting on behalf of "the people" – rather than being sued by other individuals. The crimes designated by the legislature prohibit actions that threaten orderly communal existence, so the institution of punishment is justified on consequentialist grounds. In a liberal society, the government ought to protect people's rights as best as it can – that is, it ought to minimize the infringement of rights. It does so by deterring potential criminals from committing crimes and punishing actual criminals who violate the rights of others. As I claimed in Chapter 3, the rightness of a criminal justice system depends on the rightness of the legal system as a whole. So, the moral justification of punishment policies within a liberal system depends on the justification of rights and the state's role in protecting them. In the U.S., we have agreed collectively that everyone has a *prima facie* obligation to respect basic freedoms and the rightful ownership of personal property, and that the purpose of government is to protect these rights, so murder and theft

3 My view is not to be confused with what Walker calls "a two-tier rule," which is the idea that punishment for some crimes (*mala in se* crimes, felonies, etc.) is justified on retributivist grounds and punishment for other crimes (*mala prohibita* crimes, misdemeanors, etc.) is justified on utilitarian grounds (1991, 125).

(among other things) are illegal. If the state did not protect people's lives and property, then the state would in effect cease to exist, since the social contract would be broken and people would have to defend themselves. It would, to one extent or another, be a state of nature.

In the United States, state and federal legislatures write the laws, including the criminal code. Working within the constraints of state and/or federal constitutions, they decide which actions ought to be prohibited in order to protect public safety. Crimes fall into three categories: felonies, misdemeanors, and infractions (or violations). The most serious crimes are felonies, such as murder and burglary, and in the U.S. they are punishable by one year or more in prison. Misdemeanors such as simple assault and shoplifting are less serious, with punishments of less than one year in prison. Infractions are the least serious. The term is ambiguous, since it sometimes refers to legal violations that are not considered criminal offenses and are punishable by a fine, such as most traffic violations and violations of city ordinances (e.g., walking an unleashed dog). At other times, infractions are defined as petty offenses that do not require a jury trial, which in some states include misdemeanors for which the punishment is less than six months in jail. The classification of crimes as felonies, misdemeanors, or infractions categorizes them based on the seriousness of the offense and the corresponding severity of punishment.

Lawmakers also establish the conditions of guilt under the law. That is, they determine what must be proven regarding defendants' culpability in order for them to be found guilty of crimes. For example, a first-degree murderer must have killed someone with malice aforethought. A public official who misused campaign money must have done so "knowingly and willfully" to be charged with a crime but may face civil penalties even if the violation was the result of negligence or lack of understanding of the relevant statutes (*United States v. Danielczyk*, 917 F. Supp. 2d 573, 578–80 [E.D. Va. 2013]). Someone who is careless in supervising a child, resulting in harm, may be found guilty of negligent child endangerment even if there is no intent. If the prosecutor can prove to a judge or jury that the defendant committed the illegal act and met the relevant conditions of culpability as set out in the statute, then the person should be found guilty. The judge's or jury's job is to apply the law as written.

Once crimes and their corresponding penalties are established by the legislature, police and other enforcement agencies ensure that the law is being followed, and they work with county, state, and federal prosecutors to apprehend and convict lawbreakers. In the United States, someone can be arrested if a judge issues an arrest warrant or if the police have probable cause that the suspect has committed a crime. Usually, because of the right to due process, police must first identify the suspected crime and have evidence of the person's guilt, as determined by a trial court, before an arrest or search, although they exercise some discretion. For example, a person who commits a minor offense such as jaywalking or speeding may get a warning instead of a ticket. Police also have some discretion regarding how they enforce the law, including which witnesses to interview, whether to detain a suspect, and how to maintain a safe environment in their neighborhoods, even in the absence of obvious criminal activity. The worse a crime is, however, the less latitude police officers have in deciding not to pursue it. They are not legally allowed to disregard a court order, such as an arrest warrant. Ignoring a murder, as some police did in cases of lynching, would be morally and legally wrong according to the criteria set out in Chapter 3.

Like judges and police officers, public prosecutors exercise discretion – in their case, when making charging decisions. For example, a prosecutor decides whether to charge someone with drug possession or possession with intent to distribute, the latter of which is more serious. A required minimum amount is set under the law – an amount of drugs beyond what someone would typically have for personal use – but in most states the law does not require prosecutors to charge the person with either possession or intent to distribute based solely on the amount. Indeed, they can bring a lesser charge and avoid mandatory minimum sentences by not specifying the drug amount in the charge. In the U.S., a prosecutor will often bring lesser charges against a defendant as part of a plea bargain. For example, someone who is charged with murder may agree to plead guilty to manslaughter in order to avoid the risk of a trial, have a lesser crime on their record, and receive a lighter sentence. It is now much more common for defendants to agree to plea deals than to go to trial: 97 percent of federal cases and 94 percent of state cases end in plea bargains (Goode 2012; see also Bachner and Ginsberg 2021, 100, 107, 116).

Whether defendants plead guilty or are found guilty as a result of a trial, judges (and juries, in the case of the death penalty) decide what punishment the defendant should receive. Their decisions, however, are not unconstrained. In writing criminal law, the legislature also sets statutory penalties – maximum and sometimes minimum sentences – for each offense that restrict what judges can give to defendants as a result of a guilty plea or verdict.[4] With authority delegated to them by the legislature, state and federal sentencing commissions also devise sentencing guidelines that advise judges on what penalty to give within the legislatively mandated range, depending on the circumstances of the crime and the offender's criminal record. Judges consult the guidelines and determine sentences in individual cases that fall within the statutory ranges. In *United States v. Booker* (543 U.S. 220 [2005]), the U.S. Supreme Court concluded that, although sentencing guidelines are not mandatory, judges have a *prima facie* obligation to follow them: sentences that adhere to the guidelines are assumed to be reasonable by appeals courts, and judges who depart from them must justify the imposition of lesser or greater sentences (*Rita v. United States*, 551 U.S. 338 [2007]).

4 Unless otherwise noted, when I refer to judges and courts, I am referring to criminal courts that determine the guilt of the accused and assign punishments. Appeals courts, including the U.S. Supreme Court, do not determine guilt or innocence under the law (primary law) and do not evaluate the evidence presented at trial. In reviewing the application of criminal law, appellate courts determine whether a criminal's rights have been violated and thus confirm that the rules laid down by the legislature have been followed, and also that the legislature itself is acting in conformity with the rules that are set out in the Constitution (secondary law).

In the United States, the legislature and the courts have struggled for years with two competing demands. The first demand is to standardize punishments so that defendants are treated equally under the law. This pushes the legislature to list mandatory sentences so as to limit judicial discretion. When discretion is allowed, judges' and juries' decisions are almost inevitably based in part on extra-legal factors. For example, if, all else being equal, a Black defendant who kills a white victim is much more likely to be sentenced to death than a white defendant who kills a Black victim, then the punishments are informed by irrelevant factors, with no relation to either retribution or deterrence.[5] This is one of the concerns that led the U.S. Supreme Court to impose a de facto moratorium on the death penalty in *Furman v. Georgia* (408 U.S. 238 [1972]), where the Court held that the discretion afforded to the jury led to sentences that were too severe (because the same effect could be produced by lesser sentences) and that offended our common sense of justice.

The second, competing demand when it comes to punishment is to allow for individualized sentencing – that is, sentences that are tailored to a specific defendant, given their character and the circumstances of the crime. Two defendants who are guilty of the same offense may pose different levels of threat, may not be equally deserving of punishment, and may have different prospects for rehabilitation, in light of aggravating and mitigating factors as well as their criminal histories. Having a mandatory sentence for each crime – e.g., all shoplifters get a year in jail – would run the risk of punishing people too much or too little. A rich forty-year-old who shoplifts for the tenth time to feel the rush of excitement is very different from a poor twenty-year-old who, in an isolated act of desperation, steals food to keep their family from starving – even though both are guilty of shoplifting. Allowing judicial discretion in punishment provides latitude for treating different defendants differently, based on their different degrees of guilt.

In response to *Furman*, state legislatures tried to balance the demand for equal treatment with the demand for individualized sentencing by separating criminal trials into two phases: first to determine guilt, and then to assign punishment. During the guilt phase, the jury or judge decides whether the defendant committed the crime.[6] This is purely a factual question of whether two elements have been fulfilled: *mens rea* (guilty mind) and *actus reus* (guilty act). As noted in Chapter 1, in most cases the defendant must have intentionally committed an overt act in furtherance of the crime. Merely having bad thoughts is not enough. During the second phase, the sentencing hearing or penalty phase, the judge assumes that the charge has been proven, since the defendant has been found

5 Needless to say, this is in fact the case. For detailed statistics, see Baldus et al. (1998). More up-to-date data can be found at Death Penalty Information Center (2020d).

6 In *Baldwin v. New York* (399 U.S. 66 [1970]), the U.S. Supreme Court held that the right to a jury trial, guaranteed under article III, section 2, and the Sixth Amendment of the Constitution, pertains only to trials for serious offenses, defined as crimes with possible punishments of more than six months of incarceration, and not petty offenses, which have lesser punishments. In the latter case, guilt and punishment are both determined by judges.

guilty. At this point, the judge (or the jury, in cases where the death penalty is an option) sets the appropriate punishment.

Having a range of punishments provided under each criminal statute allows judges to determine defendants' relative culpability based on whether they have committed prior criminal acts, whether they feel remorse, how much harm was caused to the victims and their families, and so on. To make such a determination, judges consider pre-sentence reports, statements from victims, and statements from the defendants and attorneys. As mentioned earlier, judges also consult sentencing guidelines about how to weigh aggravating and mitigating factors. Sentencing commissions have attempted to balance the competing demands for uniformity and individualized sentencing by setting out objective criteria that advise judges on how to determine appropriate sentences. Judges use a scorekeeping procedure to determine the "offense gravity score" (OGS) (aggravating and mitigating factors, such as whether the offense "involved a large number of vulnerable victims" [U.S. Federal Sentencing Guidelines, §3A1.1(b)(2)]) as well as the "prior record score" (PRS) (for example, someone who had previously been sentenced to long prison sentences is given more "points" than a first-time offender [U.S. Federal Sentencing Guidelines, §4A1.1]). Some jurisdictions use sophisticated actuarial risk-need assessment tools to predict recidivism and provide for more evidence-based sentencing. And judges also review the punishments that convicted criminals received in previous and similar cases – again, for the purpose of consistency and uniformity. The upshot of all this is that judges have discretion to assign appropriate sentences within the constraints of primary or statutory law (set by the legislature) and secondary law (the constitution), while also considering sentencing guidelines (established by sentencing commissions) and common law (judicial precedent).

Most decisions by state and federal courts are subject to appeal, where appellate courts initially review the trial for any procedural errors that could have affected the outcome. The direct appeal considers only possible errors or negligence during the trial (trial court error), such as the admission of evidence that should have been excluded or improper jury instructions. In addition, a decision can be reversed if the judge departed from precedent and legal custom so dramatically that it constitutes an abuse of discretion. Defendants can also petition the trial judge (and up to the state supreme court) regarding issues that are outside of the court record, such as ineffective counsel or newly discovered evidence. Federal habeas corpus petitions are limited to federal and constitutional issues, such as whether a punishment is "cruel and unusual" and thus in violation of the Eighth Amendment. With capital convictions, most states require a direct appeal to the state supreme court, and it is often followed by collateral review of habeas corpus issues by the state supreme court and federal appeals courts, possibly up to and including the U.S. Supreme Court.

Resolving the antinomy (1): The role of the legislature

The U.S. criminal justice system has many parts to it and, when there is a proper separation of powers, different people serve different functions. There is no one person or political body that establishes the laws, determines guilt, and administers punishment. This separation provides the key to resolving the antinomy of punishment: on the two-tiered model, some agents within this system are tasked with using consequentialist reasoning in their decisions regarding criminal law (general justifying aim), while other agents are tasked with representing the community's reactive attitudes with regard to individual criminals (distribution).[7]

First, lawmakers should pass laws that preserve the public order, and that public order should be a just social arrangement. The purpose of the law is to maintain the state, so the legislature acts rationally when it effectively promotes that end. It acts reasonably (or rightly) when the system it maintains is a good one. In a liberal system – if, for the sake of argument, we assume it is just – that includes the protection of individual rights primarily, but the law may also attempt to maximize happiness insofar as doing so is consistent with a respect for rights. Laws against murder and theft, and the accompanying punishment, deter people from violating people's rights to life and property. Speed limits and other traffic laws are methods of coordinating people's behavior so as to promote public safety. Drug laws protect people against choices that harm themselves and others, and they minimize costs to the nation's health, safety, and productivity. Crimes are defined as those actions that are inimical to social functioning and that inhibit just relationships. Statutory penalties deter criminal offenses in order to minimize rights violations.

Criminal liability

As I mentioned earlier, the legislature also establishes the conditions for criminal liability. It is here that the legislature's actions seem most to be grounded in retributivism rather than consequentialism. After all, the relevant statutes define who is guilty and says that only the guilty should be punished, and it designates worse punishments for worse crimes. However, if we read this as equivalent to the claim that only the guilty *deserve to be punished*, then we beg the question in favor of retributivism. There is a correspondence between crime and punishment, but the reasoning behind that correspondence is not obvious. From the perspective of the law in general, why should only the guilty be punished? Why should murderers be given harsher punishments than shoplifters? Can these practices also be justified on consequentialist grounds?

There are several ways to defend consequentialism here. First, as a general and publicly established rule or institution, a legal system in which one's guilt

7 Tasioulas claims that any "top-down" mixed theory, which attempts to combine consequentialism and retributivism, is nothing but "a cut-and-paste assembly of disparate principles," committed to consequentialism but with retributivism "bolted on," artificially and arbitrarily, in order to produce desired results (2006, 282). The fact that the approaches map onto separate state functions – a well-known and generally endorsed separation of powers – belies the criticism that it is artificial. Furthermore, in Part III, I give three arguments that justify such an arrangement, showing that it is not arbitrary.

is necessary for legal punishment is likely to maximize the common good more than a system in which their guilt is incidental to whether they are punished. This is a rule-consequentialist approach: as Rawls (1955) claims, there are broad consequentialist reasons for us to apply retributivist principles in particular cases. Second, what counts as guilt with regard to a particular crime depends on what the legislature is trying to accomplish. The examples given in the previous paragraphs show that there is not some absolute standard of "*inner wickedness*" that determines a criminal's punishment, since the kind of culpability varies depending on the purpose of a given statute (Kant 1996b, 6:333). Laws against child endangerment are meant to motivate parents to be vigilant in the protection of their children, which is a positive or affirmative act, whereas potential murderers do not have to do anything except refrain from killing. If a society had a shared sense of obligation for children rather than entrusting them to their parents, then carelessness may be more tolerated and the laws less strict, since children would have numerous adults to take care of them in the event that one adult is negligent. The state defines individual culpability in light of the social conditions it is trying to maintain. This is consequentialist reasoning.

Restrictions on the legislature

The legislature must also establish kinds and degrees of penalties for each criminal statute – that is, statutory penalties or a punishment schedule.[8] Kinds of punishment include such things as execution, prison, probation, fines, and community service.[9] Degrees of punishment are set by sentencing ranges, which allow different criminals to receive more or less severe penalties for the same crime.

Again, the aim of the punishment, as part of the criminal law, is to preserve the public order or promote the common good, but this aim is ambiguous and should not be misconstrued. Not all crime must be eradicated, and certainly not at any cost. As Michael Davis puts it, the criminal law "does enough if it holds the commotion of life below a roar," such that crime is "relatively rare"; "the rules need only forbid the more substantial harms and regulate major conflict" (1992, 72). If the penalties were so great as to be "too frightful to risk," then the criminal law would not be protecting our autonomy, giving us a space in which we are free from the interference of authority. Such a law "pretends to be the work of a god" (72). The acceptable level of criminal activity is determined with reference to the principles that the system of punishment is trying to maintain.

8 As the U.S. Supreme Court asserts in *Gore v. United States* (357 U.S. 386 [1958]), "Whatever views may be entertained regarding severity of punishment, whether one believes in its efficacy or its futility, … these are peculiarly questions of legislative policy" (393).

9 The *Wolters Kluwer Bouvier Law Dictionary* includes the following categories of legal punishments: execution (loss of life), incarceration (loss of freedom), parole (regulation of freedom), other regulation out of prison such as loss of the right to vote or the right to live near children (loss of equal privileges), civic works or free labor, shame and loss of status, fines and forfeitures, and ceremonial demotion (Sheppard 2012, 2261).

For one thing, not all crimes are equally threatening to the social order, so we would be willing to tolerate more instances of lesser crimes. Edmund Pincoffs phrases it like this:

> The arrangement in question is not required to be one which equally discourages the violation of all rules; some rules are more important for survival and well-being than others; and the effectiveness needed in the prevention of some rule-violations is not demanded for the prevention of all rule-violations. (1966, 120)

We do not need to discourage shoplifting as strongly as we discourage murder, so the punishment for shoplifting does not need to be especially severe.

Furthermore, a punishment is morally justified if the social ideal is justified, but the social ideal itself prohibits certain punishments and limits how harsh they can be. In a liberal state, we cannot execute people for simple assault or cut off their hands for shoplifting. While this may reduce rates of these crimes, it does so by imposing punishments that are inhumane and wildly disproportionate, and thus cruel and unusual (prohibited under the Eighth Amendment). We adhere to these limits on principle, and the cost of restraining ourselves is some amount of criminal activity that we could otherwise prevent. Minimizing rights violations, under a consequentialism of rights, is more important than achieving maximum deterrence. But, in a liberal system or otherwise, it is also the case that not every increase in severity decreases the crime rate, so choosing a lesser punishment may also avoid unnecessary suffering, as dictated by the principle of parsimony.

There are many instances throughout the world of punishments that go beyond what is necessary or humane. For example, Singapore's draconian laws regarding drug possession – up to ten years in prison for possessing small amounts and the death penalty for larger amounts – is not only excessive but also violates the rights of the accused. Under the liberal system that we are assuming here, the government does not have absolute authority over people's lives. Note too that, because the goal is to preserve the public order or promote the common good, then kinds of punishment must be evaluated in addition to degrees. For example, if incarceration- and community-based drug treatment programs would decrease the rate of drug use, with a lower cost, less suffering, and greater success than imprisonment alone, then we ought to prefer them on consequentialist grounds (see Mitchell, Wilson, and MacKenzie 2007; and Przybylski 2009).

Setting the scale of penalties

To set statutory penalties, lawmakers should consider the findings of criminology and other social sciences to identify trends in criminal behavior and effective methods of crime prevention. Some of this will be obvious. If the punishment for embezzling a million dollars (felony theft of property) were a $100 fine and ten days in jail, then a lot of people would risk it; this would not deter anyone who needs to be deterred. But some punishments will be less obvious. People disagree about whether drug possession and use should be treated harshly, with fines and prison time; whether it should be decriminalized, with addicts receiving mandatory drug treatment and counseling; or whether (some or all) recreational drugs should be legalized. This question involves both theoretical considerations about the extent of people's rights over their own bodies, social scientific considerations about how the illegal drug trade impacts communities, and psychological and medical considerations about how best to address drug addiction. In any event, lawmakers' decisions should be driven by the best data available: "The knowledge of the criminologist may be exiguous, but it is ample indeed compared with that of those who are responsible for our legislation and practice in this field" (N. Morris 1966, 628n1). On the two-tiered model, legislators are consequentialists. Social science, although it is imperfect, is better at informing public policy than whatever assumptions and prejudices elected officials may bring to their offices, or the feelings of their constituents.

Statistical criminological analyses help lawmakers to determine the statutory penalties they should adopt. The low end of the range (the minimum sentence) is set at that point below which the level of criminal activity would be unacceptable. That is, if the punishment were less harsh, "the commotion of life" would be above what is reasonable for citizens to expect of their government, and the crime would not be "relatively rare" – with acceptable rarity relative to different crimes (e.g., shoplifting versus murder) (M. Davis 1992, 72). The high end of the range (the maximum sentence) is set at that point above which the crime rate would be unchanged or there would be a greater marginal cost overall. If criminal activity would not be affected by a harsher penalty or if there would be undesirable collateral costs, then that penalty serves no social purpose and is therefore morally prohibited, gratuitous harm.

Every legal prohibition and every punishment imposes a kind of cost, and that cost may or may not be worth it given the benefit. The relevant costs and benefits depend on the good that the law is designed to promote. For example, on the utilitarian view regarding the aims of the state – that is, the idea that the state ought to promote overall happiness – legislators would do a utilitarian calculus to determine whether making a given penalty more severe would cause more pain and less pleasure than a lesser alternative. That sets the upper limit. They would set the lower limit at that point below which, overall, the pleasure gained would not outweigh the pain avoided. In short, the decisions are about marginal utility. On the liberal view, by contrast, the government's purpose is to protect rights, not to minimize harm. The highest penalty is set at the point above which the damage done to the rights of criminals and others would outweigh the benefit (in terms of rights) gained by the community, including potential victims. The lowest penalty is the penalty under which rights are lessened or more at risk, such that the state is not adequately performing its protective function under the social contract. The legislature would not try to balance rights and overall well-being, because rights entail a duty-based obligation that trumps the obligation to promote happiness (Dworkin 1977, 197–200). Regardless of the good that we value, punishment ought to further our collective aims, so its kind and amount ought to be set to effectively deter criminals and potential criminals, both generally and specifically.

An example will help to illustrate how a legislature is supposed to determine sentencing ranges. Before I give the example, however, I want to stress that this is for illustrative purposes only. My hypothetical imagines a correlation between the severity of a punishment and its deterrent effect, and it considers those as the only two relevant factors when setting legal punishments. This is not realistic, and social science tells us so. There are many other variables at work that must be considered in any legislative decision regarding the criminal law. Different kinds of costs and benefits must be assessed, not only the rate of deterrence (which benefits communities) but also the financial costs to the state and burdens on the legal system, the economic and social costs of removing people from their communities, and collateral impacts on their families, among other things. The deterrent effects of punishments depend not only on their severity (i.e., whether they are sufficiently disliked to be truly aversive), but also on their likelihood (i.e., certainty, or the credibility of the threat) and their immediacy (i.e., celerity, or how quickly the state carries through on its threat), which vary depending on enforcement techniques. Potential offenders are affected differently by incentives because of their demographic characteristics, and some crimes may be more deterrable than others. Since we are also trying to minimize unnecessary suffering (i.e., we are trying to act parsimoniously), we need to consider alternatives to punishment, including social reforms that would make crime less likely and rehabilitative programs that would more effectively reduce recidivism. The complexity of the calculation is daunting, and indeed it has turned some theorists away from consequentialism. However, all these problems are tractable, and, especially recently, there are reliable enough empirical studies to guide legislative decisions (a claim that I defend in detail in Part IV).

For the sake of argument, then, consider the following: Imagine that we as a society believe that one hundred reported robberies per 100,000 population is "acceptable."[10] Again, we would prefer that there be zero robberies, but if there are up to one hundred robberies, we would think that the government is doing its job. We are not in a state of nature, the government is maintaining the social order well enough because it "holds the commotion of life below a roar," and robberies are "relatively rare" (M. Davis 1992, 72). Now imagine that the following punishments would restrain and rehabilitate actual criminals and deter potential criminals such that the corresponding crime rate was the result:

1) Execution → Ten robberies per 100,000 population
2) Life in prison → Ten robberies per 100,000 population
3) Twenty-five years in prison → Ten robberies per 100,000 population
4) Ten years in prison → Ten robberies per 100,000 population

10 In actual practice, the legislature would establish more specific crimes, such as first-, second-, and third-degree robbery, with sentencing ranges for each. I set this aside for the purposes of illustration.

The idea here is that some people will commit crimes no matter the threatened consequence because they are desperate enough to risk it, they believe that they will not be apprehended, and so on. Not everyone is "minimally prudent" (Ackerman 1980, 83–84); some criminals are "incorrigible," or not deterrable (Pogarsky 2002; Jacobs 2010). Therefore, the deterrent effect of a punishment must only be enough to "induce most prudent people to conform to the behavioral condition for citizenship" (Ackerman 1980, 83–84). Ten years in prison is severe enough that anyone who can be deterred would be deterred by that sentence and would be no more deterred by harsher sentences. If potential criminals will not commit robbery when threatened with ten years in prison, they are no less likely to commit robbery when threatened with twenty-five years, life in prison, or execution.

5) Five years in prison → Fifty robberies per 100,000 population
6) Two years in prison → One hundred robberies per 100,000 population
7) Two years of probation plus a $5000 fine → 500 robberies per 100,000 population
8) $5000 fine → 1,000 robberies per 100,000 population

Ten years in prison is a more severe penalty than five years in prison, five years in prison is a more severe penalty than two years in prison, two years in prison is a more severe penalty than probation and a fine, and so on. Each increase in penalty deters more potential criminals (to a point) and keeps the convicted robbers from committing more crimes than they otherwise would.

9) No punishment → 5,000 robberies per 100,000 population

If there were no risk of punishment at all, then no one who can and needs to be deterred would be deterred. There would be many more robberies, but not an astronomical number. I have assumed 5,000 for the sake of the illustration. Other forces, such as having strong moral convictions about the wrongness of stealing or worries about social disapproval, keep most people from robbing or wanting to rob anyone.

With these numbers and with the acceptable rate of one hundred reported robberies per 100,000 population, the legislature would set the sentencing range. Two years in prison would be the minimum punishment that the courts could impose for robbery, since a lower sentence than the minimum would not hold "the commotion of life below a roar." Execution, life in prison, and twenty-five years would be ruled out as excessive, since going beyond ten years in prison would inflict gratuitous suffering. Ten years in prison would be the maximum.

I mentioned earlier that this illustration simplifies things by assuming a direct correlation between the severity of a punishment and its deterrent effect. But another caveat is necessary here, and it is crucial for understanding the task of the legislature: the crime rate is not the only effect to consider in the cost-benefit analysis. An excessive punishment is not just one that is more severe than other possible and equally effective punishments; rather, it is too much given the costs. Another way of putting it is that it is a bad tradeoff, or introduces marginal costs. As an analogy, consider the speed limit. With a seventy-mile-per-hour speed limit on most interstate expressways, there are many more traffic fatalities and worse gas mileage (more environmental harm) than we would have if the speed limit were fifty-five miles per hour. We are willing to accept those harms because lowering the speed limit would make it less convenient to travel by increasing travel times. However, we are not willing to accept the additional fatalities that would result if the speed limit were eighty, ninety, or a hundred miles per hour. In addition, there is a minimum speed: a driver must not go so slow as to impede the flow of traffic. We force people to go faster (above the minimum) for the sake of convenience (and safety), and we force people to go slower (below the maximum) for the sake of safety. Similarly, maximum and minimum sentences for a crime are imposed so as to constrain illegal activity, but only if it is worth it.

Imagine that, in the example above, having the option of giving robbers life in prison would make us marginally safer than setting the maximum at ten years:

2′) Life in prison → Nine robberies per 100,000 population

The one fewer robbery is only one of the consequences of such a large increase in penalty. There are economic, social, and psychological costs associated with the additional years of prison. Not only is there the monetary cost to house and care for offenders for longer amounts of time, but having more people in prison for longer negatively impacts families and communities. It may also violate other values that the society is trying to promote, such as treating its citizens as rights-bearers who can be rehabilitated rather than as expendable things. All of this is to say that more deterrence is not necessarily better, even on consequentialist grounds.

After a certain point, increasing the severity and number of punishments actually instigates criminal behavior. Having a parent in prison increases the likelihood of aggression and criminality among the sons of incarcerated parents throughout their lives (Murray and Farrington 2005; Murray and Farrington 2008; Wildeman 2010; Roettger and Swisher 2011). The loss of large numbers of individuals from particular communities, especially communities of color, also affects social cohesion and weakens informal social controls that effectively reduce crime. Social scientists have identified three kinds of social control: private control within intimate groups such as families and friends, parochial control within neighborhood associations, and public control by the state. According to Dina Rose and Todd Clear (1998), mass incarceration erodes shared values and creates prison subcultures, which affect communities when offenders are released; increases mobility in and out of neighborhoods; and reduces socioeconomic status – forcibly removing people as family members, socializing agents, parents, and wage-earners. These factors lead to more social disorganization. The use of prisons to incapacitate criminals and deter others concurrently has the effect of creating an environment where crime is more likely. Indeed, research shows that crime increases when the incarceration rate is between 3.25 and 4.92 inmates per 1,000 persons in the general population, a number that most American states have reached (Liedka, Piehl, and Useem 2006).

2″) Life in prison → Eleven robberies per 100,000 population

A life sentence may deter some potential criminals more than a ten-year sentence, but, as the research indicates, the additional number of long-term incarcerations, spread over multiple offenders, may affect society in ways that make it more likely that other at-risk individuals, who would otherwise not commit robberies, turn to crime. Assumptions about punishment severity and crime deterrence must be qualified in these different ways. The bottom line is that, on my view, the legislature should set the maximum penalty at that point above which no additional marginal benefit would be achieved.

Of course, legislators may feel – wrongly – like they need to represent their supporters' resentment toward criminals. This is a particular risk because they are elected and, presumably, believe that they ought to be responsive to the people. However, legislators are supposed to establish laws within the framework of the constitution in order to advance the common good, rather than simply channeling the desires of their loudest constituents or their largest donors. Procedures may have to be put in place (by legislators themselves) so that they will fulfill their proper role.

One way to avoid retributivist populism in the setting of punishment policies, for example, would be to establish more expert agencies and commissions, along the lines of the U.S. Sentencing Commission, that would be tasked with assessing the available research and determining its public policy implications. Such agencies could be a resource for policymakers as they write criminal statutes or could even be empowered to make criminal policy decisions on their own by interpreting and implementing broad directives from the legislature. As Rachel Barkow argues, such an approach would be more effective at insulating institutional criminal justice decisions from political pressures, which are improper bases for broad social policies. Instead, such agencies would render decisions based on experts' assessments of the most reliable criminological research, in an effort to maximize the public good (2019, 165–85).

Improving outcomes

Of course, this illustration assumes that the legislature can specify the impact that punishment alone has on crime rates. Although there are doubts about the ability of social scientists to provide us with this kind of precision – doubts that I address in more detail in Chapter 9 – I will mention here that the obligation of criminologists is to approximate this ideal as much as possible and for legislators to act reasonably on the basis of the data they have. It is a longstanding objection against consequentialism, and utilitarianism in particular, that it is impossible to know what the consequences of an act or policy will be. But, as John Stuart Mill notes, "the whole past duration of the human species" provides us with information about what does and does not tend to produce happiness (2001, 23). States and communities within states have been veritable testing grounds for different kinds and degrees of punishment, and they have recorded the effects on crime rates and recidivism. One running example throughout the book is the different ways that governments have tried to combat recreational drug use. Another example is the effect of the death penalty on murder rates – that is, the question of whether the death penalty is an effective deterrent – for which there is substantial comparative data. I will address capital punishment in detail in Chapter 12. For now, it suffices to say that there are more and less reasonable positions to take based on the historical evidence. And, if we act in good faith based on the information we have, Mill says, then even if the policy turns out to be the wrong one – if the punishment schedule does not maintain the social order as well as some alternative – we can still say that the legislature acted rightly (2001, 18–20).

Consequentialism is a normative theory that defines the right in terms of the good: there is some good (happiness, rights, perfection, virtue, etc.), and the right thing to do is to maximize the good. Based on this understanding of the theory, it seems that the legislature should not establish sentencing ranges but should instead set one effective penalty for all criminals, since that penalty, applied institution-wide, would maximize positive outcomes. For example, why allow for the possibility of one hundred robberies per 100,000 population, by having a minimum sentence of two years, if a set penalty of ten years in prison would keep that number to ten? There would be consequences to such a policy, as noted already, and consequentialist reasons not to set specific mandatory sentences. On an individual level, someone in less need of restraint and rehabilitation would get as much prison time as a hardened criminal, which would amount to unnecessary suffering and a wasteful use of public funds. Not allowing for individualized sentencing would also have deleterious effects on the justice system. One could imagine a prosecutor bringing lesser, inappropriate charges against someone because the possible sentence for the actual crime they committed would be disproportionate to the offense. Alternatively, if someone were put on trial for a crime they did commit but faced what the jury considers to be a disproportionate or otherwise unjust sentence, the jury may nullify the application of the law. The legislative and judicial branches of government would come apart.

If all things were equal, however, and if the best outcome, across the state or country as a whole, could be achieved with one specific, mandatory punishment, then it would seem to be required by consequentialism. And that would restrict our retributive impulses, because it would not allow judges to tailor sentences to defendants with different degrees of guilt. What distinguishes the two-tiered model of punishment from unalloyed consequentialism is that there is also a competing moral demand to give criminals what they deserve. Unlike Rawls's (1955) view, on my view the duty to give people what they deserve is not derived from and dependent on its maximization of positive outcomes. That is, the legislature recognizes that it is part of a whole system, another part of which is bound to act on nonconsequentialist, retributive principles, so the legislature must not act in a way that makes it impossible for the courts to act according to what ought to guide their decisions. The obligation of criminal courts to express the community's moral resentment places limits or side constraints on what the legislature can do. According to Paul Robinson's taxonomy of mixed theories, this is a "contingent priority" approach: the legislature sets priorities in terms of social outcomes but also sets conditions to ensure that its priorities do not exclude a reasonable range of punishments understood in terms of desert (1987, 30).

So, in some cases – namely, when maximizing the good would render a reasonable assignment of desert impossible – less-than-maximally-good consequences are preferred so that, collectively, we can achieve other moral and legal objectives. Michael Slote calls this "satisficing consequentialism" rather than maximizing consequentialism (1985, 35–59). While the legislature constrains what the judiciary can do, the judiciary also places a demand on the legislature to allow judges latitude in assigning individualized sentences. So, the legislature is not bound to achieve the *best* outcome for the country as a whole, but only a *good enough* outcome below which the legislature would be thought, reasonably, to have failed to preserve the public order.[11]

Resolving the antinomy (2): The role of the criminal judiciary

As Stanley Benn notes, there are two senses of distribution that we must keep separate so as not to confuse what, under a mixed theory of punishment, involves two different kinds of justification:

> To ask "How much punishment is appropriate to a given offence?" is ambiguous: it may refer either to the punishment allotted by a rule to a *class* of acts, or to a particular award for a given act, within that class. The distinction is pointed by the practice of laying down only maximum (and sometimes minimum) penalties in the rule, leaving particular determinations to judicial discretion. (1958, 335)

Keeping this distinction in mind is especially important for the two-tiered model of punishment. Both the legislature and the criminal judiciary are concerned with distribution, broadly speaking. But the different bases of their distributions mark their distinct penological functions: the legislature passes laws with "the punishment allotted by a rule to a *class* of acts," while a judge assigns "a particular award

11 "Could not someone who held that rightness depended solely on how good an act's consequences were also want to hold that less than the best was sometimes good enough, hold, in other words, that an act might qualify as morally right through having good enough consequences, even though better consequences could have been produced in the circumstances?" (Slote 1985, 36).

for a given act, within that class." The former decisions are justified by their consequences, while the latter decisions are justified by retribution.[12]

The idea that lawmakers should be driven by consequentialist concerns is more controversial than the idea that judges and juries should be driven by retributivist concerns. According to retributivism, only the guilty deserve to be punished, and they deserve to be punished in proportion to the seriousness of their crimes. As we conceive of criminal trials in the United States, a judge or jury is tasked with evaluating the evidence that is presented to them to determine if it is sufficient to prove, beyond a reasonable doubt, that the defendant is guilty. If the defendant is proven to have committed the crime, the judge or jury should find the person guilty and then hand down a punishment, informed by sentencing guidelines, that is within the statutory range and appropriate given the mitigating factors, aggravating factors, and criminal history.

Judges and juries should not decide whether someone is guilty based on the social consequences of a conviction, such as whether punishment for the defendant will deter other potential criminals; how much incarceration will cost the state, and whether that money could be better spent on social programs; or the effects of a conviction on race relations in the community. The legislature and the courts have different aims: "Consequences are the primary concern of legislators, not of judges or juries" (Mabbott 1955, 263; see also Ewing 1970, 66). The judge's or jury's only question ought to be whether the defendant committed the crime. If they are proven to have done so, then they deserve to be punished. If they are not proven to have done so, then they do not deserve to be punished. Or, more properly speaking, they do not deserve to be punished by the state, even if they are a bad person in other ways (who, perhaps, deserves to be punished by their parents or by God).

In Chapter 4, I defended retributivism in terms of its expressive function. Antony Duff describes the trial and the resulting punishment as a "communicative enterprise":

> Punishment is now continuous in its meaning and purpose with the criminal trial and the criminal law: it seeks to communicate to the offender that judgment on, and that condemnation of, his conduct which his trial has justified

12 Like me, Miceli (2019) distinguishes the roles of the legislature and the criminal judiciary, and he understands their guiding principles as consequentialist and retributivist, respectively. One difference is that he portrays both of their functions in economic terms. Following Gary Becker (1968), he says that the legislature maximizes overall welfare by means of deterrence; and, following Adelstein (2017), he says that the judiciary oversees the involuntary transfer of rights between victim and offender (corrective justice). Miceli thus conceives of both approaches to punishment as economic transactions. On my view, the punishment-as-price view correctly describes consequentialist reasoning but not retribution. Adelstein's analysis seems more like an economic description of the practice of giving people what they deserve, not a justification. For Miceli, retribution is a "criminal exchange," but for me it is the expression of resentment, and the expression of resentment is not an economic transaction.

> and which his conviction also expresses; to bring him to accept that judgment, to condemn himself, and to modify his future conduct accordingly; and thus to persuade him not merely to *obey* the law, but to *accept* its justified demands and judgments. (1986, 238)

The trial establishes the truth – or our justified belief in the truth (probative instead of material guilt) – of the cognitive content underlying the feeling of resentment. The punishment communicates the community's feeling of resentment both by conveying its sense of having been wronged and, ideally, by instilling in the offender a recognition of that condemnation and the rightness of the state's judgment.

On the two-tiered model, the legislative branch checks the power of the judiciary, limiting the expression of community resentment in ways that further the aims of the state. W. D. Ross claims that having retributivism as an aim would undermine the state's ability to achieve its goals (2002, 60). In a mixed theory such as mine, however, consequentialist aims are moderated rather than undermined by retributivism, and vice versa, because the principles operate at different tiers in the system. Primary rules, such as the Federal Rules of Criminal Procedure and the Federal Rules of Evidence, and secondary (constitutional) rules, such as the Fifth and Eighth Amendments, set out the expectations of and constraints on criminal trials that, collectively, further the law's purpose, which, in a liberal system such as the United States, is the protection of rights. The judge is there to make sure that the law is followed during the trial. Guilt is then determined by judges and juries within the parameters set forth by the legislature and the constitution. In other words, judges are not out to get defendants whom they think are guilty. Judges remain neutral throughout the process, with the idea that probative guilt is determined by means of a trial, and whether a defendant deserves to be punished depends on the outcome.

If the government's aim were the simple maximization of happiness, then there would probably be laxer rules and fewer protections for the accused than there are in the U.S., because the harm done to an innocent person who is wrongly convicted may be outweighed by the harm that is avoided by not letting guilty people go free.[13] If an authoritarian ruler used the law to maintain their hold on power, they would make a similar calculation: innocents who are imprisoned usually pose less of a risk than guilty people who are set free. In a liberal system, however, according to Blackstone's ratio, "it is better that ten guilty persons escape, than that one innocent suffer" (Blackstone 2016, 231). Again, using Ronald Dworkin's (1977) formulation, rights impose a stronger obligation on us than the obligation to make people happy. We are not supposed to find a balance between rights and happiness. Instead, rights protect our fundamental

13 Smilansky's (1990) objection that laxer standards in criminal trials would be justified on utilitarian grounds may be correct, but it does not impact consequentialism more generally, especially a consequentialism of rights.

values against collective political justifications in terms of well-being, so they protect the minority against the majority by trumping their demands. Rights of the accused are codified in primary and secondary law, which constrains the actions of the judiciary. When lawmakers and judges fulfill their assigned roles in a liberal system, rights are maximized even though overall happiness may not be.

It is crucial for a judge or jury to determine whether the defendant is guilty on the basis of the evidence. Resentment as a reactive attitude is based on the claim that one has been wronged, that the harm done was not deserved, and that the wrongdoer ought to suffer for it. Theoretically, a trial determines whether that feeling of resentment is properly directed. Is the defendant the one who wronged the community and who deserves the burden of punishment (as an expression of resentment)? That is, did they commit the act (*actus reus*), and did they have the state of mind that the statute requires to establish guilt (*mens rea*)? As the U.S. Supreme Court says in *Witherspoon v. Illinois* (391 U.S. 510 [1968]), the jury is "the conscience of the community" and expresses public condemnation at the transgression of social norms (510, 519; also 528, 536):

> one of the most important functions any jury can perform in making such a selection [of punishment] is to maintain a link between contemporary community values and the penal system – a link without which the determination of punishment could hardly reflect "the evolving standards of decency that mark the progress of a maturing society." (519n15)

After the defendant is convicted, the judge in the sentencing phase assumes guilt and makes sure that the offender gets what they deserve, expressing the reactive attitudes of the community. The judge determines the kind and amount of burden that is proportional to the seriousness of the crime, following what Andrew von Hirsch calls the principle of "commensurate deserts" (1976, 66). This is where Joel Feinberg's claim regarding punishment is most apparent: as meted out by judges and juries, punishment has an expressive purpose (1970, 95–118).

Resolving the antinomy (3): The role of police and prosecutors

Whitley Kaufman claims that mixed theories of punishment that depend on a separation of powers are untenable because there are *two* theories being related (utilitarianism and retributivism) and *three* branches of government (legislative, judicial, and executive branches) (2008, 44). However, the executive power does not need its own theory of punishment because it does not punish anyone. Plea deals made with public prosecutors must be accepted or rejected by judges. And if police were to inflict punishment on the people they arrest, they would be guilty of abusing their power and acting as vigilantes – as when an officer publicly executed George Floyd on the streets of Minneapolis. The two-tiered model of punishment has implications for how the executive power behaves, but there need not be a third, independent theory of punishment that governs its conduct.

Police and prosecutors stand between two powerful forces, the legislature and the judiciary, that, respectively, enact our collective will in furthering the aims of the state and express our communal conscience in the treatment of individual defendants. Police enforce the law, and prosecuting attorneys represent the state's interests and conduct the prosecution of the accused. Police and prosecutors carry out the will of the legislature; and judges and juries, when they confirm guilt and assign punishment (or not), follow the will of the people in giving offenders what they deserve. In enforcing the law, then, the actions of police and prosecutors are justified on consequentialist grounds, just as the actions of the legislature are. The difference is that police and prosecutors follow primary law as established by the legislature (e.g., by enforcing only existing statutes) and secondary law as established by the constitution (e.g., by respecting suspects' Miranda rights). Historically, political philosophers refer to the legislature as the sovereign or supreme power (although it need not have absolute sovereignty) because the legislature, by making laws, sets the parameters within which the executive works to enforce the law and the judiciary works to interpret and apply the law.[14]

This is a form of rule-consequentialism. According to rule-consequentialism, people ought to follow the rule that, in general, tends to maximize the good (however it is defined) even if acting contrary to the rule in a particular case would seem to be better. Applied here, the idea is that police and prosecutors should carry out the will of the legislature in enforcing the law and trying the accused, within the constraints set out by primary and secondary law, even if violating those rules in specific instances would seem to preserve the state more effectively. For example, police may want to search someone's house without a warrant or probable cause because they sincerely believe that the person poses a threat to the community. A prosecutor may not want to turn over exculpatory evidence to the defense if it would make it less likely that the defendant will be convicted. In both cases, they should follow the law because not doing so tends not to turn out well. On the liberal view, for instance, such well-meaning actions violate the rights of the accused. Even if the suspects are in fact guilty, one should not protect the community's well-being by violating people's rights, which, according to Dworkin, override that concern. Such actions would make it more likely that an innocent person will be punished, among other things.

As I mentioned earlier, some police and prosecutorial discretion is inevitable, and some discretion in enforcing the law is morally appropriate. Legislatures are unable to describe precisely all conduct that is covered under the law, so police

14 For example, John Locke writes: "there can be but *one supreme power*, which is *the legislative*, to which all the rest are and must be subordinate" (1980, §149 [p. 77]; see also §§143–58 [pp.75–83]). See also Rousseau (1978), Bk. I, ch. 7 (pp. 54–55), Bk. II, ch. 1–2 (pp. 59–61).

officers and prosecutors must interpret and classify what they encounter; many outdated statutes remain on the books, so they must decide what to enforce as a matter of fairness; and limited resources make it impossible to enforce all laws against everyone (LaFave 1965, 61–143). However, it is also true that discretion is prone to abuse, including discrimination against minorities. For example, police discretion often results in racial profiling (National Academies of Sciences, Engineering, and Medicine 2018, ch. 7), and prosecutorial discretion in plea bargaining has led to racial disparities in convictions and sentencing. Even when controlling for prior arrest record, studies have found that racial bias affects prosecutors' decisions at every level, including case screening, bail recommendations, charging, and sentences in pleas. Minority defendants are more likely to receive worse outcomes than similarly situated white defendants (Applegate 1982; Crew 1991; A. Davis 1998; Johnson 2003; Ulmer, Kurlychek, and Kramer 2007; Kutateladze, Lynn, and Liang 2012; Smith and Levinson 2012; Berdejó 2018). This, coupled with racial bias in policing practices, accounts for some of the disproportionate impact of mass incarceration on the Black population: "African Americans are more likely than white Americans to be arrested; once arrested, they are more likely to be convicted; and once convicted, and they are more likely to experience lengthy prison sentences" (Sentencing Project 2018, par. 2). If their purpose is to maintain the social order by enforcing the law, and if (on the liberal view) that social order involves a commitment to equal rights, then discretionary actions by police and prosecutors should be limited.

In fact, U.S. appeals courts have both limited police activity and granted broad discretionary powers that are, in some cases, prone to abuse. For example, in the landmark decision *Yick Wo v. Hopkins* (118 U.S. 356 [1886]), the Court concluded, based on the equal protection clause of the Fourteenth Amendment, that laws cannot be arbitrarily enforced in a prejudicial manner, even if the laws themselves are nondiscriminatory. Subsequent cases have held police to a standard of reasonableness that gives them broad discretionary powers: to stop and frisk a pedestrian who has not committed a crime just because police have a "reasonable suspicion" that they will (*Terry v. Ohio*, 392 U.S. 1 [1968]); to use aggressive force against a suspect so long as the officer's fear of grave harm is "objectively reasonable" in that moment (*Graham v. Connor*, 490 U.S. 386 [1989]); and to use a traffic stop as a pretext to allow search and seizure of a vehicle provided that there is "reasonable suspicion" that a traffic violation has occurred (*Whren v. United States*, 517 U.S. 806 [1996]), to name only a few examples. Such policies have sometimes permitted or excused the use of excessive force, discriminatory treatment, and abuse of power. On the two-tiered model, a reasonableness standard is best understood in terms of what efficiently accomplishes the just aims of the state, which, in the case of the liberal state, includes not only a concern for "law and order" but a fair concern for people's rights (against unreasonable searches and seizures, to equal protection under the law, etc.).

U.S. courts have imposed even fewer restrictions on prosecutors. They have consistently upheld broad powers for prosecutors to decide, almost unilaterally, whether to charge people, the crimes with which to charge them, when to terminate a prosecution, and the conditions of guilty pleas (Applegate 1982, 35–36n2). In most states, prosecutors can choose from a wide range of options in each case, especially when dealing with low-level drug offenses and theft. In Oklahoma, for example, someone who is arrested with a small amount of marijuana and a pipe may be given a deferred sentence, so nothing appears on their criminal record if they stay out of trouble; a misdemeanor and probation; or felony possession with intent to distribute and possession of drug paraphernalia, which could result in up to ten years in prison (Gentzler 2019). When prosecutors perceive mandatory minimums as too harsh, they can (but need not) undo statutory requirements by charging offenders with similar crimes that do not trigger the mandatory minimum sentences (Tonry 1996). Elizabeth Magill concludes that giving prosecutors such broad discretion threatens the separation of powers between the legislative and executive branches:

> decisions by prosecutors about how to enforce a statute are indistinguishable from lawmaking. That is, given that the range of permissible enforcement actions under criminal laws (and many other laws) is extremely broad, it is the prosecutors' pattern of decisions that shape the meaning of the law, not the underlying statute itself. (2000, 1193)

The statutory penalties established by the legislature, which are supposed to limit possible punishments, do not mean much if a prosecutor can choose from among different crimes, with very different ranges of punishments, for a single defendant.

The fact that prosecutors have broad discretion does not mean that their power is unlimited, however. Prosecutors are legally prohibited from vindictive, retaliatory, or discriminatory prosecutions, and they may not bring criminal charges to achieve civil objectives ("Right to Nondiscriminatory Enforcement" 1961). Many executive branch offices also have administrative rules with criteria to distinguish acceptable and unacceptable uses of discretion (K. Davis 1969, pt. 3). A summary of the implications of Supreme Court precedents for prosecutorial discretion was written by the U.S. Department of Justice Office of Legal Counsel in 2014 (Thompson 2014).[15] In defense of President Barack Obama's DACA policy,[16] the memo describes four principles that ought to guide discretionary actions when enforcing the law:

1) The factors that are considered in the decision about how to enforce the law should be in the enforcement agency's area of expertise. The memo specifically talks about the allocation of resources and prioritizing cases, as necessary (Thompson 2014, 5, 7).

15 The memo focuses primarily on *Heckler v. Chaney*, 470 U.S. 821 (1985).

16 Deferred Action for Childhood Arrivals (DACA) is a policy, not a law, under which the executive branch does not enforce immigration laws for undocumented immigrants who were brought to the United States illegally as children and meet other conditions.

2) The enforcement agency should not simply impose its will in place of the legislature. That is, "an agency's enforcement decisions should be consonant with, rather than contrary to, the congressional policy underlying the statutes the agency is charged with administering" (Thompson 2014, 5).
3) The enforcement agency cannot abdicate its legal and professional responsibility (Thompson 2014, 6).
4) The enforcement agency cannot make a blanket decision not to enforce, which would amount to ignoring the legislature entirely. Rather, it must examine each case individually so that it is carrying out the will of the legislature as best it can, given the agency's priorities and limited resources (Thompson 2014, 6).

Whether DACA meets these criteria is a matter of debate. One challenge is that enforcement agencies must try to balance a need for individualized assessments with a general policy that treats people equally and in accordance with the law – the same dilemma that judges face in sentencing. The U.S. Supreme Court's decision in *Reno v. Flores* (507 U.S. 292 [1993]) states that, although the executive branch's "exercise of discretion ... requires 'some level of individualized determination' ... this does not mean that the Service must forswear use of reasonable presumptions and generic rules" (313). People have a right to equality under the law. Thus, prosecutors must fulfill two competing demands: making "determinations that are specific to the individual and necessary to accurate application of the regulation" (313).

These competing demands entail that prosecutorial discretion ought to be restricted in some ways and expanded in others. An example of the former approach, using "reasonable presumptions and generic rules," is New Jersey's utilization of plea-bargaining guidelines in drug cases.[17] Whenever a prosecutor wants to offer a defendant a plea, they need to consult a chart and consider the defendant's criminal history as well as mitigating and aggravating factors – similar to sentencing guidelines. The process results in a list of allowable plea bargains (Lantigua-Williams 2016). An example of the latter approach, using

17 New Jersey is one of the few states where prosecutors are appointed, not elected. One driver of increased sentences is the fact that most local prosecutors and judges are elected in the United States, and the public often demands harsh treatment of criminals. Research shows that trial judges are more likely to impose harsher sentences when they are in competitive judicial elections (Huber and Gordon 2004; Berry 2015; Dippel and Poyker 2020), and that state appeals court judges are more likely to affirm death sentences when there is strong public support for the death penalty and they are competing in elections, whether they are partisan or non-partisan (Canes-Wrone, Clark, and Kelly 2014). In general, people who are elected will have more incentive to express the public's sometimes arbitrary, abstract, and illegitimate anger rather than focusing on justified feelings of resentment. The judiciary and, perhaps, prosecutors, should be more insulated from public emotional responses, so there is a case to be made for their appointment rather than their popular election. A full investigation of this issue would go beyond the scope of this book.

"individualized determination," is the U.S. Attorney General's Smart on Crime Initiative (U.S. Department of Justice 2013). Prior to its appearance in 2010, many prosecutors had been focusing only on drug quantity in charging people with drug crimes. As a result, low-level drug offenders often pled to felonies with steep mandatory minimum sentences. The new guidelines allow prosecutors to distinguish between drug dealers and drug users, without looking only at the quantity of drugs. As a result, it has significantly reduced the number of low-level drug offenders in prison, since many of them can be given deferred sentences (Lantigua-Williams 2016).

In light of the two-tiered model of punishment, one way of understanding the four principles in the DACA memo is that prosecutors should advance the overall aim of the legislature in furthering the common good. They should follow the spirit of the law, not (or not only) its letter. A police officer who decides not to give someone a ticket for speeding is deciding that a warning is sufficient to motivate the driver not to do it in the future. If the officer decides not to charge someone with a violent crime, however, that is contrary to the legislature's aim to maintain public safety. Similarly, a prosecutor who works out a deal with a defendant to plead to voluntary manslaughter rather than murder could be doing it for several reasons, many of which are consistent with the law's intent. The prosecutor may doubt whether they can prove to the jury that the crime was premeditated, or they may want to be sure to get the criminal off the street rather than taking a chance at trial. They may be thinking about how best to spend their office's limited resources, including on trials for people who are unwilling to plead guilty. This is very different from the prosecutor during the civil rights era who refused to bring charges against white people for hate crimes against Black people.

Another promising corrective to the pitfalls of prosecutorial discretion in the U.S. would be to incorporate elements of the European and Latin American civil law traditions in order to restrict the American prosecutor's ability to decline prosecution, reduce charges, and engage in plea bargaining. In the civil law tradition, prosecutors are bound by a code of criminal procedure that defines their role narrowly. They do not fight to "win" cases against defendants and defense counsel, as they do in the American adversarial tradition. Instead, the prosecutor's primary job is to oversee the criminal investigation; assemble a dossier that summarizes the results of the investigation, including all relevant inculpatory and exculpatory evidence; and file appropriate criminal charges if warranted. Under a system requiring compulsory prosecution, charges must be filed if there is sufficient evidence; there is no American-style plea bargaining. Any decision not to file is reviewed by prosecutorial superiors and, in some civil law systems, victims can challenge the decision. When charges are brought, a panel of judges, not the attorneys, is responsible for developing the facts at trial, deciding who will testify, and asking most of the questions. The judges' ruling explains the factual and legal conclusions that they reached and why, and, if the defendant is found guilty, explains why they imposed a particular sentence. Plea bargaining is rare because it bypasses the judges' ability to weigh the evidence and determine guilt, and because it introduces variation instead of equal treatment of accused criminals.[18]

The civil law tradition cannot simply be superimposed onto the American system, for several reasons: the right to a jury trial guaranteed under the Sixth Amendment, the separation of powers between the executive and the judiciary, the desire for local control of criminal trials, and faith in the democratic method of selecting judges and prosecutors by popular vote, among other things (Pizzi 1993). However, there are elements of the European tradition that could be incorporated into the U.S. without completely overhauling the existing system. Currently, if an American prosecutor does not file a criminal charge, usually there is no mechanism for judicial review.[19] And, although plea bargains must be accepted or rejected by judges, "judges almost automatically ratify prosecutorial charge reductions and sentence recommendations" (Alschuler 1976, 1065; see also 1065–66n25). One possible remedy is to develop stricter guidelines that would constrain prosecutorial discretion and subject it to more judicial oversight (K. Davis 1969; K. Davis 1976; Vorenberg 1976; Vorenberg 1981).[20] Lippke (2016) argues that abuses could be curtailed if a defendant who expresses an interest in plea bargaining is given a settlement hearing before a judge who determines if there is sufficient evidence to support a guilty plea and sets a presumptive sentence for all remaining charges. Sentence discounts for pleas would be restricted so as to avoid arbitrariness in sentencing having to do with, for example, how busy the prosecutor is and how risk-averse the defendant is (see also Lippke 2011). Although this stops short of the European model – victims cannot challenge a prosecutor's decision not to charge a defendant, for example – such guidelines and oversight would protect against arbitrary and discriminatory treatment by providing a way to review and evaluate prosecutors' decisions.

18 For an overview of the civil law tradition, see Merryman and Pérez-Perdomo (2018).

19 "An initial decision not to prosecute may be reached by the prosecutor without his being required as a matter of course to explain his decision to or obtain the approval of a judicial officer" (LaFave et al. 2009, §13.3[c]). In one of its rulings, the appeals court for the D.C. circuit stated:

> Few subjects are less adapted to judicial review than the exercise by the Executive of his discretion in deciding when and whether to institute criminal proceedings, or what precise charge shall be made, or whether to dismiss a proceeding once brought. (*Newman v. United States*, 382 F.2d 479 [D.C. Cir. 1967], 480)

20 Pizzi does not think that such guidelines would inappropriately constrain prosecutors or violate the separation of powers (1993, 1363–64). Former U.S. Supreme Court Justice Anthony Kennedy agrees that discretion should reside with a judge more than a prosecutor:

> in my view, a transfer of sentencing discretion from a judge to an Assistant U.S. Attorney, often not much older than the defendant, is misguided. The policy gives the decision to an assistant prosecutor not trained in the exercise of discretion and takes discretion from the trial judge. The trial judge is the one actor in the system most experienced with exercising discretion in a transparent, open, and reasoned way. (Quoted in "Kennedy Discusses Sentencing" 2003, par. 5)

Of course, we should also consider more radical alternatives; the restrictions I have mentioned may not be good enough. Perhaps the American system, with elected prosecutors and adversarial criminal trials, would better achieve the country's collective goals if it were replaced with the civil law system or something else. Perhaps some of the "public safety" funding that now goes to police should be reallocated to social programs such as education, housing, and community health. Trained mental health professionals are more likely to deescalate mental health crises, most of which do not involve crimes or violence, or require emergency apprehension, than heavily armed police officers on their own (Wood, Watson, and Fulambarker 2017). If going beyond mere reforms to the current system would better support a just social order and minimize harm – and whether they would is a matter to be sorted out by empirical studies – consequentialist legislators ought to create such policies and police and prosecutors ought to implement them.

The two-tiered model of punishment illuminates the roles of police and prosecutors, and it provides the rationale for limiting their discretion. Since both police and prosecutors enforce the law, and since the law is designed to further the aims of the state, their actions are justified under rule-consequentialism. They ought to enforce the law as written because doing so carries out the will of the legislature and, in principle and on the whole, protects the community of citizens (increasing happiness, preserving rights, or accomplishing whatever other goals the state has). The legislature and the courts allow them a range of discretion that is consistent with our collective aims.

Murphy's criteria

Theories have to explain things, and if they do not explain what they ought to explain, then we should not base our understanding and judgments on those theories. Jeffrie Murphy has developed a series of questions that any theory of punishment must answer in order to be a theory of punishment at all, let alone a true one (1987, 510–12). In addition to demonstrating the viability of my mixed view of punishment as a theory, showing how it satisfies Murphy's five conditions will help to summarize my position prior to justifying it in Part III.

1) "*What is the Nature of Crime and Punishment?*" (Murphy 1987, 510)

Murphy means by this question that a theory of punishment should be able to explain certain distinctions, especially the distinction between criminal law and civil law, and the difference between criminal punishment and civil penalties. One risk of the two-tiered model is my claim, in Chapter 1, that there is no fundamental difference between punishments and penalties. This would seem to elide the distinction between civil and criminal law. However, the distinction between criminal and civil law cannot rest on the distinction between punishments and penalties, for several reasons:

a) Some criminal violations receive what we would call penalties, and some civil violations receive what we would call punishments. For example, someone who intentionally runs a red light may be charged with a misdemeanor (a crime) because of the risk it poses to others, but as a result they may be given a fine (a penalty). A parent who refuses to pay court-ordered child support (a civil matter) may be held in contempt of court and given jail time (a punishment).

b) It would be a circular explanation: civil violations are defined by the fact that violators receive penalties, not punishments; and violators receive penalties rather than punishments because they violate civil law, not criminal law.
c) Legislatures establish criminal and civil laws and assign appropriate statutory punishments or penalties. There must be some independent criteria that they use to make the distinction between criminal and civil laws. The distinction cannot follow from the nature of the coercive response, or else lawmakers would have no way to make the distinction in the first place.

There must be a different way of distinguishing criminal and civil law, not in terms of the coercive measures that the state inflicts in each case. On my view, the purpose of punishment is to enforce the law and thus to promote the aims of the state. Criminal law, taken as a whole, provides a picture of what the state wants to be, because it shows what the legislature thinks is crucial to the state's very existence. A theocracy would strictly limit religious freedom and would severely punish violations of religious edicts. A liberal democracy would protect people's rights to life and property through laws against murder and theft, but it would allow for free religious expression as part of its commitment to personal freedom. The difference between the former and the latter reveals their different aims. The values of a society are written in its criminal law.

Criminal violations contradict the aims of the state, while civil violations contradict the aims of individuals (persons, corporate entities, etc.). Criminal punishment furthers the general aims of the state by restraining criminals and deterring potential criminals, while civil penalties further the aims of specific individuals by compensating them for damages done and restoring them to some approximation of their original states, prior to the violations. Giving a large fine for intentionally running a red light is meant to deter the motorist and other motorists from doing that. The state is protecting people's rights by reducing the threat that reckless drivers pose to themselves, to others, and to property. Sending a deadbeat dad to jail is meant to motivate him to pay the child support, which the court had found to be fair and necessary to maintain the children in the way to which they had been accustomed. The intended benefit is for the father's dependents, not society as a whole. The two-tiered model, then, allows us to explain the nature of crime and punishment in consequentialist terms, related to the aim that a given punishment or class of punishments is trying to accomplish.

2) "*What is the Moral Justification of Punishment?*"
3) "*What is the Political Justification of Punishment?*" (Murphy 1987, 510)

The two-tiered model answers both questions. According to the distinction introduced in Chapter 3, a system of punishment is justified politically if it furthers the aims of the legal system. It is morally justified if the aims of the legal system are morally right. If we assume, for example, that people have rights and that those rights ought to be protected, then punishments that deter people from violating rights and that restrain and rehabilitate criminals so that innocents are protected would be morally justified. The punishments would be legally (or politically) justified if the state adopts the protection of rights as its aim and establishes laws that effectively further that aim. A theocracy that punishes people for not adhering to required religious practices – e.g., giving a woman jail time if she does not wear a hijab in public, as they do in Iran – would be politically justified, since there is a law (primary law) that was put in place by a constitutionally prescribed process (secondary law), but, assuming that we have a right to religious freedom, it would not be morally justified.

Some forms of retributivism cannot seem to answer these questions well – or, more specifically, they can usually answer one question but not the other. Kant, for example, says that wrongdoers ought to be punished in proportion to their "*inner wickedness*," and he says that the state should execute people even if it serves no social purpose (1996b, 6:333). Murder eliminates completely the victim's ability to act, which makes it punishable, but the specific punishment that Kant demands (death) is determined not based on what will maximize outer freedom for the community, but on desert. For Kant, penal justice is a categorical imperative rather than a hypothetical imperative that depends on the state's aims (the latter of which he deems "eudaimonism") (1996b, 6:331–34; see also Murphy 1987, 521–22). Since only moral obligations can command unconditionally, Kant seems to collapse the distinction between moral justification and legal justification, at least when it comes to the death penalty. Kant answers the moral question but not the political question.

Other forms of retributivism can answer the legal question but not the moral question. Legalistic retributivism, for example, is the view that criminals deserve to be punished because they broke the law and that punishing them supports our collective political goals (e.g., treating people as responsible citizens) rather than achieving some moral good (moralistic retributivism). Mabbott defends such a view: "Punishment is a corollary of law-breaking by a member of the society whose law is broken" (1939, 160–61). Alan Brudner argues that it is permissible to punish offenders because the state is respecting them by holding them accountable for their actions, not based on what they morally deserve, but based on what is required under the law, namely "the connection between the recipient's wrong and the wrong he suffers" (2009, 39). Legalistic retributivism seems to have recently become a popular position in the United States with regard to undocumented immigrants, for whom punishment follows logically from the fact of their having done something illegal. On this view, there is no moral quandary about what to do about illegal immigrants now living in the United States. Their legal status entails that they should all be punished.[21] This sets aside the moral question

21 One example is from a letter to the editor in the *New York Times*, written in response to an editorial calling for a path to citizenship: "Illegal immigrants deserve punishment for breaking a law" (Guinn 2006).

entirely – namely, the question of whether the laws, in this case immigration laws, ought to be in place and ought to be enforced. Legalistic retributivists attempt to foreclose these questions simply by ignoring the morality of law and punishment.

4) "*What are the Proper Principles of Criminal Liability?*"
5) "*What are the Appropriate Punishments?*" (Murphy 1987, 511)

Murphy describes these questions in terms of excusing conditions and degrees of culpability. What sorts of mental states or reasons would justify, mitigate, or excuse what would normally be a criminal act, and how can we establish different punishments based on different states of mind? For example, premeditated murder by someone acting with their full capacities (unjustified, very blameworthy killing) is different from intentionally and knowingly killing someone in self-defense (justified, not blameworthy killing), which is different from unintentionally killing someone because of a negligent act (unjustified, less blameworthy killing), which is different from a schizophrenic killing someone while in a state of extreme mental distress and delusion (unjustified, excused killing). A form of retributivism that would not be able to handle these distinctions would measure guilt purely in terms of the act committed, without any reference to the criminal's state of mind – for example, that anyone who kills another person deserves to die. So-called "same-actions retributivists" want offenders to be victimized in the same way that the offenders' victims were: death for death, rape for rape, and so on (Honderich 2006, 29–30). Because such a theory would not allow for justifications and excuses, it is either a very bad theory (Honderich 2006, 29–30) or no theory of punishment at all (Murphy 1987).

In the two-tiered model, classes of crimes would be defined and the requisite intention or state of mind would be identified based on what would best preserve the public order. In other words, the state would have to define the actions that are susceptible to deterrence, and which actions it hopes to deter, and then define the requisite liability based on those considerations. For example, to establish the crime of statutory rape, the state does not have to prove that the defendant intended to have sex with a minor. This is a case of strict liability, which requires no element of intent (*mens rea*). A state may require this standard of liability in order to impose a positive obligation on would-be statutory rapists: they must establish that their partners are not minors; the mere absence of evidence is not enough. The idea here is that we all have a positive obligation to protect the welfare of minors, and the law encourages that through the threat of punishment. By contrast, intent is required for crimes such as murder or theft because our obligation in those cases is negative: we must simply refrain from intentionally killing or stealing from others. By prohibiting those intentional actions, the law has a deterrent effect on sufficiently rational agents – that is, those who are capable of forming intent.

The two-tiered model can also explain why some people are not held responsible. The state allows excusing conditions, such as having mental problems that render defendants incapable of understanding the difference between right and wrong, because prohibiting insane actions serves no deterrent purpose, and being found guilty by reason of mental disease or defect subjects defendants to psychiatric treatment. This serves a rehabilitative purpose and incapacitates them while they pose a threat to themselves or others. All of this is to say that, on my view, there are consequentialist grounds for our differing standards of criminal liability.

The two-tiered model considers the effects of state policies regarding liability and compares those policies with the alternatives. In some cases, the state should restrict how we can punish individuals because of the social consequences. For example, there is a common practice in the United States of trying, sentencing, and incarcerating juvenile offenders as adults. In most states, offenders who are seventeen or older are automatically tried in adult courts. However, all fifty states allow younger juveniles to be tried as adults under certain circumstances. In some states, minors as young as thirteen may be subjected to a judicial waiver whereby the juvenile court judge sends the case to adult court, based on the seriousness of the crime.

The punitive approach to juvenile crime does not recognize young offenders' capacity to be reformed rather than merely restrained. Diverting young offenders from juvenile facilities and age-appropriate rehabilitative programs, and redirecting public funding to house juveniles in adult prisons, have a number of long-term negative effects. It does not deter juvenile crime, it increases recidivism, and it leads to higher rates of rearrest for juveniles who are released than for adult offenders. Without educational, vocational, and other development opportunities, juveniles who are later released are even more likely to feel trapped in a life of crime (UCLA School of Law 2010).

There is not much of a retributivist case for trying juveniles as adults either. Although there may be some cases where juveniles are fully responsible, rational agents, studies show that juveniles, as a class, do not have fully developed control centers in the brain. As the U.S. Supreme Court found in *Roper v. Simmons* (543 U.S. 551 [2005]), "the susceptibility of juveniles to immature and irresponsible behavior" results in "diminished capacity," such that their "culpability or blameworthiness is diminished" (570–71). In such cases, "the case for retribution is not as strong with a minor as with an adult" (571). Although *Roper v. Simmons* only ruled out the death penalty for juveniles, there is no compelling enough retributivist argument that would override an institutional prohibition (or near-prohibition), based on consequentialist grounds, on trying juvenile offenders as adults as a general policy, even in non-capital cases. This is only one example of the implications of the two-tiered model for issues regarding criminal liability.

As for appropriate punishments (Murphy's question #5), sentencing ranges for classes of crimes are established by the legislature based on what would effectively produce the best (or good enough) outcomes – among other things, deterring potential criminals in order to maintain an acceptable level of criminal activity. Specific sentences are given to individual criminals within those ranges based on their degrees of culpability. For example, someone found guilty of first-degree murder may get life in prison, while someone found guilty of criminally negligent manslaughter may get probation. Probation is not an option for a judge when a person has been convicted of first-degree murder, and a lifetime prison sentence is not the only option; and the same is true, in reverse, for manslaughter. The reason for the different statutory punishments for murder and manslaughter ("the punishment allotted by a rule to a *class* of acts") is because of their social consequences, as determined by the legislature; and the reason for different punishments for two people, each convicted of criminally negligent manslaughter ("a particular award for a given act, within that class"), is because judges determine that they deserve different burdens (Benn 1958, 335). It makes sense that the state would want to impose harsher punishments for intentional murder than for culpable negligence because the former is more dangerous and more threatening to the social order. It also makes sense that a judge would want to punish a repeat offender or someone who victimizes innocents more harshly because the person deserves it.

The conditions of legal liability in general are determined legislatively, while the culpability of individual defendants is determined by judges in specific cases. The two-tiered model thus avoids a problem with other mixed theories when it comes to varying capacities for moral agency. According to Lippke (2006), retributivists assume that offenders are full moral agents who can be held responsible for their crimes and punished proportionally, while crime reduction theorists have lower standards, since purely self-interested agents can be deterred and even completely irresponsible people such as the insane and the severely mentally challenged should be incapacitated. Lippke claims that many mixed theorists (Hart, Rawls, and Von Hirsch) thus confront an irresolvable tension when trying to decide whom to punish. On my view, though, the standard of culpability for classes of crimes, and its exceptions, are spelled out in the law, while decisions about whether specific offenders meet that standard, and what to do with them, are determined on a case-by-case basis in the criminal courts. Someone who is found not guilty because of a mental disorder has committed one of the kinds of acts that the state prohibits, but because they are not fully responsible for their actions, they receive mandatory psychiatric treatment rather than prison time. There is no tension because, although the system as a whole is mixed, neither legislators nor judges are being asked to be both retributivists and consequentialists.

Conclusion

No one is creating a system of criminal justice from the ground up. The two-tiered model of punishment provides a framework against which we can judge existing systems and state actors (legislators, judges, police, and prosecutors), and it shows how governments' different approaches to criminal law ought to be justified. In other words, it sets out the standards that any state ought to meet. Both the legislature and the criminal judiciary have justice as their aim: the legislature ought to create policies that advance the aims of a just society, and the criminal judiciary ought to give individual defendants what they deserve. To evaluate their systems, then, we should ask the following questions:

- What are the state's aims, and are they good aims to pursue? This is a question about whether the state is acting reasonably, rightly, or morally.

- Does the criminal law, if it is properly enforced, effectively advance the aims of the state? This is a question about whether the state is acting rationally, effectively, or efficiently.
- Is the legislature performing its proper role by basing its decisions regarding criminal laws and statutory penalties on their consequences?
- Is the criminal judiciary performing its proper role by basing its decisions regarding the punishment of individual defendants on what they deserve?

Any criminal justice system is extremely complicated. The two-tiered model is not a simple theory because it reflects this complexity. It also illuminates the key philosophical and justificatory issues that lawmakers ought to consider when they formulate coercive policies, and that judges and juries ought to consider when they inflict state-sanctioned harm on their fellow citizens.

Part III
Three arguments

H. L. A. Hart identifies three separate questions that are often conflated in philosophical arguments about punishment:

1) What justifies the practice of punishment? (general justifying aim)
2) To whom may punishment be applied? (liability)
3) How severely may we punish? (amount) (2008, 3)

Using this distinction, Hart arrives at a mixed view according to which the general aim of punishment is utilitarian prevention and the reason for punishing individual people is because of their guilt. However, as Ted Honderich notes, Hart seems to believe that the mere separation of these questions makes their answers obvious, when in fact many people could (and do) dispute Hart's position: "The existence of separate questions does not constitute any argument for the conclusion that punishment must be justified by several principles" (Honderich 2006, 169). Similarly, Whitley Kaufman objects to mixed theories, in part, because their defenders do not explain why consequentialism and retributivism must answer different questions, rather than allowing that both theories may be relevant to all three of Hart's questions (2008, 51–52). Consequentialism and retributivism have to be justified, but the way of arranging them in a mixed system, with one operative at the institutional level and one operative at the distributive level, also has to be justified.

In Chapter 5, I described one way that consequentialism and retributivism could be combined within a system that distinguishes the role of the legislature from the role of the criminal judiciary: the practice of punishment is justified on consequentialist grounds, while particular punishments are justified on retributivist grounds. However, this is only one possible approach. The most obvious mixed alternative would be to say that, in all cases of legal punishment, any desire we have to give people what they deserve may be overridden by the moral obligation that representatives of the state have to protect society at large. We have a *prima facie* duty to punish those (and only those) who deserve it, but we can give people what they deserve if and only if it does not significantly diminish the common good. Kai Nielsen defends a view like this in "Against Moral Conservatism" (1972), where he challenges our moral intuition that an innocent person could never be punished; if it promotes some great public good, the sacrifice would be worth it. Another alternative would be for the legislature to make laws that give people what they deserve by establishing a graduated system of statutory penalties and a graduated list of crimes, where more severe punishments are matched with more serious offenses. Each crime would have a range of possible, not undeserved penalties. The criminal courts could then assign punishments within those ranges based on what will best promote the common good. This is Norval Morris's "limiting retributivism," and it is the mirror image of what I am defending (see esp. N. Morris 1981). There are other examples besides Nielsen and Morris. The bottom line is that, even if a mixed view is correct, the two-tiered model does not necessarily follow.

In the following three chapters, I argue that the two-tiered model is the best way to incorporate consequentialism and retributivism, and in a way that does not simply subsume one to the other. The different epistemic capacities of the legislature and the criminal courts make them better able to fulfill the community's consequentialist and retributivist obligations, respectively (Chapter 6). The compatibilist account of freedom is consistent with both a broader view of human actions as caused events and the more specific assignment of personal blame (Chapter 7). And the implications of the two-tiered model track our moral intuitions regarding proportional burdens and the punishment of innocents, among other things (Chapter 8). The two-tiered model of punishment thus accords with some epistemic, metaphysical, and ethical views that we generally hold to be true.

The following arguments provide reasons to believe that my view is better or more plausible than alternative theories. They not only show that, if we adopt a mixed theory, then this is the proper way to arrange consequentialism and retributivism. They also provide independent justification for combining the two views in a mixed theory. Consequentialism or retributivism alone cannot accommodate our intuitions regarding knowledge, freedom, and justice as well as the two-tiered model of punishment can.

6 The epistemic argument

Among other things, our moral obligations depend on what we can reasonably be expected to know. If we cannot tell what ought to be done, because we cannot determine what our obligations are or how to fulfill them, then we are not morally blameworthy when we fail to act that way. This follows from "ought implies can." With regard to punishment in particular, not all participants in the criminal justice system are equally able to determine the consequences of a given punishment or the guilt of the accused, so consequentialism and retributivism as justifications of punishment do not bind all moral agents equally.

In this chapter, I argue that, when it comes to punishment, legislators are in a better position to assess the consequences of general policies, while judges and juries are in a better position to determine particular defendants' degrees of guilt. It follows that the former are obligated more strongly by consequentialist principles and the latter are obligated more strongly by retributivist principles. This conclusion supports the two-tiered model. The legislature and the criminal courts play different roles in the system that track their different kinds of epistemic authority.

The inconclusive calculus

A common criticism of consequentialism, and utilitarianism in particular, is that we cannot possibly calculate all the consequences of any given action. And if we cannot predict what will result from our decisions, then we cannot be obligated by the principle of utility (e.g., Kagan 1998, 64–66). John Stuart Mill responds to this objection by saying that human history has given us the information needed to make many accurate predictions: "During all that time mankind have been learning by experience the tendencies of actions; on which experience all the prudence as well as all the morality of life are dependent" (2001, 23–24). When we are talking about particular actions, such as adultery or stealing, this may be true. These things tend not to turn out well, so we do not need to do a new calculation every time we think about whether to cheat on our spouses or take things that do not belong to us.

We can also justify general legal principles on the basis of their consequences. Concerning punishment, there are three kinds of such principles, which can be distinguished based on their level of generalization:

1) The most general claim that criminals ought to be punished.
2) Rules of criminal procedure that govern the actions of police, prosecutors, judges, and juries.
3) Low-level generalizations about the kinds and degrees of punishment that ought to be available to judges when assigning punishments to individual defendants for specific crimes (i.e., statutory penalties or a punishment schedule).

With regard to the decision to punish criminals as a rule (#1), it is better for society to punish wrongdoing than not to punish wrongdoing, as a matter of public policy. Although fines and prison sentences harm criminals, that harm is worth it because it leads to a net benefit for everyone who is affected, better than any of the alternatives. Of course, I am not claiming here that the suffering of any actual criminals is outweighed by the public good that it produces in a specific, existing society. Instead, I am making the more general claim that, without any state-imposed punishments, people would live in constant fear, would commit illegal acts at will, and would resort to vigilantism. The alternative to this anarchic situation is to threaten potential criminals and to punish those who break the law, on the assumption that doing so will deter at least some of them from committing crimes. And, when they are punished, it will deter others from committing crimes (general deterrence), will keep criminals from committing more crimes during the period of incarceration (incapacitation), and will make it less likely that they will offend again (specific deterrence).

There are also benefits for the social order when the criminal justice system is governed by publicly acknowledged procedural rules, including the proper roles and limited functions of the legislative, executive, and judicial powers (#2). In a liberal system, for example, the presumption of innocence and the rules of evidence are designed to constrain the actions of police, prosecutors, juries, and judges in order to protect our basic liberties. In Chapter 5, I mentioned some ways that police are constrained by constitutional protections for the accused and that prosecutorial discretion could be limited by providing for more judicial review. The actions of juries are constrained in several ways: they must disregard statements that the judge tells them to disregard (as a result of sustained objections), they must consider only the evidence presented at trial, and so on. All these rules are designed to ensure that the defendant gets a fair trial as defined under the law. For example, if a piece of evidence against the defendant was discovered as a result of an illegal search, then the jury is not allowed to consider it, even if the evidence is publicized in the local paper. The idea is that, in a liberal system such as the United States, the protection of rights, including the right against unreasonable searches and seizures, is more important than increasing the chance that defendants will be found guilty (even if they are). As Ronald Dworkin says, we are not balancing rights against well-being; instead, rights trump utility (1977, 197–200). The rules governing criminal trials maintain the liberal arrangement by maximizing rights protections, even though other things that we value, such as public safety, may be compromised as a result. This is a consequentialism of rights.[1]

Low-level generalizations regarding acceptable punishments (#3) are also possible based on consequentialist principles. For example, as I mentioned in Chapter 2, Tom Tyler's (1990) large-scale study found that people tend to follow the law when they share its values or trust in the legitimacy of the authorities, rather than simply out of fear. He makes several policy suggestions based on his findings. Throughout the book, I reference numerous studies that show that the death penalty does not deter more than life in prison, that trying juveniles as adults leads to higher recidivism rates, that correctional education programs lower recidivism rates, and that there are more effective methods of dealing with nonviolent drug offenses than merely punitive treatment, among other things. When dealing with whole populations, there are all sorts of comparative data to consider because different local, state, and federal governments have tried different things over many years.

Of course, these are all statistical generalizations. Social scientists take a broad perspective regarding general trends, but they cannot tell us as reliably whether a specific criminal will respond to correctional educational programs or the threat of execution. Even the procedures and principles that we think are fundamental to the criminal legal process may seem doubtful in a specific case. Occasionally violating general legal principles may produce better outcomes, so consequentialism seems to dictate that we violate them even though they are justified as rules of thumb. For example, purposely punishing an innocent person usually causes the person unnecessary harm without any foreseeable benefit to society, so, as a general rule, the utilitarian condemns it. However, there are specific cases where utilitarianism would seem to justify victimizing the innocent. Philippa Foot gives a classic example:

> Suppose that a judge or magistrate is faced with rioters demanding that a culprit be found for a certain crime and threatening otherwise to take their own bloody revenge on a particular section of the community. The real culprit being unknown, the judge sees himself as able to prevent the bloodshed only by framing some innocent person and having him executed. (1967, 8)

1 Dworkin's view is consistent with a consequentialism of rights:

> The "rights as trumps" theory seems to fall into the deontological camp since, within its framework, rights serve as constraints on the pursuit of desirable goals. Yet there is a way of framing its conclusions in consequentialist terms. If the value of states of affairs is determined not only on the basis of the overall utility, or well-being of individuals, but also on the basis of whether more or fewer rights are respected, then, arguably, the language of rights can be reconciled with consequentialism. (Harel 2005, 198)

Hypothetical cases like this have been given by numerous philosophers, and often they are used to argue against utilitarianism.[2] Framing an innocent person seems obviously wrong, so if a theory condones it, then the theory must be mistaken – a *reductio ad absurdum*.

In his defense of utilitarianism, Kai Nielsen responds that such a situation would in fact seldom be justified since news of the framing would likely get out, confidence in the justice system would be eroded, and the positive effects would not be realized (1972, 223–25). T. L. S. Sprigge (2015) says that the hypothetical utilitarian in this case is acting on "hunches" rather than well-confirmed generalizations: that they do not consider better alternatives, undervalue the suffering caused to the framed man and his family, and cannot calculate the effects it will have on the mob. Nielsen, Sprigge, and J. J. C. Smart question whether it would ever be possible to come up with a real-world example that would justify victimization. Sprigge says that, although it is conceivable (logically possible), such an example is "fantastical," "fanciful," and is "not serving as a preparation for any actual situation" (2015, 70; see also Nielsen 1972, 225; Smart 1973; and Smart 1991).[3] In actual situations, utilitarianism conforms to our commonsense moral beliefs.

Setting aside the question of whether things would turn out well or badly, the more important issue, at least for the purposes of this chapter, is not whether the information would get out or whether a scenario could be devised that would justify victimization. The problem is that the judge in such a case cannot know which outcome is more likely given their limited perspective, and any decision they make about the probability of bad consequences is going to be clouded by a focus on the immediate risks. Rule-utilitarians claim that, in such a case, the person ought to defer to the rule that tends on the whole to produce the most utility. However, as Smart (1956) observes, any rule is merely a general guideline that, on utilitarian grounds, should be disobeyed when the consequences of following the rule would be worse than the consequences of breaking the rule. The utilitarian cannot justify blind rule worship. In this case, the judge obviously knows that it is wrong to frame innocent people *in general* but thinks that *in this case* the negative consequences of following the rule

2 Philosophers who use the punishment of the innocent to try to refute utilitarianism include: Mabbott (1939, 152); Hawkins (1944, 206), Carritt (1947, 65), C. Lewis (1954, 227–28), McCloskey (1957, 468–69), Anscombe (1958, 15–17), Armstrong (1961, 485–86), Donagan (1968, 196–98), D. Lewis (1972), Schedler (1977, 73–103), Greenawalt (1983, 353–54), Ten (1987, 13–37), Primoratz (1989, 42–61), Braithwaite and Pettit (1990, 46, 52–53), Smilansky (1990), Gavison (1991, 352, 356), Cragg (1992, 48–51), Bagaric and Amarasekera (2000, 140–43), Matravers (2000, 17), Golash (2005, 43–44), Honderich (2006, 89–109), Kaufman (2013, 29–32), and McCloskey (2015, 131–32).

3 In addition to Smart (1973, 1991) and Sprigge (2015), similar claims that a utilitarian would not frame the innocent are given by Rawls (1955, 10–13), Ewing (1963), Pincoffs (1966, 34–36), Lyons (1974), Hare (1981, 163–64), van den Haag (1981, 709–10), Duff (1986, 158–64), Hardin (1986, 63–67), Hare (1986, 220), and Binder and Smith (2000).

(violence against a vulnerable population) outweigh the possible negative consequences of breaking the rule (the public may find out). So, if the judge makes what turns out to be an erroneous calculation and frames the innocent person, then this is at least justified on utilitarian grounds *from the judge's perspective*. The utilitarian judge may choose wrongly, but, even if their action results in worse overall consequences, the judge cannot be blamed for choosing wrongly because they are doing what seems right given their limited understanding of the circumstances.

Uncertainty about desert

In contrast to utilitarianism, retributivism is very clear about who ought to be punished and how much. According to retributivism, a punishment is justified when an offender deserves to be punished and when the severity of the punishment corresponds to the seriousness of the offense. Although there are conceptual difficulties with determining when an offense and a punishment are equivalent or proportional (and what it means to be equivalent or proportional), this duty-based theory is at least clear in its prescription to punish only the guilty, and it does not face the same difficulty of calculating outcomes that utilitarianism faces. Guilty people should be punished because they are guilty, and innocent people should not be punished because they are innocent.

Although the moral aim of retributivism is well-defined, it, like utilitarianism, runs into our epistemic limitations. Retributivists often overlook this problem, as if only consequentialists have to appeal to facts in their moral decision-making. Predictions are difficult, and consequentialists in principle must be prepared to perform a calculus that tallies up the good and bad of the possible outcomes and considers their probability so that they can arrive at a morally required course of action. But backward-looking retributivists face difficulties of their own in determining what to do. To establish guilt and the seriousness of the offense, we have to reconstruct the past and establish a person's "*inner wickedness*" on the basis of what is available to us in the present (Kant 1996b, 6:333). Our judgments regarding a person's guilt and degree of guilt are made with varying levels of uncertainty, even when we make a good faith effort to discover them. Witnesses may be purposely lying or mistaken, DNA evidence may be corrupted or misleading, and forensic psychiatrists may fail to properly assess the person's mental state at the time of the crime. Even the defendant may not know what motivated them, or whether they were fully in control (or enough in control) of their actions. Given these inevitable uncertainties, we cannot know what to do on retributivist grounds – whether the person deserves to be punished, and how much – even if the defendant seems guilty. These problems are compounded when we are distanced from the specific case – when, for example, we try to make blanket claims about the culpability of whole classes of offenders, or standard assumptions regarding the reliability of testimony from jailhouse informants.

The variable force of moral constraints

Mistakes can be made and people can be unjustly or disproportionately harmed under either theory of punishment. That is, whether we are trying to maximize positive outcomes or give people what they deserve, assigning justified punishments to accused criminals depends on facts that are not easily ascertained. The United States' track record when sentencing people to death – one in twenty-five are innocent, according to a recent study (Gross et al. 2014) – is a particularly disheartening example, especially since capital convictions are so thoroughly reviewed in appellate courts. And Sprigge is right to question how anyone would be able to predict the effects of a conviction on the actions and attitudes of a threatening mob.

Because of the inevitable uncertainty in our moral decision-making, philosophers often distinguish the evaluation of the action from the evaluation of the agent, or the evaluation of the agent's action from the evaluation of the agent's motive. As Richard Brandt (1963) puts it, people's actions may be subjectively right – and therefore excusable, justifiable, or blameless – even if they are not objectively right.[4] For the retributivist, there is an important moral difference between a jury that endeavors to determine actual guilt but fails through no fault of their own (because of inaccurate testimony, for example), and a jury that purposely goes along with framing an innocent defendant because they want to achieve some social outcome. In both cases, the act is wrong because the law of retribution is violated, but only in the former case is the jury blameless. That jury punishes the defendant based on what it believes they deserve beyond a reasonable doubt. In ethics too we must adopt the common epistemic distinction between justified belief and truth: even if people act in a way that is not right in fact, they may be justified in doing so because of what they could reasonably be expected to know based on the evidence.

Because of our epistemic limitations, we cannot be obligated to maximize utility or punish only the guilty, even if those are the requirements of utilitarianism and retributivism, respectively. If either of these theories is correct, then it would only constrain us to do what is right as best we can, in light of what can be reasonably expected of us. Having the right motives would make us virtuous agents, even if things go awry (as they do in 4 percent of capital convictions).

In Part I, I argued that legal punishment is justified both on consequentialist grounds and on retributivist grounds. The question then becomes: given the structure of the criminal justice system, which agent or set of agents is best able to maximize utility (or other consequences), and which agent or set of agents is best able to give people what they deserve, because of their different epistemic limitations? In other words, which agents are more strongly obligated by the law

4 Similarly, Duff says: "An agent acts justifiably (reasonably) if the expected or reasonably expectable consequences of her action are good; her action is objectively right only if its actual consequences are good" (1996, 4n5). See also Mill (2001, 17–18), Railton (1984), Kagan (1998, 65), and Scanlon (2008, 47–52).

of retribution, given what they can reasonably be expected to know, and which are more strongly obligated by the principle of utility (if either moral principle is right)?

Scenarios in which innocents are framed reveal a problem with utilitarian reasoning at the level of the individual case. In such situations, people are more likely to miscalculate the consequences of their actions. In Foot's example, the utilitarian judge is attempting to calm the riots without taking seriously the risk of a backlash when the lies are almost inevitably discovered. There are other sources of potential miscalculation as well. When considering specific cases from a utilitarian perspective, individuals are less likely to be dispassionate calculators of overall outcomes and are more likely to privilege their own interests and to be swayed by their own biases. For example, jurors may believe that it benefits their community to imprison a gang member who is on trial, even if they are sure that the accused is innocent of the crime. Their opinion may be racially motivated or driven by fear or self-preservation. But convicting the wrongly accused person would not only fail to remove the actual criminal from society. It may also encourage criminality by hardening the defendant's and his acquaintances' feelings of helplessness under the law. Jury instructions are written to disabuse jurors of making these kinds of calculations: "You must not substitute or follow your own notion or opinion as to what the law is or ought to be. It is your duty to apply the law as I explain it to you, regardless of the consequences" (Committee on Pattern Jury Instructions 2019, 1.04 [p. 8]). Juries are constrained in this way precisely so that they do not attempt to do the job of the legislator. They should determine only whether the guilt of the defendant has been proven and thus whether the person deserves to be punished. Although jury members are not what R. M. Hare calls "proles," who are incapable of critical thinking and must always follow the rules – jury nullification is a possibility – for the most part, their knowledge is limited, so they must keep to the rules that define their function (1981, 44–64).

In contrast to juries and judges, legislators who establish general policies regarding punishment are better able to make the kinds of impartial judgments that utilitarianism requires (Mill 2001, 11, 17, 19–20).[5] Self-interest and personal prejudices are less likely to enter into legislators' reasoning because, unlike judges and juries, they do not confront particular defendants who are accused of crimes against their own communities. The legislature has a broader view of things. Statistical data regarding the deterrent effects of prison will not tell a jury whether imprisoning a specific defendant will rehabilitate them or deter other criminals, so it gives the jury no guidance in that case. But, even if the data is inconclusive, the data do give legislators some sense of whether imprisonment has a cumulative deterrent effect, and how much of an effect it has in the aggregate. In other

5 This is a comparative claim about the epistemic positions of juries, judges, and legislators. I am not assuming that legislators act reasonably and avail themselves of social scientific research. Whether legislators actually do what they are more capable of doing and what they ought to do are historical questions, not philosophical questions.

words, the findings of social science, and the policy recommendations that are based on those findings, apply to criminals and potential criminals in general, not to any individual defendant. One former inmate may want desperately to avoid prison, while another may find the familiarity and security of prison life safe and comforting. So long as there is a typical response – prison is usually a negative reinforcer – the legislature can devise more effective penalties at maintaining the social order.

On the other hand, whether and how much a specific defendant deserves to be punished is unknown to legislators, who are unfamiliar with any particular case. They do not hear the evidence against a defendant and evaluate the trustworthiness of witnesses, and they do not deliberate about whether the different elements of the crime have been proven beyond a reasonable doubt. Thus, although ranges of statutory penalties are established by legislators to preserve the public order, judges are given sentencing discretion that allows them to impose a deserved punishment, or the most deserved punishment available, for the specific criminal:

> In life, no two offenders are identical and any system of sentencing that takes account only of the statutory labels of the offender's crime alone or together with some measure of his past involvement in crime will be too crude to be morally compelling. Statutory labels simply tell too little about the moral gravity of individual acts. (Morris and Tonry 1990, 87)

Although judges and juries may make mistakes for the reasons noted above, their opinions are more justified because of their focus on and exposure to the facts of the case, including the physical evidence, eyewitness testimony, and so on. Legislators are not in the privileged epistemic position that judges and juries are to determine whether a defendant is guilty or to determine the person's degree of guilt for the purpose of assigning proportional punishment.

Application: Three-strikes laws

Federal and state habitual offender (or "three-strikes") laws are a prime example of the failure of legislatures to accurately determine the guilt of offenders in particular cases, and they illustrate why legislators should not set statutory penalties on retributivist grounds. In defense of legislative retributivism, Don Scheid thinks that lawmakers ought to base their decisions on assumptions about typical degrees of guilt:

> In order to assign different punishments to different categories or types of crimes, the legislator needs only consider standard cases of each type of crime. The legislator may simply assume some standard level of culpability, say, the intentional, voluntary commission of the crime. The question for the legislator is then: "What should the punishment be for crime C, assuming a

> standard case in which the offender who commits C is standardly culpable?" (1997, 484–85)

Scheid says that the judge would then modify the punishment at sentencing so that it accords with the actual culpability of a given offender. But there is no reason to assume that the statutory penalties would provide the opportunity for the judge to assign an appropriate punishment, especially for atypical defendants. One could say – indeed, many people have said – that someone who is convicted of a felony after committing two or more violent or serious crimes deserves to get life in prison. This is the legislator's opinion regarding "the standard level of culpability" for persistent offenders, and it has resulted in excessive mandatory minimum sentences, including, in most U.S. states, three-strikes laws.

This is the reverse of the two-tiered model: legislators are determining offenders' degrees of guilt and taking discretion out of the hands of judges, who are more familiar with the defendants and the circumstances of their crimes. Under three-strikes laws, the mere fact that a defendant commits a felony establishes a high degree of guilt that warrants a severe penalty. The two distribution questions ("who?" and "how much?") are being conflated. Legislators are not well-positioned to know what these people deserve. There are numerous examples of criminals receiving wildly disproportionate sentences (twenty-five years to life) for relatively minor third offenses such as stealing a slice of pizza, lying on the written portion of a driver's license test, having a stolen computer, or possessing 0.14 grams of meth (Egelko 2003, Taibbi 2013). Three-strikes laws do not have a deterrent effect (King and Mauer 2001; Kovandzic 2001; Zimring, Hawkins, and Kamin 2001; Kovandzic, Sloan, and Vieraitis 2004; Parker 2012), so, if legislators instead acted on consequentialist grounds, judges would be able to assign punishments that are proportional to the offenders' actual degrees of guilt. What an offender deserves is determined through the more epistemically justified process of a criminal trial rather than mere "assumptions" about how guilty third-strike offenders tend to be. I will return to this in Chapter 11: instances of jury nullification (Chiang 1996) and backlash from judges (Kilgore 2015, 46–47) when it comes to excessive mandatory minimums and three-strikes cases lend support to the idea that legislators are acting inappropriately.

Limiting retributivism

Norval Morris's mixed view puts judges and juries in a similarly untenable position. According to Morris's limiting retributivism, legislatures establish a range of acceptable punishments for a given crime because our moral intuitions regarding desert are not clear or specific enough to identify a precise punishment. Retribution thus serves as a "limiting principle" rather than a "defining principle," the latter of which "would give the exact sanction to be imposed" (N. Morris 1982, 182). Utilitarian concerns such as deterrence or incapacitation can then inform a judge's decision about which of those punishments to select (N.

Morris 1966, 639; Tonry and Morris 1978, 447; N. Morris 1981, 259, 264; N. Morris 1982, 198; Morris and Tonry 1990, 104–5).[6]

On Morris's view, the judge may (perhaps should) adjust a sentence within the appropriate range in order to deter potential criminals, or to accomplish other social aims. So, imagine that Morris's judge is in the United States and presides over a criminal trial in a state where the death penalty is an option, and the defendant has been found guilty of first-degree murder. During the sentencing phase, the jury is supposed to decide what punishment to give them. According to Morris, the jury should select the punishment that will have the most positive impact by, among other things, deterring other potential murderers. To make this decision, then, the jury would have to know whether the death penalty deters more than life in prison. As I show in Chapter 12, there are conflicting studies. The jury would have to be in a position to evaluate those studies. They would have to determine whether the additional cost of an execution over life in prison is worth it and would have to predict whether the legislature would spend the money saved on other, more effective crime-prevention strategies. And that may depend on who is in the legislature or who is administering the budget. Furthermore, does the deterrent effect depend on how much the execution is publicized? Will the news cover it? And how likely are potential murderers to follow the news anyway? It is unclear whether the deterrent effect of the death penalty, if there is one, is correlated with capital sentences or with executions that are actually carried out. In the latter case, the jury would have to assess the likelihood that the verdict will be overturned on appeal. They have to think about whether the judge's rulings before and during the trial were appropriate, whether the defense attorney was competent, how often appellate courts overturn cases (in this state or district and for this judge!), and so on. How likely is it that the appellate court judges will change by the time the defendant's case is heard, and will the new judges be more protective of defendants' rights or will they be "law and order" types? Who is appointing them (a Democrat or a Republican) and how likely is the legislature to confirm them? And how long will it take? Because the appeals process is so slow, an old defendant will be more likely to die on death row than be executed. Should the defendant's age figure into the jury's calculation? There are other factors as well. A study by Joanna Shepherd (2005) found that deterrence rates vary among states because there is a threshold – nine executions annually – over which the death penalty begins to have a deterrent effect. Lower numbers of executions do not deter, and in some cases actually increase the murder rate (a "brutalization effect"). If these results can be trusted – the jury would have to evaluate Shepherd's methodology, too – it would have to consider how many people have been executed in their state. If it is near nine, would executing this defendant push the state over the threshold? If it would be the seventh execution, the jury would have to think about how many more murder

6 Frase (2004, 2005b, 2013) has defended an "expanded" version of limiting retributivism, which, he claims, already informs most state guidelines systems.

trials are likely that year, how likely it is that other defendants will be convicted, how likely it is that the other juries will give the death penalty, and so on. If two capital cases are going on at once and there have already been eight executions this year, what should the two juries do?

The considerations are endless, and many of them are things that no judge or jury could possibly know. By contrast, in making policy decisions regarding whether to allow the death penalty as an option, lawmakers can consider the deterrent effects of the death penalty in the aggregate and over time. That view of overall trends can tell us whether the death penalty deters *in general*, which is very different from knowing whether the death penalty deters *in this case*.

It makes more sense for a judge or jury to base their sentencing decision on what the defendant deserves. Having heard the testimony and examined the evidence, the judge or jury makes a decision about whether the defendant is guilty during the guilt phase of the trial, and they also know the defendant's degree of guilt, which can inform their decision in the sentencing phase. Assessing the seriousness of the crime in terms of aggravating and mitigating factors, and determining what this individual criminal deserves, is more within their grasp.

Conclusion

We are fallible beings, and, with regard to punishment, there are a number of mistakes we are prone to make. Among other things, we may not know what someone deserves (whether they are indeed guilty, or what their intentions were), and we may miscalculate in our prediction of likely consequences (for example, in being willing to sacrifice innocents for the greater good). By establishing different institutions with different roles, we recognize that all of us are limited in our knowledge and fallible in our moral judgment. A government of checks and balances is predicated on the idea that no one person or political body is absolutely epistemically and morally privileged.

The preceding epistemic considerations and their moral implications support the two-tiered model of punishment, according to which the consequentialism that informs the legislature in setting up institutions of criminal law is separate from the retributivism that justifies the verdicts of judges and juries in particular criminal cases. Because legislators are better able to devise broad institutional policies that improve social well-being in the aggregate and over time, it is more reasonable for them to be bound by consequentialist principles than judges, who would be acting on "hunches" rather than "well confirmed generalizations" (Sprigge 2015, 73–74). Because judges and juries are better able to consider the individual defendant's degree of guilt, it is more reasonable to expect them to determine guilt than legislators, who can only assume some "standard level of culpability" that may be inappropriate in a given case (Scheid 1997, 484–85). Because "ought implies can," legislators can be constrained by consequentialist principles in a way that judges cannot, and judges can be constrained by the law of retribution in a way that legislators cannot. Neither of them can be obligated to do something that they are unable to do.

7 The compatibilist argument

The two-tiered model justifies legal punishment by appealing to both consequentialism and retributivism. These theories seem to be mutually exclusive, since they have different reasons for imposing burdens on wrongdoers. Yet I have been claiming that they can work together in the same system, provided that consequentialism is used to justify legislative policies (legal prohibitions and statutory penalties) and retributivism is used to justify particular criminal judgments (verdicts and sentencing).

In this chapter, I argue that the two-tiered approach is consistent with a compatibilist theory of freedom. According to compatibilism, even if people's actions are causally determined, they can still be held morally and legally responsible. This provides us with two alternative but compatible approaches to agents, corresponding with the two alternative but seemingly incompatible approaches to punishment. As determined things, people's actions are caused (not just affected or influenced) by incentives, so public policies can be designed to maximize positive consequences. As responsible subjects, people's actions are attributable to them, so they can be said to deserve punishment in proportion to their guilt. On the compatibilist view, then, consequentialism and retributivism are both viable theories of punishment, corresponding with the two different ways of considering people's actions.

What is compatibilism?

Compatibilism is not so much one theory of freedom as a set of approaches that share a core claim: although all events, including all human actions, are determined, people can still be held responsible for at least some of them. One kind of compatibilist asserts that an action is free if it is caused in the right way. David Hume, for example, says that the same conditions that define causal determinism (constant conjunction and subjective association) also characterize human actions, which are in principle predictable. An agent can be held responsible for those actions that are traceable to their character (1975, §8 [pp. 80–103]). Similarly, A. J. Ayer (1954) says that an action belongs to the person if it is motivated internally rather than being forced on them by external forces. If I push my friend into a ditch on purpose because I think it would be funny, that is very different than if I trip on a rock and bump into them, or if someone puts a gun to my head and forces me to do it. Thus, Ayer says, the real contrast is not between freedom and determinism but between freedom and coercion. Harry Frankfurt (1988) argues that free actions are ones where our first-order desires are in accordance with our second-order volitions. We are free when we not only want X, but we want to want X, and we want our desire for X to be effective in determining our actions. All three of these philosophers – Hume, Ayer, and Frankfurt – identify some causal chain that gives rise to the action that is attributable to the agent as a particular kind of cause, even though the agent does not act as an uncaused cause.

Another group of compatibilists, led by John Martin Fischer, understands freedom in terms of an agent's responsiveness to reasons. If a person tends to be responsive to an appropriate range of reasons, as a mental disposition, and if their actions follow from the reasons they have (i.e., it is a volitional state), then they are acting freely (Fischer 1994; Fischer and Ravizza 1998). Still another group of compatibilists asserts that actions are free if they are socially situated in the right way. P. F. Strawson (2008), for example, claims that we hold people morally responsible for their actions when they elicit certain morally reactive attitudes from others, such as resentment felt by a person who is wronged or moral indignation by third parties. And Gary Watson (1987) says that morally responsible agents have the potential to communicate about moral issues with other members of the ethical community. In doing so, they can serve as moral interlocutors because they exercise moral judgment and engage in shared moral practices. For Fischer, Strawson, and Watson, whether there is personal responsibility depends on how we engage with reasons and with one another, regardless of the ultimate causes of our dispositions, attitudes, and communication practices, and regardless of whether there is any sense in which the agent could have done otherwise under the same conditions.

There are many varieties of compatibilism, and I have mentioned only a few of the most prominent. For the purposes of this chapter, it is unnecessary to evaluate compatibilism as a theory of freedom and to compare the strengths and weaknesses of the different alternatives. It is enough to focus on what all forms of compatibilism have in common: the thesis that a kind of freedom, enough to justify the attribution of moral and legal responsibility, is possible even if universal causal determinism is true.

Libertarianism and desert

Compatibilism as a theory of freedom is contrasted with incompatibilism, which holds that freedom and determinism are incompatible. This is an assumption behind libertarianism, according to which freedom is only possible if some actions are nondeterministically caused, either by reasons – which, they claim, are not amenable to causal explanation (Kane 1996) – or by the agent – agent-causation, as opposed to event-causation (O'Connor 2000). Libertarianism lends itself to a retributivist theory of punishment because only agents are responsible for voluntary actions; there is no other cause. To be sure, somebody who grew up with violence is going to have violent responses as a real alternative to nonviolent responses in a way that people who did not grow up with violence do not. But, barring severe mental impairments, the person, rather than their psychological, physical, social, and historical circumstances, is "ultimately responsible" for their actions (Kane 1996, 35). If agents act nondeterministically, then praise or blame should fall to them.

Not holding agents personally responsible for their actions would be a kind of category mistake, not treating them with the respect they deserve as responsible agents. As Immanuel Kant puts it, deterrence theory treats the criminal merely as a means to an end (1996b, 6:331; 1997, 27:553; see also Kaufman 2013, 27–33). This is known generally as the "use objection." If we were concerned only with future consequences of the punishment rather than the guilt of the agents, then we would be construing their actions as just other points in the causal nexus, with effects that we want to control in order to produce some social benefit. Because libertarian agency distinguishes moral agents, as uncaused causes, from other things in the world, people have a right to be punished, while dogs and rocks do not (H. Morris 1968).

Retribution makes sense for the libertarian, but deterrence poses more of a problem. Not only is it morally inappropriate in some sense, per the use objection, but it is also more difficult to explain the predictability of our responses, in the aggregate, to the threat of punishment and other crime-reduction strategies. Although we cannot know how such strategies will affect individual people, social scientific research, which I discuss in more detail later in the book, allows us to measure, to some extent, their overall effectiveness. How is that possible?

On the compatibilist account, incentives are a kind of cause, and since our actions are caused, the effects of punishment on human behavior are predictable:

> All laws being founded on rewards and punishments, it is supposed as a fundamental principle, that these motives have a regular and uniform influence on the mind, and both produce the good and prevent the evil actions. We may give to this influence what name we please; but, as it is usually conjoined with the action, it must be esteemed a *cause*, and be looked upon as an instance of that necessity, which we would here establish. (Hume 1975, §8, pt. 2 [pp. 97–98])

When a person acts unexpectedly, it is a sign that we do not know everything about the relevant causes and effects rather than a sign of indeterminism. We can better predict a person's actions the more we know them, because we are more aware of the character from which their actions follow (Hume 1975, §8 [pp. 80–103], esp. pp. 83–91).

The libertarian's explanation is more complicated. The grounding assumption behind the event-causal libertarian view is that agents' reasons give rise to actions, but that reasons are nondeterministic causes of physical actions that result from nondeterministic processes. According to Kane (1996), for example, an agent is responsible for an action (a "self-forming willing") only if the action is not causally determined (that is, the agent's present choice explains the action) or it is causally determined by the results of other undetermined actions by the agent (that is, the agent's prior choices, on their own or coupled with the present choice, explains the action). Any initial decision that "is not required by my past" is what Kane calls "a 'value experiment' whose justification lies in the future" rather than being arbitrary (1996, 145). To be sure, the desires, beliefs, expectations, and incentives are not all up to the agent, but such psychological attitudes are indeterminate, making the effects of these mental processes merely probable – such is Kane's account of probabilistic causation.

The compatibilist and libertarian explanations of the effectiveness of deterrence differ primarily on why we cannot predict people's behavior with certainty. According to Hume, this is because of a lack of knowledge, while Kane thinks that there is nothing to know, and that probability is the best we can do given the nature of free will. Punishments and threats of punishments are more effective either because they cause more law-abiding behavior or because they are more likely to inform people's undermined choices. I set aside the question of whether probabilistic causation is consistent with indeterminism and the idea of self-forming willing. Deterrence theory assumes that people in general tend to give predictable weight to incentives and that there is enough uniformity among people's responses that, although sociological and psychological laws are elusive, more informed public policy decisions are more scientifically grounded. Insofar as indeterminism sits uneasily with such assumptions, libertarianism seems comparatively less amenable to deterrence theory than compatibilism does.

Hard determinism and deterrence

While deterrence theory is less appropriate under libertarianism, retributivism is inappropriate under hard determinism. The hard determinist claims that human actions, like all other events in the world, are the result of prior causes. There is no uncaused causation, including no agent-causation, so there is no such thing as personal moral or legal responsibility. If freedom is impossible, desert theory is nonsensical. As Sam Harris puts it, "the urge for retribution depends on our not seeing the underlying causes of human behavior" (2012, 55); it "rests on a cognitive and emotional illusion," namely a metaphysically independent and undetermined agent (58; see also Waller 2018 and Waller 2019). If we could identify the natural bases of our actions instead of attributing them to some unintelligible, almost magical spontaneity, we would see that there is no guilt on the part of agents, so it would not make sense to punish people in accordance with their degrees of guilt.[1] On this view, human actions are a kind of natural event, like trees growing or rocks rolling downhill, nothing more.

1 Ewing disputes this point. He says that determinism "is not incompatible with the admission that some acts are very harmful or even intrinsically evil, and that the infliction of punishment

Some philosophers claim that hard determinists must be abolitionists regarding punishment (e.g., Smilansky 2011; Corlett 2013, 25–49). Since no one is responsible for anything, no one deserves anything. However, this objection rests on the assumption that punishment is necessarily retributive.[2] For the hard determinist, punishment can still be used to improve people's future behavior, so it can serve an important social purpose. For example, Richard Brandt (1958) claims that censure may be used, not as an expression of resentment, but to change people's behavior by reminding them of what is prohibited and instilling in them a fear of disapproval. Bruce Waller (2018) says that, once we recognize that moral responsibility is nonsense, the best alternative is a therapeutic "no-blame system model" that seeks to correct the social causes of criminal activity rather than inflicting harm on individual offenders. When the latter is needed in the case of especially dangerous criminals, it is an "unjust necessity." And free will skeptics Derk Pereboom and Gregg Caruso[3] argue for "an incapacitation account built on the right to harm in self-defense" (2018, 204; see also Caruso 2019 and Pereboom 2019).[4] They view imprisonment as analogous to quarantine. Like carriers of dangerous diseases, criminals are not responsible for the danger they pose to others in the basic desert sense, but with both disease-carriers and criminals, we can separate them from the general population based on "the right to self-protection and the prevention of harm to others" (Pereboom and Caruso 2018, 205). And just as we take antibiotics to kill bacterial infections and improve our health, we can imprison people and try to rehabilitate them in order to

---

can be a useful means to lessening the frequency of such acts." On that point, he seems to conflate retributivism and deterrence theory. However, he continues: determinism

> is not even incompatible with the appropriateness of blame; to blame a man is to say that he has chosen to do something bad or neglected to choose to do something good, and this is perfectly sensible even if a determinist view be assumed, provided only if it is granted that among the causes which determine action is choice. (1970, viii–ix).

Depending on how he defines choice, Ewing is either assuming compatibilism rather than hard determinism, in which case he is right, or he is espousing an indeterministic version of determinism, which is confused.

2 For example, Harris distinguishes what he calls punishment from deterrence, rehabilitation, and containment (2012, 1, 59); and Perlmutter (2014) claims that punishment *per se* must be backward-looking, based on what a person did rather than what will be accomplished by the harm.

3 Pereboom and Caruso are, strictly speaking, not hard determinists but hard incompatibilists. Hard determinists believe that causal determinism is true so no one has free will. Hard incompatibilists believe that, regardless of whether causal determinism is true or false, our modern scientific theories show that it is extremely unlikely that we could have the qualities that would make free will and personal responsibility possible. For the purposes of this chapter, I elide this distinction.

4 Other theorists who derive the state's right to punish from the right to self-defense include Farrell (1985, 2004), Quinn (1985), Montague (1995), and A. Ellis (2005).

decrease the likelihood of reoffending.[5] None of these presuppose free will, personal responsibility, or desert. The hard determinist can introduce punishment as another cause to improve outcomes, what Harris calls "punishing people purely for pragmatic reasons" (2012, 59).

Soft determinism, desert, and deterrence

Unlike libertarianism and hard determinism, compatibilism poses a quandary when it comes to the appropriate justification of punishment because it seems to push us in two different, seemingly contradictory directions. On the one hand, human actions are caused by prior events, are in principle predictable, and are subject to manipulation by other causes. On the other hand, people are responsible for some of their actions, namely the actions that are traceable to their characters or to reasons. As I noted earlier, deterrence seems more appropriate for the former than the latter, in the sense that we are trying to introduce punishment as another cause in the chain of causes leading to improved social outcomes; and retribution seems more appropriate for the latter than the former, in the sense that we are punishing someone based on their degree of guilt, including whether the action was up to them and how malicious the intent was. Compatibilism is the view that we can be both determined and free, so it is consistent with both deterrence and desert. This raises the question of how these seemingly incompatible theories of punishment can be brought together – if, as I argued in Part I, they are both justified.

One way to accommodate the idea that the person is both determined and free, and subject to both deterrence and blame, is to separate the aims of punishment, as I have, based on the differing functions of the legislature and the criminal courts, as well as their different perspectives on the agent. Legislators form policies regarding punishment, including appropriate kinds and ranges of punishments for classes of crimes, in light of their effectiveness in deterring future crimes. Punishment as a social practice or institution is justified by its consequences. By contrast, judges dole out punishments in accordance with a person's degree of guilt, within the ranges and under the policies established by the legislature. The distribution of punishments is justified by what is deserved. Under the law, then, people are treated as means but not merely as means.

5 Pereboom raises several traditional objections to utilitarian deterrence theory, including the claim that innocents could be punished if the consequences were good enough, as well as the use objection. He presents nonpunitive incarceration as an alternative (2001, 158–86). However, Pereboom defines deterrence more narrowly than I do, as general deterrence and distinct from rehabilitation and incapacitation. Furthermore, as Murtagh (2013) argues, Pereboom's objections, even when they are telling, apply only to classical utilitarianism and not to deterrence theory more generally, the latter of which aims at crime reduction rather than maximizing happiness overall.

Punishment as social engineering

The purpose of the legislature is to create law, and the purpose of law is to preserve the public order and achieve our collective aims. Both the threat of punishment and the actual punishment of criminals help to promote the common good by means of general and specific deterrence. In the former case, the social order is not disrupted because crimes are prevented from occurring, and in the latter case, convicted criminals are kept from committing more crimes (in cases of incarceration or execution) and are rehabilitated so that they are less likely to commit crimes in the future. The legislature takes no position on particular criminals. Potential criminals are considered in the aggregate, as impersonal forces that could disrupt social harmony.

Because the purpose of legislative action is to achieve certain consequences – namely, the preservation of the public order – it is appropriate to view people impersonally as means to that end. And a presupposition of policies around punishment is that they will predictably change people's behavior, or that the manipulation of the conditions under which people act determines the outcome of those actions. Of course, criminologists cannot predict people's behavior with the level of probability that chemists can predict a chemical reaction. On the deterministic view, group behavior is the result of complex social forces (at the group level) and psychological forces (at the individual level). The legislature seeks to manipulate those forces as best they can, with the knowledge they have, for the common good. So, the reasoning of the legislature must also remain probabilistic, considering which social policies *tend to* improve outcomes rather than which social policies *will* improve outcomes.

Punishment as personal blame

Courts are tasked with assessing criminal liability and determining appropriate punishments based on people's degrees of guilt. According to Stephen Darwall (2007), criminal processes are justified by the fact that the legal authority represents the community of equal moral persons, and the state and offenders engage one another in a relationship of mutual accountability. The judge confronts the defendant from what Darwall calls the "second-person standpoint," which is "the perspective you and I take up when we make and acknowledge claims on one another's conduct and will" (2006, 3). The accused is interpellated as a subject in the Althusserian sense: the court demands a plea, and in making a plea, the defendant identifies themselves as someone who can be addressed by the state as a defendant, as someone who can take responsibility or deny responsibility for the crime. The resulting trial is a case of claim-making against the accused criminal: the prosecution tries to convince the jury that the defendant not only caused the crime to happen but was also blameworthy. By demanding reasons and having in mind excusing conditions that would absolve them of responsibility, we hold them to account for their actions in a way that is distinctive of rational agents. By giving people what they deserve – convicting them only if they are guilty and assigning proportional punishments – judges treat the accused as responsible people who were free to choose whether to commit the crimes, based on their characters.

To be sure, we do not need to assume that the accused performed an absolutely self-determined act; that is, we need not presuppose libertarian freedom. In any trial, the jury or judge must determine three things:

1) whether a crime was committed and the accused is the person who did it (*actus reus*);
2) whether the crime is traceable to the person's character, there are mitigating circumstances that reduce their legal culpability, or they suffer or suffered from a mental disorder that made them unable to appreciate the wrongness of their actions (*mens rea*); and,
3) in general, whether our collective sense of disapproval is appropriate given the facts of the case.

Condition #1 is a straightforward ascription of causal agency.[6] Condition #2 requires only that the action was up to the agent rather than attributable to, say, a physical spasm or some mental defect. Using Ayer's language, the action must be uncoerced, not uncaused. To be criminally liable, an offender had to have acted wrongly as a result of reasons, based on their characteristic ways of prioritizing those reasons, which is what defines freedom for Hume, Fischer, and others. Finally, reactive attitudes are felt in the context of social expectations and fault ascriptions. As Strawsonian compatibilism makes clear, condition #3 is independent of any metaphysical commitments, including beliefs in uncaused causes. Because it can accommodate these three conditions, compatibilist freedom is sufficient for criminal liability.

Application: Neuroscience and the law

This distinction between the state's view of its citizens as incentive-driven machines and the court's view of defendants as self-determining agents makes sense in light of the compatibilist theory of freedom. And, setting aside the philosophical question of whether compatibilism is the best theory of freedom to hold, there is good reason to find this theory of freedom compelling in the legal sphere given our assumptions around legal and moral culpability. One has only to set our (mostly Newtonian) scientific commitments and our folk psychological concepts of personal responsibility alongside one another to see how we often use the compatibilist approach – for example, as our legal system is confronted with advances in neuroscience.

On some accounts, neuroscientific research has begun to undermine our notion of criminal responsibility. For example, we now know that the capacity for

6 Some of the terminology in this paragraph is borrowed from Feinberg (1970, 119–51).

self-control is associated with activity in the dorsolateral prefrontal cortex, and if that part of the brain is diminished, then a person is less likely to be able to hold themselves to social expectations and ethical obligations. Brain scans have shown that this part of murderers' brains tends to be underdeveloped. One could argue, then, that a person's homicidal impulses are the result of abnormal neurochemistry rather than some free choice. If the criminal act is attributable to the brain rather than to the "person" (whatever that is), then they are not responsible for what they did: there is no such thing as intentional action, they could not have done otherwise, and so on. Eliminative materialists conclude that we ought to do away with folk psychological explanations in terms of mental states and mental causation, and replace them with descriptions of brain states discovered by scientific psychology. There are no reasons or agency, only neurochemical reactions that we label with inexact talk of "the mind."

We resist this implication not (or not only) because of some anti-scientific bias but because it fails to capture how we conceive of ourselves – and must conceive of ourselves – in practical contexts, when making moral and legal judgments.[7] Indeed, folk psychology is foundational to our conception of the law. In the words of Stephen Morse,

> Doctrine and practice implicitly assume that human beings are agents, creatures who act intentionally for reasons, who can be guided by reasons, and who in adulthood are capable of sufficient rationality to ground full responsibility unless an excusing condition obtains. (2015, 40; see also Morse 2006, 399–400; Sifferd 2006; Morse 2008, 3–13; Morse 2013; and Sifferd 2018, 71–77)

This notion of an excusing condition is crucial. In a typical case, free choice is presupposed unless the defendant can prove that they were not in control. That is what makes insanity (or diminished capacity) an affirmative defense. Hard determinists claim that there is fundamentally no difference between intentional and pathologically motivated actions, or between choices and reflexes. However, criminal trials only make sense if, in general, we act on the basis of reasons and those actions are attributable to us, because only then can we be legally responsible and motivated by incentives. Thus, the law presupposes what Morse calls the "causal theory of action": the view that we have beliefs and desires, that those mental states cause or otherwise generate the actions that result, and that we can distinguish normal, morally responsible adults from others who suffer from rational or motivational deficiencies (2015, 48; see also Morse 2013, 35–39).

If, as Morse claims, the law presupposes folk psychological concepts, including freedom and responsibility, then there must be some way to accommodate that presupposition alongside neuroscientific and other causal claims that threaten

7 I discuss the practical standpoint in ethics and its implications for the theory of punishment in Altman (forthcoming).

to reduce people to the sum total of their psychological, biological, social, and historical circumstances. We cannot be put in the position of rejecting either the latest science or centuries of common law. The problem is that they seem to presuppose very different approaches to freedom: deterministic physicalism or libertarianism.

We need not see this as a real dilemma if we adopt compatibilism as our theory of freedom. On that view, we can be physicalists while also acknowledging mental states, mental causation, and different degrees of responsibility. Morse, who is himself a compatibilist, concedes that our actions have physical causes and our actions are determined by those causes (2006, 398; 2013). But, he says, we can be held responsible for our actions so long as they are determined in the right way. The law distinguishes between kinds of causes, not between caused and uncaused actions. Morse follows Ayer in claiming that "causation – including brain causation – is not the equivalent of compulsion" (Morse 2015, 57; see also Morse 2014, 844). All actions are caused, but there are varying degrees of responsibility based on whether an action is caused by my own mental states, coercion, or insanity. Some are intentional and others are not. Only intentional actions can be attributed to the agent, and that attribution is all that is required under the law. Although mental and physical states are identical, they are relevant to what Katrina Sifferd (2018) calls different "levels" of understanding human behavior – namely, the macrobehavioral level of responsibility assessments and the microphysical level of brain states. In most criminal cases, a person either meets or does not meet the behavioral criteria for responsibility, depending on whether they are responsive to reasons (à la Fischer), so neurological evidence to explain their intentions is simply unnecessary (Morse 2006, 405–6). The law is not concerned with where the intention came from; judges and legislators are not doing metaphysics. As Morse says, free will is a "non-problem" in law (2008, 3–4; see also Morse 2013, 27–28, 39).[8] Even if none of our actions are free in the libertarian sense, we can still be responsible in the legal sense.

Conclusion

The two-tiered model and the compatibilist theory of freedom mutually support one another. If there are reasons to adopt both retributivist and consequentialist theories of punishment (as I argued in Part I), and if those theories are more appropriate under two different standpoints on human action (as free and determined, respectively), then that provides support for compatibilism. From the other direction, if compatibilism is the right theory of freedom, it lends support to the two-tiered model of punishment. The two-tiered model resolves a seeming

8 There are different theoretical explanations of why physicalism and folk psychology are compatible, including Morse's non-reductive physicalism (Morse 2008) and Sifferd's non-eliminative reductive physicalism (Sifferd 2018). Exploring this debate would take me too far afield.

tension facing compatibilism, namely the demand for both consequentialism and retributivism if people are both determined and free. Both approaches to punishment are possible within a mixed theory in which the legislature aims to shape outcomes and criminal courts aim to give accused criminals what they deserve. Together they form a unified legal system within which both personal responsibility and advances in neuroscience are accepted without contradiction.

8 The moral argument

Over the last two chapters, I have appealed to epistemic considerations and the compatibilist theory of freedom to argue that the two-tiered model is the correct approach to legal punishment. In this, the final chapter of Part III, I provide a moral argument for the two-tiered model by showing that its implications accord with our moral intuitions. Each of the component theories, on its own, entails conclusions that are morally objectionable. The two-tiered model uses consequentialism to constrain retributivism and retributivism to constrain consequentialism, in ways that make both of them, together, more acceptable on moral grounds.[1]

Restricting the retributivist impulse

Retributivists say that people ought to be punished because they deserve it, and they assume that legal punishment ought to be directed only at criminals and that it ought to be proportionate to their crimes. However, the theory faces three potential problems that would make retributivism unacceptable as a theory of legal punishment:

1) First, criminals are not the only people who deserve to be punished. People with bad characters or bad intentions are unworthy of happiness, regardless of whether they act on their intentions. Yet we think that legal punishment should be restricted to those who act or attempt to act wrongly.
2) Second, people who act immorally but not illegally – by, for example, committing adultery or breaking promises – ought to be punished somehow, perhaps by their spouses or social groups. Yet we think that state-sponsored

1 Tasioulas says that any mixed theory is "little better than an *ad hoc* compromise among radically disparate concerns … explicitly manufactured to yield results more attuned to our settled moral convictions" (2006, 281–82). As I showed in Chapters 6 and 7, there are nonmoral reasons to arrange the theories in a two-tiered model. Furthermore, the fact that the results of the model accord with our moral intuitions is reason to support the theory, not reason to be suspicious of what motivated the mixed theorist.

punishment should be restricted to a subset of wrong actions that also are prohibited by law.[2]

3) Third, if we follow the *lex talionis* strictly, then the punishment should be equivalent, not just proportionate, to the crime – "an eye for an eye." Yet we prohibit state-sponsored punishment that is inhumane in its method or excessive in its degree.

The question, then, is how we can be committed to retributivism while restricting both what the state does to people and to whom it does it. I cover each of these issues in turn.

First, a feasible form of retributivism would have to explain why only convicted criminals, and not all bad people, deserve to be punished by the state. Immanuel Kant says that only someone with a good will is worthy of happiness (1996a, 4:393) and that people ought to be punished in accordance with their "*inner wickedness*" (1996b, 6:333; see also Kant 1997, 27:434). That implies that plenty of non-criminals ought to suffer, such as those who undertake the "greatest efforts" to do wrong but fail only because they "lack the capacity to carry out [the will's] purpose" (1996a, 4:394). As noted in Chapter 2, on some religious views, God metes out justice in the form of punishments for the wicked and eternal rewards for the righteous, based entirely on what they deserve. And what they deserve depends not (or not only) on what they do, but on the kinds of people they are. People such as the would-be arsonist who are deterred from doing wrong only by the threat of punishment or other social circumstances are not morally praiseworthy, even if they act in ways that are legally permissible. If the state sees itself as retributivist, doling out punishments according to what people deserve, then restricting harm only to people who have committed crimes seems contrary to the theory that is supposed to justify punishment.

In response to this problem, many retributivists focus on legal punishment as the paradigm case of punishment. One form of retributivism, legalistic retributivism, says that people deserve to be punished for no other reason than the fact that they break the law. Being found guilty of a crime is both necessary and sufficient for justifying punishment (e.g., Mabbott 1939). However, as C. L. Ten puts it, "to restrict the justification of punishment to illegal acts, irrespective of the moral quality of these acts, would ... sever the link between punishment and moral wrongdoing which lies at the heart of retributive theories" (1987, 72). Legalistic

2 Moore (1997) claims that, even though a law based on retributivist principles should not punish lack of virtue, it ought to enforce moral obligations. This elides the distinction between moral and legal wrongs. Moore limits the scope of punishment not by restricting it to legal rather than moral matters, but by narrowly defining the scope of morality. For example, the law should not prohibit consensual sexual relationships. But the law should be uninvolved here not because our private moral and immoral behavior is no business of the government, but because there are no morally wrong consensual sexual relationships. If we did have moral obligations around sex, Moore says, then the government would be justified in intervening (esp. 756).

retributivism entails both that the morally guilty need not be punished so long as they do not break the law, and that the morally innocent may be punished so long as a law is broken – regardless of the morality of the law itself (Christopher 2002). In doing so, legalistic retributivism defines what I call the reasonable in terms of the rational. It neither morally justifies nor morally obligates the state to punish anyone.

Alternatively, the retributivist could say that, in making criminal law, we identify all the bad actions for which it would be good to punish people. Then, because the bad consequences of punishing people for some of those acts would outweigh the good that would come from punishing them, those would be designated as non-crimes. Bad consequences could include state overreach, errors in determining what actions are in fact bad, interference in familial self-regulation, difficulty in establishing guilt, and so on. In short, the retributivist could say that all bad actors deserve punishment, but it is worth it to the state only to punish some of them. The problem with such an approach is its commitment to competing, non-retributivist values that may override the duty to give people what they deserve. There would have to be an account of why, say, the regulation of morality would amount to state overreach, why the possibility of error is allowed in some cases and not others, why and when self-regulation is more important than desert, and so on, all without begging the question in favor of the status quo.

According to the two-tiered model, the state punishes only actions, including inchoate crimes that risk harmful actions, because the consequences are better than the alternative. That is, we have a considered preference for a system in which our retributive impulses are restricted as a matter of policy, at the institutional level, because that most effectively preserves the public order and promotes the common good. On the liberal view, for example, a system in which people are punished for immoral thoughts and character, or private actions that do not impact the functioning of the state, would unduly restrict personal freedom of thought, association, and religion; and the minority population would be subject to the moral views of the majority. Because it is so difficult to know about someone's character, the rules of evidence would be loosened to the point where innocents are convicted of thought-crimes. It would be nearly impossible to discover a person's degree of guilt absent any actions that reveal it: as Cesare Beccaria writes: "The gravity of a sin depends on the inscrutable malice of the heart, which finite beings cannot know without special revelation. How, then, could it be used as a guide for the punishment of crimes?" (1995, 23). God may know whether someone has a good or bad character, but the government does not.

The same reasons also justify excluding private moral transgressions from coverage under the criminal law. If the purpose of government is to preserve the rights of the people, then the criminal law is designed to deter, restrain, and rehabilitate people who violate or would violate the rights of others. Acting immorally may be contrary to a person's duties to others or oneself but, if it does not also fall into one of the criminal legal categories – for example, murder is both illegal and morally wrong – then the agent is not subject to state sanctions because of their immoral actions. W. D. Ross explains the rights view succinctly:

> [The state's] proper work is that of protecting rights. Now rights are … rights to be treated in certain ways and not to be treated in certain ways from certain motives; what the state has to take account of, therefore, is not morally bad actions, but wrong acts, and it has to take account of them in such a way as to diminish the chance of their repetition. (2002, 60)

If the state's aim is to maximize the good (e.g., the protection of rights), then it ought to deter actions that undermine the good (e.g., that violate rights) and need not interfere with actions that do not, even when those actions are wrong in other ways. It is illegal to punch someone for no good reason because we all have the right to noninterference, but it is not illegal to cheat on one's spouse because there is no right to fidelity – that is, the cheater has a duty not to cheat, but there is no correlative right.

The two-tiered model of punishment, then, explains why, on consequentialist grounds, retributive punishment on the part of the state (in the courts) ought to be restricted to those who commit (or are thought to commit) criminal acts. But the definition of criminal actions would vary depending on the aims of the state. My theory does not by definition rule out criminalizing thoughts or immoral actions. To be sure, the aims of the liberal state would not be accomplished with such a system. Under a theocracy, however, religious expression that is contrary to state dogma or private actions that violate the government's official moral positions would be subject to punishment. In Iran, for example, adultery is punishable by death by stoning, and blasphemy of the Prophet Muhammad is punishable by death or imprisonment. To show why these crimes and punishments are wrong, we must separately explain why the aims of the Islamic Republic of Iran are wrong.

My theory also rejects equality retributivism – the view that the crime and punishment must be equivalent – in favor of proportional retributivism. Divine punishments in the afterlife would presumably be equivalent to the wrongdoings of the sinner. For example, Dante depicts those who are guilty of uncontrollable lust during their lifetimes as spending eternity being tossed about by ever-changing cyclones of wind (1971, Canto V, ll. 28–49 [pp. 110–11]). However, allowing for this kind of equivalence in criminal courts would be morally problematic. Judges and juries may be angry enough to want rapists to be raped and murderers to be brutally tortured to death. One could even grant that they deserve these things. But that does not mean that the state ought to do it – and my theory explains why. These kinds of punishments, in addition to being excessive, would have a coarsening effect on the country. Jeffrey Reiman makes this kind of argument against the death penalty. He says that, even though murderers deserve to die, we should refuse to execute them because not brutalizing people who deserve to be brutalized and not executing people who deserve to be executed would have a "civilizing effect" (1985, 145):

> If civilization is characterized by lower tolerance for our own pain and that of others, then publicly refusing to do horrible things to our fellows both

> signals the level of our civilization *and, by our example, continues the work of civilizing.* (135–36)[3]

Reiman speculates that the effects of not carrying out an execution, even if the criminal deserves it, may have more of a deterrent effect than execution because the state would be modeling mercy for its citizens (146). Indeed, there is some empirical evidence that the death penalty increases the number of murders because of a brutalization effect (Bowers and Pierce 1980; Bowers, Pierce, and McDevitt 1984, 271–335; Cochran and Chamlin 2000; Shepherd 2005). One can only imagine how it would affect society if the government trained and employed professional rapists and torturers to inflict equivalent punishments on the worst criminals.

On the two-tiered model, lawmakers would prohibit punishments, even if they are deserved, that would be barbaric or would increase rather than decrease criminal acts. As I said in Chapter 4, the state's control over criminal justice purifies the community's feelings toward wrongdoers by focusing on resentment rather than anger or revenge, and it symbolically expresses resentment in the form of legal punishment. Here I explain why and how the state does that. Using consequentialist reasoning to set the punishment schedule that judges must follow rules out the excesses of equality retributivism, forcing them to assign appropriate punishments, proportional to the offenses, within a range of legislatively mandated punishments. Worse crimes would get worse punishments, not equal punishments.

Not only are there reasons to limit the retributive impulse that courts express, but there are also reasons only to allow the expression of the retributive impulse within the courts. If retributivism is true, it seems to justify vigilantism. During demonstrations against Chinese rule in Hong Kong in 2019, following the shooting of a protester by police, another protester gave voice to this position: "'If they killed someone, that means we get to kill them. An eye for an eye and a life for a life'" (Su and Kilpatrick 2019). If murderers deserve to die, there is no obvious nonconsequentialist reason why the state should execute them rather than someone else doing it. There are, however, consequentialist reasons to restrict vigilantism and defend the state's monopoly on coercion. If these restrictions were not in place, there would be chaos: accused criminals would be subject to the whims of the mob (rather than the strict rules of evidence and other rights that the state provides), and multigenerational blood feuds between groups would be commonplace (see Diamond 2008). Everyone would exact their own revenge as they see fit and, as John Locke notes, a sense of impartial justice would be lost because people would be biased in their own favor (1980, §§13, 125 [pp. 12, 66]). Having consequentialism inform legislative actions with regard to punishment allows the courts to express the community's resentment within reasonable limits and to assign punishments in a way that accords with our considered moral intuitions.

3 Reiman (1985) not only gives a consequentialist argument about the effects of acting civilized. He also says that we ought to be civilized, as a kind of duty.

Restricting consequentialist calculations: Innocence and guilt

A longstanding objection to consequentialism is that it commands us to perform actions that are inherently wrong or contrary to duty so long as the consequences are good enough. If we ought to pull the lever so that the runaway trolley runs over one person instead of five, then should we also cut up a healthy loner and distribute their organs to five people who need transplants (Thomson 1985)? Defenders of consequentialism have tried in different ways to avoid its apparent approval of using people merely as means for the benefit of others – by, for example, invoking the distinction between killing and letting die (Foot 1967) or appealing to rights as a restriction on utility-maximization (Thomson 1985). John Stuart Mill (2001) defends a version of utilitarianism according to which rules, not individual actions, ought to maximize utility. A rule that we should divert runaway trolleys to minimize casualties would, in fact, maximize utility, while a rule that has us abduct and kill healthy individuals would cause widespread panic and more suffering overall.

With regard to punishment in particular, the most common objection to consequentialism is that it "might not allow punishment of all those who deserve it" and it might "warrant punishments beyond those deserved," specifically the punishment of innocents (Goldman 1981, 721–22). I mentioned this in Chapter 6. Kai Nielsen illustrates the problem with the case of the magistrate and the threatening mob (a version of Philippa Foot's hypothetical [1967, 8]):

> A magistrate or judge is faced with a very real threat from a large and uncontrollable mob of rioters demanding a culprit for a crime. Unless the criminal is produced, promptly tried, and executed, they will take their own bloody revenge on a much smaller and quite vulnerable section of the community (a kind of frenzied pogrom). The judge knows that the real culprit is unknown and that the authorities do not even have a good clew as to who he may be. But he also knows that there is within easy reach a disreputable, thoroughly disliked, and useless man, who, though innocent, could easily be framed so that the mob would be quite convinced that he was guilty and would be pacified if he were promptly executed. Recognizing that he can prevent the occurrence of extensive carnage only by framing some innocent person, the magistrate has him framed, goes through the mockery of a trial, and has him executed. (Nielsen 1972, 223)

Nielsen himself says that the utilitarian or consequentialist could say that the judge should not frame the innocent man because what he did would probably be found out eventually, which would set a dangerous precedent for other magistrates, corrupt the institution of justice, and cause distrust of the legal system, among other things.[4] Nevertheless, Nielsen concedes that utilitarians

4 See Chapter 6, note 3 for a list of other authors who argue that a utilitarian should not frame the innocent.

could disagree about this, with some condoning the execution of the innocent man (223–25).[5] Although he argues that we ought to get over our resistance to accepting this, which is a result of a misplaced moral conservatism (223–25), many people take this to be a damning objection, a *reductio ad absurdum* of the consequentialist justification of punishment.[6]

In principle, consequentialism could also justify not punishing the guilty. J. D. Mabbott claims that, for deterrence theory, what matters is that people think the criminal is punished, not that the person is actually punished (1939, 152). Bentham seems to admit as much when he says that "the idea only of the punishment (or, in other words, the *apparent* punishment) … really acts upon the mind" (1970, ch. XV, §9 [p. 178]), and "real punishments" ought to be inflicted only if and to the extent that it succeeds in "producing the *appearance* of it" (1830, Bk. I, ch. 5 [p. 29]). One could tweak Nielsen's case so that the outcome is nearly as objectionable, even though no one is actually punished:

> A magistrate or judge is faced with a very real threat from a large and uncontrollable mob of rioters demanding a culprit for a crime. Unless the criminal is produced, promptly tried, and executed, they will take their own bloody revenge on a much smaller and quite vulnerable section of the community (a kind of frenzied pogrom). The judge knows the real culprit, who is a friend of hers. Stunned by the intensity of the public outrage, the offender is scared enough never to commit another crime again; he will follow the law in the future. The judge recognizes that she can prevent extensive carnage without killing her friend, so she goes through with the trial, convicts him, and convincingly stages his death before the friend escapes to a remote island, where he lives a tranquil life, never to be seen or heard from again.

Like the previous case, the consequentialist could argue that this would be the wrong thing to do. The charade is likely to be discovered, resulting in more public anger and distrust of the system. However, as with the first case, one could imagine a way that this could work, and, if it did, the consequentialist would condone it. After all, the criminal is happy, the judge is happy, and the public is happy; the pogrom is avoided; justice seems to have been done; other potential

5 Others who say that, if consequentialism warrants it, then supposedly unjust punishments would in fact be justified include Smart (1973, 69–72), Gerber (1975), and Bagaric and Amarasekara (2000, 141–43).

6 See Chapter 6, note 2 for a list of authors who argue against utilitarianism because it entails that innocents may justifiably be punished. Christopher argues that retributivism is not immune to the charge that punishing the guilty would be justified in some cases. He claims that moralistic retributivism justifies the punishment of legal innocents, that legalistic retributivism justifies the punishment of moral innocents, and that, by invoking the doctrine of double effect to excuse the unintentional punishment of innocents, retributivism justifies the punishment of defendants without regard for fault or culpability (2002, 869–924). Since my purpose here is to defend my mixed theory against this charge, I set aside this criticism of retributivism.

criminals are deterred – everyone wins. But this seems wrong because justice was not in fact done. The criminal did not get what he deserves. Consequentialism seems to be missing something crucial about how committing a crime and receiving a punishment should be related. Criminals ought to be punished *because of* their crimes.

The two-tiered model of punishment avoids both these implications of consequentialism as a standalone theory. First, the legislature would not create an institution of punishment that allows the innocent to be framed and the guilty to go free. Such a policy would not preserve the public order. People would not know whether to trust the courts' judgments. The angry mob would know that the legislature has deemed it appropriate to frame innocent people in such circumstances, so framing the innocent would do nothing to pacify them. This is where the consequentialist gives the typical response: doing this would have bad consequences. The difference with my view is that it is not a contingent matter of whether the news gets out. Since consequentialism is operative at the institutional level – since the legislature is making policy – it is necessarily public because it is promulgated as the law.[7]

Second, judges ought to give people what they deserve, not do whatever it takes to achieve some social aim, such as pacifying an angry mob or deterring potential criminals. The legislature considers the impact of large-scale policies on people's behavior in general, including the deterrent and rehabilitative effects of punishment, but the courts consider whether the individual defendant is guilty of a crime and which punishment is warranted by their degree of guilt. An innocent person who is brought before a judge or jury would be found not guilty and escape punishment because they do not deserve to be punished. The pressure of the mob does not change that fact. And a guilty person would not escape punishment because the goal of the trial is not to make the offender and everyone else as happy as possible or otherwise to maximize socially desirable ends. As Michael Davis puts it, "the judge who, though imposing the right sentence, does so only to discourage other criminals, or only to satisfy the victim, or only for some combination of these or other practical reasons would, it seems, have misunderstood her job" (1992, 32). Similarly, as is made clear in instructions to juries, their job is "to decide whether the government has proved beyond a reasonable doubt that the defendant is guilty of the crime charged" (Committee on Pattern Jury Instructions 2019, 1.21 [p. 31]). The fact that offenders broke the law is sufficient reason for the jury to find them guilty and for the judge to punish them in accordance with how guilty they are, within the range of appropriate punishments as set by the legislature.

An example from John Kleinig will help to illustrate this point: A Nazi war criminal escaped to an uninhabited island, where he lived peacefully for thirty years until being discovered. Although he does not repent his crimes, he has no

7 My response here is similar to the response that Rawls gives in "Two Concepts of Rules" (1955).

desire to leave the island or cause further trouble. It has been so long since he committed the crimes that punishing him, Kleinig says, will do no good. No one is demanding that he suffer. Should he be punished, and would he have any right to complain if he were punished (Kleinig 1973, 67)? A utilitarian could reply that not punishing him would set a bad example, namely that someone who successfully escapes and hides for long enough will get off the hook. But even if we dismiss this idea, as Kleinig asks us to, what should be done? On the two-tiered model, the legislature sets appropriate penalties for kinds of crimes. And, provided that the laws promote a just arrangement and there is no less harmful alternative that would as effectively maintain the state, then the punishment he receives is also just. The Nazi, assuming that he committed murder or other war crimes, falls under one of those classes, so he should be charged. The legislature has deemed that it furthers the common good to hold offenders to account for those offenses – presumably without statutes of limitations. The judge, then, determines whether the defendant is guilty of the crime and sentences him accordingly. It is not up to the judge whether punishing the defendant would do any good, or whether he poses any further threat. The verdict is backward-looking in that sense. So, like Kleinig, I believe that the Nazi would not be justified in complaining about his punishment, because it is just that he should suffer.

One advantage of the two-tiered model is not only that it prohibits punishing the innocent, but that it does so for the right reasons. Even if Nielsen could rule out victimization, it seems that he would have judges and juries decide the outcome of the case based on facts that are beyond the scope of their authority. Consequentialist judges and juries would deliberate not about whether the state has proven its case against the defendant, but about how likely it is that the public will find out if they frame an innocent person. Perhaps Nielsen would have opposing counsel present arguments regarding just how angry and inquisitive the public is and the probability of their discovering any miscarriage of justice, rather than whether the defendant committed the crime. As Alan Goldman says, consequentialists could rule out the punishment of innocents, but in doing so they misconstrue the nature of the wrong that would be committed by framing them. If an innocent person is (purposely) punished, it is not that the judge has made an incorrect calculation or that society has been wronged. Rather, the innocent person has been victimized (1981, 722; see also Duff 1986, 160–61). The two-tiered model makes sense of this: accused criminals should get what they deserve because, in a certain sense, consequentialism becomes silent once we step into the courtroom. It would be wrong for a judge to punish an innocent person or to let a guilty person go free because such treatment is disproportionate to their degrees of guilt, not because people will be upset.

Judges and juries may be tempted to consider the social consequences of their actions, but doing so would violate their designated roles in a system of punishment that is justified, as a whole, when the actions of the legislature and the courts are grounded in different theoretical principles. Nielsen may consider this a form of moral conservativism. However, the fact that my theory of punishment does not ask us to violate our considered moral intuitions regarding the punishment of innocents lends support to its rightness.

Restricting consequentialist calculations: The therapy world

Talk of preserving the public order may worry people. If crimes cause suffering and punishment imposes burdens on people, then it seems like the best way to reduce harm would be not merely to deter potential criminals, but to do away with crime altogether by reeducating or drugging the entire populace. Herbert Morris (1968) describes this as a "therapy world" in which no one is held responsible for anything; everyone's behavior is available to be manipulated. This is a specific version of the more general worry that consequentialist theories of punishment do not respect people's moral standing – the use objection. Indeed, Antony Duff thinks that this is a "conclusive" moral objection against them (1996, 87). Under consequentialism, potential criminals are being coerced rather than reasoned with, and actual criminals are being forcibly incapacitated and "fixed" (i.e., rehabilitated) rather than being called upon to recognize their wrongs and reintegrate into the community. From the institutional perspective, people are treated as means to the end of peaceful coexistence.

There are several responses to this worry. First, this misapplies the utilitarian theory. Mill (1978) famously argues that respect for people's rights is fully consistent with – in fact, it is entailed by – the principle of utility. He describes three "regions" of human liberty – liberty of conscience, liberty of pursuits, and freedom of assembly – and claims that society is better off when it protects these freedoms than when it forces people to believe certain things or live certain ways. Mill makes a case for the value of nonconformity and says that allowing people to decide for themselves tends to maximize happiness in general (1978, esp. 11–12, 50, 60).

Second, this objection is not necessarily applicable even to the consequentialist part of the two-tiered model. Institutional decisions regarding punishment need not be utilitarian. As I said in Chapter 3, a consequentialism of rights is one possible institutional approach, according to which decisions about government intervention and coercion could be based on a rights calculus. In this case, a policy of social engineering that violates people's rights in order to maximize overall happiness, even if it could do so, would not be optimal. We should reject a therapy world in favor of the kind of treatment that Morris himself recommends: "In our system of punishment an attempt was made to maximize each individual's freedom of choice by first of all delimiting by rules certain spheres of conduct immune from interference by others" (H. Morris 1968, 485; see also Nozick 1981, 381). This is the liberal arrangement that would be required under a consequentialism of rights, which also has us maximize individual freedoms.

Finally, the two-tiered model is a mixed view in which there are two separate obligations: the legislature ought to form policies that promote the common good, and criminal courts ought to hold individual defendants accountable for their criminal acts. Morris imagines a strictly utilitarian deterrence theory, not a mixed view. As I showed in the previous chapter, having a justified feeling of resentment toward wrongdoers depends on conceiving of the person as free. Making the population unfree would mean that the government is not fulfilling one of its obligations: to express the community's resentment toward wrongdoers. Offenders who are brought to trial are treated as potentially responsible agents. The expression of resentment is based on claims of culpable wrongdoing. Thus, the government is limited in its institutional decisions by the (sometimes) competing claims of the community. Judges and juries check the power of the legislature – in this case, not allowing for the dehumanization of free agents. A threat system (as opposed to a brave new world) is sufficient to maintain an acceptable level of social order that is consistent with our treatment of one another as persons.

Conclusion

As I mentioned earlier, a common objection to consequentialism is that it does not properly conceive of punishment as an imposition of burdens because of a wrong act (see esp. Perlmutter 2014). The fact that it is forward-looking flattens the distinction between it and any other calculus-based decision, such as how much to invest in public education, when to lie, and whether to eat ice cream late at night. Retributivism, it is claimed, is a proper theory of punishment because it focuses on desert. One advantage of the two-tiered model of punishment is that it acknowledges and accommodates two seemingly competing realities. First, legal punishment is only one tool that the state uses to maintain itself. Considering legal punishment as a unique thing, different from all other public policies, ignores the ways that punishment *is* like other public policies. It is a state institution, which makes legal punishment different from parental or divine punishment. However, the two-tiered model also makes room for the desert-based assignment of burdens through the criminal courts. I can agree with retributivists that there is something distinctive about backward-looking punishment, but at the level of distribution rather than policy. The two-tiered model thus keeps what is distinctive of punishment – the fact that, unlike other calculations, it involves desert – *and* what is distinctive about legal punishment – the fact that, like other public institutions, it serves a social purpose.

Part IV
Decision procedure

In the previous three parts of the book, I defined punishment, argued for consequentialism and retributivism, and explained and justified the two-tiered model as the best way to combine them in a mixed theory. In the final two parts, I explain how the model can be used to set punishment policies and statutory penalties, and to resolve conflicts between the legislature and the criminal judiciary (Part IV); and I apply the model to two controversial topics in the theory of punishment: capital punishment and restorative justice (Part V).

In Chapter 9, I defend criminology against critics of consequentialism who exaggerate the failures of the social sciences. Criminological research can provide clear (or clear enough) guidance for policy decisions that promote the common good through general and specific deterrence. In Chapter 10, I explain how consequentialist legislators should set statutory penalties that are proportional to their crimes, in contrast to the retributivist alternative described by Michael Davis.

Having defended legislative consequentialism against some common objections, I devote Chapter 11 to what may broadly be characterized as the two-tiered model's decision procedure. How do consequentialism and retributivism function together in a single system, and what happens when there is a conflict? In most cases, legislatively established statutory penalties constrain criminal courts' distribution of burdens. In those rare cases where statutory penalties are unreasonably excessive, jury nullification is a kind of check on the power of the legislature to impose undeserved punishments on individual offenders. This is part of a collective process of deliberation that arrives at reflective equilibrium and establishes the comparative importance of desert and efficiency at achieving our social aims.

9 In defense of criminology

> It would be a disservice to exaggerate our lack of knowledge of the efficacy of certain penal sanctions. Cynicism is a cheap commodity and gives a spurious air of wisdom.
>
> – Norval Morris (1966, 645n28)[1]

Because consequentialist theories appeal to the deterrent effects of punishment, the question of which punishments are justified, for whom, and under what circumstances could in principle be answered scientifically with some version of Jeremy Bentham's felicific calculus. We would calculate the costs and benefits in the short and long terms, using different variables such as intensity and duration to determine a scale of crimes and corresponding punishments that would deter potential criminals. For example, assault and battery is more harmful than theft, so we ought to deter it with a punishment that is sufficiently motivating for potential batterers. That assumes that batterers would be deterred by a given punishment and that the appropriate punishment – the one that would in fact deter – could be established empirically.

Yet, Robert Martinson (1974) observes that social scientists have been unable to isolate and measure the effectiveness of specific punishments and rehabilitative programs, and these empirical failures cast doubt on the ability of consequentialists to make even low-level generalizations that would be action-guiding (see also Lipton, Martinson, and Wilks 1975). More recently, Robert Forde (2018) has criticized criminology as it is currently practiced, claiming that it rests on correlational analyses with no scientific validity and that it is driven by biased researchers with little accountability. Michael Davis puts the situation starkly:

> If even relatively crude tuning of penalties to empirical consequences is in practice impossible, empirical preventive theories cannot justify punishment as an institution, much less choosing any institution of punishment others, or choosing one punishment over another, except in some counterfactual world

1 Originally appearing in the *University of Chicago Law Review*, 33 U. Chi. L. Rev. 627 (1966). Reprinted with permission from the *University of Chicago Law Review* and the University of Chicago Law School.

> in which we would know much more than we do know here. (2009, 84; see also Paternoster 2010)

Davis attributes the general decline in popularity of consequentialist theories and the subsequent rise of retributivism in the 1970s to this empirical failure of the social sciences (2009, 84).[2]

In expressing their doubts about the viability of consequentialism, Martinson, Forde, and Davis focus on three separate levels of generality regarding punishment and its attempted consequentialist justification:

1) Punishment as an institution that sets out a system of incentives for criminals and potential criminals.
2) Lower-level generalizations about which punishments are appropriate and effective for kinds of crimes and classes of criminals (i.e., statutory penalties, or a scaling of crimes and punishments).
3) Specific judgments about what punishments particular criminals ought to get for the crimes they commit (i.e., distribution of individual sentences).

When we examine each of these in turn, it becomes clear that critics of consequentialism are exaggerating its supposed shortcomings. Despite claims to the contrary, consequentialists can appeal to empirical social science research to justify both (1) the institution of punishment and (2) statutory penalties. On the two-tiered model, (3) individual offenders ought to be judged based on what they deserve (retributivism), so empirical calculations regarding consequences are unnecessary and inappropriate at that level. In this chapter, then, I defend consequentialism against the objection that it provides little guidance for policymakers regarding criminal law (1 and 2), as opposed to judges (3).

Consequentialism and the general justifying aim of punishment (1)

As defined in Chapter 1, legal punishments are established by a recognized legal authority and acknowledged by potential criminals as constraining. Regarding what H. L. A. Hart calls the general justifying aim of punishment, the question is whether a system of *ex ante* incentives actually works to change behavior. At this broad level, it is not necessary to quantify how effective disincentives are, only that they are effective in general. That is, an institutional consequentialist must show that criminal activity is less likely when there are punishments than

2 For a list of sources that describe recent historical changes in our theoretical opinions regarding punishment, see Introduction, note 8.

in a hypothetical society where there are no punishments. In short, are people motivated by pains and pleasures and by threats and enticements?

When phrased like this, institutional consequentialism seems obviously correct. Although the picture of human beings as *homo economicus* has rightly been challenged, one does not need to believe that we are ideal optimizers of personal utility in order to accept the truism that people generally try to avoid bad outcomes. Bentham reminds us that, although our decisions may not reflect accurate cost-benefit analyses, they are informed by a basic concern with our own well-being:

> When matters of such importance as pain and pleasure are at stake, and these in the highest degree (the only matters, in short, that can be of importance) who is there that does not calculate? Men calculate, some with less exactness, indeed, some with more: but all men calculate. I would not say, that even a madman does not calculate. (1970, ch. XIV, §28 [pp. 173–74])

The very fact that criminals try to get away with their crimes is evidence of their preferences – namely, their desire to avoid the harms of punishment. Although researchers disagree about the most effective ways to modify behavior, there is a vast body of literature on deterrence which confirms that we respond to incentives and that the perception of risk affects what we do (see, e.g., Nagin, Cullen, and Jonson 2018). Indeed, evolutionary theory itself is based on the idea that we weigh risks and benefits, even if the calculation is not made perfectly or explicitly. As Ernest van den Haag puts it,

> It is impossible to understand the survival of the human race without realizing that people habitually tend to avoid or minimize natural and social dangers (costs) in proportion to both the severity of the injury threatened and the risk of actually suffering that injury. (1982, 771; see also van den Haag 1975, 112–15)

The idea that deterrence is ineffective in general defies common sense.[3] If people did not care about consequences at all, everyone would be trying to fly from rooftops.

3 Many theorists express surprise that anyone would call this obvious claim into doubt. They refer to common sense and our everyday assumptions. For example, in their classic study on deterrence, Zimring and Hawkins write: "It is a matter of common observation that men seek to avoid unpleasant consequences, and that the threat of unpleasant consequences tends to be a deterrent" (1973, 5). In defense of his own deterrence theory, Andenaes says:

> it seems reasonably safe to evaluate the general-preventive effects of punishment on a common sense basis. Modern psychology has shown that the pleasure-pain principle is not as universally valid as is assumed, for instance, in Bentham's penal philosophy. Nevertheless,

Not all people want to commit crimes, and some people cannot be deterred no matter the threat, but a subset of the population is prone to break the law *and* is capable of being deterred. Greg Pogarsky (2002) identifies these groups, respectively, as the "acute conformists," the "incorrigible," and the "deterrable" (see also Zimring and Hawkins 1968). Bradley Wright et al. (2004) find that, in general, perceptions of risk have a deterrent effect for a majority of people who are prone to criminal activity. That is, few criminals are incorrigible; most are deterrable. They are less likely to violate the law if conformity is believed to be in their self-interest.[4]

> it is still a fundamental fact of social life that the risk of unpleasant consequences is a very strong motivational factor for most people in most situations. (1974, 147)

Andenaes makes a similar claim in another work:

> The strongest basis for the belief in general prevention is still the well-known experience that fear of unpleasant consequences is a highly motivating factor in most walks of life, and the more highly motivating the more serious the feared consequences are. The notion that this well-known mechanism were to be without importance when the issue at hand is that of whether or not to commit a criminal act, is almost fantastic. (1982, 229; translated and quoted in Mathiesen 2006, 57)

Wilson echoes this idea:

> People are governed in their daily lives by rewards and penalties of every sort. We shop for bargain prices, praise our children for good behavior and scold them for bad, expect lower interest rates to stimulate home building and fear that higher ones will depress it, and conduct ourselves in public in ways that lead our friends and neighbors to form good opinions of us. To assert that "deterrence doesn't work" is tantamount to either denying the plainest facts of everyday life or claiming that would-be criminals are utterly different from the rest of us. (1983, 121)

Morris and Zimring have us consider a hypothetical:

> there are many examples of the threat of punishment under the criminal law clearly influencing human behavior. Honest reader, consider your income tax return, and what it would be like were you assured that it could not be checked. If we have misjudged you, consider the impact on your neighbor's tax return! (1969, 138)

4 Brooks seems to think that, because many people are acute conformists with no interest in breaking the law, there is no way to measure the effects of threatened punishments on deterrable offenders. He imagines that criminals may be deterred by other factors such as guilt (2012, 164). It is an odd argument to make. Most people do not want to commit murder because of their moral scruples (which includes guilt for wrong actions), but the deterrent effect (or lack thereof) of the death penalty is discoverable in principle and in practice by comparing crime rates, for example, of socioeconomically and geographically similar counties in neighboring states with and without the death penalty. If the murder rate were lower in the county with the death penalty, the more reasonable explanation is that the death penalty deters, not that the people in that state just happen to feel guiltier about murder than people in the other state. Based on the data, we would be justified in believing that the threat of capital punishment is deterring deterrable offenders, and we would have a sense of how much it deters, even if it is not needed to deter everyone.

So long as some people are deterrable, the threat of punishment serves a purpose. As Andrew von Hirsch notes, punishment does not need to deter everyone in order to be an effective method of crime prevention:

> the crime-preventive mission of the criminal law is not necessarily that of preventing the most recalcitrant from offending. The criminal sanction cannot achieve anything near one hundred per cent efficiency, and fulfils its proper function if it helps induce most people to comply. My conception of prevention is one that would give ordinary persons good reasons for compliance. (1993, 44)

This is one reason why the law cannot have perfect compliance as its ideal. Even at its most effective, not everyone will obey the law, no matter what the incentives are. This fact does not undermine the proposition that deterrence is the general justifying aim of punishment.

That most people are deterrable is not only a commonsensical idea but is also supported by historical evidence. Defenders of deterrence theory often reference the steep increase in crime during blackouts, when detection is less likely, and when there is a sharp reduction in police presence.[5] For example, during World War II, the crime rate in England and Wales rose by 57 percent. Although some of it (e.g., forgery, black markets, theft) was due to desperation and restrictions during wartime, the lack of police and periods of near-total darkness also led to increases in looting, gang activity, and murder (M. Ellis 2018). Conversely, violations of blackout rules, such as not fully covering windows at night, were easily detected, strictly enforced, and subject to steep penalties, so such rules were almost uniformly followed. Another example: In Copenhagen in 1944, the German occupiers arrested the entire Danish police force, leaving the city with nothing but an improvised, ill-prepared, and unarmed civilian force under German control. Crime dramatically increased, including terrorist acts by the security officers themselves, who were subject to little oversight (Holbraad 2017, 46–47; see also Andenaes 1974, 16–17). More recently, when France instituted stay-at-home rules to slow the spread of COVID-19, President Emmanuel Macron initially called on people's "individual and collective discipline." When people ignored the request, more than 100,000 police officers were deployed and thousands of fines were issued. People who repeatedly flouted the confinement rules were charged with endangering the lives of others, with a maximum punishment of up to a year in prison and a €15,000 fine. Violations of the lockdown order dropped precipitously ("France Arrests People" 2020, 15; "Lockdown and the Long Haul" 2020).

These are extreme cases, of course, but they lend empirical support to what seems obvious to many people: the threat of punishment is an incentive not to commit crimes, and without it more people would be criminals, and criminals

5 Several examples are given in Andenaes (1974, 3–33).

would commit more crimes. Although offenders and would-be offenders do not use the classic expected utility model, evidence suggests that they do think in terms of gains and losses (Kahneman and Tversky 1979).[6] Coupled with the fact that there are deterrable, would-be criminals, punishment as an institution can be justified by its effects on human behavior.

Consequentialism and statutory penalties (2)

Most critics of consequentialism (including Davis, as I show later) are willing to grant this general point concerning the institution of punishment.[7] Their main objection usually regards "low-level generalizations" – that is, statutory penalties (M. Davis 2009, 85). Davis claims that the social sciences cannot "*quantify* the costs and benefits of punishment enough to defend any empirical preventive theory" (2009, 85). Consequentialists must not only make general, conceptual claims about people's motivation by incentives, but must talk about which incentives deter crime, how much, and whether the costs of inflicting specific punishments on specific classes of criminals are worth the benefits. If there is no reliable empirical data on which to base criminal justice policies and statutory penalties for specific crimes, then we must look to another theory for guidance. Retributivists only have to pair up crimes and punishments on a scale of proportionality that matches the seriousness of a crime with the severity of a punishment. The fight between consequentialists and retributivists, and among different kinds of mixed theorists, is all about this middle ground.

6 An opposing view is voiced by Kleck et al., who say that information about punishment is so obscure that potential criminals cannot perform the typical cost-benefit analysis that we all do in most situations:

> It may therefore be useful to view prospective offenders' responses to punishment levels as characterized by a severely constricted rationality. Although many people are capable of weighing perceived risks and rewards when deciding whether to commit crime, they typically have so little accurate information about key risks and rewards that this capacity for rational decision making remains to a great extent inoperative. (2005, 655; see also von Hirsch 1985, 32)

Their conclusion does not follow from their premises. Prospective offenders' knowledge is not so limited that cost-benefit analyses are impossible. They still have beliefs – some accurate, some inaccurate – about the risk and severity of legal punishments, and that influences their actions. Furthermore, Kleck's argument would not entail that we should abandon consequentialism, only that we should inform people more accurately about the criminal law.

7 For example, von Hirsch, in his defense of retributivism, says the following:

> We are considering here whether deterrence is reason for having *any* system of criminal sanctions at all. For that purpose, our evidentiary requirements are modest: only that (for some offenses, at least) the threat and imposition of punishment induces more compliance than if there were no punishment. We are persuaded that punishment does deter, at least in this minimal sense. (1976, 40)

To evaluate and respond to this objection, it is important to remind ourselves that deterrence (or prevention) is not a simple, homogenous concept. If the purpose of the law is to maintain the social order by, among other things, minimizing crime, then there are different ways to use punishment in order to achieve that end. In addition to restraint (which is easily measurable), punishment may aim at (a) general deterrence and (b) specific deterrence:

a) Punishment deters generally when it causes *potential* criminals to refrain from criminal acts, for fear of being punished.
b) Punishment deters specifically when it causes *actual* criminals to refrain from additional criminal acts because of either fear or reformed character (rehabilitation).

If empirical research can effectively guide us with regard to each of these separate aims, it can reliably inform consequentialist reasoning regarding statutory penalties.

General deterrence (2a)

There are different "levels" of "low-level generalizations" concerning general deterrence, and at each point, there is enough empirical guidance to support consequentialist reasoning. First, with regard to general deterrence at its broadest level, we can do a rough calculation to determine that, in states that attempt to do what is right, punishment promotes the good more effectively than not punishing. The harm that is averted by condemning criminal behavior and deterring potential criminals outweighs the harm that is inflicted on convicted criminals. One way that legal punishment deters is by communicating society's shared standards of approval and disapproval, thus fostering a sense of right and wrong in people and making them respect the law's moral authority (Andenaes 1974, 7–8, 110–28; Robinson and Darley 1997; Robinson 2000; Robinson 2008b, 175–212; Robinson, Barton, and Lister 2014, 314–30). If wrong acts are not censured or are even publicly accepted, then they become more common. On this point, social scientists have little work to do that historians have not already done. Genocides in Nazi Germany from 1938 to 1945, in Cambodia under the Khmer Rouge from 1975 to 1979, in Rwanda under the Hutu-majority government in 1994 – history is full of examples of state-sponsored atrocities that would not have happened (at least in such magnitude) without their being ignored, condoned, or supported by the ruling authorities. At the institutional level, the practicality of consequentialist reasoning is not undermined just because social scientists cannot calculate precisely how many Jews would have lived had the German government defended their natural rights instead of instituting the Nuremberg Laws.

If we get more specific, it becomes clear that contemporary social scientists have provided insight into the factors that increase or decrease punishment's deterrent effects. In fact, criminological research has supported some classic philosophical speculation regarding human motivation. Bentham lists several "circumstances" that affect the calculation of pleasures and pains: intensity, duration, certainty or uncertainty, propinquity or remoteness, fecundity, purity, and extent (1970, ch. IV, §§2–3 [pp. 38–39]; see also ch. XIV, §27 [pp. 173–74]). These variables impact the desirability of a given outcome. One reason why obesity is such a problem is because food that is bad for us often tastes good and the health effects of a poor diet are usually not immediate. We wrongly emphasize short-term benefits over long-term costs. Similarly, the fact that the burden of legal punishment is uncertain (criminals may not get caught or convicted) and remote (punishments do not happen immediately) influences potential criminals' decisions. Occasional and delayed punishment may function like an intermittent reinforcement schedule if criminal behavior more often and more quickly results in getting rewards (i.e., whatever is gained by the crimes). This partial reinforcement pattern can create especially strong misbehavior that is resistant to intervention.

There are ways to make threats more effective in deterring potential criminals, and this insight can guide public policy. For example, Cesare Beccaria says that punishments must be prompt and certain (1995, 48–49, 63–65); and van den Haag (1982) says that punishments ought to be mandated, determinate, and flat. Formal punishments often fail to deter not because punishment does not deter, but because legal punishment is an abstract reality for most offenders. The immediate forces in their daily lives, such as economic desperation, matter more than the remote possibility of legal sanction.

Criminological studies have confirmed that the effectiveness of punishments depends on several factors, including their severity, certainty, and celerity. Steven Levitt (1996) compared states that had court-ordered reductions in sentences with those that did not and found that states with longer statutory sentences had lower crime rates than those who shortened them. This supports the idea that severity has an impact on the deterrent effect of punishment – that is, that increases in the amount of punishment lead to decreases in crime. This study is an outlier, however. Many other studies have challenged the importance of severity, at least on its own. A review of research by Anthony Doob and Cheryl Webster concluded that "sentence severity has no effect on the level of crime in society" – the null hypothesis (2003, 143).

The effectiveness of punishment seems to depend more on its swiftness and certainty. Most contemporary studies of deterrence presuppose the framework posited by Gary Becker (1968), who claims that criminals are subject to the same decision-making forces that all of us are – specifically, that they seek to maximize utility by evaluating marginal costs and benefits. Becker claims that those who are risk-averse are deterred more by a punishment's severity, and those who are risk-acceptant are deterred more by a punishment's certainty. Since criminals have more of a preference for risk than the average citizen, Becker concludes that certainty is more influential than severity.[8] Furthermore, offenders and potential offenders have "limited rationality," meaning that the comparisons and calculations they make are highly subjective and usually less than optimal.

8 For an analysis and evaluation of Becker's approach, see Chalfin and Tahamont (2018).

They are "psychological persons" rather than "economic persons" (Carroll 1978). Certainty and celerity relate to offenders' expectations, so, unlike severity (which is an objective property of punishments), they are epistemically meaningful and more likely to inform their decision-making. Such thinking has been used to justify criminal justice reforms. For example, Washington state's Swift and Certain policy allows community corrections officers to apprehend and incarcerate offenders on their caseloads for up to three days without a judge. The policy has reduced recidivism rates and increased offender participation in treatment programs (Hamilton et al. 2015; Hamilton, Campbell, et al. 2016; Washington State Department of Corrections 2018).

The deterrent impact of these three factors has been tested and evaluated innumerable times.[9] Research is complicated by the fact that severity, certainty, and celerity combine to increase their deterrent effect, beyond what they would achieve individually (Howe and Brandau 1988; see also Mendes 2004).[10] Setting aside the more specific question about which factors are most important for deterring potential criminals – that is a question to be answered by criminologists rather than philosophers – the very idea that punishment can be improved as a deterrent presupposes that it *can* serve as an effective deterrent, if only we focus on the right characteristic or set of characteristics.

9 Well-designed studies that investigate the deterrent effects of severity, certainty, and celerity include: Chambliss (1966) (certainty and severity deter); Gibbs (1968) (certainty deters; severity deters somewhat); Gray and Martin (1969) (certainty and severity deter); Tittle (1969) (certainty deters; severity only affects homicide rates); Logan (1972) (certainty and severity deter); Antunes and Hunt (1973) (certainty and severity deter); Bailey, Martin, and Gray (1974) (certainty deters; severity only affects homicide rates); Tittle and Rowe (1974) (certainty deters when it reaches a "critical level"); Grasmick and Bryjak (1980) (certainty and severity deter); Selke (1983) (celerity deters); Pestello (1984) (celerity affects fear of consequences); Clark (1988) (celerity deters when combined with severity or certainty); Howe and Brandau (1988) (certainty and severity deter; celerity deters somewhat); Klepper and Nagin (1989) (certainty and severity deter); Decker and Kohfeld (1990) (certainty deters; severity does not deter); Farrington, Langan, and Wikström (1994) (certainty deters); Howe and Loftus (1996) (certainty and severity deter; celerity does not deter); von Hirsch et al. (1999) (certainty deters; severity does not deter); Maxwell and Gray (2000) (certainty deters); Mendes and McDonald (2001) (certainty and severity deter); Nagin and Pogarsky (2001) (certainty deters; severity deters somewhat; celerity does not deter); Eide, Rubin, and Shepherd (2006) (certainty deters; severity deters somewhat); Pogarsky (2007) (certainty and severity deter); Nagin (2013) (certainty deters; severity deters somewhat); and Zettler et al. (2015) (celerity deters). U.S. courts have also recognized that a punishment's deterrent effects depend on its certainty and celerity. See *United States v. Panico*, 308 F.2d 125 (2nd Cir. 1962), 128; and *Harmelin v. Michigan*, 501 U.S. 957 (1991), 989. Some studies also indicate that the effects of certainty vary depending on the crime: for example, see Chambliss (1967), Silberman (1976), and Geerken and Gove (1977). Critical studies claiming that certainty, severity, and celerity have no causal deterrent impact or only a weak association include Paternoster (1987), Pratt et al. (2006), and Pratt and Turanovic (2018).

10 Mendes (2004) claims that, in the aggregate, we cannot say that criminals are more risk-acceptant, and therefore we cannot say whether certainty deters more effectively than severity (as Becker would have us believe).

The different factors that are related to a punishment's deterrent effect (severity, certainty, and celerity) explain the success of so-called truth-in-sentencing (TIS) laws. TIS legislation reduces or eliminates parole so that offenders are incarcerated for the period of time to which they have been sentenced (or some substantial portion of that time, e.g., 85 percent of maximum), rather than being released earlier. For example, if someone is sentenced to five to ten years for burglary and aggravated assault, they would not be eligible for release until after five years. Prior to TIS, they may have been released after four years. TIS legislation is correlated with a decrease in both violent and property crimes (Long 2018; Li and Long 2018; see also Shepherd 2002). One reason is that criminals are incapacitated for longer, but there is also a deterrent effect. The sentence is not only longer (more severe) than prior to TIS, but offenders also have clearer expectations regarding the extent of their punishments (more certain),[11] as opposed to a system where they may or may not be released early, depending on parole boards' recommendations. Of course, this alone does not justify TIS, since keeping people in prison longer has other, negative effects as well, mostly associated with mass incarceration. But it gives us a *prima facie* reason to support TIS laws on consequentialist grounds.

Studies such as the ones that examine severity, certainty, and celerity represent more specific and rigorous investigations of the connections between incentives and behaviors that, in many cases, have already been revealed historically in actual crime rates and policies. When critics of utilitarianism argued that individuals could not do a utilitarian calculation before every action, John Stuart Mill responded that human beings have been testing different kinds of actions for the whole of human history: acting in different ways, experiencing the consequences, and establishing social norms that tend to produce the best outcomes (2001, 23–24). Similarly, different countries and communities, in having different punishments for different classes of crimes, have been testing their effectiveness in modifying behavior and preserving the public order. Social scientists do not need to develop complex hypothetical scenarios or imagine a "counterfactual world in which we would know much more than we do know here," as Davis demands of them (2009, 84). Since societies have instituted different punishments and approached criminal activity in different ways, we can chronicle the actual effects of these different policies and do a comparative analysis of their relative effectiveness. For example, comparisons of violent crime rates in countries with and without the death penalty, socioeconomically and geographically similar states with and without the death penalty, bordering counties in neighboring states with and without

11 When criminologists talk about certainty, they usually mean how likely it is that someone will be caught and punished. I am shifting the meaning a bit here. "Certainty" in this context refers to how confident a person is that they will receive a longer punishment. Absent TIS laws, it is uncertain how long the offender will remain in prison because of the possibility of early parole. It is unclear whether Bentham would call the effect of TIS laws greater certainty or longer duration, but in any event, it does make offenders want to avoid the punishment more (1970, ch. VI, §§1–3 [pp. 38–39]).

the death penalty, the same state before and after prohibition, and the same state before and after highly publicized executions all show that the death penalty does not deter more than life in prison. Although this does not have the scientific rigor of most criminological research – there are many confounding factors, for example – our experience with different approaches to punishment, historically, is in many cases enough to inform public policy. Is it more likely that the death penalty does not deter more than life in prison *or* that it does deter but, in every one of these cases, there are other socioeconomic factors that negate the effect? Given the evidence we have, it is more reasonable to believe that the death penalty does not deter more than life in prison and that, therefore, it is unnecessarily severe.

Davis says that consequentialism needs to justify even more specific (or even "lower-level") generalizations regarding crimes and punishments if it is to validate its appeal to deterrence. To be action-guiding, we must have reasons, in terms of consequences, why, for example, a particular crime should get three years rather than two years in prison, or vice versa (1992, 75). One thing to note at the outset is that Davis focuses almost exclusively on severity. The fact that "the rate of crime certainly does not respond … inversely to severity of statutory penalty" is not a reason to reject social science or consequentialism as a whole, but only the belief, disproven by criminology itself, that the crime rate is correlated with severity alone (M. Davis 1992, 5). More importantly, however, Davis is asking something of criminology that it does not need to do. His directive would seem like an impossible task if we were founding a new society and had to establish punishments from the ground up, based on nothing but findings of the social sciences. However, we exist in communities that have established crimes and punishments, and our task at this point is to evaluate and improve them. That is, we must determine whether existing penological practices are functioning well and figure out how to make them more effective.

No existing society is beginning from a state of nature. The consequentialist does not need to discover the ideal system of criminal justice and have a foolproof plan for how to implement it. Instead, there has to be a standard of success, a way to measure the outcomes of different policies, and a method for making things better. In 1967, the President's Crime Commission described the situation like this:

> Information about the consequences of actions by the criminal justice system is essential for improving those actions. In this sense the criminal justice system may be compared to a blind man far down the side of a mountain. If he wants to reach the top, he first must move. And it matters little whether his first move is up or down because any movement with subsequent evaluation will tell him which way is up. A step by step process of experimenting, evaluating, and modifying must be undertaken. Both innovation and the subsequent evaluation of its consequences are essential to climbing up. (Institute for Defense Analyses 1967, 2)

Evaluating punitive practices is always comparative. Colorado's experiment with community-based drug treatment programs, for example, does not need to be optimal compared to any possible option, but only better than the other live alternatives, in order to produce marginal utility (Przybylski 2009).

Davis's alternative is no better than this. The retributive approach to crime is comparative – how much of a burden does one crime deserve compared to another? – and the answer to this question is settled by an appeal to intuition. The fact that consequentialism is similarly comparative – how effective is one policy compared to another? – is not an objection to it, especially since such a policy decision can be based on empirical evidence rather than intuition. The social sciences have established processes for "experimenting, evaluating, and modifying" existing penological practices. And, when existing social scientific methods are unreliable, there are processes to improve them within the disciplines themselves.

As noted earlier, certainty and celerity have more of an impact on a punishment's effectiveness than severity alone; severity has an impact in conjunction with the other two factors. And if increased penalties do nothing to decrease the crime rate, then, even if we cannot isolate that from all other predictors of crime, it would be reasonable to assume, barring any dramatic demographic or socioeconomic changes, that increased penalties would be excessive. Simply adding an additional year to a statutory penalty (three years instead of two) would, on its own, have little if any additional deterrent effect. If we are unhappy with the occurrence rate of a particular crime, perhaps investment should be made in targeted enforcement (e.g., increased police) and a more efficient plea or trial process rather than simply tacking additional years onto a statutory minimum sentence – increasing certainty and celerity rather than severity.

Another thing that criminologists have discovered is that formal punishments such as imprisonment have less of an impact on criminal behaviors than informal social controls such as loss of friendship. In fact, many criminologists have developed models to explain how less coercive institutions (private controls within intimate groups such as families and friends, and parochial controls within neighborhood associations) act in conjunction with the threat of legal punishment (public controls by the state) to reduce crime and disorder (Taylor and Covington 1988; Bursik and Grasmik 1993; Taylor 1996; Sampson, Raudenbush, and Earls 1997; Rose and Clear 1998; Taylor 1999). Along with the threat of legal punishment, the expression of disapproval by the community (e.g., the stigma of incarceration, shame, and embarrassment) has been shown to have an additive effect on deterring criminal behavior (Grasmick and Green 1980; Williams and Hawkins 1986; Grasmick and Bursik 1990; Apel and DeWitt 2018; Wilcox and Cullen 2018). This is one reason why, as I argue in Chapter 13, introducing restorative practices in addition to traditional punishments may be valuable. More work needs to be done to figure out how the state can use these informal mechanisms to achieve its ends, and also how legal and social sanctions impact one another,[12] but criminology does give us direction as we develop public policy

12 Some researchers tend to assume that we ought to focus on *either* legal constraints *or* social constraints, but Morris and Zimring remind us that they are not isolated from one another:

– instead of just talking about severity (e.g., two- versus three-years' imprisonment), as retributivists tend to do.

Evidence or intuition?

There are better and worse criminological studies, their scientific methods are subject to public and professional scrutiny, and other researchers can improve upon those methods to arrive at more justified conclusions.[13] One can question whether a particular study correctly isolates the relevant predictor, and we can revise the study in the future. The transparency of experimental design allows us to develop improved methods, which leads to more reliable results.[14]

By contrast, how would we settle a disagreement between two people – say, a "law-and-order Republican" and a "bleeding-heart Democrat" – one of whom thinks that three years is "fair" or "deserved," while the other thinks that two years is sufficient? What would an improved methodology look like when we are trying to determine desert or fairness? Criminology helps to discover what effectively motivates people. It turns our attention to the certainty and celerity of punishment, as well as informal methods of social control. John Barnes does a good job of expressing both the limitations and promise of social scientific methodology:

> It seems to me important that we should not abandon the search for a fuller understanding of the nature of order and disorder in social life merely because the natural science paradigm used by the early positivists and by most later mainline sociologists has proved to be inadequate and largely unrewarding. Without some effort to adapt the rigorous methods of scientific testing and validation to the more difficult field of social life, we have to fall back on traditional wisdom, common sense and rules of thumb, on social technology, as it were, rather than social science. (1990, 191)

Retributivists' almost exclusive focus on the severity of punishments is an example of "traditional wisdom, common sense and rules of thumb." In light of the evidence, retributivism, with its focus on severity, seems to be after a red herring, at least when it comes to public policy. But retributivists would never be able to discover that on their own because they appeal to intuition rather than empirical evidence, and intuition is not testable in principle.

"it would be hard to deny that there is a relationship between the precepts of the criminal-justice system and the values supported by less formal social sanctions, or to deny that the former may influence the latter" (1969, 139). Legal punishment influences public values through its expressive function, for example.

13 One example of what this kind of professional self-scrutiny looks like is Farrington, Ohlin, and Wilson (1986). The authors examine past experimental research, assess the current state of the discipline, and suggest a new methodology using longitudinal-experimental studies.

14 Nagin (1998, 2013) provides valuable overviews of how the study of deterrence has improved and the ways it has yet to improve.

The question is not what is right unconditionally and ahistorically, but how we can best make progress in improving our own imperfect system of crimes and punishments. Criminology does not give a definitive answer to every question, but it can guide discussion about criminal justice reform in productive ways. Again, the death penalty is a good example of how useful the social sciences can be, in a consequentialist framework, compared to retributivism. Questions about whether a murderer deserves to die are amorphous. How would one go about critiquing the common view, asserted as a kind of basic premise by van den Haag and others, that murderers deserve to die? Although this question is perfectly sensible within a criminal trial process that allows the death penalty as an option, voicing differing opinions on what is deserved leads to a stalemate when it comes to public policy. One person says that murderers deserve the death penalty, another person says that life in prison is sufficient ... and then what? Instead of simply stating our competing intuitions, policy decisions should be data-driven, and the decision about whether to have capital punishment should be based on its deterrent effect and its cost-effectiveness. This is a more promising approach when it comes to deciding together how best to accomplish our social aims. It is exactly why a growing number of Democratic and Republican officials in the U.S. are united in their opposition to the death penalty: they are convinced by studies showing that it is not a greater deterrent than life in prison and that the extra money it costs to pursue a capital case could be better spent on more effective crime-prevention efforts (McCausland 2018; Carlisle 2019). Appealing to facts discovered by the social sciences helps us to build consensus rather than reinforcing a political divide based on different assessments of desert.

Increasingly, state legislatures in the U.S. are drawing on social science research to make data-driven decisions. For example, regarding sentencing, eighteen states now require specialized corrections impact statements when the legislature considers changing criminal statutes and punishments. Twenty-five states and the District of Columbia have sentencing commissions that oversee sentencing practices and conduct research to analyze program performance. They look at recidivism rates and operational costs to evaluate programs and make recommendations to the legislature. And a public-private partnership between the U.S. Department of Justice and the Pew Charitable Trusts has helped more than half of U.S. states by collecting data regarding prison populations and cost of imprisonment, developing initiatives to address recidivism and prison population growth, and measuring the impact of policy changes.[15] Efforts such as these have led to widespread sentencing reform (Lawrence 2015, 3).

15 Although I and most criminologists focus on recidivism as the measure of success, there are other measures that could be considered. Crime prevention could be measured by the number of criminal events, criminal offenders, the amount of harm prevented, the number of victims, or the increase or decrease of risk factors or protective factors for crime (Sherman 1997, 2–3). Duff and Garland suggest that we could also measure "rehabilitative effects in more partial, qualitative ways – such as a slowing down in subsequent rates of offending, or a

Public institutions are tasked with furthering our collective aims. The difficulty of discovering the way forward is no reason to abandon that basic conception of what these institutions do. As an analogy, consider the Federal Reserve's decision to raise or lower interest rates. The reasons to do so include regulating inflation and avoiding recession. Given all the macroeconomic factors at work, it is difficult to know exactly how to do that. But that does not mean that the Chair of the Federal Reserve should give up on the science of economics, become a Kantian, and suddenly start lending money based on desert. Instead, they try to get better data, perform better economic analyses, and, if necessary, hire better economists.

It seems strange that a group of philosophers working in this field would give up on consequentialism and become retributivists in large part because criminology has not yet perfected its methods. Apparently, because we do not know how best to use punishment to maintain the social order, punishment does not need to maintain the social order. It would be like saying that the principle of utility makes sense, but because we cannot perform a utilitarian calculus with as much accuracy as we would like, then we should just be relativists; or that doctors in the nineteenth century should have gone back to talking about the four humors just because they did not fully understand the germ theory of disease. With regard to punishment in particular, the (current) imprecision of criminology is no reason to abandon empirical research in favor of an (often question-begging) appeal to moral intuition. Why would that do a better job of justifying punishment, both as an institution and with regard to statutory penalties, than peer-reviewable studies of human behavior? The consequentialist's methodology is subject to public scrutiny, evaluation, and improvement in a way that the retributivist's appeal to "commonsense" intuitions is not, no matter how deeply held those intuitions are. This is not to say that intuitions should play no role in philosophical arguments – they should. But intuition should be used sparingly, and its comparative advantages over social scientific research should not be exaggerated.

As I noted in Chapter 6, permissibility (in this case, the permissibility of punishment) is not directly related to what is objectively justifiable ("the objective 'ought'") but what principles we have reason to accept (Scanlon 2008, 47–52; see also Brandt 1963; Railton 1984; and Kagan 1998, 65). We are not morally required to choose the best alternative to further our collective ends, but to choose what we reasonably believe to be the best alternative based on the most reliable data we have. Consequentialism is consistent with the general claim that we are motivated by incentives, which everyone accepts; research has given us some indication of which incentives are most effective, and the factors that increase and decrease their effectiveness; and we can, in many cases, have reasonable assurance, based on historical and experimental evidence, about which policies are comparatively more effective than others. Where the research is unclear, we can improve it. Under the circumstances, criminology gives us a relatively

decrease in the seriousness of subsequent crimes, or even collateral improvements in aspects of the offender's conduct and life-style" (1994, 24).

reliable method for discovering consequences, and consequentialism can be action-guiding regarding general deterrence.

Specific deterrence (2b)

Much of what I said about general deterrence also applies to specific deterrence. In fact, research on rehabilitation has perhaps made even more dramatic strides in the last four decades. Risk-assessment instrumentation has evolved in a way that many retributivists who object to consequentialism on methodological grounds still fail to recognize.

Misinterpretations of meta-analysis, specifically, have had an outsized impact on philosophers' overall assessment of criminology. Martinson's objections to what he thought was meta-analysis in his famous 1974 article "What Works?" (the answer: nothing works) provided a pathway for the destruction of the rehabilitative model (see also Lipton, Martinson, and Wilks 1975; and Brody 1976).[16] In *Doing Justice* (1976), for example, von Hirsch says that the failure of rehabilitative programs is one of the reasons why he adopts retribution over rehabilitation (xxxvii–xxxix).[17] But Martinson would later recognize the limits of his 1974 study, modify his analysis, and claim that action-guiding work could be done, especially regarding rehabilitation, so long as we have a clear understanding of what criminologists are doing:

> it was misleading to judge criminal justice on the basis of these evaluation studies. ... [Martinson's earlier work] focused on summarizing evaluation research which purported to uncover *causality*; in our current study we reject this perspective as premature and focus on uncovering *patterns* which can be of use to policymakers in choosing among available treatment programs. These patterns are sufficiently consistent to oblige me to modify my previous conclusion. (Martinson 1979, 244n6, 253; see also Wilks and Martinson 1976; and Martinson and Wilks 1977)[18]

16 The title of Martinson's work was recently echoed in Schell-Busey et al., "What Works? A Systematic Review of Corporate Crime Deterrence" (2016). However, Schell-Busey concludes that there *are* effective corporate crime deterrence strategies, including regulatory policies such as inspections and education, and multiple intervention strategies that can be used in conjunction with one another. Thus, Martinson's and Schell-Busey's meta-analyses reach opposite conclusions.

17 To be precise, von Hirsch argues that the threat of punishment serves a general deterrent purpose but that, once a crime has been committed, the offender ought to be punished because they deserve it. Rehabilitation and incapacitation, as justifications of punishment, would not respect the criminal's fundamental rights. So, general deterrence is the general justifying aim of punishment, but retribution justifies the distribution of punishments (von Hirsch 1976, 35–55). Von Hirsch, then, is a mixed theorist.

18 In the 1979 article, Martinson says that we ought to be cautious in undertaking sentencing reform, but that we can identify, empirically, the different conditions under which treatment programs are beneficial, neutral, or detrimental. He explicitly rejects his earlier

Methodologies in correctional management have become even more sophisticated since Martinson's reversal, with quasi-experimental approaches that can go beyond his modest, but still action-guiding, conclusions.

Unfortunately, the same thematic undertones of Martinson's 1974 dismissal of rehabilitation programs can be found in Forde's (2018) more recent critique of forensic psychology.[19] Forde assumes that meta-analyses are simply large-scale summaries of previous research. He argues that this is a problem because combining the findings of many weak or less robust studies does not somehow produce a robust outcome. However, what real meta-analysis does is calculate a grandiose effect size based on an amalgamation of the data, including the samples. That is, it uses numerous studies to enlarge the sample size and strengthen the evidence for their shared conclusion. Standards for including a study in a meta-analysis are also far more selective than Forde suggests. Criminologists rely heavily (perhaps exclusively) on the Maryland Scientific Methods Scale (SMS) to assess the robustness of a study for inclusion in a meta-analysis (Farrington et al. 2002). The SMS requires studies to be at least quasi-experimental, with comparable units of analysis to meet the cutoff. Along with meeting the standard for rigor set by the SMS, studies included in a meta-analysis must present raw (unstandardized) effect sizes in order for researchers to use those numbers in the calculation of the grandiose effect size.[20] Such a methodology increases the predictive power of the models rather than masking weak outcomes, as Forde says it does, and it can come closer to demonstrating causal relationships between rehabilitative programs and recidivism.

While Forde is right to criticize some older research for flawed study designs and more wide-reaching conclusions than the evidence warrants, he also attacks criminology for not being able to do things that researchers never claimed to be able to do. Efforts in the discipline are oriented into three general areas: theory, policy, and practice. Research regarding punishment policies is mostly aligned with the positivistic approach to social science. It relies on large samples and advanced group-matching to demonstrate cause and effect. Forde is critical of such studies because they lack classic experimental design. However, limitations in quasi-experimental designs do not completely diminish the inferences of those

---

conclusion that treatment had no effect. Nonetheless, Michael Davis describes the 1979 piece only as "a useful short discussion of these empirical failures," which is misleading (2009, 85n25).

19 Roger Schaefer assisted me with the following three paragraphs, including some of the specific phrasing.

20 When effect sizes are standardized, they allow for comparison between variables in a given study, which is often done by transforming the coefficient into standard deviation units. Such standardized measures cannot be used in meta-analysis, however, because the standardizing is unique to that sample/study. Most studies that employ inferential analyses will report both the standardized and unstandardized coefficients – yet most discussions will emphasize those standardized measures. This is done for an important reason: it allows for comparison across variables (reported as Beta in ordinary least squares [OLS] regression). In the event that a study only provides standardized effect sizes, it cannot be used in meta-analysis.

studies so long as the data and analysis are properly contextualized. In the past, criminologists had assumed universality of contextual factors – for example, doing a study of an urban population and assuming that the results could inform policy in rural areas – even though two populations may not be comparable. Martinson (1979) is especially critical of studies for failing to recognize that disparities in outcomes may be due to the fact that offenders are differently situated (low-risk or high-risk, juvenile or adult, etc.). But criminologists are addressing this.

The evidence-based movement in criminology in general and penology in particular has renewed efforts to improve inferential or prediction modeling with regard to rehabilitative programs. While the actuarial approach to correctional discourse did not become mainstream until the late 1990s, the foundation for such advancements was developed in the 1980s and first formalized in 1990 by Donald Andrews and James Bonta (Andrews, Bonta, and Hoge 1990; see also Bonta and Andrews 2007; and Bonta and Andrews 2016). Guided by their risk-needs-responsivity (RNR) model, correctional systems embraced the use of actuarial assessment instruments to predict an offender's likelihood of recidivating.[21] Prior to the inclusion of statistically derived instruments, assessments of risk and/or needs were based on clinical judgment, which became known as first-generation risk assessment. While many clinicians favor this method of assessment, it has routinely been shown that statistical models provide a more reliable prediction of recidivistic outcomes (Cullen and Johnson 2017). Subsequent generations of risk-assessment instruments followed an evolutionary path that began with the measurement of static risk factors such as prior offenses and age (second generation), followed by the inclusion of dynamic needs factors such as antisocial attitudes and unemployment (third generation), while the most robust instruments assess risk and needs, and are gender responsive (Hamilton, Kigerl, et al. 2016; Hamilton et al. 2020). These instruments utilize the most reliable scientific procedures for both construction and validation, and they are tailored based on jurisdictionally defined outcomes, making these the most robust of the current fourth-generation assessment instruments.[22]

The U.S. Department of Justice has committed itself to instituting "evidence-based rehabilitation strategies" in order "to reduce recidivism and strengthen

21 The RNR model includes three principles:

> 1) the *risk principle* asserts that criminal behaviour can be reliably predicted and that treatment should focus on the higher risk offenders; 2) the *need principle* highlights the importance of criminogenic needs in the design and delivery of treatment; and 3) the *responsivity principle* describes how the treatment should be provided. (Bonta and Andrews 2007, par. 1)

22 That Davis has overlooked these developments in criminology is clear from the fact that, when he talks about the "empirical failures" of the social sciences in his 2009 article, he refers to Barnes's collection of essays, *Models and Interpretations* (1990), as "a fuller, more nuanced, and more recent discussion of what the social sciences can do now" (M. Davis 2009, 85n25) – even though the essays where Barnes talks most explicitly about the methodology of the social sciences were originally published in 1967 (ch. 8), 1970 (ch. 11), and 1971 (ch. 9).

public safety" (2017, par. 1). Rigorously designed criminological studies are shaping public policy to improve rehabilitative outcomes, despite Martinson's initial skepticism. To take just one set of examples, researchers have found that inmates who participate in correctional education programs are 43 percent less likely to be reincarcerated than those who do not (Davis et al. 2013; see also Drake, Aos, and Miller 2009). On the basis of this and other evidence, states have instituted vocational, educational, and behavioral programs (to address dynamic needs) that are rigorously monitored and assessed to determine their effects on recidivism. Many such programs have been shown to be more beneficial for criminals and better at lowering crime rates than prison alone (see, e.g., Gaes et al. 1999; Wilson, Gallagher, and MacKenzie 2000, Steurer and Smith 2003; Mitchell, Wilson, and MacKenzie 2007; and Przybylski 2009). For example, Washington state administers the Correctional Industries (CI) offender work program, a vocational and cognitive behavioral program that allows inmates to learn technical skills that make them more employable and "soft skills" that help them interact positively with others. An evaluation of the program found that CI participants were significantly less likely than non-CI participants to commit a new crime leading to a conviction and significantly more likely to have a legal source of income and remain in the community (Lutze, Drapela, and Schaefer 2015). In an improvement over earlier research designs, the researchers did not simply compare the two groups (CI and non-CI), but used propensity score matching to balance the differences between the groups on all relevant pre-intervention characteristics – that is, they have addressed Martinson's concern about class disparities.

In light of the extensive research done by social scientists and the resulting development of actionable rehabilitative strategies, Martinson, Forde, and Davis wrongly dismiss the promise of consequentialist reasoning based on criminological research. Criminology has progressed significantly since philosophers largely abandoned it in the 1970s. There is a way forward for consequentialism that is not available to alternative positions such as desert theory or fair-play theory. As criminological methods improve, we will get an even clearer picture of how to reduce crime.

Example: Punitive versus rehabilitative drug treatment

The treatment of nonviolent drug offenders is another example of how criminology can be action-guiding when it comes to specific deterrence. In the United States, there were about 1,841,200 state and local arrests for drug abuse violations in 2007, four-fifths of which were for simple possession. In the twenty-year period from 1987 to 2007, drug arrests increased from 7.4 percent of all arrests to 13 percent of all arrests (Bureau of Justice Statistics 2020). There was also a fourfold increase in the percentage of drug offenders who were sentenced to prison rather than having their cases dismissed or being sentenced to community service or probation (M. Alexander 2012, 60). Despite the increase in number and severity of punishments, the punitive approach to drug crimes has not reduced overall drug use, which has increased from 8.3 percent of the population in 2002 to 10.6 percent of the population in 2016 (Substance Abuse and Mental Health Services Administration 2017).

The punitive approach to drug possession in the United States is in contrast to the way that many other Western democracies deal with substance abuse. Portugal is a prime example. In 2001, Portugal decriminalized the possession of all drugs for personal use. Instead of a criminal violation, drug possession is an administrative violation, and users are summoned to appear before a Commission for the Dissuasion of Drug Addiction:

> Rather than being arrested, those caught with a personal supply might be given a warning, a small fine, or told to appear before a local commission – a doctor, a lawyer and a social worker – about treatment, harm reduction, and the support services that were available to them. (Ferreira 2017, par. 6)

This health-centered, nonpunitive approach to drug dependency has, along with other social shifts, had many well-documented positive consequences, such as a drop in drug use over all measures, including those most indicative of drug use trends (drug use among people aged 15–24, past-year and past-month drug use among the general population, continuation of drug use, etc.); a large drop in new cases of HIV among those who inject drugs; a substantial decrease in deaths due to drug use; and a much lower proportion of drug-related offenders in prison (Transform Drug Policy Foundation 2018). Several European countries have also established supervised drug consumption rooms, which "primarily aim to reduce the acute risks of disease transmission through unhygienic injecting, prevent drug-related overdose deaths and connect high-risk drug users with addiction treatment and other health and social services" (European Monitoring Centre 2018, 1). These have led to a reduction in risky behaviors that increase HIV transmission and overdoses, a reduction in drug-related deaths, and increased enrollment in detoxification and drug dependence treatment (European Monitoring Centre 2018; see also Belackova and Salmon 2017).

The United States has slowly begun to move in a more European direction. For example, despite increased prison sentences for simple drug possession and use, some counties have established drug courts, which now operate in all fifty states. County governments work with community organizations to provide treatment for drug users and to monitor their progress with frequent drug testing, all with rehabilitation as their aim. This method of dealing with drug addiction in the U.S. has been shown to reduce rates of recidivism substantially more than prison (Roman, Townsend, and Bhati 2003; Carey et al. 2006). For example, Colorado's community-based treatment programs for low-level drug offenders are more cost-effective and avoid some of the major problems associated with incarceration, the latter of which has lower rates of deterrence (higher rates of continued drug use upon release) than treatment (Przybylski 2009). New York's Family Justice program uses informal networks to monitor offenders and reintegrate them into the community – family and friends who support ex-prisoners' drug treatment – thus providing private reinforcement of social norms, an effective strategy for behavior modification (Shapiro and Schwartz 2001; see also Liddle and Dakof 1995). Evidence-based strategies are being used by lawmakers to devise policies that are more effective than merely increasing the severity of punishments. Critics of consequentialism decry the therapy model that, they say, does not fully respect offenders' personhood. But helping drug offenders to overcome their addictions and reintegrate into the community shows a healthier respect for their ability to live freely than incarcerating them and expecting them to be rearrested again and again for drug possession.

This is just one example of a class of crimes (low-level drug offenses) and a type of criminal (nonviolent offenders who possess and use illegal drugs) for which social scientists can generate reliable data regarding the relative effectiveness of different interventions. Martinson and Forde are dismissive of correlational studies, but criminologists now use better techniques to determine the effectiveness of different approaches by controlling for confounding predictors in different jurisdictions. That is, criminologists can compare different groups receiving different treatments in different communities without simply ignoring other (e.g., socioeconomic) factors that affect deterrence. By using advanced group-matching for comparative analyses, criminologists are able to establish probabilistic causal claims about groups of offenders and potential offenders. Such research has been shaping public policies for the better.

Do retributivists also depend on the social sciences?

The two-tiered model justifies the institution of punishment and statutory penalties based on their consequences. Davis and others object that the required calculations and predictions regarding deterrence and rehabilitation cannot be done. In the absence of a reliable social scientific methodology for determining the comparative costs and benefits of different punishments, we ought to abandon consequentialism entirely – or at least that is the usual argument. In fact, however, only a specific kind of desert theory is a real alternative to consequentialism. Most theories, including most retributivist theories, rely in part on a calculation of consequences, in spite of their objections.

Desert theorists could claim that the guilt of the offender is either necessary or sufficient to justify punishment. If guilt is sufficient to justify punishment, then that means that punishment would be positively justified on that basis. But that by itself does not entail that the punishment is justified, all things considered. For it to be justified, all things considered, then either giving someone what they deserve must be the only value – the only thing worth doing – or fulfilling the obligation to give someone what they deserve must be more important, comparatively speaking, than other, competing obligations. In other words, following Lawrence Alexander's (1980) taxonomy, there are three possible versions of retributivism:

1) Weak retributivism, which is the view that desert is only a necessary condition to justify punishment;

2) Moderate retributivism, which is the view that desert is a necessary and sufficient condition to justify punishment, and we *may* punish the deserving just because they deserve it; and
3) Extreme retributivism, which is the view that desert is a necessary and sufficient condition to justify punishment, and we *must* punish the deserving just because they deserve it.[23]

Consequences are relevant in determining what to do for both weak and moderate retributivism, which are the most commonly defended versions of the theory.

Few people hold that giving someone what they deserve is the *only* valuable thing we can do, such that there are no other values that compete with it (extreme retributivism). At some points, Immanuel Kant seems to defend this position, such as when he says that "the law of punishment is a categorical imperative" (1996b, 6:331), that we must execute someone even if it serves no social purpose (6:333), and that "if justice goes, there is no longer any value in human being's living on the earth" (6:331–32). G. W. F. Hegel likewise says that the state must punish offenders or else it would be condoning criminal action: "it would be impossible for society to leave a crime unpunished – since the crime would then be posited as right" (1991, §218 [p. 251]). This is a hard position to defend. The proponent of extreme retributivism would have to say not only that innocent people should never be punished – which makes sense even if guilt is only a necessary condition of punishment – but that guilty people should *always* be punished, even if doing so would be hugely socially detrimental. On this view, we ought to execute murderers even if the money spent on capital trials would bankrupt the government, precipitate its collapse, and lead to anarchy – and more murders.

Again, it is difficult to justify such a singular focus on desert. Even Kant talks about the deterrent purpose of punishment and the "pragmatic" functions that it serves for the state (1997, 27:286). Although only the guilty can be punished, and punished because they are guilty – guilt is necessary and sufficient for punishment – that does not rule out additional aims. In Kantian terms, the guilty can be used as a means, but not merely as a means. This is consistent with a mixed view such as mine, according to which judges can only punish the guilty, even though the institution of punishment, collectively, promotes the common good.

A retributivist could claim that desert is a sufficient reason to punish someone (moderate retributivism) without being committed to the idea that all criminals must be punished, and punished in proportion to their degree of guilt. On one version of this view (though, again, one that few people would hold), there is only one kind of value: justice. However, even that one value imposes different kinds of obligations on us. There are competing justice claims and we have to weigh them against one another in order to determine the strongest obligation. Under the duty of justice, we ought to inflict just suffering and prevent or correct unjust suffering. We have an obligation to punish the guilty, but we also have

23 I discuss these versions of retributivism in more detail in the Introduction.

an obligation to defend the innocent, and sometimes those obligations can conflict. If there are two punishments, one of which is deserved and one of which is less than what is deserved, but the less severe punishment actually deters better, then the less severe punishment may do a better job overall of achieving justice because it would prevent more undeserved suffering. For example, someone who is addicted to drugs and has burglarized homes to feed their habit may deserve more prison time. But if drug treatment and a more restorative approach would effectively rehabilitate the offender, thus preventing future burglaries, then the aim of justice could be best achieved – less deserved suffering for the offender, but less undeserved suffering for potential future crime victims – by giving the offender a punishment that, strictly speaking, is less than perfectly just. To determine this, however, we need to measure and compare the deterrent and rehabilitative effects of different interventions.

This is a version of W. D. Ross's (2002) duty-based approach: we ought to give people what they deserve, but we also have other duties that may, in different situations, be more pressing.[24] Michael Moore, for instance, defends a form of retributivism according to which we have a *prima facie* reason to punish moral violations, rather than desert being necessary or sufficient for punishment (1997, 189–229, 403–19). Desert gives us a positive reason to punish people, but we have positive reasons to do other things as well – and those duties may conflict. Again, the death penalty is a good example. There are different claims that the duty of justice can make on us. A criminal may have a right to be punished, but people may also have a right to healthcare or education. We ought to fulfill all these obligations. If we can only accomplish some of them, given our limited resources, then we have to weigh those different obligations against one another. For example, we ought to punish offenders and we ought to provide good education for our children. If giving murderers exactly what they deserve depletes the state's budget, then the right thing to do may be to divert that money away from capital punishment in order to meet the obligations to our children. We must know the cost of the death penalty, the amount of resources we have, and how those resources can be most effectively deployed before we can know what to do, even under most versions of retributivism.

What becomes apparent here is that, if we are not exclusively concerned with punishment as our only moral obligation, then we must consider consequences, either indirectly or directly. Kant pointed out that we cannot rationally will an end without also willing the means to that end, and that willing something is "summoning of all means insofar as they are in our control" (1996a, 4:394). The means we have at our disposal and their effectiveness at accomplishing the aims of justice are questions that cannot be answered *a priori*. Perhaps murderers deserve to die and drug offenders should go to prison. Potential crime

24 On the difference between what we ought to do (fulfill all our *prima facie* duties) and what is right to do (fulfill the most pressing *prima facie* duty, or our duty proper), see Ross (2002), 1–47.

victims do not deserve to suffer. Children deserve an education and, perhaps, they deserve healthcare, clean air, and clean water – all of which place demands on our resources. Is sending murderers to prison for life and placing drug offenders in treatment programs good enough in terms of justice? Does it censure them enough (von Hirsch 1993) or adequately correct the unfair advantage they took (M. Davis 1996)? How do we correct – or, more properly speaking, how much do we correct – for that unfair disadvantage while also fulfilling the aims of distributive justice by correcting for the unfair disadvantage that poor children have when they get substandard education or polluted drinking water? These questions only arise when we realize how much more executions cost and we can assess the social benefit of capital punishment against the social benefit of life in prison for them plus clean water for the poor. None of this implies that retributivists are closet consequentialists. We have a duty to promote justice, which is good in itself. It does mean, however, that we are always comparing options, even if all we want to do is achieve justice as best we can. The question of how to use our resources most effectively as means to the end of justice is, in part, an empirical question.

Not all retributivists are extreme retributivists, who say that we ought to punish the guilty, come what may. More common is the idea that desert is merely a necessary condition for punishment (weak or negative retributivism), with retribution as a side constraint. On this view, we should not punish the innocent, but whether to punish the guilty is an open question, as is whether to punish them in ways that are equivalent to their degrees of guilt. The reason for the relative popularity of this version of retributivism is that few desert theorists are axiologically monistic. That is, like Ross, they believe that justice is only one value among others, and that we sometimes need to sacrifice justice for other goods. With innocents, that is a particularly high bar, but it is not unreachable. Moore says that, despite his nonconsequentialist moral views, torturing, killing, and (presumably) punishing an innocent person would be justified to avert catastrophic consequences (1997, 719–26). The bar is lower for proposals not to punish the guilty, or not to punish them quite as much as they deserve. It may be incumbent on us to punish a person who deserves it, even though it serves no social value, such as the Nazi who is discovered living peacefully on a desert island (Kleinig 1973, 67). But if appropriately punishing the guilty has a negative social value, the question of what to do is more complicated. For example, Jeffrey Reiman agrees that murderers deserve to die: "In my view, the death penalty is a just punishment for murder because the *lex talionis*, an eye for an eye, and so on, is just" (1985, 119). But he concludes that we should not kill murderers because doing so would be uncivilized, and there is value to civilization that overrides the value of giving them precisely what they deserve (134–42). A proportionally severe punishment – life in prison – is enough. Likewise, Davis says that we should rule out punishments that are "inhumane" or "morally shocking," even if they are deserved (1992, 78–79). All retributivists need to do is grant that we have other obligations, in addition to imposing harm on the deserving, in order for research on costs and benefits to be relevant to their decision-making. Despite concerns over the reliability of the social sciences, most retributivists cannot leave criminology behind.

Conclusion

The turn to retributivism, just when criminology was made aware of its shortcomings and set out to improve its methodology, reflects a more general tendency among philosophers to police their own disciplinary boundaries. According to Hallvard Lillehammer, philosophy's "institutional paradigm" includes the "frequently coercive refusal to allow that philosophical enquiry is empirically tractable." However, he says that we should:

> be suspicious of the tendency of this institutional paradigm to postulate truths that are "basic," "ultimate" or "fundamental" just at the point where things begin to look interesting [or] problematic from the point of view of those we in the profession pretentiously refer to as "non-philosophers." (2009, par. 36)

The idea that criminology, because of its limitations, should have no say in determining morally and legally appropriate punishment policies is overly dismissive. The turn to "obvious" truths such as desert and proportionality, often asserted as intuitive, basic, or commonsensical claims, is not philosophical progress. Indeed, it hinders progress on the theory of punishment. The part of this field that addresses the general justifying aim of punishment, the part having to do with incentives and comparative outcomes, ought to be naturalized, or at least as naturalized as the social sciences can make it.

Whether perceived failures of the social sciences led to consequentialism's decline in popularity is a historical question. Once we delineate the different foci of criminal law, it becomes clear that consequentialism is on a firm foundation when considering the institution of punishment in general as well as lower-level principles regarding statutory penalties. Deterrence is a viable aim of punishment, given the nature of human motivation. And social scientists have had enough success in comparing the consequences of different possible or actual punishments that, although there may be a lack of data in some areas, there is reason to continue the research and to use the data we have to promote the common good.

10 On proportionality

In Chapter 5, I explained how a punishment schedule would be set in theory. Statutory penalties would be justified on consequentialist grounds. Worse crimes get more severe, more certain, or swifter punishments because the community is keener to deter them in order to preserve the public order and promote the common good. On the two-tiered model, the punishment for a particular offender would then be imposed within the sentencing range based on what they deserve.

One may still wonder, however, whether the process for setting statutory penalties that I described, for the sake of argument, in Chapter 5 could be devised in reality. One implication of the criticisms leveled against criminology and other relevant social sciences is that they could never give us enough information to reliably inform our decisions on specific penalties for specific crimes. Retributivists claim that they can produce a well-founded punishment schedule, and many of them give more or less detailed descriptions of how to do it. In this chapter, I explain why consequentialism is better equipped than retributivism to justify a system of statutory penalties and show how it, like retributivism, arrives at punishments that are proportional to the corresponding offenses.

Davis's retributivist alternative

Michael Davis defends a mixed but mostly retributivist view, and a comparison of the two theories will illustrate how my two-tiered model answers some of the problems to which he thinks consequentialism is susceptible.[1] In "How

1 Davis (2009) endorses a kind of practical pluralism regarding punishment. He says that the institution of punishment is justified in many different ways, and all of those different justifications – retributivism, utilitarianism, preventative theory, restorative justice, expressivism, and so on – lead to roughly the same structure of punishments and penalties. Therefore, disagreements among punishment theorists need not be resolved. If all of them entail most of the same things, both at the policy level and the level of specific punishments, then there is no need to settle on any one theory of punishment. His own position is complex: "my theory of punishment …, if I have one, is a mix of the fairness theory, some moralistic theories (a wholly internalist 'mixed view'), and perhaps an internalist (or externalist) version of enforcement"

to Make the Punishment Fit the Crime" (1983),[2] Davis makes a distinction between justifying the criminal law in general and justifying particular systems of criminal law – that is, statutory penalties for kinds of crimes. Davis claims that the purpose of the law is to maintain order (or "at least a modicum of order") by setting a "price" to be paid when a crime is committed (M. Davis 1992, 72). Punishment serves as a kind of social control. So, despite his defense of retributivism, Davis does not claim that "deterrence is *entirely* irrelevant to justification." It "may plausibly be treated as a mere *side constraint* on the institution of criminal punishment": "any system of criminal punishment that set penalties so low as to threaten the desired level of social order would be disqualified," as would any excessive or inhumane punishments (M. Davis 1992, 27). The institution of punishment is justified on consequentialist grounds. Davis and I agree on this.

Davis then wonders whether a community could appeal to utilitarianism to set statutory penalties, since the reason for preferring one penalty over another seems to be that there is some advantage to choosing one over the other. The utilitarian calculus considers different options and compares the outcomes to determine the right action to perform or the right policy to adopt. If twenty years in prison for kidnapping would deter better than fifteen years in prison, then the former is preferable to the latter because of its overall advantage. However, Davis argues that this approach faces an insurmountable problem: to determine the preferability of one penalty over another, "we would compare two complete systems differing only in a single penalty" (1992, 73).

Although Davis does not clearly distinguish them, he gives different, related reasons for why such a comparison is impossible when it comes to punishment:

1) Evaluating a punishment within a particular system is impossible because no social scientist can compare the effectiveness of punishments here and now to the effectiveness of different punishments in some imagined state where nothing is changed but the one punishment. Societies are complex systems composed of ever-changing groups of individuals, each with their own preferences and expectations, varying histories and political institutions, and so on. It is impossible to control for all these other factors and isolate only one predictor – the penalty for a particular crime – and compare the consequences of different punishments (M. Davis 1992, 76–77). For example, we could not determine how the murder rate in Michigan would be affected

(M. Davis 2009, 93–94). The scale that he describes in "How to Make the Punishment Fit the Crime" is not intended to justify punishment but to set the standards for how much criminals should be punished (M. Davis 1992, 69–97). It is consistent, he says, with a number of different theories, including the retributivist position (fair-play theory) that Davis defends in *To Make the Punishment Fit the Crime* (1992, 235).

2 The article was originally published in 1983. I cite page numbers from the book in which the article is reprinted, Davis's *To Make the Punishment Fit the Crime* (1992), pp. 69–97.

by adopting the death penalty as a maximum punishment because Michigan constantly changes in other ways – socioeconomically, demographically, etc. – that also impact the crime rate: "There is no mathematical model of society from which to make deductions about the actual or probable consequences of such a penalty" (M. Davis 1992, 74).

2) Even if we could consider the effectiveness of a punishment in a particular society, that would tell us nothing about the preferability of that punishment elsewhere or in general. Perhaps better consequences would accrue with the same punishment in a different legal system, or a different punishment in a different legal system. A utilitarian evaluation of the consequences of a particular punishment has nothing "directly to do with the actual or probable consequences of the penalty" on its own because "such talk goes on *within* the criminal law" (M. Davis 1992, 77; see also Brooks 2012, 41–42).
3) The possible punishments for a given crime are so numerous that it would be impossible to test all the options, even if we could isolate the one predictor. Davis asks a rhetorical question: "What are we to do when the choice is between two and three years imprisonment?" (M. Davis 1992, 75).

Because of these problems, criminology lacks predictive power. Davis concludes that "predicting the effect of any statutory penalty remains at least as risky as predicting next year's stock prices" (1992, 5). These are well-worn criticisms of utilitarianism: the world is too complex, so the mathematical precision demanded by the utilitarian calculus is impossible, especially for prescribing large-scale social policies.

As an alternative, Davis establishes a ranking system that matches penalties to crimes (1992, 69–97). His process is typical of what retributivists say we should do to establish proportional, deserved punishments (e.g., Mabbott 1939, 162; von Hirsch 1976, 132–40; von Hirsch, 1985, 61–101; Scheid 1997; von Hirsch 1998; Corlett 2001). First, Davis would have us list penalties, exclude inhumane penalties, classify the remaining penalties into different types (fines, imprisonment, corporal punishment, capital punishment, etc.), and then rank them within the different types (e.g., five years in prison is worse than four years in prison). Second, we would do the same thing with crimes: we would list all crimes, classify them into different types (homicide, assault, theft, drug offenses, etc.), and then rank them within the different types (e.g., murder, manslaughter, and justifiable homicide, with distinctions within each of these classes). The ranking is done by taking on the perspective of a hypothetical "rational person."[3] A lesser penalty is one a rational person would rather risk than the next higher penalty (a prison sentence is worse than a fine, three years in prison is worse than two years in prison, etc.), and a lesser crime is one that a rational person would rather risk than the next higher crime (it is better to have someone pick your pocket than to

3 Feminist epistemologists have long challenged the notion of a generic "rational person," who is often implicitly gendered male and privileged in other ways (race, class, etc.). See, e.g., Lloyd (1993) and Alcoff (1999).

be assaulted, better to be assaulted than murdered, etc.).[4] Finally, the two scales are related to one another, so that the most severe penalty is assigned to the most serious crime, the least severe penalty is assigned to the least serious crime – so-called "anchor points" – and all the crimes and penalties between the two extremes are also paired together. This amounts to a retributive system, specifically a form of proportional retributivism according to which worse crimes are given worse punishments (M. Davis 1992, esp. 77–83).

Problems with Davis's retributivist alternative

One problem with this approach is identified by Ted Honderich: why is this preference scale "in itself any reason for subjecting such an offender to such a punishment?" (2006, 35; see also Brooks 2012, 31–32). The mere fact of the ranking, even if it accords with our retributivist intuitions, does not entail that assigning the corresponding penalty to some criminal is actually justified, only "appropriate" relative to the scale. We could not justify punishing a criminal by telling them, "You're getting ten years in prison because that's how the scales line up." What Davis does here is consistent with the letter of retributivism but not its spirit. To be sure, he says that punishing criminals is justified because they deserve it, in proportion to their offenses – specifically, that they deserve the punishment because they have taken unfair advantage by not following the shared rules (fair-play theory) (M. Davis 1992, esp. 29; M. Davis 1996). Although that is why criminals are punished and it is why they receive greater or lesser punishments, relative to other crimes, the specific punishments they receive (e.g., two or three years in prison) are determined and justified with reference to the scale. One could say that someone who is guilty of assault causing bodily harm should get less of a penalty than someone who commits aggravated assault and more of a penalty than someone who commits simple assault. But one could not say that someone who is guilty of aggravated assault deserves ten years in prison. On Davis's view, that is established by the scale, not by the *lex talionis.*

Davis accuses the consequentialist of not being able to decide between two years in prison and three years in prison for a particular offense, since the outcomes could not be isolated and compared (objection #3 above) (1992, 75). But the retributivist's singular focus on severity poses a similar problem. There are hundreds of crimes defined under the law. The idea that we could arrive at a consensus about their ranking is far-fetched. Would this be done state by state? And would it be a problem if people in different states had different scales? What is deserved would not seem to change when someone crosses an artificial border. Even if we were able to settle on a shared ranking, the idea that there would be some one-to-one matchup between the penalty scale and the crime scale is highly unlikely. There are an infinite number of penalty options: three years is more severe than

4 Research has shown that there is broad consensus in the ranking of crimes. See Hamilton and Rytina (1980), Jacoby and Cullens (1998), and Robinson and Kurzban (2007).

two years, of course, but three years is also more severe than thirty-five months and three weeks, which is more severe than thirty-four months and two days, and so on. Davis gets around this by enjoining us to simplify our penalties:

> Where a type of penalty has a huge number of degrees, these should be reduced to a manageable few. That may be done either by selecting certain round number[s] (e.g., ten dollars, fifty dollars, and so on) or by grouping the penalties into ranges (e.g., one to ten dollars, eleven to fifty dollars, and so on), or by some combination of these. (1992, 79)

Setting aside the fact that "manageability" is a vague standard, what results from this process is an assignment of a penalty for a crime based not on desert, but on the arbitrary choice of "round number[s]." What does Davis himself do when the choice is between two and three years' imprisonment for a crime that falls between a more serious crime that gets four years in prison and a less serious crime that gets one year in prison? The right thing to do is no more obvious on his view than it is under consequentialism.

Davis's punishment schedule depends on a clear rank ordering of crimes and punishments, yet there is no reason to believe that such a ranking system is possible. The reason why the legislature typically establishes a range of punishments for each kind of crime is to allow for discretion in sentencing, since crime A may be worse than crime B in some cases, and in other cases crime B may be worse than crime A. Is simple battery always worse than petty theft? It depends on what is stolen or who is hurt. Stealing someone's computer may not be as bad as stealing someone's insulin, even if they cost the same; and punching a professional boxer is different from punching someone who has never been hit, even if they both get black eyes. Davis wants to allow for three different possibilities: either (1) crimes are classified by type, ranked within each type, and then paired with precise penalties (identified as "round numbers"); (2) penalties are grouped into ranges; or (3) "some combination of these" (which is actually many options, depending on the combination) (1992, 79). In the case of sentencing ranges, there would often be overlap between the ranges of penalties associated with two closely related crimes on the scale. For example, someone guilty of disorderly conduct gets up to sixty days in jail and someone guilty of disobeying a police officer gets up to one year in jail. The latter crime is worse ... or is it? The ranges of penalties allow for the former offender to get more jail time than the latter offender, if the first is especially disorderly and the second is a minor infraction. So, whether one is worse than the other – what each criminal deserves – is decided case by case, as it is under the two-tiered model, rather than by a strictly ordered punishment schedule. What does this do to Davis's scale?

This is part of the larger problem that, despite appearances, Davis's fair-play theory provides little guidance on how much punishment criminals should receive. According to his theory, criminals should be punished in proportion to the unjust advantages they receive from their crimes, in order to inflict offsetting disadvantages. But, as von Hirsch has pointed out, it is difficult to measure unfairly appropriated degrees of freedom, to compare those degrees of freedom for various crimes, and to match what is unfairly appropriated to a particular punishment (1993, 8). Like von Hirsch (1985, 40–46; von Hirsch and Ashworth 2005, 137–43), Davis concedes that we can only give an ordinal ranking of punishments rather than cardinal judgments about what precise punishment is appropriate for a given crime. But even for this kind of ranking to work, we would have to commit ourselves to a simplistic theory of value: "Only someone gripped by the utterly implausible idea that all values are reducible to some single final (and measurable) good could suppose that such a unitary ranking of wrongdoings is even in principle possible" (Duff 1996, 61). Given the vagueness of the values involved in fair-play theory, reasonable people can disagree about how much punishment is deserved, and there is no objective standard against which to measure their conflicting intuitions. A clear ranking system, even one involving a comparative judgment of the relative seriousness of two different crimes, faces its own set of challenges.

To get around this problem, Davis defers to the preferences of a generic "rational person." To determine what a "rational person" would prefer, Davis describes a kind of social agreement that is arrived at through the legislative process (1992, 81). To test whether the legislature is acting rationally, Davis mentions only the intuitions of a typical citizen: "he has only to go to a statute book and ask himself whether the rankings generally mirror his fears" (81). This process seems to rank punishments by the actions of democratically elected representatives, or perhaps by poll. But commonly held beliefs can be wrong. Davis criticizes Anthony Ellis (2005) for appealing to opinions about what works when Ellis defends his own preventive theory:

> He does not explain how we are to distinguish between the fads that overwhelm common sense now and then (which an externalist should ignore) and a true rational assessment of evidence (which they are bound to respect). He does not even ask how such a common opinion could be justified (if it actually exists). (M. Davis 2009, 86n29)

Ellis could perhaps be accused of inconsistency for appealing to consequences and to people's opinions about consequences, which are two different things. But retributivists do not get a free pass just because they do not rely on empirical evidence. Retributivists who claim to express common opinions regarding desert are just as likely to get caught up in fads and repeat prejudices as consequentialists are, perhaps even more so.

The racially motivated panic over the crack epidemic was just such a fad. When the U.S. Congress passed the Anti-Drug Abuse Act of 1986 (Pub. L. No. 99–570, 100 Stat. 3207), it established much tougher sentences for crack cocaine than powder cocaine (21 U.S.C. §841[b] [2000]). This disproportionately affected Black defendants, who are more often arrested, prosecuted, and given harsher sentences for crack offenses, even though there are more white powder cocaine users and the drugs are pharmacologically identical (Vagins and McCurdy 2006). On the scale of crimes, the United States, through its elected representatives, ranked possession of crack cocaine as much worse than possession of powder cocaine, but there was no good basis for their 100-to-1 sentencing disparity. After the U.S. Sentencing Commission and Congress reduced the penalties for crack offenses in 2007 and 2010, settling on an 18-to-1 disparity, the Commission's own research found that there was no statistically significant difference in the recidivism rates for those who served their full sentences under the 1986 law versus those who were released early under the amended statute (U.S. Sentencing Commission 2014). A robust sense of rationality should include a standard of reasonableness in addition to mere efficiency at satisfying preferences, which, although no "mathematical model," would be justifiable to others. And, certainly, the evidence that one could draw upon in justifying preferences – whether, for example, crack possession ought to be punished more severely, or the death penalty ought to be paired with murder – should include evidence found in the social sciences.

Davis's rational person can hardly ignore empirical research into the very punishment about which they are expressing a preference. If criminological research has improved to the point where we can reliably predict the relative effectiveness of different punishments, as I have argued, does Davis still want us to determine the proper punishments solely by agreement? This is a kind of "penal populism," which dismisses the authority of criminologists in favor of an appeal to intuition (Pratt 2007). In principle, social scientists can provide us with actual standards, or reasonable belief in actual standards, against which to measure our legislative judgments, based on consequentialist considerations. If, say, the death penalty is shown not to deter more than life in prison, and it has no other positive social impact, then noting that "rational people" prefer life in prison over the death penalty, or having a poll regarding how much people fear being murdered, would do nothing to justify the punishment. We should not leave punishment decisions up to popular opinion (expressed as ranking), and we should not adopt an alternative theory of punishment just because criminology does not have the precision that chemistry has. Social scientific methodologies have an advantage over Davis's appeal to "intuitions of gravity of offense" (1992, 63). Michael Shaffer claims that the latter kind of argument often amounts to mere assertion:

> Positing theories is not confirming theories. Traditional philosophy tries to pretend positing and confirming are the same thing by sliding intuition into the equation as a source of putative evidence. But philosophical theories so understood are merely speculative takes on what might be true devoid of real evidence. All evidence is empirical and scientific evidence is the most dependable (i.e. safe) form of empirical evidence. (2019, par. 33)

To be sure, criminology can still refine its methods and increase its predictive power. But the ultimate appeal in such a case is to our interpretation of the empirical evidence rather than speculation or intuition.

Answering Davis's criticisms of consequentialism

According to consequentialism, some crimes are assigned steeper statutory penalties than other crimes because the effects of nonenforcement would be worse for more serious crimes than for less serious crimes, not because one crime is more deserving than others according to some shared intuition. Worse crimes must bring about worse punishments, if only to make the transgressions bad bets in the minds of criminals, or so the state can take a stronger stand against the most heinous crimes in communicating social norms to its citizens. Jeremy Bentham argues that the principle of proportionality is justified on consequentialist grounds because we as a society have a stronger preference for avoiding worse crimes. We ought to assign harsher punishments to worse crimes in an effort to deter them more strongly, so that criminals will be more likely to commit minor crimes (or none at all), which we are more willing to tolerate (1970, ch. XIV [pp. 165–74]). Aggravated assault poses more of a threat to the social order (personal security and well-being) than assault causing bodily harm, which poses more of a threat to the social order than simple assault. The effect on the social order could be measured in terms of different outcomes, and we assign a punishment that deters it more and keeps it "relatively rare," measured in terms of the crime rate and people's tolerance for the level of offenses (M. Davis 1992, 72).

The recent interest in decriminalizing drug possession is motivated by data that shows incarceration does not work to address the problem. How would Davis explain and justify such a move? He could say that we have realized that drug users do not actually deserve hard treatment, presumably because they did not take unfair advantage of the system after all. We have discovered that addiction is not a choice for which we can hold people strictly responsible. That is purely about blame, and we leave it at that. The consequentialist's response is more compelling: imprisonment is not doing any good. Drug addiction is a disease, so the best way to address it is through treatment programs rather than or in addition to prison. Statutory penalties are not about blame but about what measures will produce the best outcomes. If punishment is a social institution, then it should serve a social purpose.

On my view, punishments need not be justified apart from a social system, as Davis claims of utilitarian justifications, but rather must be justified against a system that is assumed (or assumed to be justified) from the outset. As I argued in Chapter 3, punishments are legally justified if they support the existing system better than the alternatives and morally justified if they are legally justified, not excessive, and the system as a whole has morally justified aims. So, Davis's first two objections (#1 and #2 above) are not problems for my theory. I reject Davis's claim that a penalty for a particular crime must be isolated from its social context. Indeed, its justification *depends on* the social context, including its effectiveness for a specific population with its unique history.

I have argued that the criminal justice system as a whole is justified by its consequences, and the social scientific assessment of those consequences is the basis for developing appropriate and effective policies regarding kinds of crimes and classes of criminals. To be sure, social science falls short of Davis's ideal – a "mathematical model" – but, as I said in the previous chapter, it does guide us in making reasonable choices about how best to deter illegal behavior and rehabilitate criminals (1992, 74). Policies regarding nonviolent drug offenses are but one example where the social sciences provide better and more evidence-based guidance regarding what to do, and those findings may prompt us to revise our statutes. We are obligated to improve our punishments, not achieve an ideal state.

Although social circumstances do change, there is no reason to believe that they shift so dramatically from day to day that the social sciences could not keep up with them. Thom Brooks voices this worry when he says that "the fact that some were deterred last year or even yesterday may be no guarantee that we can expect a similar number to be deterred today or next month" (2012, 41). A Humean skeptic would say the same thing about the sun rising or the actions of billiard balls. The question is: what is reasonable to believe given the empirical evidence? Brooks is right that there "may be no guarantee" that things will be the same, but, barring a radical change such as a Nazi occupation, slight shifts in social attitudes will likely not radically alter people's measurable responses to incentives.

There are several responses to Davis's third objection (#3), that consequentialists cannot test all the options and set specific punishments for specific crimes. First, Davis assumes Bentham's version of utilitarianism, according to which the utilitarian calculus can be performed with mathematical precision in tallying up pains (dolors) and pleasures (hedons) (1970, preface [p. 9]; ch. IV, §§2–6 [pp. 38–40]). If we adopt a form of preference utilitarianism (as John Stuart Mill does [2001, 8–11]) rather than hedonistic utilitarianism, then actions and policies are right if they satisfy preferences rather than maximizing pleasures and minimizing pains. Then we would only have to establish a way to compare and order preferences. Although this faces problems of its own – especially interpersonal comparisons of preferences – Davis himself faces the same problem, since he has us order punishments based on "the preferences of rational persons," specifically which crimes and penalties the society as a whole finds better or worse (1992, 82).[5]

Proportionality and the *Weems* case

To show one of the advantages of retributivism over utilitarianism, Davis considers how his theory explains and justifies the U.S. Supreme Court's decision regarding proportionality in *Weems v. United States* (217 U.S. 349 [1910]). Paul A. Weems, a disbursing officer employed by the U.S. government, was charged with falsifying official documents. The state alleged that he had entered two small sums, totaling about six hundred Philippine pesos, as paid out so that he could

5 Von Hirsch and Ashworth use a similar "interest analysis approach" to gauge a punishment's severity (2005, 147–48). They believe that it avoids the pitfalls of subjectivism: "adopting an interest analysis approach means that the assessment of severity is made less dependent on the preferences of particular individuals" (148). But Davis specifies "rational persons," which is an attempt to avoid interpersonal variation and focus on what ought to serve our interests, so long as we are thinking clearly.

convert the funds to his own use. He was convicted in the Philippines (then a U.S. colony) of defrauding the government and was sentenced to fifteen years in prison with hard labor and a fine of four thousand pesetas, along with other penalties, such as surveillance by the government for the rest of his life. Among other reasons for legally challenging the punishment was Weems's claim that it was "cruel and unusual," thus violating the Eighth Amendment – not because any of the punishments were unacceptable practices in general, but because they were excessive for the crime committed. The Supreme Court agreed with Weems and found that the punishment was disproportionate to the offense. The statutory penalty exhibited "unrestrained power" (381) on the part of the legislature: "it is a precept of justice that punishment for crime should be graduated and proportioned to offense" (367). The majority's reasoning mirrors Davis's account of how punishments and crimes ought to be related. They seem to imagine a scale of crimes and punishments that are related to one another by proportionality, with the worst punishments reserved for the most serious crimes. The Court notes, for example, that some people convicted of homicide were not punished as severely as Weems was for falsifying documents (380).

Davis claims that this is not utilitarian reasoning, since it is about proportionality rather than ideal outcomes. However, the *Weems* decision "suggested little in the way of principle that would enable courts to apply that doctrine [of proportionality]," and the lack of any "objective standard ... continues to affect the Court's persistent failure to articulate a coherent proportionality doctrine," either retributivist or consequentialist (Raymond 2006, 254). Indeed, far from a clear endorsement of retributivism, the Court's decision in *Weems* is consistent with a consequentialist theory like the one I described in Chapters 2 and 3. A consequentialist could argue that what it means for the punishment to be disproportionate is that either (1) it does not accomplish the aim of punishment because it is not strong enough to deter the relevant crime and preserve the public order, or (2) it goes beyond what is necessary to accomplish the aim of punishment, thus violating the principle of parsimony. In other words, a punishment could be too lenient or too severe, given the offense, even for a consequentialist.

For consequentialism, of course, lack of proportionality cannot be determined apart from the social conditions and the specific aims of the state. But Davis himself also admits that we should "take into account the rational concerns of a particular society." For example, in a country that depends entirely on horses for transport, stealing a horse would be much more serious than a mere theft of property (1992, 89). The "liberal-communitarian" Antony Duff rightly notes that any penalty scale along retributivist lines must take into account "existing penal practice" and "a host of historical contingencies" (2001, 134). Proportionality must be determined holistically, and one element of this picture is what is to be accomplished by a given punishment – that is, the consequences of a given punishment for promoting the common good, whether it involves stealing horses or falsifying official documents. Although this is not strictly utilitarian – Davis may be right about the fact that the Court's reasoning was not utilitarian – it could be consequentialist. To be sure, Weems's punishment went beyond what the community's reactive attitudes would require in order to achieve retribution, but the mistake was at the legislative level in imposing a great burden to achieve something that could be accomplished with a lesser burden. The two-tiered model of punishment can, like Davis's view, explain why the punishment was excessive and why the U.S. Supreme Court's decision in *Weems* is justified.

Different kinds of proportionality

In claiming that consequentialism can justify a proportional punishment schedule, retributivists would likely object that I have missed the point of proportionality. On my view, consequentialism, grounded in social scientific findings, can provide better guidance about proportional punishments than we get from retributivist intuitions about how much punishment an offender deserves. But the reason for proportional punishments matters. Even if consequentialist proportionality happens to coincide roughly with desert-based proportionality, this is merely coincidental. Retributivists believe that punishing a person more severely than they deserve is wrong because a less heinous crime deserves a less severe punishment, not because of the bad consequences of doing so. On this view, the "justice" that the Supreme Court references in *Weems* is about what one would call desert-based proportionality rather than harm-benefit proportionality.[6]

Setting aside the question-begging assumptions behind the concept of "true" proportionality, this objection is more appropriate for a non-mixed consequentialist theory than it is for my two-tiered model of punishment. Paul Robinson defends a version of the former view. He claims that the threat of punishment will only effectively deter criminal behavior if it aligns with the community's shared moral commitments, including the belief in degrees of moral blameworthiness. It does not matter whether people's belief in retributive proportionality is justified, only that giving someone what they deserve serves a "psychological function" whose consequences in terms of crime control are better than the alternatives (Carlsmith, Darley, and Robinson 2002):

> the criminal law's moral credibility is essential to effective crime control, and is enhanced if the distribution of criminal liability is perceived as "doing

6 Justice Antonin Scalia, in two more recent cases, claims that harm-benefit proportionality is an oxymoron: "it becomes difficult even to speak intelligently of 'proportionality' once deterrence and rehabilitation are given significant weight. Proportionality is inherently a retributive concept, and perfect proportionality is the talionic law" (*Harmelin v. Michigan*, 501 U.S. 957 [1991], 989); and "Proportionality – the notion that the punishment should fit the crime – is inherently a concept tied to the penological goal of retribution" (*Ewing v. California*, 538 U. S. 11 [2003], 31). Scalia made these claims in the context of saying that the Eighth Amendment's prohibition on cruel and unusual punishment, because it is not based on one penological theory (namely, retributivism), could not be used to prohibit disproportionate sentences as unconstitutional. Frase (2005a) disputes Scalia's assertions. Frase distinguishes retributive proportionality from nonretributive proportionality, and he identifies two kinds of nonretributive proportionality: ends proportionality and means proportionality.

> justice," that is, if it assigns liability and punishment in ways that the community perceives as consistent with the community's principles of appropriate liability and punishment. (Robinson and Darley 1997, 457; see also Robinson 2000; Robinson 2008b, 175–212; and Robinson, Barton, and Lister 2014, 314–30)

This justification of proportional punishment is harm-based, not desert-based. What the public thinks offenders deserve ("empirical desert") is a fact that ought to be included in the utilitarian calculus – it has "instrumental value" – rather than being something that has independent, deontological value or is open to moral scrutiny (Robinson 2007; Robinson 2008a; Robinson 2008b, 135–74; Robinson 2011; Robinson, Barton, and Lister 2014, 314–30). Like Rawls (1955), Robinson's position is rule-utilitarianism in all but name: giving people what they deserve – or, more properly speaking, what the community "perceives" to be deserved – is justified because, as a practice, it maximizes positive outcomes. If there were no deterrent effect of giving people what they are thought to deserve, or, counterfactually, if giving offenders more or less than they deserve were somehow to lower the crime rate, then that would be justified instead.

As a truly mixed theory, the two-tiered model is different. The proportional punishment schedule established by the legislature is distinct from the appropriate punishments distributed to specific criminals by judges. Since my primary purpose in this chapter is to show how a mixed theory can justify the proportionality of statutory penalties as well as retributivism can, I have emphasized the consequentialist side of the theory. I have shown that we can establish worse punishments for worse crimes based on consequentialist reasoning: for example, murder is worse than burglary, so murder is punished more harshly than burglary because we want to deter murder more than burglary (harm-benefit proportionality). This applies to *classes* of criminals.[7] According to the two-tiered model, ***individual*** criminals are then given better or worse punishments within the statutory ranges because of what they deserve (desert-based proportionality). If burglars get up to twenty years in prison by statute, a judge will vary sentences for different burglars based on the heinousness of their crimes. As I claimed in Chapter 4, the punishment is proportional to the crime because the strength of the community's justified feeling of resentment varies depending on

7 In establishing his own principle of proportionality on consequentialist grounds, Beccaria defines the worst crimes as "those which spell the immediate destruction of society" and the least bad crimes as "those which involve the smallest possible injustice to its private participants." "Between these two extremes," there are "imperceptible gradations." Although it is impossible to construct a scale of punishments that

> measure[s] all the infinite and untoward combinations of human actions geometrically, … it is enough that the wise lawgiver signposts the main stages, without confusing the order and not reserving for the crimes of the highest grade the punishments of the lowest. (1995, 20)

the seriousness of the crime. Thus, my mixed theory accommodates desert-based proportionality when it comes to sentencing specific criminals in a way that, for example, rule-utilitarianism does not. So long as statutory penalties do not differ so dramatically from what is deserved as to be disproportionate – a possibility that I address in the following chapter – retributivists and I arrive at roughly the same conclusion about what an individual criminal deserves and why.

Conclusion

Consequentialism can be action-guiding at the institutional level to devise a punishment schedule that roughly correlates with the same scaling of penalties based on proportionality. My approach not only provides a factual basis for such decisions, rather than intuition, but it also provides an empirical method for changing statutory penalties in order to achieve marginal utility. The social sciences can guide us in setting proportional punishments, either increasing or decreasing existing punishments in order to promote the common good more effectively, and in a way that causes the least amount of harm.

11 Jury nullification and reflective equilibrium

Since the legislature constrains potential retributive excesses and the courts constrain our tendency to use people merely to achieve social ends, the two-tiered model lends support to the separation of powers, checks, and balances. If the same political body were both to make and to enforce laws, it would be difficult if not impossible for it to adopt both consequentialism and retributivism without it becoming a confused jumble of principles that are consulted selectively to support ad hoc judgments. For example, if an authoritarian ruler put laws in place to protect the regime, they would try to achieve that same end in the courts, where, in the absence of independent judges, a defendant's guilt or innocence would be secondary to the question of what would consolidate the ruler's power. Political opponents would be framed, given sham trials, and imprisoned or executed, while the leader's allies would be exonerated, even when they break the law. It would maintain the social order at the expense of justice.

Alternatively, in a system of direct democracy without any protection for individual rights – an ochlocracy, mob rule, or tyranny of the majority – the retributive impulse would be codified in the law itself. The expression of communal resentment would go unchecked. Punishments would be given regardless of whether they effectively deter and regardless of the cost. It would be chaotic. Maximilien Robespierre made the connection between retribution and democracy explicit: "Terror is nothing but prompt, severe, inflexible justice; it is therefore an emanation of virtue; it is not so much a specific principle as a consequence of the general principle of democracy applied to the homeland's most pressing needs" (2007, 115). Not only does this lead to abuses – the Terror is a pretty good example – but it also contradicts the aim of the law as a mechanism to preserve the state, which, as I argued in Chapter 2, is the reason why punishment exists as a legal institution.

On my view, the legislature and the criminal judiciary check one another because they act on different, competing principles. The primary way that this happens around punishment is that the legislature checks the retributive impulses of judges and juries so that, collectively, their application of the law helps to preserve the public order. But it is also the case that the judiciary checks the consequentialism of the legislature by punishing only the guilty and only in proportion to their degree of guilt, even if occasionally punishing the innocent or excessively punishing the guilty would have deterrent effects. Judges attend to the individuality of criminals rather than to the general category of criminality.

Assigning different theoretical principles to the legislative and judicial powers seems to follow the template that John Rawls describes in "Two Concepts of Rules" (1955). For Rawls, the legislature creates punishment policies in order to maximize utility, and the criminal courts give offenders what they deserve. Our views diverge, however, because of the theoretical bases of the different powers' authority. For Rawls, retribution is not good in itself. It is justified in the courts because, when carried out collectively by judges as a practice (rather than as a summary of what tends to work), it maximizes happiness. According to the two-tiered model, by contrast, retributivism is justified separately and is not derived from the principle of utility, so judges and juries only have a *prima facie* obligation to carry out the will of the legislature. There is a strong obligation simply to apply the law, but the obligation is not absolute because, in a given case, there may be a conflict between consequentialism and retributivism. When there is such a conflict, it is possible for retributivist concerns to be more pressing. Therefore, the relationship between the legislature and the judiciary is more complicated on the two-tiered model than it is for Rawls.

Because punishment is driven by different values at the institutional level (general justifying aim) and at the case-specific level (distribution), inevitably there will be occasional tensions between the punishment designated under the law and the punishment that seems appropriate given our reactive attitudes. These tensions are settled and the proper punishments determined through a back-and-forth social and political process that tests laws against our moral intuitions, including court cases, and restrains our moral attitudes by means of the law – a kind of wide reflective equilibrium.

The law as a strict constraint

When lawmakers act justly, the legislative power strictly limits what a community can do to express its resentment. A common objection to some forms of retributivism, especially equality retributivism, is that the position leads to absurd implications: we should rape rapists, torture torturers, and so on. Because we should not punish people in those ways, it seems that equality retributivism must be wrong (Nathanson 2001, 72–75). In fact, raping rapists may be the most appropriate punishment given the heinousness of the crime. Dante's hell is filled with sinners whose wrongful acts are repaid with appropriate and equivalent punishments. In a legal context, however, things are different. We as a society refuse to rape rapists not because it is undeserved, but because, without divine justice as our goal, the state has other obligations that override the *prima facie* duty to give people precisely what they deserve. In other words, we need not reject retributivism, even equality retributivism. Instead, we only need to claim that we have other, more important goals that limit how we ought to behave when punishing convicted criminals – specifically, a concern for preserving the public order. We should avoid punishments that are deserved but are inconsistent with a society's values. And if the punishment is wrong in itself or the system it supports is immoral, then it should not be carried out, regardless of how effectively it controls crime.

Under the two-tiered model, this limitation on retributive punishment is provided by the legislature, which decides which actions ought to be prohibited and establishes statutory penalties for those who are found guilty. In a liberal political system such as the United States, the purpose of the law is to protect the rights of its people, and any power the government has derives from the consent of the governed. The Eighth Amendment's prohibition on "cruel and unusual punishment" recognizes that even convicted criminals have some fundamental rights that should not be violated; we owe them certain protections even though they have forfeited some of their rights in committing crimes. Such rights serve as a moral side constraint on how we can permissibly express our retributive impulses. Inflicting retributive harm on a person may be good, but we are limited in what we can do to individuals even when pursuing things of value, given that protecting people's fundamental rights is one of the aims of the liberal state. Rapists may deserve to be raped, but the state should not be in the business of raping people. Prohibiting such punishments preserves what I assume, for the sake of argument, approximates a just arrangement.

Narrow reflective equilibrium

In a perfectly just political system, the law would place constraints on criminal trials, including statutory penalties, that judges ought to follow without deviation. If such a system were wholly governed by utilitarian principles, for example, then it would restrict judges so that they would be allowed to give people what they deserve only if it maximized happiness or minimized unhappiness. Judges and juries would be expected to convict innocents if doing so advanced society's overall welfare. Rawls makes the case that such a practice could not be justified on rule-utilitarian grounds (1955, 8, 12–13; see also Binder and Smith 2000), and Kai Nielsen argues that, with great probability, the deliberate framing of innocents would cause more harm than good (1972, 223–25).[1] However, my point here is that *if* the principle of utility were the right principle to guide public policy, and *if* policies regarding punishment, including the punishment of innocents, were established to effectively promote the greatest happiness, *then* judges ought to follow those rules without exception. Any deliberation – for example, about whether this is a case where the rules allow us to frame the innocent – is not about questioning the principle of utility or its secondary principles, but about how best to follow those principles, which are absolutely constraining. Using this method of narrow reflective equilibrium, we test and revise our specific intuitions and policies against some general theory of value that itself remains unchanged.

1 See Chapter 6, note 3 for a list of authors who claim that utilitarianism does not justify framing the innocent.

This is the process that Rawls (1955) describes. For the sake of argument, he presupposes that rule-utilitarianism is right. People who engage in practices are merely applying established principles – principles that are ultimately justified by the principle of utility – to specific cases. He says, for example, that someone can deliberate whether to keep one's promise, "but to do so is to deliberate whether the various excuses, exceptions and defenses, which are understood by, and which constitute an important part of, the practice, apply to one's own case" (17). He assumes that "the (ideal) legislator" is forming policies based on the principle of utility, that they have made the correct utilitarian calculations, and that the resulting practices include the rules and exceptions that, if they are followed to the letter, will maximize happiness (6). This is why Rawls (1955, 16), like Beccaria (1995, 14–15), says that judges must follow the rule without using their own discretion.[2] Rules are "definitive" (Rawls 1955, 24). A person who performs an action falling under a rule only needs to explain their action rather than justify it (27). If the practice of punishment is justified by the principle of utility, then particular punishments that follow the practice are justified, provided that judges correctly follow the rules.

Mistakes in the exercise of legislative power (1): Unjust laws

In Chapters 2 and 3, I explained that punishment as an institution ought to maintain the social order, so it is justified on consequentialist grounds, relative to the aims of the state. But we can also judge the aims of the state and can judge punishment as a means to that end against independent moral principles. In the first case, it is a practical judgment regarding the efficacy of the punishment, with relative goodness. In the second case, it is a moral judgment regarding the ultimate rightness or wrongness of the punishment as a means to an end. Corresponding to these two judgments are two different ways that the legislature can go wrong: either by making incorrect calculations about what would best promote the public good (a practical mistake) or by furthering aims that are unjust (a moral wrong). As I mentioned in Chapter 3, this distinction is analogous to Immanuel Kant's distinction between hypothetical and categorical imperatives: the former obligates us to do something *if* we adopt a certain end (in this case, the legislature's taking on the obligation to maintain the state), and the latter obligates us to do what is right regardless of our aims (1996a, 4:414–17).

One way that punishments can be wrong is if they further unjust aims or they are wrong in themselves (moral wrongness). As I said in Chapter 3, my theory of punishment is defensible apart from a specific theory of justice. Although the ultimate rightness of punishment depends on whether it is furthering a just system, its justification *as punishment* is relative to a particular set of social and political

2 Similarly, Feuerbach says that, because laws are formed to maintain the state, judges must simply apply the law as written: "the judge is but the servant of the law [*der Richter aber nur Diener des Gesetzes ist*]" (1801, §83 [p. 64]).

institutions. If a system were absolutely just, then it ought to be enforced without exception; any exception would contravene the demands of justice. However, if a legal system is morally flawed – if it is unjustified legislation – then the rules that identify bad behaviors and their punishments will come into conflict with principles of justice and, in some cases, with people's retributive intuitions. Since our reactive attitudes provide a separate justification for holding people to account, what justice requires for individual defendants could diverge from what the law requires.

When laws are unjust, our reactive attitudes ought to limit what we do to people in the name of the law. Because of the inevitable imperfection in our political institutions – bad principles, bad interpretation of principles, bad application of principles, and so on – legislation only serves as a *conditional* constraint on actual punishments. In some cases, judges and juries themselves push back against the legislature by refusing to enforce laws that are contrary to a society's deeply held moral values. Juries can find defendants not guilty even though proof of their guilt is established under existing laws, thus nullifying the law's authority. For example, prior to the Civil War, Northern juries in the U.S. sometimes acquitted defendants who were charged with violating the Fugitive Slave Act of 1850. The federal legislature was ostensibly protecting the property rights of slave owners, but abolitionists in the North resisted applying the law in order to further the cause of protecting the human rights of escaped slaves. In such cases, judges and juries acted on moral principles that contradicted the law as written and thus restricted the reach of the sovereign legal power.

To be sure, there is disagreement about whether jury nullification is morally justified, especially in a democratic system where the people have the power to change the laws. And we should not be sanguine about risks of jury nullification. There are also cases where juries fail to impose just sentences in refusing to carry out the law as written. Juries have acted wrongly in acquitting white defendants of lynching, of murdering civil rights activists, and of violating fair housing laws (Relman 1991; Conrad 2014, ch. 7). In such cases, the law was just and it should have restricted the actions of the jury. To allow for the rightness of jury nullification in some cases, one only has to grant that the legislature *can* get it wrong (of which there are many historical examples) and that the *prima facie* duty to follow the law, even a law created by elected representatives, *may* conflict with and be outweighed by the *prima facie* obligation to give defendants what they deserve. People who did not turn in fugitive slaves did not deserve to be punished.

Note, however, that jury nullification involves finding defendants not guilty even though the elements of a crime have been proven. Condemning defendants for something they did not do or punishing them for actions that are not prohibited under the law are not cases of jury nullification, but mob justice. This reflects the fact that, under the two-tiered model, the prohibition on excessive harm (the principle of parsimony) is strongly constraining. As W. D. Ross says, the duty of nonmaleficence is "a duty of a more stringent character" than other duties (2002, 21). Judges cannot inflict suffering on defendants that goes beyond the statutorily defined penalties, even if it is deserved. Such sentences would be overturned on appeal.

For these reasons, retributivism under the two-tiered model is both negative and positive, but at different levels. Considered from outside the model, as it were, desert is only a necessary condition for punishing an offender. It is not a positive obligation, since an offender's guilt does not sufficiently justify legal punishment, in the absence of applicable laws, and criminal statutes are justified on consequentialist grounds. However, judges, who apply the laws to specific criminals, are positive retributivists, in the sense that actual guilt is sufficient to find them guilty and to punish them in accordance with their degrees of guilt, within the statutorily defined punishment schedule. Another way of putting this is that I, as a defender of the two-tiered model of punishment, am a negative retributivist, but judges, as agents who are bound by the theory's constraints, are positive retributivists.

Because the jury expresses the community's sense of justice, jury nullification can serve as a check on the actions of the legislature and an impetus to change the law. As Nancy Marder puts it, the jury is part of an interpretive and political process, and jury nullification is one way that they provide "feedback" to the other branches of government:

> Under a process view, the jury not only participates with the judge in the process of interpreting the law, but also is engaged in a "dialogue" with the legislative and executive branches through which it informs them when they have overstepped their bounds, and it does this through nullification. (1999, 925)

This notion of "overstepping their bounds" presupposes that there is some limit to legislative action. Specifically, lawmakers can act wrongly in attempting to preserve an unjust system. The U.S. Supreme Court extended the right to a jury trial to the states in part because it allows the people, through their representatives on a jury, "to prevent oppression by the Government" and to provide the accused with "an inestimable safeguard against the corrupt or overzealous prosecutor and against the compliant, biased, or eccentric judge" (*Duncan v. Louisiana*, 391 U.S. 145 [1968], 155–56). Juries can push back against injustice from legislators, prosecutors, and judges, all of whom purport to represent the state.

Jury nullification is an example of the community undergoing a process of wide reflective equilibrium, in which it is not only testing beliefs against other beliefs and bedrock principles (narrow reflective equilibrium), but it is also testing general principles – in this case, legislative decisions that purport to advance the aims of justice – against our moral intuitions. In ethics, sometimes a compelling moral theory ought to correct our intuitions, and, if the theory is wrong, sometimes our moral intuitions ought to correct the theory. Similarly, sometimes cogent public policies regarding punishment ought to correct our retributive inclinations, and, if the law is wrong, sometimes our recognition of what someone deserves ought to correct the law. People who assisted fugitive slaves did not deserve to be punished, and that judgment indicated that the law was not properly weighing a concern for the property rights of slaveowners against the right of all people to be free. Punishment thus serves as a lens through which to evaluate the actions of the sovereign power. Punishing the guilty tends to establish a more just arrangement by deterring criminals, but not punishing someone, even someone who is guilty, may help to establish a more just arrangement if it is an act of resistance against an unjust law.

Mistakes in the exercise of legislative power (2): Bad calculations and retributivist legislators

The second way that the legislature can act wrongly is by ignoring the consequences of its social policies and making laws based on different, nonconsequentialist principles. In that case, the legislature is not filling its proper role and is not using punishment as a means to accomplish the aims of the state (a practical mistake). Often legislatures overstep their bounds by enacting policies on retributivist grounds. In an effort to appear tough on crime, for example, legislators may try to give people what they deserve, or, beyond that, to express their anger at the intractability of a complex social problem by lashing out at criminals. Not only does this mistake retribution for revenge, but it also usurps the role of judges and juries. The legislature is determining how despicable particular criminals are, even though, as I noted in Chapter 6, they are epistemically ill-equipped to make such a judgment. The result of such misguided reasoning is that the legislature tries to force judges and juries to assign punishments that do nothing to maintain the state: either they must convict defendants of acts whose performance does not erode the public order, or they must assign excessive sentences, within the range of statutory penalties, that cause harm to society rather than furthering the common good.

Example: Three-strikes laws

As I mentioned in Chapter 6, three-strikes laws are one example of lawmakers trying to force judges and juries to impose disproportionate statutory penalties. Under federal law, a defendant must be given a mandatory life sentence if they are convicted of a serious violent felony and have either two prior serious violent felony convictions or one such conviction and one or more prior serious drug convictions. Qualifying violent felonies are listed in the statute (murder, kidnapping, sex offenses, violent robberies, extortion), but any offense that includes an element of force and is punishable by ten years or more in prison also qualifies (18 U.S.C. 3559[c]). Twenty-eight states have similar laws that require heavier sentences for repeat offenders, even for nonviolent felonies.

Three-strikes laws are supposed to prevent crime. Legislators assume that would-be third-strike offenders will see that the potential cost (life in prison) outweighs any benefit of committing a third felony: according to the California Supreme Court, "the basic purpose" of "enhanced punishment" provisions in the law is "the deterrence of recidivism" (*People v. Jackson*, 37 Cal.3d 826 [1985], 832–33). The U.S. Department of Justice says that longer prison sentences for repeat offenders are also designed "to take violent criminals off the streets," an act of restraint that prevents them from committing more crimes (J. Harris 1995).[3] The U.S. Supreme Court itself has said that three-strikes laws are "justified by the State's public-safety interest in incapacitating and deterring recidivist felons" (*Ewing v. California*, 538 U.S. 11 [2003], 12). The assumption is that the consequences of imposing life sentences on this subclass of repeat offenders will be better than the consequences of imposing the standard penalties for the crimes they commit, considered individually.

The facts, however, do not support the assumed consequentialist justification. Research shows that three-strikes laws are ineffective deterrents (King and Mauer 2001; Kovandzic 2001; Zimring, Hawkins, and Kamin 2001; Kovandzic, Sloan, and Vieraitis 2004; Parker 2012).[4] A detailed survey by Michael Vitiello (1997) shows that proponents of three-strikes laws overestimate the amount of crime prevented and the resulting social savings, and he argues that other, less expensive approaches, based primarily around rehabilitation, would have comparatively better outcomes. Other studies go further than that, claiming not only that other alternatives are comparatively better, but that three-strikes laws actually make us less safe than the status quo. For example, in states with three-strikes laws, criminals who commit otherwise nonlethal felonies such as armed robbery are more likely to kill civilians who resist them and other witnesses in order to reduce the chance of arrest and conviction. A review of the relevant data found that the rate of civilian murders increased 16 to 24 percent in cities with three-strikes laws (Kovandzic, Sloan, and Vieraitis 2002). In addition, criminals who face third strikes are more likely to murder police officers to escape arrest. States with three-strikes laws each have an additional police murder roughly every other year, compared to states without such laws (Marvell and Moody 2001; Moody, Marvell, and Kaminski 2002). Legislatures who claim to be doing a utilitarian calculus are ignoring the data and miscalculating the consequences.

Although most of the rhetoric around habitual offender laws involves their supposed crime-prevention benefits, state and federal legislators also claim that they are being tough on crime by giving violent criminals what they deserve, which is an appeal to retribution. These laws have traditionally had broad public support, as a way for society "to express its moral outrage" at repeat offenders (DiIulio 1994). Criminals who are eligible for life sentences because of third strikes are thought to be more culpable because they not only committed additional crimes but also failed to appreciate the wrongness of their first two offenses: according to the Maryland Court of Appeals, "repeat offenders may be more morally blameworthy than first-time offenders, and hence deserve a stronger measure of

3 In *People v. Edwards* (97 Cal.App.4th 161 [2002]), the California Fourth District Court of Appeal found that a third-strike offender "has demonstrated an imperviousness to deterrence which it would be folly to ignore" (165). So, the only way to keep the person from offending again is to imprison them for life.

4 Some authors claim that three-strikes laws do deter, but they are in the minority. For example, see Helland and Tabarrok (2007).

retribution" (*Collins v. State*, 381 Md. 673 [2004], 732).[5] In other words, criminals are being punished for the new crime and for residual guilt from their earlier crimes. Because application of a three-strikes law results in a life sentence, this substitutes punitive treatment for rehabilitation. California, for example, counts some juvenile offenses toward a person's three strikes, expressly rejecting the rehabilitative aim of the juvenile justice system (Packel 2002; *People v. Nguyen*, 46 Cal.4th 1007 [2009]).

Such laws force judges to give criminals punishments that they may not deserve. There are many examples of this across the country: Texas's habitual offender law led to a fifty-year sentence for someone who stole a rack of ribs ("Willie Smith Ward" 2013), and California's three-strikes law sent someone to prison for twenty-five years for shoplifting a pair of socks (Taibbi 2013). One study found that 85 percent of the defendants sentenced under three-strikes laws are convicted of nonviolent offenses, such as burglary and petty theft, and drug crimes (Dickey 1996, 6–7).[6] Judicial discretion allows criminals to be treated as individuals, based on the facts of their specific cases. Three-strikes laws take away that discretion in favor of a blanket policy that equalizes punishment for unequal crimes. The legislature is substituting its retributivist judgment for that of judges and juries. Because judges and juries are better positioned to know what defendants deserve, as I argued in Chapter 6, three-strikes laws are "premised on circumventing specific retributivist measurements. The statute explicitly ignores the calibration of criminal punishment to fit the particular felony" (Yankah 2004, 1029n35). That is, the legislature's attempt to give all repeat felons what they think is deserved forces judges to assign punishments that are often disproportionate to offenders' degrees of guilt.

5 In *People v. Williams* (49 Cal.App.4th 1632 [1996]), the California Sixth District Court of Appeal described a mixed justification of enhanced sentencing involving both deterrence and desert:

> The purpose of section 667 (b)-(i) is to deter and punish recidivism by making repeat offenders serve longer sentences. … When the deterrent effect of the law fails and the defendant subsequently commits another felony, he or she becomes a repeat offender and deserves harsher punishment. (1638)

In an earlier decision, *People v. Arwood* (165 Cal.App.3d 167 [1985]), the Court attributed the same mixed purpose to the voters who supported felony enhancement provisions: "the voter's intention [was] to deter certain criminal conduct regardless of whether it refers to specific criminal offenses because it is perceived as dangerous and deserving of additional punishment when committed by recidivists" (175).

6 A more recent study found that 56 percent of third strikers in California were convicted of nonviolent offenses (Brown and Jolivette 2005). California has worked harder than most other three-strikes states to correct this problem. Proposition 36 (2012) revised the three-strikes law to exclude most nonviolent offenses, Proposition 47 (2014) reclassified some non-violent felonies as misdemeanors, and Proposition 57 (2016) made nonviolent felons eligible for parole after they have served the full sentences for their primary criminal offenses, even if they were given life sentences under the three-strikes law.

The threat of mandatory minimums also leads to the conviction of innocents. Michelle Alexander notes that it is common for people to plead guilty to crimes they did not commit because, in addition to having inadequate legal representation, they are worried about excessive penalties if they are found guilty as the result of a trial:

> Never before in our history ... have such an extraordinary number of people felt compelled to plead guilty, even if they are innocent, simply because the punishment for the minor, nonviolent offense with which they have been charged is so unbelievably severe. (2012, 87)

Imprisoning innocent people does nothing to reform them, and harsh punishments for nonviolent offenders does little to protect the public.

There have been many constitutional challenges to three-strikes laws, to no avail (Mandinach 2016). One objection has been that such mandated sentencing violates the separation of powers guaranteed in the Constitution because it limits, by legislative fiat, the prerogatives of criminal courts. In fact, three-strikes laws are a kind of perfect storm of two mistakes in reasoning regarding punishment. The legislature, remember, is supposed to create laws and statutory penalties that advance the aims of the state, constraining judges and juries so that their retributive impulses are limited to a range of options that allow for differing punishments tailored to specific criminals but that, collectively, reduce crime through deterrence and rehabilitation. In many states, three-strikes laws were enacted as a result of public initiatives. In such cases, the public is either wrongly using resentment (or possibly revenge) to guide public policy, or it is doing an ill-informed and inaccurate cost-benefit analysis. And the legislature is failing to restrict the public in expressing its reactive attitudes in the proper forum, with the proper guidance, and within the proper limits. In the middle of this, judges are calling for caution in order to preserve individualized sentencing – again, with little effect.

Judicial discretion

Judges who are left entirely to their own devices are also liable to make mistakes, which is one reason why they are constrained by statutory provisions. If judges are given wide latitude, then different offenders could get different punishments depending on which judges they draw (and when during the day they appear[7]), despite committing the same crimes. Judges' decisions may be infected with racial bias, or their sentences may be overly punitive so they appear tough on crime during an election year.

Just as unreasonable actions on the part of the legislature are corrected by judges and juries (e.g., through jury nullification), unreasonable actions on the

7 Danziger, Levav, and Avnaim-Pesso (2011) famously discovered that judges made less favorable parole decisions the longer it had been since they had a food break.

part of judges and juries are prevented by the legislature (primary law) and the constitution (secondary law). Judges act more or less reasonably depending on the extent to which, collectively, their judgments and sentencing further the just aims of the state. A pattern of racial prejudice would, for example, be inconsistent with liberal values because people have a right to equal protection under the law. Judges who exhibit detectable racial prejudice in their sentencing decisions would have their decisions overturned on appeal. Appellate courts also check excessively punitive sentences (e.g., *Weems*). And, although judges may depart from presumptive sentencing guidelines, they must give reasons for doing so, and such decisions are subject to appellate review. I echo Rawls (1955) here: legal practices are justified by our collective aims, and the practices dictated by institutional structures coordinate judges' behavior so that their sentencing achieves those aims. To this end, judges are constrained by statutory sentencing ranges, directed by sentencing guidelines, and overseen by appellate courts, the latter of which, through their engagement with the criminal judiciary, establish the beginnings of a common law of sentencing, itself a result of reflective equilibrium.

The problem of indeterminacy

One advantage of utilitarian and retributivist theories of punishment is that they seem to give us clear guidance regarding how justifiably to treat the guilty. Bentham's felicific calculus sets out the seven variables to consider when calculating pain and pleasure, and once we tally up the hedons and dolors and compare the outcomes of the different options, it becomes clear what we should do based on the principle of utility (1970, ch. IV, §§2–6 [pp. 38–41]). And, according to retributivism, we ought to give offenders what they deserve, either equivalent or proportionate punishments relative to their degrees of guilt.

One problem with mixed theories is that, when one of the component theories (consequentialism or retributivism) is not prioritized over the other, usually there is no algorithm from which to derive a specific punishment as *the* justified response to a given act. A punishment justified on consequentialist grounds could be challenged on the grounds that it is inconsistent with what the person deserves. And a person's deserving to suffer underdetermines whether they should be punished, depending on whether it falls under a general practice that supports the common good. The methods of such constraint include, among other things, jury nullification and constitutional protections, respectively. Policies that advance the common good serve as side constraints on judges' imposition of just sentences, and justice is a side constraint on the legislature's statutory decisions.

When there is a conflict, the legislature and the courts determine the appropriate punishment through a back-and-forth, dialogic process that, hopefully, arrives at a kind of reflective equilibrium. To be sure, this is not a simple process, but the complexity of the issue demands it. Although retribution and deterrence are intuitively correct aims of punishment, assigning punishment to specific criminals is more an art than a science. In this way, my theory of punishment is like Ross's deontological ethics, where we know what ought to be done (our *prima facie* duties) but we only have "more or less probable opinions" about the right thing to do (our "duty proper") based on those sometimes competing principles (Ross 2002, 19–20, 31).

Don Scheid (1997) has claimed that any mixed theorist faces a choice between two ways of understanding how consequentialism and retributivism are related. On the "composite approach," which he compares to Ross's moral theory, principles are given different weights and we determine which principle is overriding through an appeal to intuition. The decision process is "amorphous." By contrast, the "goal/constraint approach" conceives of the goal of punishment as crime control but also says that that general purpose is constrained by desert claims about individual criminals, "at least for all standard situations" (446–51).

Scheid's distinction is an oversimplification. For one thing, most non-mixed theories also have to weigh valued outcomes against one another; they are not any simpler or less amorphous. Unless one is an extreme retributivist, for whom justice must be done no matter the consequences, any other retributivist theory is going to recognize the existence of different, sometimes competing obligations. Both the weak retributivist, for whom desert is merely a necessary condition, and the moderate retributivist, for whom desert is a necessary and sufficient condition, recognize that other values may compete with the value of giving people what they deserve. Desert may constrain us in the sense that we can (almost) never punish the innocent – remember Michael Moore's refusal to rule it out absolutely (1997, 719–26) – but whether to punish the guilty, and how much, is a complex moral equation – arguably, just as complex as it is for mixed theories.

Like Scheid (following H. L. A. Hart), I distinguish the general justifying aim of punishment from its distribution. So, it is not a composite approach in which the two principles are applied to the same thing and then weighed against one another. Consequentialism relates to the institution of punishment and statutory penalties (as established by the legislature) and retributivism relates to the allocation of punishments for individual offenders (as determined by criminal courts). Scheid and I agree on this. However, he also says that what someone deserves is absolutely constraining on the state's pursuit of crime control. Scheid imagines a system in which the state wants to reduce terrorist activity, so it proposes torturing its citizens for information. Assuming that such torture is undeserved – perhaps torture is always undeserved – then the system as a whole would be unjust: he says that "it would be the package – the overall effectiveness of the agency in its achievement of a worthy goal by acceptable methods – that we would ultimately have to evaluate" (Scheid 1997, 451). The two-tiered model justifies the same conclusion: torture is not only an unreliable way of getting accurate information (thus inefficient and gratuitous), but, if we assume a liberal political system, then it is contrary to the values that the state ought to promote (thus unjust).

Although he does not put it like this, Scheid also seems to think that the general justifying aim of punishment constrains the penalties we can give offenders. Scheid rejects the retributivist claim that there are absolute or context-independent amounts of punishment that offenders deserve. Instead, "the overall magnitude of the punishment scale will depend on the empirical requirements of crime control," while the specific punishments assigned to different criminals on that scale depend on what they deserve (Scheid 1997, 488). For example, if the death penalty increases crime because it has a brutalizing effect, then the range of punishments would exclude execution, even if the case could be made, on retributivist grounds, that murderers deserve to die. Scheid says that, in an imaginary world where murder cannot be deterred, "since the general justifying aim of punishment is deterrence or crime control … then the act should not come within the ambit of punishable crimes" (502n118). So, the constraint goes in both directions: the general justifying aim limits retributive distribution, and retributive distribution limits crime control.

Although Scheid emphasizes how desert claims limit pursuit of the common good and I emphasize how consequentialism limits the distribution of punishment, we arrive at the same place. The question is what to do when there is a conflict between those two values. Each aim cannot constrain the other in a strict sense, because that would entail a contradictory conclusion: for example, that we should execute murderers and not execute murderers. Perhaps such conflicts are not "standard situations" as Scheid defines them. In any event, evaluating which punishments are "appropriate," determining which methods are "acceptable," and figuring out whether a punishment is "fair" enough given our broader aims – these are Scheid's terms – are tasks that can only be accomplished through a dialogic process and the achievement of reflective equilibrium (Scheid 1997, 449, 451). Scheid may not like the appeal to intuition (any more than I do – see Chapter 9), but, when resolving conflicts, it is the best we can do – and the best he can do.

Joel Feinberg has a more complex picture of the situation than Scheid does. Feinberg says that, when individual justice and social utility are both valued in a legal or moral system, they can stand in one of four different kinds of relations:

1) The two principles can never conflict.
2) When they do conflict, social utility trumps individual justice.[8]
3) When they do conflict, individual justice trumps social utility.
4) When they do conflict, we cannot tell in advance which claim will be strongest. They must be "balanced" by considering the specific case and weighing the principles against one another. (1972, 1006)

The first option is unrealistic, the second option can be attributed to Rawls, and the third option is typified by Norval Morris's limiting retributivism. Like

8 Zaibert claims, wrongly, that this is the only option available to mixed justifications. He says that, according to mixed views, retributivism inevitably must give way to "the intricate workings of some State institutions": they are left with "a deflated version of retributivism, precisely tailored to fit in an overarching consequentialist agenda" (2006, 16–17). Similarly, Wood says that a mixed theory such as mine amounts to "confining retributivist considerations to the second level, and so giving them … a lesser role" (2002, 306). According to the two-tiered model, however, jury nullification may be right precisely because desert can justifiably check our collective attempts to preserve the public order.

Scheid's position,[9] the two-tiered model falls into the fourth category, with some caveats. Like Ross's *prima facie* duties, our competing obligations regarding punishment are not equally weighty. In earlier chapters, I explained how the general justifying aim of punishment is consequentialist, with the idea that we ought to minimize suffering and choose the policy that most efficiently achieves our social aims, and that those social aims ought to be just. Within the range of statutory penalties, judges assign punishments to the guilty in proportion to their degrees of guilt. Therefore, consequentialism constrains retributivism through the punishment schedule. The possibility of justified jury nullification introduces a caveat. We ought to select the most deserved punishment within the range of statutory penalties *unless* doing so would be so disproportionate as to be unreasonable.

Consider the case of a shoplifter who steals bread to feed their starving family. The judge would likely give them the minimum sentence, which in most states is a small fine. The judge may believe that the offender is a good person who acted out of desperation, but, since they did commit the crime and the state is obligated to deter stealing, it is worth the burden imposed on them, even if, on some accounts, the person does not deserve it. By contrast, in cases of jury nullification, the penalty is thought to be excessive given what the person did, thus not only violating our retributive obligation but also the obligation to reduce suffering. The punishment in such a case is unnecessarily harsh and so undeserved that any judge or jury who imposes it would be acting wrongly. There have been several illustrative cases related to three-strikes laws. For example, a Los Angeles jury found a defendant guilty of possessing one rock of crack cocaine, but then discovered that it would result in a sentence of twenty-five years to life in prison. When the jurors were polled to confirm the verdict, two jurors changed their minds, resulting in a hung jury (Chiang 1996). The defendant committed the crime, but the sentence would have been so disproportionate to the actual offense that the jury thought the community's resentment could be better expressed by freeing the offender, despite his guilt. Thus, jury nullification happens with regard to distribution of punishment both in terms of what Hart calls title and amount (2008, 4) – that is, both in terms of who is punished (e.g., the defendant who is guilty of not turning in a fugitive slave) and how much (e.g., the defendant who would get twenty-five years for low-level drug possession).

Such extreme cases of conflict between consequentialism at the institutional level and retributivism at the individual level are very rare, especially since the principles are relevant to different parts of the legal system. Indeed, most such conflicts can be avoided if the principles are properly applied. I argued that three-strikes laws have not benefited the community, so they are not in fact justified on consequentialist grounds. The same is true of fugitive slave laws. The conflict that precipitates jury nullification is often between an erroneous calculation about the

9 Scheid claims that he identifies with the fourth option (1997, 446n12). He says that a system has to be evaluated as a "package," considering both its general deterrent purpose and its retributive function (451).

benefits of such laws and a proper assignment of guilt. Still, however infrequent, there are some cases where our competing obligations must be weighed against one another. Consequentialism and retributivism are separately justified obligations, so one cannot simply override the other in every case. This is in contrast to Rawls's view and more in alignment with Hart, who says that "our main social institutions always possess a plurality of features which can only be understood as a compromise between partly discrepant principles" (2008, 10).

Does this mean that the two-tiered model gives us "a shifting patchwork of compromises and arbitrary decisions" (Duff and Garland 1994, 5)? On my view, there can be disagreement among people who hold competing but equally reasonable views, and there is no algorithm to settle that disagreement. But that recognition hardly renders us directionless. In most cases, the statutory penalties established by the legislature appropriately constrain the retributivist impulses of judges and juries. In those rare cases where statutory penalties are unreasonably severe or weak, there is a deliberative process by which we arrive at reflective equilibrium. That is no vaguer than what the retributivist would have us do when one desert theorist says that murderers deserve to be executed and another desert theorist says that life in prison is good enough. All we can do is examine the arguments and try to figure out which is best, based on the principles that we hold, which, in the case of the two-tiered model, are consequentialism and retributivism.

The paradox of punishment

This is also why the two-tiered model is not plagued by the so-called paradox of punishment. The idea behind the paradox of punishment is that, in order to deter crime, punishments must be increased well beyond what is deserved to account for the fact that getting caught and convicted is unlikely. Punishments are supposed to serve as incentives not to commit crimes, but if criminals are only caught half the time, for example, then the punishment for a given class of offenses would have to be twice what it would be if everyone were caught. If we would typically give a burglar two years in prison but burglars are only caught half the time, then we would have to double the sentence to four years in order to incentivize potential criminals not to do it. It would not be worth it to commit burglary if the offender receives a two-year sentence every time, but it may be worth it to them if they only get a two-year sentence every other time. The problem for mixed theories is that, if punishments are increased to account for this, then individual criminals are getting more than they deserve; and if they are not increased, then punishment does not serve its deterrent purpose – hence the paradox (Goldman 1979).

Under the two-tiered model, the separate obligations will usually not compete since they apply to different things: deterrence applies at the institutional level and at the level of statutory penalties, and desert applies at the level of individual allocations. A concern with deterrence limits our retributive impulses within statutory boundaries. Provided that the punishment is within the range of reasonably appropriate allocations, a criminal who gets more or less than what they deserve, strictly speaking, would not be a problem. Judges would simply give the criminal the least or the most severe punishment within the legislatively designated range. The paradox of punishment depends on there being a specific, mathematically determined punishment established by means of deterrence and a specific, preferentially determined punishment established by means of desert-allocation. However, for neither view must punishment be exact, only good enough given our other obligations – satisficing consequentialism rather than maximizing consequentialism – and relatively deserving rather than absolutely deserving (Slote 1985, 35–59). These are made consistent with one another through a collective process of deliberation, including public discussion, elections, and jury nullification.

Conclusion

Legal historians are well aware that, in most democracies with constitutional governance, neither the legislature nor the courts are wholly responsible for the criminal law. The legislature sets statutory penal codes, which are interpreted and applied by the courts. When the law is silent, the courts innovate and extend existing law in ways that establish common-law precedent. This often prompts legislative changes, which are then interpreted by the courts – and the cycle continues. The fact that this back-and-forth process takes place does not mean that the criminal law is arbitrary. As a social endeavor, this is what practical reasoning looks like.

When we as a community hold two distinct and contrary justifications of punishment, conflict is inevitable. But that does not leave us rudderless. The legislature and the criminal judiciary check one another's power to intentionally inflict harm on their own citizens. Policies that preserve the public order are limited by how much people deserve, and the distribution of punishments is limited by legislative decisions about what will advance the common good. This mutual constraint occurs through an imperfect and open-ended process of collective practical reasoning that arrives, temporarily, at reflective equilibrium. The goal is to maintain a just social arrangement while also validating the community's warranted reactive attitudes, thus fulfilling both *prima facie* obligations and doing what is right.

Part V

Applications

There are no mathematical algorithms to solve the problems posed by practical philosophers. Still, a theory of punishment should help us to sort things out. As Michael Davis says, "insofar as theories help us to see phenomena more clearly, a theory of punishment should help us resolve practical problems of punishment more easily" (2009, 77). And things do need to be sorted out. Take the United States as an example. Although in principle the U.S. conceives of the law as an enforcement mechanism for protecting people's rights, its current criminal justice system is a complicated amalgam of historical precedent, well-meaning legislation, political posturing, reform movements, and legal responses to constitutional challenges. As far as theory goes, lawmakers and judges appeal to retribution and deterrence almost interchangeably, depending on their mood.

Part V transitions from the philosophy of punishment to something more like penal theory. I show that the two-tiered model of punishment is action-guiding, that it can be used as a theoretical framework with which to identify reasons for or against particular legal practices around punishment, and that it can be a tool of reform. As examples, I discuss two controversial legal and moral issues: the death penalty (chapter 12) and restorative justice (chapter 13). The two-tiered model can explain why the death penalty ought to be abolished: as a statutory penalty, it does not promote the public good. It can also explain how restorative practices can accomplish the aims of retribution, and in ways that are more socially constructive than incarceration alone.

12 Consequences of capital punishment

One implication of the two-tiered model of punishment is that lawmakers should be using consequentialist reasoning to decide on statutory penalties. If a punishment inflicts more suffering than is necessary to accomplish its end – that is, if it does not deter potential criminals more than a lesser alternative – then it is not parsimonious and should not be an option for judges and juries to impose. That is one way that the legislature restrains the community's retributive impulses.

Hundreds of studies have been conducted to determine whether the death penalty deters, and their conclusions vary. Some studies claim to show that the death penalty has no impact on murder rates, others insist that it deters murderers and saves lives, and still others conclude that the death penalty actually increases rates of violent crime. Researchers criticize the study designs of those on the other side of the debate, who then defend their methods – and during all this back-and-forth, people continue to be executed.

In this chapter, I make two separate arguments against the death penalty: (1) it does not deter more than life in prison, and (2) resources that go toward executions would be better spent on more effective crime-prevention measures. These are both consequentialist reasons why state and federal legislatures should abolish capital punishment. In jurisdictions where the death penalty is an option, legislatures are either appealing to erroneous data regarding deterrence or wrongly justifying the practice with an appeal to desert. Thus, in states with the death penalty, the legislature is not fulfilling its proper role, distinct from judges, in furthering the aims of the state without inflicting gratuitous suffering on its citizens.

The argument for deterrence

Punitive and nonpunitive methods of social control are both necessary to preserve the public order, so that people are motivated to follow the law. The institution of punishment, specifically, is a kind of threat system that establishes costs for committing crimes. For economists, it is obvious that raising the cost of an activity will lower demand, and recently economists have been the primary defenders of the view that the death penalty, by raising the cost of committing murder, has a deterrent effect. As Kenneth Avio puts it, "Economists have tended to view the risks of apprehension as well as the threatened punishments as implicit prices which are hypothesized to elicit a supply response" – in the case of capital punishment, to drive down the number ("supply") of killings (1988, 1253).[1] Several recent econometric studies have concluded through statistical analysis that the death penalty saves the lives of potential victims, with totals ranging from three to eighteen innocents spared for each execution.

A study by economists Naci Mocan and Kaj Gittings (2003) is a representative example. They examined the effect of several different factors on the homicide rate: execution rate, commutation and removal rates, homicide arrest rate, sentencing rate, imprisonment rate, and prison death rate. Rather than compare each of these factors to the homicide rate in a given year, Mocan and Gittings introduced a time lag, since executions in the latter half of the year would be more likely to affect homicide rates in the following year. The authors examined 6,143 death sentences between 1977 and 1997 and concluded that each execution "reduces," "decreases," or "generates a reduction in" homicides by about five and that each commutation "increases" homicides by the same amount (Mocan and Gittings 2003; see also Mocan and Gittings 2010).

An argument against the argument for deterrence: Faulty assumptions

Many social scientists, psychologists, and philosophers have challenged studies like Mocan and Gittings's, and those challenges fall into two broad categories: first, regarding their conceptual assumptions about potential murderers' decision-making; and, second, regarding their study designs and methods of data analysis. These sorts of difficulties plague most of the economists' research in this area, and they call into doubt the consequentialist basis of their support for the death penalty.

The first problem with these studies is that their inference to the deterrent effect of the death penalty depends on a conception of the person that is least accurate in describing potential and actual murderers. Although punishment as an institution is necessary as a kind of threat system, the idea that all criminals or classes of criminals are equally deterrable does not follow from that. Most contemporary deterrence theories (including mine) are based on a Beckerian model of crime according to which people are driven by a decision-making calculus where they weigh potential benefits against potential risks. In other words, researchers consider potential criminals to be consumers in a competitive marketplace, albeit ones who are risk-acceptant (G. Becker 1968).

The problem with this assumption is that, while none of us are ideal optimizers of personal utility (*homo economicus*), murderers are often impaired in ways

1 At the end of his own study that purports to show a deterrent effect, Layson concludes, "Even murderers appear to obey the law of demand" (1985, 88).

that make them even less so than the average citizen, and indeed other criminals. Hugo Adam Bedau explains why:

> Most capital crimes are committed in the heat of the moment. Most capital crimes are committed during moments of great emotional stress or under the influence of drugs or alcohol, when logical thinking has been suspended. Many capital crimes are committed by the badly emotionally-damaged or mentally ill. In such cases, violence is inflicted by persons unable to appreciate the consequences to themselves as well as to others. … It is impossible to imagine how the threat of any punishment could prevent a crime that is not premeditated. (2012, pars. 24–25)

Murders committed in the heat of the moment, by people who are mentally unbalanced or are impaired by drugs and alcohol (or both), are done without a serious consideration of the possible consequences. Studies show that violent crimes tend to involve less self-control than nonviolent crimes (Heilbrun, Knopf, and Bruner 1976), most impulsive murderers (93 percent) have a history of drug or alcohol abuse and/or were intoxicated at the time of the killing, and most impulsive murderers (59 percent) are developmentally disabled (Hanlon et al. 2013). Because impulsive murders are more prevalent than premeditated murders, the majority of murderers are not engaging in rational reflection to calculate whether killing someone will benefit them in the long run.

In *Gregg v. Georgia* (428 U.S. 153 [1976]), which reinstated the death penalty in the U.S., the Supreme Court concedes that impulsive murderers will not respond to incentives in a rational way. However, the justices claim that some members of the subclass of instrumental or predatory murderers are capable of being deterred by the threat of execution:

> Although some of the studies suggest that the death penalty may not function as a significantly greater deterrent than lesser penalties, there is no convincing empirical evidence either supporting or refuting this view. We may nevertheless assume safely that there are murderers, such as those who act in passion, for whom the threat of death has little or no deterrent effect. But for many others, the death penalty undoubtedly is a significant deterrent. There are carefully contemplated murders, such as murder for hire, where the possible penalty of death may well enter into the cold calculus that precedes the decision to act. (185–86, note omitted)

There are a number of qualifications here: the data are inconclusive, some (impulsive) murders are not deterred by the death penalty, and *some* people who commit *some* (planned) murders *may be* deterred. Setting aside these important caveats, the Court's reference to a "cold calculus" presupposes that some hypothetical agents act rationally in deciding whether killing would ultimately be to their benefit. Other defenders of the death penalty make similar claims. Ernest van den Haag, for example, speculates that the death penalty motivates some potential murderers to refrain from killing: "I believe the death penalty, because of its finality, is more feared than imprisonment, and deters some prospective murderers not deterred by the threat of imprisonment" (1986, 1665–66). The idea is that, because people are motivated by *ex ante* incentives, a greater incentive (i.e., a more severe penalty) will be more motivating. People do not want to die, so the threat of death keeps some potential murderers – the ones who are deterrable rather than incorrigible – from carrying through on their desire to kill.

Defenders of the death penalty here make several questionable assumptions. The first assumption is that there is a strict distinction between impulsive or expressive murders (e.g., as a result of unexpected, confrontational disputes) and instrumental or predatory murders (e.g., robbery-homicides) (Miethe and Regoeczi 2004, 101–29). They imagine that impulsive murderers decide on the spot, in the heat of the moment, to kill someone, while instrumental murderers plan ahead for weeks or months and weigh the costs and benefits. However, premeditation is defined differently in different states, and in many states it means that the person could have decided to do it mere seconds before the murder. An armed robber may never have intended to use violence, only to threaten it, until things went unexpectedly wrong. Under the circumstances, even someone who is guilty of premeditated murder under the law's definition may not have had the ability to do a complex calculus that considers whether their state has the death penalty, their chances of getting caught, the likelihood of a death sentence, how successful appeals tend to be, the state's execution rate, and so on. In a country where only 38 percent of the people know that their state has a constitution (Bachner and Ginsberg 2021, 5), many potential murderers probably cannot even say whether the death penalty is an option, let alone the chances that they will be executed.[2]

A second assumption is that, unlike impulsive murderers, would-be instrumental murderers are thinking rationally. But even instrumental murderers tend on the whole to be psychologically impaired. Unlike impulsive murderers, murderers who commit their crimes with malice aforethought are not lacking in neurological and cognitive functions; their IQs tend to be in the normal range. However, they suffer from other psychiatric disorders, and at a much higher rate than their impulsive counterparts. In one study, two-thirds of prisoners who were found guilty of premeditated murder had mental disorders such as schizophrenia or bipolar disorder, or personality disorders such as antisocial, histrionic, or narcissistic disorders (Woodworth and Porter 2002; Hanlon et al. 2013). Among other things, such disorders affect their capacity to empathize with their victims and thus undermine their ability to calculate the effects of their actions, especially on others.

It is true that impulsive murderers are less likely to consider the consequences of their actions than instrumental murderers. By definition, instrumental murderers

2 As far as I can tell, no one has polled people to determine the level of awareness regarding the legal existence of the death penalty in their states. Most polls have to do with whether people support it.

are looking for some kind of gain: to get money or drugs, improve their social status in a gang, or some such thing. But because these crimes are not committed in the heat of the moment, it also means that these criminals are less likely to be caught, or less likely to believe that they will be caught. The fact that they have a plan for succeeding at the crime means that they think they are careful enough to get away with it, so the possibility of execution does not pose much of a threat to them. If they believe that they will not get caught and if the threat of life in prison without parole (which is no small punishment!) is not enough to deter them, adding a more severe penalty, as a remote possibility, will not deter them either.

The deterrent effect of a punishment, remember, depends more on its certainty and celerity than its severity. If potential murderers knew that they would be immediately executed following a killing, then many of them would be less likely to do it. But that is hardly the case. Although the death penalty is "the ultimate punishment," it is also the least certain of any punishment and the most distant. A survey of fifty-five major U.S. cities found that only 50 percent of homicides result in an arrest ("Murder with Impunity" 2020). Even if a murderer is caught, what follows in about 60 percent of capital cases is a plea agreement for a lesser charge or a lesser punishment (Thaxton 2013). And in those cases where a trial takes place, there is uncertainty about whether they will be found guilty and, if they are, whether they will be sentenced to death. If they do receive a capital conviction, most states require a direct appeal to the state supreme court, where the inmate challenges the claims made at trial. They must wait until a state-appointed lawyer is assigned to them – an average of three to five years – and then the appointed counsel must research the case, study case law, file an opening brief, wait for the state to file a responsive brief, and file a reply brief – a process that usually takes another few years (Alarcón 2007; Latzer and Cauthen 2007; California Commission 2008, 121–25). And if the state supreme court hears the case, it is usually two or three years before the case is scheduled and a judgment is made. The direct appeal is often followed by collateral review of habeas corpus issues by the state supreme court and federal appeals courts, possibly up to and including the U.S. Supreme Court. At each step in the process, there are similar delays in appointing counsel, in researching the case and petitioning the court, and in the court's review. The complete federal habeas review process takes about ten years. And each step makes it less likely that the person will get the death penalty. James Liebman, Jeffrey Fagan, and Valerie West (2000) found that, in capital cases from 1973 to 1995, 41 percent of convictions were reversed during direct appeal at the state level, 10 percent of the remaining decisions were overturned through the state post-conviction review process, and 40 percent of the cases that survived state challenges were reversed as a result of federal habeas corpus proceedings. In total, U.S. appeals courts discovered serious, reversible error in 68 percent of the capital convictions.

Even if their convictions are not overturned or they are successfully retried (and the new verdicts are not also reversed on appeal), that does not mean convicted murderers will be executed. According to the U.S. Department of Justice, prisoners executed in 2017 had been on death row an average of twenty years and three months (Bureau of Justice Statistics 2019). A more efficient review process is nearly impossible because of our underfunded death penalty system, especially budget cuts to public defenders' offices. Because of the numerous and long delays, many of those who are sentenced to be executed die of natural causes before the execution takes place – basically, serving life in prison. All told, the Bureau of Justice Statistics (2014) found that, of the 8,466 people who were sentenced to death in the U.S. between 1976 and 2013, only 1,359 (16 percent) were actually executed. The rest had their sentences or convictions overturned (38 percent), had their sentences commuted (5 percent), remained on death row at the time of the study (35 percent), or died of natural causes or suicide (6 percent) (20). In short, execution is a distant and unlikely possibility, lacking both celerity and certainty.

Consequentialist defenders of the death penalty make an improper inference. The fact that some general practice of punishment (as a threat system) is necessary to deter crime does not mean that the deterrent effect of any particular punishment such as the death penalty is directly proportional to its severity.[3] The factors that affect a punishment's deterrent ability vary depending on the crime (Chambliss 1967; Silberman 1976; Geerken and Gove 1977). And, given capital punishment's uncertainty and lack of swiftness, the threat of execution poses little real risk for offenders. As H. L. A. Hart says, the death penalty for a potential murderer may mean

> a not very high probability of death in the future. And futurity and uncertainty, the hope of an escape, rational or irrational, vastly diminishes the differences between death and imprisonments as deterrents, and may diminish it to a vanishing point. (2008, 86)

While the cost is high in terms of severity, murderers are extremely unlikely ever to have to pay that cost (lack of certainty) and extremely unlikely to pay it anytime soon (lack of celerity).

Do these objections imply that murderers are undeterrable, so we should not punish them at all? No. What it implies is that the death penalty is unlikely to deter more than life in prison – a comparative question regarding marginal utility rather than absolute utility.[4] Since the state has a *prima facie* obligation not to inflict excessive harm on its citizens, the burden of proof is on proponents of capital punishment to demonstrate that it is necessary. Another purpose of

3 Flanders makes this inference:

> To question whether *death deters* is ultimately to question the foundation of general deterrence theory, the idea that the harsher a penalty, the greater the deterrence value. If we accept general deterrence in other areas of punishment, which we by and large do, there is no reason to suddenly reject it in the death penalty context. (2013, 601)

4 Incidentally, this would be true even if neither execution nor life in prison has any deterrent effect.

punishment, restraint, could be accomplished as well with imprisonment (life without parole) as with execution.[5] The claims I have made do not cast doubt on the need for punishment in general, but on the assumptions that underlie the pro-death penalty argument. Most murderers do not make rational calculations based on the severity of the death penalty. In behavioral psychology terms, the contingency between murder and execution (the operant and its consequent) is weak or nonexistent.

Of course, Mocan and Gittings claim to show that it does deter: each execution – actual execution, not death sentence – saves five innocent lives, and each commutation leads to five additional homicides. But these claims defy logic. In Texas, for example, executions are common enough that they get scant news coverage. And commutations are even less publicized. In a country where only 19 percent of the people know who their state senator is (Bachner and Ginsberg 2021, 5), it is unlikely that criminals and potential criminals, most of whom are drug users with mental problems, are reviewing the results of appellate cases and deciding what to do based on the judges' rulings. In short, these econometric studies depend on "incomplete or implausible models of potential murderers' perceptions of and response to the capital punishment component of a sanction regime" (Committee on Deterrence and the Death Penalty 2012, 3).

Another argument against the argument for deterrence: Fragile inferences

There are also problems with the economists' methodology, which casts their conclusions into doubt. Their studies indicate that the death penalty is an effective deterrent – specifically, that it lowers the homicide rate more than incarceration – but they disagree about how much of a deterrent it is. The most well-known of these studies and their findings are as follows:

- In 1975, Isaac Ehrlich concluded that each execution saves eight lives (that is, eight more than if the offender were given life imprisonment).
- In 2003, Hashem Dezhbakhsh, Paul Rubin, and Joanna Shepherd concluded that each execution saves eighteen lives.
- In 2003, Mocan and Gittings concluded that each execution saves five lives.
- In 2004, Joanna Shepherd concluded that each execution saves three lives (see also Dezhbakhsh and Shepherd 2006).[6]
- In 2004, Paul Zimmerman concluded that each execution saves fourteen lives.

5 In this chapter, I have been discussing general deterrence primarily, and here I reference restraint. Specific deterrence is not an aim for either life in prison or execution. People who are executed cannot be rehabilitated. And it is irrelevant whether people are rehabilitated while they spend their lives in prison without the possibility of parole, because they will never be reintegrated into society.

6 The fact that, only a year earlier, Shepherd herself was coauthor on a study that found six times the deterrent effect than her 2004 study indicates that something is wrong with these econometric studies.

Social scientists cannot conduct controlled, experimental studies that would allow them to isolate a single variable related to the murder rate. For example, they cannot execute murderers in a treatment group and refrain from executing murderers in a control group, all while controlling for other socioeconomic and demographic variables. So, strictly speaking, they cannot say that executions "save" lives or "reduce" homicides, which are causal claims.[7] Instead, these researchers can only claim to show that executing convicted murderers (the predictor variable) is correlated with a lower number of homicides (the criterion/outcome variable). That is, when a state executes someone, there are fewer murders in that state compared to a state that does not execute someone who would be eligible for it elsewhere. Any causal claim based on that correlational data would require an additional inference and would depend on assuming that other predictors (per capita income, age, drug use, etc.) are adequately accounted for in their study designs.[8]

Ehrlich's (1975) article was revolutionary because it was the first study to use advanced econometric techniques to examine deterrence, and it broke with the many previous studies that seemed to show that the death penalty does not deter more than life in prison. His work was so well received that it may have impacted public policy. U.S. Solicitor General Robert Bork's amicus brief on behalf of the state in *Gregg v. Georgia* relied heavily on Ehrlich's findings in claiming that the death penalty is not excessive because it does deter (Bork, Randolph, and Easterbrook 2008, 24–26; see also Bork 2008, 81).[9] And the Supreme Court referenced Ehrlich in their opinion (*Gregg v. Georgia*, 428 U.S. 153 [1976], 184n31), claiming that, because empirical studies were inconclusive regarding the death penalty's deterrent effect – this despite the fact that nearly every study prior to Ehrlich consistently showed no effect – it ought to be left to the states to decide whether to adopt it (155, 184–87).[10]

Immediately after Ehrlich's work was published, it was subjected to several criticisms. Among other things, the FBI data he uses to measure homicides and

7 Ehrlich uses the language of "saving" lives by executing murderers (1975, 398). Dezhbakhsh, Rubin, and Shepherd say both that executions "save" victims (2003, 373) and that they "result in" fewer murders (344, 369). Mocan and Gittings say that each execution "decreases" (2003, 453, 474), "reduces" (456, 466), or "generates a reduction" in homicides (469). Shepherd says that each execution "results in" fewer murders (2004, 283, 308). And Zimmerman says that the death penalty "deters" murder (2004, 163, 166).

8 Although I focus on the econometric studies using panel data, there is another set of studies, called "event studies," that use granular time series data to see whether the *timing* of executions affects the murder rate. Evidence of deterrence was discovered by Land, Teske, and Zheng (2009). No evidence of deterrence was found by Cochran, Chamlin, and Seth (1994); Stolzenberg and D'Alessio (2004); and Zimring, Fagan, and Johnson (2010). I focus on the econometric studies using panel data because the findings are purported to be more robust, they consistently indicate a deterrent effect, and they have had more of an influence on public policy discussions. Few event studies show a deterrent effect. They also have several methodological and conceptual problems. For a discussion of these problems, see Charles and Durlauf (2013).

9 Bork says that the Ehrlich study provides "strong empirical evidence that the threat of imprisonment deters crime (including murder)" (Bork, Randolph, and Easterbrook 2008, 24) and that Ehrlich's work "is respectable academic evidence on the side of deterrence" (Bork 2008, 81).

10 Justice Thurgood Marshall criticizes Ehrlich's study in his dissent in *Gregg v. Georgia* (428 U.S. 153 [1976]), 233–36.

punishments are unreliable, especially for the 1930s; his assumptions about which explanatory variables to include and exclude are questionable and, along with his model's functional form, greatly impact the outcomes; his regressions are unstable over the 1960s;[11] his findings rely too much on estimates (of offenses, arrest rates, conviction rates, and murder convictions); and he confuses cause and effect – that is, it is more likely that the homicide rate affected the probability of punishment, not vice versa (Baldus and Cole 1975; Bowers and Pierce 1975; Passell and Taylor 1977; Klein, Forst, and Filatov 1978; Bowers, Pierce, and McDevitt 1984, 303–35; Avio 1988). Still, Ehrlich's work set the terms for future studies.

The econometric studies in the 2000s purport to be more accurate than either Ehrlich's analysis or older comparative studies that found no deterrent effect. These more recent studies all use similar approaches. They use annual state- or county-level panel data on homicides in the U.S. in places that had the death penalty prior to the moratorium in 1972 (as a result of the *Furman* decision) and then reinstated it in 1976 (following *Gregg*). To analyze the data, they use fixed-effects models and operate within the ordinary least-squares (OLS) estimator framework. That is, they use a multivariate regression: they assume that the values of some predictors/regressors are fixed so that only one of the predictors (executions) changes, and, to estimate unknown parameters, they minimize the difference between observed responses and the responses predicted by the linear approximation ("fitting" the function with the data). Binary dummy variables are introduced – for example, 1 if the death penalty is legal and 0 if it is not. The studies also include a variety of predictors that are correlated with the homicide rate, such as the unemployment rate, real per capita income, proportion of the population in urban areas, age group distributions, proportion of the population that is Black, and so on. The idea is that they want to be able to measure the influence of these different predictors on the homicide rate and identify the specific effect of executions, as distinct from these other predictors.

Many academics and lawmakers have been impressed with these studies, and, like Ehrlich's work, they have been consulted when forming public policy. In her testimony before a U.S. Congressional subcommittee, Shepherd said:

> There may be people on the other side [of the death penalty debate] that rely on older papers and studies that use outdated statistical techniques or older

11 Donohue and Wolfers explain this issue:

> A particularly telling problem with the Ehrlich time-series analysis was that his finding of a deterrent effect emerged only because Ehrlich used a log specification that gave disproportionate weight to the fact that the small reduction in the execution rate from a very low level to virtually zero in the late 1960s was accompanied by a very large jump in murders. Stopping the analysis in 1962 rather than 1969 or using a nonlogarithmic model would generate no deterrent effect. This nonfinding seems more intuitively plausible in that the 80 percent decline in the execution rate over the period of 1933-1962 occurred during a period of falling murder rates (from 8.8 per 100,000 to 4.6, a decline of 47.7 percent) and the large post-1962 increase in murder rates occurred identically in states that never had the death penalty as well as those that did. (2009, 253n1)

> data, but all of the modern economic studies in the past decade have found a deterrent effect. (quoted in Kovandzic, Vieraitis, and Boots 2009, 804; see also Liptak 2007)

Although I will question these studies, it is good that legislators are consulting empirical data. This is exactly the sort of process we should follow under the two-tiered model of punishment: legislation should be guided by punishment's effectiveness in furthering our collective aims, and research in criminology and the other social sciences is needed to evaluate its effectiveness.

Before assessing the economists' empirical methods, it should be noted that their findings are qualified in important ways. For example, Shepherd (2005) finds that deterrence rates vary among states because there is a threshold – nine executions annually – over which the death penalty begins to have a deterrent effect. Lower numbers of executions do not deter, and in some cases actually increase the murder rate. According to Shepherd's analysis, the death penalty only deters in six states (22 percent of the twenty-seven states that had capital punishment at the time of the study), has no effect in eight states (30 percent), and actually increases the murder rate in thirteen states (48 percent) – a brutalization effect. Unless there are other factors that account for geographic variation, this alone casts doubt on her conclusion that, overall, the death penalty deters potential murderers. In fact, the results are mixed. In addition, Zimmerman (2006) claims that the execution method matters. He discovered that the electric chair has a deterrent effect, but lethal injection, the gas chamber, hanging, and firing squads do not impact the homicide rate at all (see also Ekelund et al. 2006). Both Shepherd and Zimmerman defend capital punishment because of its deterrent effect. However, unless we want to electrocute people, and do it to more than nine people every year in each retentionist state, it follows from their own analyses that the death penalty is a bad bet.

Even if we assume, as these researchers do, that potential murderers do a cost-benefit analysis based on potential benefits and risks (à la Becker) – an assumption that I questioned earlier in the chapter – one crucial factor is how to measure risk. Different researchers measure probability of execution differently: ratio of executions to homicides (Zimmerman), ratio of executions to death row inmates (Shepherd), or ratio of executions to death sentences (Dezhbakhsh, Rubin, and Shepherd; Mocan and Gittings). Other researchers use the ratio of executions to prisoners or to the general population. A key question regards which outcomes potential murderers are likely to consider when calculating risks (Kovandzic, Vieraitis, and Boots 2009, 807). The economists disagree on this point, which is one reason why their results vary (anywhere from three to eighteen lives saved per execution).

Researchers also choose different lag times, from approximately one to six years, in measuring the deterrent effect. Because they have different definitions of this predictor variable, it threatens the internal validity of their study designs. For some, the lag time concerns how long it takes a criminal to be executed following their arrest. Because the deterrent effect of a punishment is affected by its celerity, a shorter time would have a more pronounced effect. Researchers have to account for the delays when assessing the deterrent value by assuming longer delays would lower the deterrent effect, and then imagining that the effect would be increased if the execution were sooner. By contrast, other researchers think of the lag time in terms of how the criminal's calculus (even if there is no such thing) is affected by death sentences rather than actual executions. If someone is sentenced to death, that sentence may affect the homicide rate, even though the execution happens years later. In that case, the impact of the sentence would show up immediately after the trial rather than when (or if) the convicted murderer is actually executed. Researchers disagree, however, about whether potential murderers are more impacted by death sentences or executions, which affects the time lag they assume, which affects their results. Even researchers who agree conceptually on the kind of lag to consider (to sentencing or to execution) disagree about how much of a lag to use. And the data they use varies over time and across states. It takes longer to be executed in California than in Texas, and the average time to execution overall in the United States nearly doubled in the twenty years preceding the rash of econometric studies in the early 2000s.[12]

Sample selection also has a dramatic impact on their findings. It is important to note that, when most of these studies were done, only twenty-seven of the fifty U.S. states had capital punishment. Restriction of range lowers correlation coefficients and impacts the studies' external validity. Furthermore, among those retentionist states, there was a lot of variation: some states hardly ever executed people, some states only occasionally executed, and some states executed often. Since there is no commonly accepted basis on which to decide whether or when to exclude outliers, researchers faced a dilemma: if the high-executing outliers such as Texas were excluded simply because their reliable data would have had an outsized effect on the outcomes, then that would have reduced the number of actual executions that the researchers considered, which would have increased the margin of error; but if only states that regularly executed people were included, then those outliers would have driven the results. The first problem is addressed by Richard Berk, who examines the problem of "influence" in these studies. He found that, if Texas is not included, the results are dramatically affected by death penalty states that execute no one or fewer than five prisoners per year, which is about 1 percent of the available data: "claims of deterrence are a statistical artifact of this anomalous 1 percent" (2005, 303). Considering that all the available

12 For example, Mocan and Gittings (2003) and Shepherd (2004) use six years as their lag, with the idea that it takes an average of six years between a death sentence and execution. They based that figure on data from the Bureau of Justice Statistics in 1994 (Kovandzic, Vieraitis, and Boots 2009, 807). When they did their studies in 2003 and 2004, however, the average was 131 and 132 months, respectively, not six years. As of 2017, the average time spent on death row was over ten years (243 months), and in California it was over twenty-five years. See St. John (2016) and Death Penalty Information Center (2020e).

longitudinal data shows no deterrent effect (as we will see later), this seems to inflate their statistical importance.

If Texas is included, however, then it skews the results in the other direction. Most researchers focus on frequency of executions as a key factor in measuring execution risk. This has affected the economists' findings by overemphasizing states that execute a lot of people, or smaller states that execute a lot of people relative to their population. Between the death penalty's reinstatement in 1976 and the end of 2020, Texas executed 570 people, over 37 percent of the total executions in the United States as a whole (Death Penalty Information Center 2020c). In 2018, only twenty-five executions took place across the country, and thirteen of them were in Texas (Death Penalty Information Center 2020b). Texas is thus overrepresented in these homicide regression models. Dezhbakhsh and Shepherd estimate the effect of an execution on the homicide rate to be –0.145, which means that an execution in Texas deters about twenty murders while an execution in Delaware deters less than one (2006, 525).[13] Yet, in their 2003 study, they conclude that each execution saves eighteen lives (Dezhbakhsh, Rubin, and Shepherd 2003, 344, 369, 373). Including high-executing states expands the amount of data, but in ways that make the results unrepresentative of general trends.

Researchers who ignore these outliers and focus on more typical states – setting aside the question of what counts as "typical" – face a different problem. If we dismiss reliable data simply because it overrepresents one state, then the smaller sample size introduces a greater margin of error and less external validity. If, for example, Texas is removed from the study, this leads to a range of possible outcomes, anywhere from thirty-four lives saved per execution to forty-two lives lost (a brutalization effect) (Donohue and Wolfers 2005, 823–26). In other words, these studies produce opposite conclusions regarding the deterrent effect of the death penalty overall depending on whether Texas is excluded as an outlier or included to increase the sample size. In light of this, they cannot really tell us whether executions save lives.

In addition, all these studies are at risk of endogeneity bias because they omit relevant predictors or assume that they are fixed in their models. Edward Leamer illustrates the problem. After listing possible deterrent variables, economic variables, and social and environmental variables, he imagines different researchers devising different studies:

> Individuals with different experiences and different training will find different subsets of the variables to be candidates for omission from the equation. … A right winger expects the punishment variables [e.g., probability of capital conviction] to have an effect, but treats all other variables as doubtful. … The rational maximizer takes the variables that measure the expected economic return of crime as important, but treats the taste [i.e., social/environmental]

13 In this analysis of their data, I am following Kovandzic, Vieraitis, and Boots (2009, 810n5).

> variables as doubtful. The eye-for-an-eye prior treats all variables as doubtful except the probability of execution. An individual with the bleeding heart prior sees murder as the result of economic impoverishment. Finally, if murder is thought to be a crime of passion then the punishment variables are doubtful. (1983, 41–42)

The results of Leamer's imagined studies are very different, with some finding deterrent effects of different levels to others finding a brutalization effect. And this is not merely a hypothetical example. A study by Tomislav Kovandzic, Lynne Vieraitis, and Denise Boots (2009) uses the same methods as the economists who claimed to discover a deterrent effect. They control for socioeconomic variables that were typically included in the other studies: unemployment rate, real per capita income, poverty rate, education level, and so on. But they also control for other possible confounding factors, including crime policy variables such as three-strikes laws and right-to-carry concealed handgun laws, and historical events such as the rise of mass incarceration and the crack epidemic. With these other predictors included, Kovandzic, Vieraitis, and Boots determine that the death penalty has no effect on the homicide rate. In a regression model, this implies that the other predictors accounted for variance in the homicide rate that was previously attributed to the death penalty. As I mentioned earlier, the choice of explanatory model affects the number and type of predictors. As these models become more comprehensive by including more predictors, the relative influence of the death penalty diminishes.

To take another example, Dezhbakhsh, Rubin, and Shepherd use some variables to aggregate other variables. One of the variables in their decision rule, "Z," "contains individual-specific economic and demographic characteristics, as well as any other observable variable that may affect the individual's choice" (2003, 352). Their "murder supply equation" includes "TD," "a set of time trend dummies that captures national trends, such as violent TV programming or movies that have similar cross-county effects" (352–53). In addition, they use demographic factors as "proxies" for earning opportunities, since "earning opportunities (legitimate or illegitimate) cannot be perfectly controlled for in an empirical investigation" (351, 358). They include population density "to capture any relationship between drug activities in inner cities and murder rate" (358). And they include "judicial toughness" as a variable that "takes values 0, 1, or 2, depending on whether a state has zero, one, or two tough sentencing laws at a given year" (368, 368n24). There are many factors to consider, most of which are vague. For example, what counts as "violent TV programming" or "tough sentencing laws"? In short, researchers have to make decisions about which predictors to include, which ones to aggregate, how to measure the level of each predictor, and how much weight to give each one in the equation. Those decisions depend on educated guesswork and lead to different study designs and different results.

John Donohue and Justin Wolfers (2005) illustrate the fragility of these models. They use the same method as Dezhbakhsh, Rubin, and Shepherd (2003), who purport to show that each execution saves eighteen lives. But a few minor changes to the variables lead to very different results. For example, Dezhbakhsh, Rubin, and Shepherd try to control for "partisan influence" by using six political variables, reflecting the Republican vote shares in six different presidential elections (Donohue and Wolfers 2005, 826).[14] If, instead, the study consolidates this into one variable – the Republican vote share in the state in the most recent presidential election – then, even when using Dezhbakhsh, Rubin, and Shepherd's preferred model, the results indicate a brutalization effect: each execution leads to eighteen *additional* homicides (Donohue and Wolfers 2005, 825–26).

Another problem with these studies, and indeed with many multiple regression analyses, is multicollinearity. There are numerous predictors that affect the homicide rate, but they cannot be isolated. That is, many of the predictors affect one another, in addition to affecting the homicide rate. Here is just a sample of possible predictors:

- socioeconomic factors such as the unemployment rate, per capita income, poverty rate, job availability, social mobility, percent of single-parent families, and education level;
- demographic factors such as population density, age, gender, and race;
- behavioral factors such as alcohol and drug consumption;
- political factors such as a state's partisan affiliation;
- historical factors such as the crack epidemic or mass incarceration;
- legal factors such as three-strikes laws, truth-in-sentencing laws, and right-to-carry concealed handgun laws; and
- penological factors such as level of police presence, likelihood of apprehension, probability of capital conviction, median time served on death row, probability of execution, and how well-publicized executions are.

Many of these predictors are correlated with one or more of the other predictors. For example, the unemployment rate impacts per capita income and drug use; there are racial disparities in education level; and demographics affect a state's partisan affiliation, which affects the severity of criminal statutes. Such multicollinearity reduces the precision of the estimate coefficients – that is, it makes it harder to control for other predictors and focus on executions specifically – so it impacts the validity of the models and the significance of the results.

All of this is to say that the findings of these researchers are extremely sensitive to decisions they make in their study designs. Small tweaks to the sample periods, comparison groups, control variables, functional forms, and estimators have large effects on their outcomes. Donohue and Wolfers show that, depending on one's assumptions and the model one chooses, the results, using the exact same data and study design, could vary significantly: "with the most minor tweaking of

14 Dezhbakhsh, Rubin, and Shepherd claim to focus only on the Republican share of *the most recent* presidential election (2003, 357, 360), but Donohue and Wolfers, who had access to their data and code, discovered that was not the case (2005, 825–26).

[Dezhbakhsh, Rubin, and Shepherd's] instruments, one can get estimates ranging from 429 lives saved per execution to 86 lives lost. These numbers are outside the bounds of credibility" (Donohue and Wolfers 2006, 3; see also Donahue and Wolfers 2005, 824). One can, of course, argue about which assumptions to include. My point is that the question is not settled and that the data does not show, with any degree of stability, that the death penalty deters more than life in prison. These econometric studies are at best inconclusive and at worst misleading. As a result, "any inference from these data about the deterrent effect of capital punishment is too fragile to be believed" (Leamer 1983, 42). Death penalty proponents, including legislators, should not place so much confidence in their findings.[15]

An argument against deterrence

If executions deter potential criminals, then having the death penalty would lower the rate of murders or violent crimes more than if there were no death penalty. One challenge is that social scientists cannot isolate one predictor (executions) and measure the effect of its presence or absence on the homicide rate. By pointing out the limitations of these correlational studies, I have called into question the economists' conclusion that each execution saves between three and eighteen lives.

My criticisms do not imply that all social scientific research is flawed to a degree that renders it useless, as a rule. Because of the limits of social science, it often has to rely on a lot of comparative data when considering large-scale public policy decisions.

- Amnesty International (2013) compared countries with and without the death penalty, and it concluded that there is no correlation between the death penalty and lower rates of violent crime.

The comparative data, however, are often not definitive. Comparing two countries, even countries that are alike in many ways, may not reveal whether capital punishment specifically is having an impact or if there are other factors at work. The same may be true in different states within a country.

- *The New York Times* found that there is no correlation between the death penalty and lower murder rates in different U.S. states. In fact, states without

15 The economists have tried to defend their studies, focusing on the criticisms of Donohue and Wolfers (2005), but I do not find their defenses convincing. See Zimmerman (2009), Mocan and Gittings (2010), and Dezhbakhsh and Rubin (2011). Rubin (2009) criticizes the analysis by Kovandzic, Vieraitis, and Boots (2009). For a reaffirmation of the critiques of the econometric studies in light of these responses, see Chalfin, Haviland, and Raphael (2013). Other critical examinations of the empirical methods that underlie these studies include Fagan (2005), Fagan (2006), Cohen-Cole et al. (2009), Kirchgässner (2011), and Committee on Deterrence and the Death Penalty (2012).

the death penalty tend to have lower murder rates than states with the death penalty (Bonner and Fessenden 2000; see also Death Penalty Information Center 2020a).

States can have very different economic climates or job prospects, and the violent crime rate may be impacted by things other than the threat of execution. Even though there is no reason to believe this, perhaps the violent crime rate would be even higher in Texas (439 per 100,000 population in 2018) if they did not have the death penalty, and it would be even lower in Maine (121 per 100,000) if they did (United Health Foundation 2020).

Social scientists have tried to control for those variables by focusing on individual states or countries over time, correcting for changes that affect the crime rate, such as improvements in job prospects.

- Ruth Peterson and William Bailey (1988) compared the murder rates in the same state before and after the Supreme Court's de facto moratorium as a result of the *Furman* decision in 1972. They found that, in the same state, the murder rate was unaffected by whether or not the death penalty was in place (see also Bailey and Peterson 1997; and Katz, Levitt, and Shustorovich 2003).
- Avio (1979), using Ehrlich's multiple regression analysis, found no deterrent effect of the death penalty in Canada over a thirty-five-year period (1926–60).

These are broad, large-scale studies of the same place over long periods of time. Maybe the effects are more noticeable in the short term, and people's violent behavior is impacted immediately after an execution.

- Jeffrey Grogger (1990) found that executions have no short-term impact on the rate of violent crimes.

Perhaps the deterrent effect is felt most when potential murderers are made more aware of executions, so they know that it is a real possibility that they will be executed.

- Robert Dann (1935) and Leonard Savitz (1959) found that, in any given U.S. state, highly publicized death sentences and executions had no impact on the murder rate.
- Several studies actually discovered a brutalization effect, with highly publicized executions leading to a short-term increase in homicides (Bowers and Pierce 1980; Bowers, Pierce, and McDevitt 1984, 271–335; Cochran and Chamlin 2000).
- Although she claims that her research supports the death penalty, Joanna Shepherd (2005) also concludes that murder rates increased as a result of the death penalty in nearly half of the states that have it (thirteen of twenty-seven states).

To control for changes over time and for different demographics, comparative studies were done of socioeconomically similar states with and without the death penalty.

- Thorsten Sellin (1959; 1980) looked at states with similar social and economic conditions and similar populations, and he found that there was no way to distinguish states with the death penalty from states without the death penalty.[16]

Studies were also done of socioeconomically and geographically similar counties in neighboring states with and without the death penalty.

- Derral Cheatwood (1993) examined similar, adjacent counties in neighboring death penalty and abolitionist states and found that there is no correlation between the violent crime rate and the existence of the death penalty, number of executions, or number of people on death row.

Perhaps the effects of the death penalty are felt more strongly by police and prison guards. Some states reserve the death penalty only to punish the killing of police or prison staff, so its effects may be limited to protecting those populations. "Ordinary" murders of the population at large would be unaffected.

- Bailey and Peterson (1994) found that the death penalty has no discernable impact on the safety of police or prison guards (see also W. Bailey 1982).

All these comparative studies are in some sense simpler than the econometric studies, but they are less fragile. Considering them in the aggregate, they represent consistent findings that the death penalty does not deter more than incarceration.

Of course, none of these studies show definitively that the death penalty does not deter more than life in prison. As I noted earlier in the chapter, there are simply too many variables, and researchers have the option of choosing subsets of these variables that accord with their conceptual or theoretical biases. However, the studies that seem to show deterrence are subject to a lot of model uncertainty – that is, changing one or two small assumptions in their models yields very different results. By contrast, the comparative panel data studies and time-series studies depend on fewer assumptions, only the crime rate and the classification of states/countries as socioeconomically similar. Furthermore, dismissing all the statistical data about similar countries, similar states, the same state over time,

16 Such a comparison of neighboring states with similar populations and similar socioeconomic conditions is the only kind of study that Hart finds convincing. He rejects the comparison of different countries with and without the death penalty because there are so many other variables that may account for any difference. He also rejects studies of the same country before and after abolition, since, he says, such countries often fail to use the death penalty for many years before it is officially removed (2008, 83–85).

similar counties, and more would require some leaps of faith regarding social conditions that are hard to swallow. For example, is there any reason to believe that the same state before and after prohibition would coincidentally undergo sufficient change and the exact level of change in, e.g., economic conditions to negate the supposed additional risk from not having the death penalty? Given the evidence we have, it is more likely that the death penalty simply does not deter.

The conclusions of all this research are not based on "outdated statistical techniques or older data," as Shepherd claims (quoted in Kovandzic, Vieraitis, and Boots 2009, 804). Multiple studies over many years have demonstrated that capital punishment does not deter homicides or other violent crimes more than life in prison, and the econometric studies that seem to show a deterrent effect are flawed. Thus, Bedau concludes:

> If one must draw the balance sheet at the present moment, it appears that despite the introduction of econometric techniques, the negative judgment on the deterrent superiority of the death penalty over long-term imprisonment reached a generation ago by Sellin and other criminologists has not been seriously undermined or contradicted. (1982, 97)[17]

Michael Davis (2009, 84–86) should not be suspicious of all the findings of social science, only the ones (like Shepherd's) with suspect study designs and fragile conclusions.

Criminology does not have the precision of chemistry, but that does not mean that it can give us no guidance whatsoever. The lack of deterrent effect is not absolutely certain, but that does not entail that the data are inconclusive. People who claim as much are using the wrong standard. The question is what is more reasonable to believe given the evidence and under the circumstances. The very fact that econometric studies showing a deterrent effect have such wildly different results – three to eighteen lives saved per execution (or maybe 429 lives saved, or eighty-six additional murders) – itself testifies to the precariousness of their regression models. By contrast, there is little to no variation in the comparative studies. Most of them converge on one shared conclusion: the death penalty does not deter more than incarceration. Those are the findings that should guide public policy.

Not good outcomes, but the best outcomes

Despite disagreement in the scholarly literature, an evaluation of the evidence seems to indicate more strongly that the death penalty does not deter. However, even if defenders of the death penalty were to demonstrate that executions deter

17 Bedau's essay appeared in 1982, after the publication of Ehrlich's work but prior to the spate of econometric studies in the 2000s. Given my analysis in this chapter, Bedau's claim still stands.

potential murderers, they face a tougher challenge than they realize. According to consequentialism, a given policy must not only achieve positive outcomes but must also produce better outcomes than alternative policies (i.e., marginal utility). The utilitarian calculus, for example, says that we should maximize happiness or minimize pain, not that we should simply produce happiness or avoid pain. Even satisficing consequentialism is not a free-for-all; not any good outcome is good enough. If giving a hundred dollars to an inefficient charity will help one family eat for a week but giving a hundred dollars to an efficient charity will help five families eat for a week, then, all other things being equal, I am obligated to give my money to the efficient charity, even though my donation to the inefficient charity would have some positive impact. Analogously, even if (for the sake of argument) executing a convicted murderer were to save five lives, Mocan and Gittings would also have to show that the money and time spent on that execution would not have a greater deterrent effect if it were spent on other crime prevention methods. I doubt that they could accomplish this.

Costs vary by state, but in every case, the costs of a capital case are much higher than the costs of a non-capital case, due to several factors: the salary of public defenders (two is standard for a capital case), a longer pre-trial phase so experts can examine the forensic evidence and assess the defendant's mental health and background, a more thorough jury-selection process, longer trials and accompanying court costs (including compensation for court personnel, attorneys, and jurors), solitary confinement on death row, and the series of appeals that I listed earlier in the chapter, each of which involves more attorney fees, court costs, and so on (Roman et al. 2008, 40–59). Although the difference in cost varies among death penalty states, a clear pattern emerges:

- In Maryland, capital-eligible cases in which prosecutors do not seek the death penalty cost about $1.1 million on average, $1.8 million when they unsuccessfully seek the death penalty, and $3 million when they successfully seek the death penalty. From 1978–99, Maryland spent a total of $186 million on capital cases, resulting in five executions. So, each execution cost the state about $37 million (Roman et al. 2008).
- Florida spends $51 million a year to impose the death penalty. Each execution costs about $24 million. Sending someone to prison for life without parole costs about $1 million (Pudlow 2010; see also "High Price of Killing Killers" 2000).
- In Washington state, prior to the State Supreme Court's decision in 2018 that abolished capital punishment, the average cost of each death penalty prosecution was about $3 million, versus $2 million for sending a criminal to prison for life. The five executions completed between 1976 and 2018 cost the state on average $24 million each (Collins et al. 2016).
- As of 2011, California spent $184 million a year on the death penalty. In total, the death penalty costs three times as much as permanent imprisonment. The state spent more than $4 billion on capital punishment between

> 1978 and 2011, resulting in thirteen executions, which is almost $308 million per execution (SB 490, 2011–12 Sess. [Cal. 2011]).

Even if it were the case that actual executions deter some potential murderers, to base an argument for the death penalty on this data, one would also have to show that the many millions of dollars in additional money spent on each execution would not be better spent elsewhere.

If the maximum sentence were life in prison without parole, the additional money that now goes toward capital cases could be diverted to other methods of crime prevention, including additional police officers and community policing (Chalfin and McCrary 2013; Mello 2019), drug treatment programs (Bondurant, Lindo, and Swensen 2016), better education (Lochner and Moretti 2004), and well-designed rehabilitation programs (Gendreau, Smith, and French 2006; Cullen and Gendreau 2012), all of which have, unlike the death penalty, been shown to have a deterrent effect on crime. Many of these initiatives affect homicide rates specifically. For example, increasing the visibility of police, when it is focused on specific crime problems, heightens perceived risk of apprehension – that is, it increases the certainty of punishment – which has been shown to deter crime (National Research Council 2004; Durlauf and Nagin 2011; Corsaro and Weisburd 2018). Steven Mello found that adding 9.5 additional police officers led a reduction of one murder (2019, 175, 185).[18] Do the math: if, say, five murders can be prevented by 47.5 new police officers and each execution costs $24 million, it would be more cost effective, even if Mocan and Gittings are right, if we pay each new cop half a million dollars than if we diverted that money into capital cases. Incidentally, such a calculation, based on the aforementioned studies, confirms the opinions of law enforcement officers. A poll of police chiefs from throughout the United States found that they ranked the death penalty as the *least cost-effective* and the *least effective* method to reduce violent crime, behind reducing drug abuse, having a better economy, simplifying court rules (i.e., increasing celerity), instituting longer prison sentences (i.e., increasing severity), hiring more police officers (i.e., increasing certainty), and reducing the number of guns on the street (Death Penalty Information Center 1995).

Cass Sunstein and Adrian Vermeule claim that, even if these other things would deter crime, the death penalty would provide "further deterrence," so we ought to have it and pay for it (2005, 732). However, that overlooks the tradeoffs we would have to make in spending that kind of time and money. The question here is not so much whether it is effective (it is not), but whether it is *most* effective given our limited resources or *more* effective than other crime-prevention measures. Even if it did deter, capital punishment would not maximize overall positive consequences because it is an inefficient deterrent compared to other options.

18 Chalfin and McCrary (2013) conclude that murder is one of the classes of crimes that increased policing is most effective at reducing.

Of course, it is possible to reduce the time and expense of capital cases, but that also comes with a cost. Most of the expense comes from court costs and lawyers' salaries during the appeals process. If we limit or otherwise reduce appeals, then we are more likely not to catch errors of law or errors of fact that were made at trial, which would increase the chances of executing innocent people. Some defenders of the death penalty are fine with this: for example, van den Haag says that the loss of innocents is worth the tradeoff (1969, 142; 1985a, 967; 1986, 1664–65). But on other views, such as Ronald Dworkin's rights view, it is better to inflate a right than to infringe on a right (1977, 198–200). And if the time and money devoted to an abbreviated capital punishment process could be spent in ways that more effectively drive down the violent crime rate, if the execution of innocents left actual murderers on the street, and if people began to lose faith in the justice system, then even utilitarians would reject an abbreviated process for capital cases. Indeed, few consequentialists of any stripe would support such a thing.

Retributivists would also object to increasing the risk of executing innocents. It is true that more murderers would get what they deserve (at least according to some versions of retributivism), but more innocents would get punishments that they do not deserve. Desert-based defenders of capital punishment would have to argue that it is worth killing innocents so that we can give murderers a slightly harsher penalty (death instead of life in prison). That would be a hard case to make.

The retributivist's response

In Chapter 5, I talked about how retributivism and consequentialism are mutually constraining. According to the two-tiered model, consequentialism establishes a boundary at the high end beyond which we cannot punish people because it would be excessive, and a boundary at the low end below which the state would not be fulfilling its obligation to maintain the social order. But in Chapter 11, I also talked about how communities, through jury nullification in the courts, can push back against lawmakers when their reactive attitudes are not reflected in the law. As I also said there, retributivism checks the legislature's calculation about the crimes and level of punishment without which the state would not be said to function. It cannot commit us to gratuitous harm in the name of desert, but it can challenge punishments that are excessive given a defendant's degree of guilt.

Some retributivists may try to get a wedge in at this point and claim that our *a priori* duty to give people what they deserve may, in some cases, override the obligation not to inflict more suffering than is necessary. That is, the retributivist may argue that it would be unreasonable for lawmakers to prohibit the death penalty, even though it is an excessive punishment that is unnecessary for the purposes of deterrence. This is extreme retributivism coupled with equality retributivism: "If … he has committed murder he must *die*. Here there is no substitute that will satisfy justice" (Kant 1996b, 6:333). We must inflict the equivalent penalty as our one overriding duty.

To mount this challenge, the retributivist would have to show that, in some cases, only the death penalty is appropriate for murder and that life in prison is so disproportionate to what murderers deserve that such a punishment would be unreasonably lenient, morally inappropriate, or unjust. This line of argument against the two-tiered model depends on two assumptions, both of which are questionable. First, it would have to assume equality retributivism instead of proportional retributivism, even though the former position is ethically untenable. Most retributivists do not think that we should rape rapists and torture torturers: for example, van den Haag rules this sort of thing out as "repulsive" (1985b, 171), and Davis says that it is "morally shocking" (1992, 79). If, instead, the retributivist says that the punishment must be proportional rather than equivalent to the crime, then murder would only justify the most severe punishment on the scale. That punishment need not be death.[19]

The second assumption is that the community's resentment could not be properly expressed with anything but an execution. This is doubtful. According to Norval Morris's limiting retributivism, desert establishes a range of acceptable punishments, not just one option. And, as U.S. Supreme Court Justice Thurgood Marshall says, society's moral outrage can be expressed just as effectively with a lesser punishment than execution: "It is inconceivable that any individual concerned about conforming his conduct to what society says is 'right' would fail to realize that murder is 'wrong' if the penalty were simply life imprisonment" (*Gregg v. Georgia*, 428 U.S. 153 [1976], 233–36). According to the two-tiered model, society's reactive attitudes should be constrained by the consequentialist reasoning of the legislature. We are obligated to follow the policies that, on the whole, further the state's just aims. No retributivist could make a strong enough case that death is so important, and that life in prison accomplishes so little in terms of expressing resentment, that we should override the state's obligation both to preserve the law and to do so while minimizing the intentional infliction of harm.

Four possibilities, and the implications for public policy

Following Hart, the two-tiered model distinguishes the justification of punishment policies and statutory penalties (general justifying aim) from the justification of punishments for specific criminals (distribution) (2008, 3–4). Legislatures ought to use consequentialist reasoning, and judges ought to use retributivist reasoning. If the death penalty does not deter, restrain, or rehabilitate criminals more than an alternative, lesser punishment, then it causes gratuitous harm and

19 Nathanson makes this point in his own argument against the death penalty:

> The proportionality principle … is no help to death penalty advocates, because it does not require that murderers be executed. All that it requires is that if murder is the most serious crime, then murder should be punished by the most severe punishment on the scale. The principle does not tell us what this punishment should be, however, and it is quite compatible with the view that the most severe punishment should be a long prison term. (2001, 76–77)

ought to be prohibited (principle of parsimony). Defenders of capital punishment, such as van den Haag, often ignore the cost or effectiveness of capital punishment and claim that it is irrelevant to the decision about whether to adopt the practice.[20] Lawmakers who claim to give criminals what they deserve, who evoke "law and order," and who channel the supposed anger of victims and potential victims are acting like avenging angels, not legislators.

Assessing the deterrent effects of capital punishment, then, is crucial in deciding whether to allow judges and juries to have the death penalty as an option in sentencing. Many people assume that the evidence regarding deterrence is inconclusive. Under the circumstances, we must decide on the most reasonable policy to adopt. Consider the four possibilities:

1) The death penalty does not deter more than life in prison without the possibility of parole.

There is enough evidence that the death penalty does not deter, and enough questions about the research purporting to show that it does, that this is the most reasonable position to take. And, given the *prima facie* wrongness of intentional harm, the death penalty should not be used because it causes gratuitous suffering – additional burdens without additional benefits.

2) The evidence is inconclusive regarding whether the death penalty deters more than life in prison.

If, along with the econometric studies, the evidence that the death penalty does not deter is called into question, then the death penalty should still be rejected. The *prima facie* wrongness of intentional harm places the burden of proof on defenders of the death penalty; we should intentionally harm our fellow citizens only if there is a good enough reason to override the presumption of wrongness. One of van den Haag's mistakes with his "Best Bet" argument is that he assumes a retributive claim: a murderer's life is worth less than an innocent victim's life; it has "negative value" (1985a, 965; 1985b, 170; 1986, 1666). Yet, that kind of reasoning is out of place at the policy level. Lawmakers should consider only the effectiveness of a punishment in preserving the public order (in deterring and not brutalizing), not what the individual murder deserves. Furthermore, van den Haag does not consider alternative policies that would have more of a deterrent effect.

3) The death penalty does deter, but it is not the most efficient way to deter (or the best use of limited resources).

20 Van den Haag says: "I would favor retention of the death penalty as retribution even if it were shown that the threat of execution could not deter prospective murderers not already deterred by the threat of imprisonment" and "the actual monetary costs are trumped by the importance of doing justice" (1986, 1665, 1666; see also 1985a, 967).

Mocan and Gittings, and many other death penalty proponents, think that, if we could show that executions deter, that would be enough to justify the death penalty. For example, Chad Flanders assumes ("it seems at least plausible") that some people are deterred, and that is enough: "even if it is one or two [lives saved], the deterrence argument works on its own terms: it prevents either an equal or greater harm than the harm it causes" (2013, 601). That is faulty consequentialist reasoning. A murderer's life is not the only cost. Even if executions reduce the murder rate, supporters of the death penalty would have to show that it is the optimal method of deterrence, or comparatively better than the live alternatives, which is not the case. Because of the enormous cost of each execution and clear evidence for alternative methods that reduce violent crime, we ought to divert the funding into other crime-prevention measures, such as increased policing.[21] Indeed, we have to expand our calculus beyond policies that are explicitly designed to prevent criminal behavior. The money spent on executions may be better spent on social programs that would dramatically impact people's lives by improving education, reducing economic disparities, and addressing drug dependency, all of which would ultimately reduce criminal activity (see Kleiman 2009, esp. 117–35). As Wolfers puts it, "I honestly think it's a distraction. ... The debate here is over whether we kill 60 guys or not. The food stamps program is much more important" (quoted in Liptak 2007).[22]

The fourth possibility is the only one that would justify the death penalty on consequentialist grounds, but it is the least likely:

4) The death penalty deters, and it is the most effective way of saving the lives of potential victims.

If this were true, then the two-tiered model of punishment would allow it as an option for judges and juries for the most egregious murder cases. However, the

21 Yang and Lester, whose meta-analysis purports to show a deterrent effect, express hesitation about adopting the death penalty as the optimal public policy for this very reason: "Even if executions are shown to deter potential murderers, alternative strategies to reduce the murder rate may be more effective and more ethically acceptable" (2008, 459).

22 N. Morris also comments on the small number of executions and the fact that they accomplish nothing of value:

> One cannot look at the present situation of capital punishment in the United States, whether you are for it or against it, without disgust for the processes of its implementation, for the sensationalism of its role, or for the claims of its impact on crime rates where it could not possibly have any effect at all. It is a largely symbolic process, given the numbers we are prepared to execute. If capital punishment were thought of as a serious deterrent in this country, to have a real impact on homicide and attempted homicide, it would have to be functioning at about 10,000 executions a year. The highest that we have ever reached is 199, and we are not likely to run blood baths any bigger than that. Whether one supports capital punishment or rejects it, the country has clearly failed to make it anything more than a distasteful symbolic process. (1987, 2)

available evidence does not support this, and, under the circumstances, it would be unreasonable to believe it.[23]

Conclusion

The two-tiered model clarifies the conditions that would have to be met to justify capital punishment. Even if a judge or jury really wants to kill a defendant, or even if the defendant deserves to die, this is irrelevant to whether the death penalty should be in place as a matter of public policy. There is a lot of evidence that the death penalty does not deter, and no reliable evidence that it does. Additionally, any purported deterrent effects are outweighed by more efficient and effective alternatives. Given what we know and have reason to believe, the death penalty should be abolished.

23 Indeed, as I mentioned, police chiefs do not believe that the death penalty is the most effective way of saving lives (Death Penalty Information Center 1995), nor do members of the American Society of Criminology, the Academy of Criminal Justice Sciences, and the Law and Society Association (Radelet and Akers 1996; Radelet and Lacock 2009).

13 Retribution and restorative justice

As a mixed theory, the two-tiered model of punishment incorporates both consequentialism and retributivism. Consequentialism ought to inform legislative policies regarding punishment, including which actions to prohibit and the kinds and degrees of punishments necessary to deter them. Retributivism ought to guide judges in the distribution of burdens within those statutory ranges. In the previous chapter, I argued that capital punishment does not deter and that the resources devoted to it could be spent more effectively on other crime-prevention measures, so it is excessive and inefficient, and it ought to be rejected on consequentialist grounds. In this chapter, I consider whether restorative justice is consistent with retribution as it is conceived under the two-tiered model, as an expression of resentment by the community.

My thesis in this chapter is fairly modest compared to the previous one. Once we evaluate the different studies, it becomes clear that the death penalty does not deter. The right thing to do follows from a utilitarian-style calculus, based on the data. Things are different when it comes to expressing our reactive attitudes. Resentment is the feeling of having been unjustly harmed or neglected, and the state expresses this feeling by finding offenders guilty and imposing punishment. Among other things, the state agrees that the victim's resentment is justified, asserts that the victim is part of the community, and publicly chastises the offender for violating shared legal norms. The question I address here is whether restorative justice could accomplish these ends, on its own or in conjunction with more traditional punishments, so that the community can express its resentment as or more effectively than it does without it. In other words, can restorative processes such as victim offender conferencing achieve the same expressive purpose, and thus replace or enhance traditional punishments such as incarceration?

Because I am focusing on the compatibility and complementarity of restorative justice and retribution, I will assume for the sake of argument that restorative justice does have deterrent effects, and that the effects are at least comparable to the effects of traditional punishments that criminals would otherwise receive. Research on restorative justice and recidivism rates is encouraging, especially when comparing the effects of restorative justice practices to incarceration and probation (e.g., Coates and Gehm 1989; Umbreit, Coates, and Kalanj 1994; McCold and Wachtel 1998; Maxwell, Morris, and Anderson 1999; Sherman, Strang, and

Woods 2000; Bonta et al. 2002; Umbreit, Coates, and Vos 2002; Sherman and Strang 2007).[1] However, I am not going to evaluate the evidence for deterrence, as I did in Chapter 12. Rather, I will argue that, *if* restorative justice is acceptable on consequentialist grounds as a public policy, *then* it is also acceptable on retributivist grounds as a distributed burden. In other words, restorative justice is compatible, in principle, with a retributive theory grounded in resentment.

What is restorative justice?

Restorative justice has roots in ancient, religious, and indigenous practices (Galaway and Hudson 1996, 137–223; Weitekamp 1999; Hadley 2001; Tso 2005; Sullivan and Tifft 2008, 151–87; Zehr 2015a, 129–57), but it gained widespread popularity in the 1970s as a response to an increase in incarceration, poor prison conditions, and the perceived failure of the criminal justice system to address the needs of crime victims and communities. Used as an alternative to or in conjunction with traditional punishments, restorative justice deals with crime and other kinds of wrongdoing by bringing together victims, offenders, and community members in order to address their different needs and attempt to repair the harm that was done. What do they need in order to become whole again (or as whole as they can be) (Braithwaite 2002, 11)? The idea is that people who are affected by the crime ought to participate in the justice process and come to an acceptable resolution. On the traditional view, the offender takes on blame and ought to be punished. On the restorative justice view, the offender takes on obligations to the victim and the community and ought to make things right, whether concretely (through restitution) or symbolically (through contrition).

Restorative practices include victim offender conferencing (direct or indirect), family group conferencing, peacemaking circles, sentencing circles, reintegrative shaming, and community reparation boards.[2] Most of these practices are overseen by trained, neutral facilitators. They are distinguished by:

- who is involved, whether it is the victim and the offender, family members of the victim and the offender, or other community members;

1 The effectiveness of restorative justice depends on many factors, including whether it is court-mandated, which restorative justice techniques are being used, whether offenders are low-risk or high-risk, and whether offenders are adults or juveniles. For meta-analyses of the literature and mixed assessments of the effectiveness of restorative justice, see Bonta, Wallace-Capretta, and Rooney (1998); Nugent, Williams, and Umbreit (2004); Latimer, Dowden, and Muise (2005); Bonta et al. (2008); and Wilson, Olaghere, and Kimbrell (2017). Defenders of restorative justice often point out that traditional punishments do a poor job of deterring criminals. Restorative practices would only have to deter crime as well as or better than traditional punishments do. We should not hold restorative justice to a higher standard.

2 On the different methods of restorative justice, see especially Braithwaite (1989); Umbreit and Greenwood (2000); McCold (2001); Pranis, Stuart, and Wedge (2003); United Nations Office on Drugs and Crime (2006); Zehr (2015a, 159–77); and Zehr (2015b, 60–66).

- how the victim and the offender communicate, whether directly (face-to-face) or indirectly through a facilitator;
- their timing during the process, whether they take place pretrial, parallel with a trial, during sentencing, during the offender's imprisonment, or during probation;
- their relation to traditional criminal justice processes, whether they are alternatives to trial and sentencing or used in conjunction with the established system; and
- their goals, such as facilitating healing for the victim and offender, assisting offenders in their transition out of prison and back into the community, or both.

Restorative practices only occur pending a risk assessment and a determination that all the parties involved are informed about the processes and are willing to participate. An offender who is forced into meeting a victim with the expectation of some kind of apology may re-victimize the other party through a dismissive attitude, refusal to admit responsibility, hostility, or disregard for what the victim articulates as a harm. A period of preparation is required to manage expectations, explain the levels of volunteerism expected, and make victims aware of potential confrontations. In addition to the victim and offender, other stakeholders are often involved in the process because the offender takes on obligations to everyone who is affected – not only the victim and victim's family, but also the community and the offender's own family.

Restorative justice is past-, present-, and future-oriented because it acknowledges the offender's culpability for wrongdoing, works to repair the harm to the victim, and encourages lawful behavior moving forward. Thus it incorporates elements of both consequentialism and retributivism. As Clifford Shearing notes, restorative justice "provides opportunities for the development of a symbolic, past-oriented approach that is compatible with the instrumental, future-oriented logic of risk-management" (2001, 216). Through reintegrative shaming, for example, offenders are held accountable for performing wrong acts (backward-focused), their actions are condemned while they, as people, are respected in the process (present-focused), and they are expected to rejoin the community after they have made things right (forward-focused). It assigns blame in a way that rewards offenders with forgiveness and reintegration into their communities after restoration has been achieved.

Is restorative justice "punishment"?

In Chapter 1, I defined punishment, in part, as the imposition of burdens, which is often understood in terms of harm, suffering, or "hard treatment." The latter "involves not merely condemnation, rebuke, or censure, but some substantial imposition on a wrong-doer" (Kleinig 1998, 275). Whether restorative practices count as punishments, then, depends on how broadly we construe the burdensome aspect of punishment, whether punishment can be nonpunitive, or what constitutes a "substantial imposition" (Daly 2013). Compensating the victim and participating in victim offender conferencing are not like prison. The intent behind restorative practices is not to inflict hard treatment on offenders in proportion to their offenses but to repair the harms to victims and communities. So, some proponents of restorative justice, such as Herman Bianchi (1994), see conflict resolution as an alternative to punishment.

Similarly, David Boonin (2008, 1) and Nathan Hanna (2008) claim that punishment is defined by a punitive attitude and the intentional infliction of suffering.[3] Because there are better alternatives to purposely harming offenders, we ought to abolish punishment in favor of victim restitution and other restorative practices. According to Boonin, the thesis that harm is essential to punishment is "crucial" to the arguments he gives for abolitionism (2008, 13n14; see also 3–28). It is also the linchpin of Hanna's arguments against expressive retributivism (2008; 2009b), liberalism (2009a), and deterrence theory (2014). If the aims that these theories value can be accomplished without causing harm, he says, they cannot justify punishment. This is reminiscent of the definitional stop approach to ruling out the punishment of innocents: Hanna thinks that these theories are wrong because they can only be right theories *of punishment* if they justify the intentional infliction of harm.

However, if we define burdens more broadly (along Foucauldian lines) to include any unwanted interference with someone's freedom, then restorative practices also count as punishments. Suffering is one kind of burden, but obligations are another. Under restorative justice, offenders are blamed for their wrongdoings, and their wrongdoings create obligations. Daniel McDermott (2001) describes this as a "moral debt." The offenders did not treat their victims as rights-holders, thus withholding a moral good from their victims that they must now repay. Performing community service, attending counseling programs, having to confront victims and other affected members of the community, and being subjected to reintegrative shaming are difficult experiences to endure, even though they are not like prison (Daly 2013, 363, 367–68). Therefore, Kathleen Daly (2000; 2002) and Antony Duff (2001, 92–99; 2011) believe that restorative justice gives us alternative *forms of* punishment rather than alternatives *to* punishment (see also Zehr 2015a, 209; and Johnstone 2011, 106–10).

Duff defends an interesting position regarding hard treatment and restorative justice. He rightly claims that communicative retributivism can only justify hard treatment if it is necessary to communicate censure (1986, 233–66; 2001,

3 For a list of other theorists who claim that harm is essential to punishment, see Boonin (2008, 13–14n14) and Hanna (2014, 593, 593n5). Among proponents of restorative justice, Walgrave most clearly defines punishment by its intent:

> Painful obligations that are imposed without the intention to cause suffering are not punishments. … It is the painfulness in the intention of the punisher that counts, not in the perception of the punished. It is the punisher who considers an action to be wrong and who wants the wrongdoer to suffer for it. (2008, 48; see also 62)

29–30). Often, he says, suffering ("penal hard treatment") *is* crucial to achieving the aims of punishment, so that criminals focus on their wrongdoings and commit to reforming themselves (1986, 240–46; 2001, ch. 3).[4] Prison time not only makes them regret what they did wrong but itself constitutes an apologetic reparation, a kind of "secular penance" (1986, ch. 9; 1988; 1992; 1996, 51–57; 2001, 106–115; see also S. Garvey 1999 and Bennett 2008).[5]

However, prison, fines, and other punitive practices are not the only effective means of communicating censure and restoring wrongs. Duff also says that "criminal mediation and reparation [are] a kind of secular penance" (2003, 53). He identifies three different kinds of "suffering" or "burden" that offenders deserve and that are imposed on them through restorative processes: suffering remorse, suffering censure from others, and suffering hardship in making reparation to their victims (48–49). The latter burden "is a species of penal hard treatment" for the offender because "it is intentionally burdensome, making demands on his time, money or energies, independently of its communicative meaning" (55). As Jean Hampton claims, this is a kind of treatment based on desert:

> the demand for a wrongdoer to "make amends" to his victim is a retributive idea, arising from the retributive claim that repairing diminishment requires, among other things, repairing the wrongdoer's damage to the victim's entitlements (generated by her value). A punishment can have built into it actions or services that constitute such amends. (1992a, 1697)

Seeing offenders as being indebted to their victims and their communities because of their past actions is backward-looking, even if the obligations they must fulfill are designed to repair the wrongs in the future. And, contrary to mere imprisonment, offenders make amends directly, as a result of the agreements reached in victim offender conferencing, rather than indirectly in paying a debt to the state.

Consistent with expressivism, the emphasis should not be on whether offenders are experiencing hard treatment, but on what is being conveyed to them and the community. Joel Feinberg says that reprobation is more crucial to accomplishing the purpose of punishment than imposing prison or fines on offenders.

4 Kleinig says that using "face-to-face blame" rather than hard treatment "does not adequately register the seriousness of moral wrongdoing" (1991, 417). Bennett (2008) thinks that only hard treatment is "symbolically adequate" for public condemnation. Tasioulas says that "the seriousness of the wrong committed warrants a blaming response that operates *through* the infliction of hard treatment, since only such a response adequately reflects the gravity of the wrong that has been committed" (2006, 296). And Narayan thinks that hard treatment is appropriate because it censures the criminal, but she also thinks that it is the best form of censure because of its "role in crime prevention" (1993, 180).

5 Bennett (2008) sees an apology as crucial to making things right and also thinks that hard treatment is necessary in order properly to respond to wrongdoing, but the two actions have different purposes. The apology is primarily for the victim, but the hard treatment is necessary to do justice to the offender, in order to hold them accountable as a moral agent.

Although Feinberg says that hard treatment is part of the definition of punishment, he also says that "reprobation is itself painful, whether or not it is accompanied by further 'hard treatment'" (1970, 98).[6] There need not be an equivalence between the crime and the harshness of the punishment, only between the crime and the feeling of condemnation: "it is social disapproval and its appropriate expression that should fit the crime, and not hard treatment (pain) as such" (118; see also Christie 1981).[7] In principle, this could be accomplished with nonpunitive restorative practices, which involve the community more directly and facilitate more interpersonal communication, in conferences and circles, than criminal trials do. Hard treatment may be "a conventional device" for the expression of resentment, but other, nonpunitive conventions could in principle accomplish this just as well (Feinberg 1970, 98).[8]

At some point this becomes a verbal quibble rather than a substantive disagreement. The two-tiered model of punishment may entail either that we ought to adopt nonpunitive punishments or nonpunitive alternatives to punishment, depending on how we define punishment (or burdens specifically). At the policy level, it is consequentialist, aiming at harm reduction, rather than a narrow form of deterrence theory that is committed to the idea that harm and the threat of harm are necessary to deter. One advantage of my theory is that it is willing to follow wherever the most valid social scientific evidence leads us. I allow for the possibility of abolitionism as a result of our foundational commitment to justice and preserving the public order, provided that it would allow for the expression of resentment on behalf of the community through, for example, restorative justice practices. If victim restitution is better able to achieve our social ends with less suffering and within the bounds of what is reasonably acceptable in order to achieve retribution, then that is what legislatures should support.

False contrasts

Both defenders and critics of restorative justice often claim that it is the polar opposite of the traditional approach to crime, which aims at condemnation rather

6 Hanna objects to Feinberg's claim that reprobation is a kind of hard treatment (2008, 124–28).

7 Wringe says that suffering is not intentionally inflicted, but offenders must be treated harshly to adequately convey society's disapproval. Suffering is not the aim of punishment, but a necessary side effect (2016, 18–41, 65–87). This is a factual question rather than an evaluation per se. In this chapter, I am arguing that hard treatment, at least as Wringe understands it, is not necessary to achieve the communicative aim of punishment.

8 Hanna takes this point to be an objection to expressive retributivism (2008, 130–33), but it need not be. I agree with Hanna that conventions need to be justified, and that this may mean that punishment is not justified for the sake of retributive expression. That does not entail that expressive retributivism is wrong, only that our conventional ways of expressing resentment are not ideal. One of Hanna's points is that expressivism does not justify the "uniqueness claim" that only hard treatment could censure the wrongdoer (133–48). As should be clear from this chapter, I agree. See also Golash (2005, ch. 6).

than reconciliation. Some critics of restorative justice complain that it coddles criminals, who deserve hard treatment in response to the harm they cause. The purpose of punishment is to give criminals what they deserve, proportional to their offenses, not to work out some kind of agreement between criminals and the people they victimized. Calling victim offender conferencing a kind of "mediation" is especially troubling, since mediation implies that the two parties come to the table with equal standing and that there will be give and take on both sides (Reimund 2004, 405–6; see also Umbreit, Coates, and Kalanj 1994).[9] In the case of punishment, however, the victim owes nothing to the offender. When restorative justice proponents talk about the offender being victimized by society or by others (Richards 2005; Richards 2006, 204–13), or they describe criminal violence as an offender's attempt to achieve justice (Gilligan 1996, 11–12, 18–20), they blur the distinction between the criminal, the victim, and the community, and they engage in a false moral equivalency between individual crimes and social disadvantages. Although crimes and punishments both inflict harm, any ethical similarities are merely apparent: the victim is unjustly harmed by the criminal, and the criminal is justly harmed by the state in recompense for an unlawful action (van den Haag 1986, 1667).

Some defenders of restorative practices make the same contrast between restoration and retribution, seeing them as two different "lenses" through which we can view criminal activity and our response to it (Zehr 2015a, esp. 178–81). But they claim that restorative justice is a more constructive alternative to the intentional vindictiveness of retributive punishment (e.g., Van Ness 1993, 251–52, 258–59, 266; Wright 1996, 133, 135; Daly 2002; Walgrave 2008, ch. 2; Zehr 2015a, 67–85, 105–8, 183–201, 211–14). Wrongs are not righted and harms are not healed simply by having the state inflict hard treatment on offenders because they deserve it. The emphasis on blame and guilt, and the imposition of pain in proportion to that guilt, is an unproductive kind of backward-looking approach that does nothing to reestablish relations of right. It stigmatizes and excludes offenders, which encourages more criminal behavior rather than providing the conditions under which they can reintegrate into society (Braithwaite 1989, esp. 16–21; Braithwaite 2000).

In fact, both advocates and critics of restorative justice are interpreting retribution in uncharitable ways. Many critics of restorative justice assume that things can only be made right if pain is inflicted on offenders rather than contrition and efforts at reparation. For example, Richard Delgado (approvingly) equates retribution and vengeance, and he criticizes restorative justice for failing to satisfy this social need (2000, 761). On this view, retributivism is a kind of "magical thinking" (Nussbaum 2015, 48) or "mysterious piece of moral alchemy" (Hart 2008, 234) by which suffering is thought to rebalance the scales of justice. But harming offenders does not repair the harm that they inflicted on their victims.

9 Zehr says explicitly that victim offender conferencing is *not* mediation, for the reasons I give (2015b, 15–16).

Advocates for restorative justice, however, have a similarly distorted view of retribution. They tend to think that retributive punishment is primarily about the pain inflicted rather than the expression of moral disapproval for which punishment serves a symbolic function.

As I argued in Chapter 4, retribution need not be motivated by anger or the desire to inflict suffering. If it is interpreted along the lines that I defended there, it becomes clear that retributive justice and restorative justice can achieve much the same thing, only through different methods (Zehr 2015a, 237–40). Both serve expressive functions in communicating reactive attitudes, including resentment. Therefore, under the two-tiered model, restorative justice could, in principle, be a viable addition or, in some cases, alternative to traditional punishments.

Passive and active responsibility

In Chapter 4, I explained what must underlie the retributive impulse, if it is to be something other than the magical thinking criticized by Nussbaum and Hart. There are a few different parts to retribution, based on our reactive attitude of resentment:

1) Feeling a sense of moral indignation at having been wronged.
2) Holding someone accountable for the wrongdoing.
3) Expressing resentment by punishing the guilty, and in proportion to their degree of guilt.

As a reactive attitude, resentment involves indignation toward the offender and disapproval of the criminal act. It also has cognitive content, including the belief that the offender has violated a moral or legal obligation and is responsible for doing so. When the state punishes them as a result of the criminal justice process, it condemns the crime and the criminal. As Feinberg says, punishment holds the offender responsible, symbolically disavows the criminal act, reaffirms the force of law, and absolves innocent people of blame (1970, 101–5).

If part of the purpose of retributive punishment is to hold criminals to account and absolve others of blame, arguably this could be better achieved through restorative practices than with a purely punitive system of punishment. Many criminal trials, most notably in the United States, are designed to be adversarial. The defendant is incentivized to deny or avoid responsibility for the crime. The defense does whatever it can, within the constraints of the law, to have the charges dismissed, have incriminating evidence declared inadmissible, plead to a lesser charge and negotiate for the lightest punishment possible, and, as a last resort, convince the judge (in a bench trial) or at least one juror (in a jury trial), by means of confusion, misdirection, or any other method at their disposal, that the defendant may not be guilty – even if they are. Defendants who are convicted and sentenced may feel like they have lost a high-stakes competition, not that society is expressing its disapproval.

By contrast, restorative practices give offenders an opportunity to take responsibility for their crimes. Victims and other members of the community communicate to offenders what the crimes did to them. Accountability is not achieved through hard treatment, but by making offenders understand the consequences of their actions – the suffering crime victims have experienced and the offenders' responsibility for it (Zehr 2015b, 33). As a result, offenders assume responsibility for their actions in both the active and passive senses: blame is attributed to them for what they did (passive responsibility), and they are obligated to try to repair the wrongs (active responsibility) (Bovens 1998, 26–38; see also Braithwaite and Roche 2001).[10] The community can fulfill its commitment to justice, and the offender can fulfill their duty of reparation (Ross 2002, 21).

Under restorative justice, the sense of responsibility that is attributed to offenders must be qualified. Restorative justice differs from its traditional counterpart in its rejection of the atomistic view of society as nothing but a collection of autonomous agents. According to Jeffrie Murphy, retributivists usually presuppose a model of the person that is empirically unjustified:

> At root, the retributive theory fails to acknowledge that criminality is, to a large extent, a phenomenon of economic class. To acknowledge this is to challenge the empirical presupposition of the retributive theory – the presupposition that all men, including criminals, are voluntary participants in a reciprocal system of benefits and that the justice of this arrangement can be derived from some eternal and ahistorical concept of rationality. (1973, 241)

Traditionally, retributivism does not examine the background conditions that make crime more likely, such as social determinants, because it conceives of offenders ultimately as rational end-setters who weighed the options and chose wrongly. By contrast, victim offender conferencing not only allows victims to describe the harm that was done to them, but also allows wrongdoers to explain themselves. Many offenders do not see themselves as completely in charge of their own lives but as pressured by socioeconomic forces beyond their control. The traditional criminal justice system, where offenders are passive observers as others decide their fate, can reinforce their sense of victimization (Zehr 2015a, 39–50; Zehr 2015b, 41–42). By addressing this self-perception, restorative processes can actually get offenders to realize the extent of their own culpability and can get communities to consider how they may have failed as well. Ironically, by acknowledging this sense of victimization, participants in restorative practices encourage offenders not to deflect blame, as they do in a trial setting, but to come to terms with the consequences of their actions. And community members can be readier to monitor and support offenders in their rehabilitation so that they can be more successfully integrated into society. Traditional punishment focuses almost exclusively on passive responsibility – that is, assigning blame for

10 Zehr talks about this in terms of backward-looking "accountability" and forward-looking "responsibility" or "real accountability" (2015a, 47–48).

what people did in the past. Restorative practices expand the scope of responsibility to include future obligations that offenders assume as a result of their culpability.[11]

Communicating resentment and censure

Assigning blame is a matter of holding someone to account for their wrong actions. The expressive function of punishment involves communicating resentment to offenders and affirming the law's authority for the community at large, among other things. Duff distinguishes expressive retributivism from communicative retributivism, claiming that the former view only requires an expressor and not someone to whom the expression is addressed (1992, 51–52; 1996, 32–33). However, the distinction between expression and communication is porous.[12] Would an expressive utterance actually express anything if no meaning was communicated? Many of the examples of expression given by Feinberg are not acts of emoting that someone can do in a closet.[13] They involve disavowing criminal acts, vindicating the law, and absolving others of blame, all of which involve a demand that others acknowledge normative claims (Feinberg 1970, 101–5). Duff may be correct that expressivism ought to focus more on the addressees of our moral indignation, both the person who is being blamed and those who should share our resentment. But this is more a question of emphasis than a substantive disagreement. In fact, restorative practices can bring this aspect of expressive punishment to the fore.

As mentioned earlier, in the adversarial context of the traditional criminal justice system, defendants tend to be better off when they admit nothing and refuse to accept responsibility. By contrast, restorative practices encourage offenders to own up to their mistakes. By hearing the impact of their crimes on the victims and their communities, offenders can begin to understand the harm they have caused and to empathize with the people they harmed. Offenders talk about why the crimes occurred and how this has affected their lives, and, ideally, they come to accept responsibility. It is hard for someone to grasp the abstract idea that they

11 Gabbay claims that restorative justice and retribution are both backward-looking and forward-looking:

> Restorative justice turns to offenders … and demands their accountability. In this aspect, both restorative justice and retributivism are backward-looking, connecting past acts to present moral obligations. … But it does not stop there. Just as retributivism sees the criminal event as the basis for justifying the state's obligation, restorative justice sees it as the basis for justifying the imposition of obligations upon the offender. (2005, 376)

12 Like me, Hanna also elides this distinction, saying that "Antony Duff and Jean Hampton are among the most prominent contemporary ER [Expressive Retributivism] theorists" (2008, 133).

13 I disagree with Glasgow's understanding of what it means to express something. He says: "Unlike communication, expression is a one-way street: even if you don't receive my call, I'm still talking" (2015, 608–9). On my view, expression involves a communal space. "Audience-independent" expressivism is an oxymoron.

have wronged the state by violating our shared rules and taking unfair advantage. It is much easier to understand how they have hurt other people and to feel remorse when confronting the human impact of their bad choices.

There are both deontological and consequentialist reasons for returning at least part of the criminal justice process back to victims. Nils Christie (1977) has argued that crimes are best construed as conflicts between offenders and victims, that these conflicts "belong" to them, and that they have a right to participate in their resolution. The state has "stolen the conflict" from victims and offenders. Neil MacCormick (1978) makes the case that victims have a right of reparation when they are wronged, and that there is a corresponding obligation for offenders to repair the wrong. Victimization often involves a lack of recognition for personhood and self-determination. Although a criminal trial can correct the imbalance of power and recognition that is caused by the crime, getting victims involved in the process also allows them to reclaim some of their agency.

In addition, if we think in terms of desire-satisfaction, numerous studies have shown that crime victims are less interested in punitive punishment for offenders and more interested in being informed about their cases, participating in the process, getting some kind of emotional reconciliation (sometimes with an apology from the offender), getting material reparation, and being treated fairly and respectfully (Strang and Sherman 2003; see also Umbreit 1989). These needs are more effectively addressed in restorative practices, which explains why they have been shown to improve victim satisfaction and increase offender accountability (Umbreit and Coates 1993; Poulson 2003; Behtz 2004; Latimer, Dowden, and Muise 2005; Sherman and Strang 2007).

In the context of restorative justice, offenders may express remorse and ask victims for forgiveness, and they may offer monetary compensation, perform community service that is specific to the offenses, or participate in drug/alcohol abuse treatment programs. For example, a burglar may have to pay for the damage they did, replace the stolen items, and do job training so they develop the skills to make a more honest living. The victim and other community members may work with the offender to devise a plan to prevent future crimes and to hold the person accountable to the plan. When an offender makes an attempt to right the wrong, they not only take responsibility for the crime but also vindicate the victim's own account of events and absolve the victim of blame. Thus, restorative practices can, ideally, accomplish Duff's "three 'r's of punishment" – repentance, reform, and reconciliation – without hard treatment (2001, 107–12).

Unlike Duff, some communicative retributivists both misconstrue the function of restorative practices and overestimate the communicative effectiveness of traditional punishments. For example, Stephen Garvey (2003) claims that crime causes two kinds of injury: material harms, such as lost property or injuries; and moral harms, which result from the fact that criminals show contempt for their victims by disregarding their rights and advancing the criminals' own interests. According to Garvey, restorative justice addresses the former kind of harm, while only punishment can correct moral wrongs. He says that restorative justice focuses on restitution, such as having the offender return stolen property, while punishment "proclaims to the world – to the victim, to the offender, and to the community as a whole – that the message of superiority implicit or explicit in the offender's crime is a false message." Hard treatment such as incarceration lowers the offender's status and rebalances the scales of justice, thus providing "full restoration of the victim" (S. Garvey 2003, 308).

One problem with this account is that it overlooks the moral dynamics involved in, for example, victim offender conferencing. Although restorative justice does not force or require offenders to apologize – neither does the state when it sends people to prison – it does have offenders listen to victims in order to understand the harm they caused.[14] As a result, offenders ought to express remorse and try to repair moral wrongs as well as material harms, making things right both concretely and symbolically. When victims are able to tell their stories and have them listened to rather than dismissed, that alone helps to repair a kind of moral harm by validating their perspectives and their worth (Brison 2002). And if offenders do apologize to their victims, it puts them in a vulnerable position in which they feel shame at what they did (passive responsibility), gives victims the power to accept or reject the apologies (undoing their unfair advantage), and is a way of committing to changed behavior and restitution (active responsibility) (Van Ness and Strong 2015, 101–2). Studies have found that victims are more interested in this kind of moral, emotional, or symbolic reparation than material reparation, and that they believe this aim is best accomplished by means of restorative practices (Marshall and Merry 1990; Umbreit, Coates, and Kalanj 1994; Strang 2001). Even if the offender does not apologize, "the defiant actor is made to feel and understand the disapproval of others, whatever he himself may think of his conduct" (von Hirsch 1993, 10). One does not need to adopt an "audience-independent" version of expressivism to make sense of punishments for unrepentant and uncommunicative offenders (see Glasgow 2015). Like hard treatment, victim offender conferences and circles convey the resentment and censure of the community, even if the offender disagrees or does not want to hear it. And victim offender conferencing does it more directly and explicitly.

Putting offenders in the position of being blamed by their victims and members of their communities, who expect contrition, achieves a kind of rebalance of power. Offenders have asserted that their interests are more important than the victims' persons or property. Punishment is a way of withdrawing our solidarity with offenders, who must atone for their crimes before they are reconciled with the community. According to Christopher Bennett (2002), this cycle of alienation and reconciliation is essential to retribution. Rather than being stigmatized and excluded, reintegrative shaming allows for offenders to become part of their

14 In the Canberra Reintegrative Shaming Experiment (RISE), which involved cases of property crimes committed by juvenile offenders and middle-range violent crimes committed by young adults, offenders apologized 86 percent of the time when they participated in restorative justice conferencing. Only 16 percent apologized when they were subject to a traditional criminal trial (Strang and Sherman 2003, 28).

communities again – on the condition that they lower themselves with respect to their victims, by recognizing the extent of their wrongdoings and, perhaps, asking for forgiveness (Braithwaite 1989; Braithwaite, Ahmed, and Braithwaite 2006).

The limits of traditional punishments

Often, traditional forms of criminal justice ineffectively communicate the public censure of wrongdoing. Thomas Mathiesen (2006) has analyzed the different elements of communication and found that, when it comes to criminal prohibitions and punishment, the state is particularly bad at doing the three things that any communication must do: conveying the facts, using appropriate designations, and using an effective sign structure. That is, potential and actual criminals are unlikely to be aware of sanctioning levels, police practices, and sentencing practices, and the reasons behind them (failure to convey the facts); the meaning of the law and punishments are filtered through mass media outlets, which tend to focus on the sensational and the dramatic rather than the parts of the law that are relevant to the bulk of criminal activity (inappropriate designations); and these messages are unlikely to be heard by those who are most likely to offend, given their social experiences and acculturated attitudes toward the state and the law (ineffective sign structure) (Mathiesen 2006, 65–75).[15] For example, people who smoked crack in 1986 probably were not aware of the provisions of the Anti-Drug Abuse Act that was passed that year, except as it was inexpertly conveyed to them by their fellow drug users; they did not know about or understand the reasons for the disparities between crack and powder cocaine; and they likely felt alienated from the legal process that codified those disparities. The criminal justice system is just as likely to obscure moral censure as it is to convey that message effectively.

As I mentioned in Chapter 5, the vast majority of state and federal cases (94 and 97 percent, respectively) end in plea bargains (Goode 2012; see also Bachner and Ginsberg 2021, 100, 107, 116). When a criminal pleads to a lesser charge, "the criminal offense is not even properly named" (Moss 2013, 220). If the plea requires the defendant to give an allocution, they have to explain themselves to the court, and to the state's satisfaction, not the victim's. If a trial is held, defendants usually do not testify on their own behalf, so there is no need to explain themselves. Defense attorneys argue for the accused and try to deflect responsibility rather than accept it. Defendants are unlikely to feel remorse because they are alienated from the proceedings, having previously been alienated from the political process of creating criminal law. Defendants may not understand the full consequences of their behavior because they do not engage with victims or victims' families. The whole system may seem like a foreign imposition rather than moral communication (Moss 2013, 220).

15 Mathiesen (2006) is primarily talking about how failures of communication affect the ability of legal punishment to deter. However, the same criticisms apply with regard to its retributive function, so long as retribution is justified in terms of expression.

This is very different from the direct engagement and participation that is the hallmark of restorative justice, where people share their perspectives on the crime, ask questions, and come to a consensus about what should be done. When offenders directly engage people who are most affected by their crimes, it is more likely to convey the sense of wrongdoing, since the harm is, on some accounts, what makes it wrong in the first place. In victim offender conferencing or circles, the whole group – the victim and their family, representatives from the community, and a mediator who represents the public – can denounce the criminal's conduct and come up with a response that is tailored to the specific offender and the specific community: "By allowing the affected parties to decide on an appropriate outcome through a deliberative process, society can broaden its mechanisms of expressing public condemnation in more innovative yet equally effective means" (Gabbay 2005, 369). For Duff at least, victim offender conferencing is "an appropriate paradigm of punishment as a communicative enterprise" (2003, 55).

Restorative practices and punitive practices: Contrary or complementary?

Although legal punishment may be able to communicate some things – publicly disavowing the crime, reaffirming the law, absolving others of blame – retributive expression in particular, which is supposed to convey the resentment of the community, can be achieved effectively through restorative conferencing and circles. In fact, there are a number of low-level criminal offenses, such as property crimes and minor assaults, that could be more constructively addressed through restorative practices instead of criminal trials. For example, there is no pressing need to restrain a shoplifter, to reaffirm the law against theft, or to absolve other suspects of blame, since such crimes are hardly publicized. In cases like this, restorative justice can serve as a real alternative to the traditional court system.

For many crimes, especially the most serious, there is still a need for more traditional punishments, including hard treatment. The offender is not the only one who needs to be condemned. The act itself needs to be condemned by the state, innocents have to be publicly exonerated, and the state must announce to the citizenry that the victim is in the right: as Donald Hermann puts it,

> An approach that restricts the response to crime to restorative justice alone ignores the continuing need to take into account the requirements of public order and the felt need for censure of the offender, which requires application of retributive punishment. (2017, 103)[16]

16 Kleinig makes a similar point regarding censure:

> It seems to be a very widely shared experience of human beings that face-to-face blame does not adequately register the seriousness of moral wrongdoing. Something more demonstrative is required. … I do not think we live in a society for which hard treatment has become redundant; nor do we come near to it. (1991, 417–18)

Admonishing Billy Budd would not have served a broader purpose had it been handled only by those who were most directly affected by it, and if he had not been so severely punished. Criminal law should include what Owen Fiss calls a public dimension of adjudication (1984, 1085–90).[17]

As I said earlier, retribution and restoration are often erroneously construed as contrary positions, such that we could only choose one or the other. However, even with the most serious *malum in se* crimes, such as murder or rape, or crimes where victim offender conferencing is especially difficult, such as domestic violence or hate crimes, restorative practices can serve important communicative functions (Umbreit, Bradshaw, and Coates 1999). In many such cases, traditional retributive punishments and restorative practices should be used in conjunction with one another so that the criminal justice system can better serve its expressive purpose and address the interests of all the stakeholders:

> Restorative justice addresses the needs of the victim for reparation and restoration. Similarly, restorative justice addresses the needs of the offender for forgiveness and reintegration into the community. Furthermore, retributive justice addresses the need of the state to maintain the criminal law through enforcement and punishment. Finally, retributive justice restores the offender's moral state as a result of the imposition and acceptance of prescribed punishment. (Hermann 2017, 98)

Restoration and retribution, properly understood, serve complementary purposes in holding offenders, even violent offenders, responsible for their crimes and in giving them what they deserve, albeit in a broader sense than traditional retributivists tend to think.[18]

Conclusion

In this chapter, I am not going so far as to argue that restorative practices should replace traditional forms of punishment, especially as a response to all crimes. Even defenders of restorative justice disagree about which kinds of offenses should be addressed through restorative practices, and about whether (and

A. Morris says that hard treatment is necessary both to preserve the public order and to communicate effectively to offenders and victims: "it might be agreed that a prison sentence is required in a particular situation to protect society, to signify the gravity of the offending or to make amends to victims" (2002, 599). See also Duff (2001, 60–64), Robinson (2003), Robinson (2006), and Bennett (2008, 144).

17 Of course, given the many failures of the prison system, successfully integrating restorative practices into more traditional punishments would require substantial reforms. Brooks acknowledges this in his discussion of punitive restoration (2012, 142–43).

18 The idea that restorative practices complement rather than contradict state-sponsored retribution, and that both are needed, is defended most clearly by Zedner (1994), Gabbay (2005), and Hermann (2017).

when) restorative practices should be used as a supplement to or a replacement for hard treatment such as imprisonment. In many cases, traditional punishments are necessary to incapacitate criminals, for example, and they may be required to express society's broader reactive attitudes. What I am arguing is that the contrast between retribution and restoration, and the belief that they are incompatible, rely on misinterpretations. Through victim offender conferencing, sentencing circles, and reintegrative shaming, retributive justice accomplishes many of the aims of retribution: communities express their disapproval; participants collectively affirm the wrongness of the crimes, acknowledging the truth of the claims behind the resentment (that victims have been wronged); offenders are held accountable for what they did; and they commit themselves to reestablishing relations of right, thus reaffirming the law. When drained of anger and vengeance, the purposes of retribution can be furthered by means of restorative justice.

Conclusion

The two-tiered model of punishment is a mixed theory. Two contrary positions, consequentialism and retributivism, function together in one criminal justice system. The theory distinguishes the roles of two political bodies – the legislature and the criminal judiciary – each of which fulfills a different moral obligation. In formulating legal prohibitions and setting statutory penalties, lawmakers ought to preserve a just public order and promote the common good. In applying the law to accused criminals and imposing punishments, judges ought to give people what they deserve, punishing the guilty, and only the guilty, in proportion to their degrees of guilt. Both lawmakers and judges have public commitments: respectively, to protect the community and further its goals, and to express the individual and collective sense of resentment at having been wronged.

Philosophy is inherently interdisciplinary, and philosophy of law is no exception. The theory of punishment straddles two very different fields: practical philosophy and social science. Both disciplines are crucial for completing the two tasks that remain as a result of my inquiry. First, by defining the legislature's role in consequentialist terms, broadly construed, I have made no claims about which aims the state ought to achieve. For punishments to be right or reasonable under the two-tiered model, they must support a just system. Therefore, we must investigate the normative principles of a just society. This is a value ("ought") question, and it is especially suited to political philosophy.

Because punishment is the intentional infliction of harm and because the intentional infliction of harm is *prima facie* wrong, we must be reasonably sure that punishments are efficient and effective. So, the second task is to identify strategies that effectively and efficiently achieve our shared ends. We must empirically investigate how best to reduce criminal behaviors while also minimizing collateral social costs. This is a factual ("is") question, with practical implications. To be sure, there is a lot of progress to be made in determining the relative effectiveness of certainty, severity, and celerity and in evaluating informal social controls as mechanisms of deterrence. However, good work is being done. Philosophers of science should be involved in evaluating and improving the relevant methodologies, but the bulk of the empirical research will be done by social scientists.

Despite the claims of abolitionists, I doubt that hard treatment for offenders could ever be completely eliminated. Some people will always be both deterrable and in need of deterrence. Punishment and the threat of punishment communicate the shared values to which we have collectively committed ourselves. By restricting unlawful actions, the threat of punishment allows law-abiding people to act without hindrance, and it preserves a sphere of action free from interference by authority. As Michael Davis notes, the benefits of punishment are so great that it remains and has remained preferable to other methods of social control in just about every form of organized human society, even when penalties are set in very different ways (1992, 73).

None of this entails that we should execute criminals or put all of them in cages. Since the 1970s, the United States has responded to a growing fear of crime by making changes to the law that have dramatically increased the prison population. Mass incarceration has had a "negligible" impact on the crime rate, but it has inflicted tremendous physical, psychological, social, and economic costs on offenders and their families, communities, and society as a whole (Roeder, Eisen, and Bowling 2015). The primary legislative and institutional drivers of carceral expansion are high mandatory minimum sentences, including three-strikes laws; statutes that allow juvenile offenders to be tried as adults; severe penalties for drug offenses; and broad prosecutorial discretion. Mass incarceration is one of the defining social issues of our generation, and, since it is driven largely by policies around punishment, philosophers of law are particularly well suited to confront it. Over the course of the book (especially Chapters 5, 6, 9, and 11), I have explained why and how these policies ought to be changed. We can effectively address the problem by evaluating the institution of punishment on consequentialist grounds. The two-tiered model of punishment not only returns our focus to rehabilitation but also broadens our view to a consideration of the collateral costs of "tough on crime" policies.

For the last fifty years, psychology and the social sciences have made us increasingly aware that a merely punitive response to crime is not the most effective way to achieve general and specific deterrence. Once we identify the risk factors that lead to criminal behavior, we can begin to address crime at the root through more effective social initiatives such as better education, job training, and youth employment programs, rather than merely increasing the severity of existing punishments and hoping for the best. And many innovative, nonpunitive programs – used in conjunction with or instead of prison – show promise for helping convicted criminals to re-enter their communities and avoid recidivating, including corrections-based education, vocation and work programs, cognitive therapy, drug treatments, and restorative justice, just to name a few. It is time for rehabilitation to have a comeback.

This book should thus serve as a call to action. The two-tiered model shows that we can both give criminals what they deserve and be concerned with whether the institution of punishment promotes or inhibits the common good. Our obligations around punishment are more complex under a mixed theory than under the non-mixed alternatives, but that is appropriate given the complexity of the issue itself. We should think about our values and act in accordance with our ideals. We should view crime reduction as part of a broader effort at harm reduction. We should punish the guilty and protect the innocent. This book provides a philosophical foundation for future efforts, and there is a lot of work to do.

References

Ackerman, Bruce A. 1980. *Social Justice in the Liberal State*. New Haven, CT: Yale University Press.

Adelstein, Richard. 2017. *The Exchange Order: Property and Liability as an Economic System*. New York: Oxford University Press.

Aeschylus. 1961. *Seven against Thebes*. In *Prometheus Bound and Other Plays*, translated by Philip Vellacott, 88–121. New York: Penguin.

Alarcón, Arthur L. 2007. "Remedies for California's Death Row Deadlock." *Southern California Law Review* 80, no. 4 (May): 697–752.

Alcoff, Linda Martín. 1999. "On Judging Epistemic Credibility: Is Social Identity Relevant?" *Philosophic Exchange* 29, no. 1: 73–93.

Alexander, Lawrence. 1980. "The Doomsday Machine: Proportionality, Punishment and Prevention." *Monist* 63, no. 2 (April): 199–227.

Alexander, Michelle. 2012. *The New Jim Crow: Mass Incarceration in the Age of Colorblindness*. New York: New Press.

Alighieri, Dante. 1971. *The Divine Comedy*. Vol. 1: *Inferno*. Translated by Mark Musa. New York: Penguin.

Allen, Francis A. 1981. *The Decline of the Rehabilitative Ideal: Penal Policy and Social Purpose*. New Haven, CT: Yale University Press.

Alschuler, Albert W. 1976. "The Trial Judge's Role in Plea Bargaining, Part I." *Columbia Law Review* 76, no. 7 (November): 1059–1154.

Altman, Matthew C. Forthcoming. "Kant's Compatibilism and the Two-Tiered Model of Punishment." In *The Court of Reason: Proceedings of the 13th International Kant Congress 2019*, edited by Camilla Serck-Hanssen and Beatrix Himmelmann. Berlin: de Gruyter.

Amnesty International. 2013. *Not Making Us Safer: Crime, Public Safety and the Death Penalty*. London: Amnesty International. https://www.amnesty.org/download/Documents/8000/act510022013en.pdf.

———. 2018. "Iran: Authorities Amputate a Man's Hand in Shocking Act of Cruelty." January 18. https://www.amnesty.org/en/latest/news/2018/01/iran-authorities-amputate-a-mans-hand-in-shocking-act-of-cruelty/.

Andenaes, Johannes. 1974. *Punishment and Deterrence*. Ann Arbor: University of Michigan Press.

———. 1982. "Nyere forskning om almenprevensjonen – status og kommentar." In *Fra spredte felter: Et utvalg artikler og foredrag*, 196–239. Oslo: Tanum-Norli

Andrews, D. A., James Bonta, and R. D. Hoge. 1990. "Classification for Effective Rehabilitation: Rediscovering Psychology." *Criminal Justice and Behavior* 17, no. 1 (March): 19–52.

Anscombe, Elizabeth. 1958. "Modern Moral Philosophy." *Philosophy* 33, no. 124 (January): 1–19.

"Anti-Swearing Law Unconstitutional, Appeals Court Says." 2002. *Midland Daily News*, April 1. https://www.ourmidland.com/news/article/Anti-swearing-law-unconstitutional-appeals-court-7132716.php.

Antunes, George, and A. Lee Hunt. 1973. "The Deterrent Impact of Criminal Sanctions: Some Implications for Criminal Justice Policy." *Journal of Urban Law* 51, no. 2 (November): 145–61.

Apel, Robert, and Samuel E. DeWitt. 2018. "Informal and Formal Sanctions." In *Deterrence, Choice, and Crime: Contemporary Perspectives*, vol. 23 of *Advances in Criminological Theory*, edited by Daniel S. Nagin, Francis T. Cullen, and Cheryl Lero Jonson, 139–56. New York: Routledge.

Applegate, Amy G. 1982. "Prosecutorial Discretion and Discrimination in the Decision to Charge." *Temple Law Quarterly* 55, no. 1: 35–88.

Aquinas, Thomas. 1964–81. *Summa Theologiae*. Translated by Thomas Gilby. 61 vols. Cambridge: Blackfriars.

Armstrong, K. G. 1961. "The Retributivist Hits Back." *Mind* 70, no. 280 (October): 471–90.

Austin, John. 1995. *The Province of Jurisprudence Determined*. Edited by Wilfrid E. Rumble. Cambridge: Cambridge University Press.

Avio, Kenneth L. 1979. "Capital Punishment in Canada: A Time-Series Analysis of the Deterrent Hypothesis." *Canadian Journal of Economics* 12, no. 4 (November): 647–76.

———. 1988. "Measurement Errors and Capital Punishment." *Applied Economics* 20, no. 9 (September): 1253–62.

Ayer, A. J. 1954. "Freedom and Necessity." In *Philosophical Essays*, 271–84. London: Macmillan.

Bachner, Jennifer, and Benjamin Ginsberg. 2021. *America's State Governments: A Critical Look at Disconnected Democracies*. New York: Routledge.

Bagaric, Mirko. 1999. "Suspended Sentences and Preventive Sentences: Illusory Evils and Disproportionate Punishments." *University of New South Wales Law Journal* 22, no. 2 (December): 535–63.

Bagaric, Mirko, and Kumar Amarasekera. 2000. "The Errors of Retributivism." *Melbourne University Law Review* 24, no. 1: 124–89.

Bailey, Victor. 2019. *The Rise and Fall of the Rehabilitative Ideal, 1895–1970*. Abingdon, UK: Routledge.

Bailey, William C. 1982. "Capital Punishment and Lethal Assaults against Police." *Criminology* 19, no. 4 (February): 608–25.

Bailey, William C., J. David Martin, and Louis N. Gray. 1974. "Crime and Deterrence: A Correlation Analysis." *Journal of Research in Crime and Delinquency* 11, no. 2 (July) : 124–43.

Bailey, William C., and Ruth D. Peterson. 1994. "Murder, Capital Punishment, and Deterrence: A Review of the Evidence and an Examination of Police Killings." *Journal of Social Issues* 50, no. 2 (Summer): 53–74.

———. 1997. "Murder, Capital Punishment, and Deterrence: A Review of the Literature." In *The Death Penalty in America: Current Controversies*, edited by Hugo Adam Bedau, 135–61. New York: Oxford University Press.

Baldus, David C., and James W. L. Cole. 1975. "A Comparison of the Work of Thorsten Sellin and Isaac Ehrlich on the Deterrent Effect of Capital Punishment." *Yale Law Journal* 85, no. 2 (December): 170–86.

Baldus, David C., George Woodworth, David Zuckerman, and Neil Alan Weiner. 1998. "Racial Discrimination and the Death Penalty in the Post-Furman Era: An Empirical and Legal Overview with Recent Findings from Philadelphia." *Cornell Law Review* 83, no. 6 (September): 1638–1770.

Barkow, Rachel Elise. 2019. *Prisoners of Politics: Breaking the Cycle of Mass Incarceration.* Cambridge, MA: Belknap.

Barnes, J. A. 1990. *Models and Interpretations: Selected Essays.* Cambridge: Cambridge University Press.

Baron, Dennis. 2020. *What's Your Pronoun? Beyond He & She.* New York: Liveright.

Beccaria, Cesare. 1995. *On Crimes and Punishments and Other Writings.* Translated by Richard Davies, Virginia Cox, and Richard Bellamy. Edited by Richard Bellamy. Cambridge: Cambridge University Press.

Becker, Gary S. 1968. "Crime and Punishment: An Economic Approach." *Journal of Political Economy* 76, no. 2 (March–April): 169–217.

Becker, Lawrence C. 1974. "Criminal Attempt and the Theory of the Law of Crimes." *Philosophy & Public Affairs* 3, no. 3 (Spring): 262–94.

Bedau, Hugo Adam. 1978. "Retribution and the Theory of Punishment." *Journal of Philosophy* 75, no. 11 (November): 601–20.

———. 1982. "Deterrence: Problems, Doctrines, and Evidence." In *The Death Penalty in America*, 3rd ed., edited by Hugo Adam Bedau, 93–103. New York: Oxford University Press.

———. 2012. *The Case against the Death Penalty.* Washington, DC: American Civil Liberties Union. www.aclu.org/case-against-death-penalty.

Behtz, Sarah Anne. 2004. "Justice for All? Victim Satisfaction with Restorative Justice Conferences." Master's thesis, East Tennessee State University. www.antoniocasella.eu/restorative/Behtz_2004.pdf.

Belackova, V., and A. M. Salmon. 2017. *Overview of International Literature: Supervised Injecting Centers & Drug Consumption Rooms.* Sydney: Uniting Medically Supervised Injecting Center.

Benn, S. I. 1958. "An Approach to the Problems of Punishment." *Philosophy* 33, no 127 (October): 325–41.

Bennett, Christopher. 2002. "The Varieties of Retributive Experience." *Philosophical Quarterly* 52, no. 207 (April): 145–63.

———. 2008. *The Apology Ritual: A Philosophical Theory of Punishment.* Cambridge: Cambridge University Press.

Bentham, Jeremy. 1830. *The Rationale of Punishment.* London: Heward.

———. 1970. *An Introduction to the Principles of Morals and Legislation.* Edited by J. H. Burns and H. L. A. Hart. Oxford: Clarendon.

Bentley, Kristina A. 2000. "Suggesting a 'Separate' Approach to Utility and Rights: Deontological Specification and Teleological Enforcement of Human Rights." *Sapientia* (September). citeseerx.ist.psu.edu/viewdoc/download?doi=10.1.1.581.7674&rep=rep1&type=pdf.

Berdejó, Carlos. 2018. "Criminalizing Race: Racial Disparities in Plea Bargaining." *Boston College Law Review* 59, no. 4 (April): 1187–1249.

Berk, Richard. 2005. "New Claims about Executions and General Deterrence: Déjà Vu All Over Again?" *Journal of Empirical Legal Studies* 2, no. 2 (July): 303–30.

Berns, Walter. 1979. *For Capital Punishment: Crime and the Morality of the Death Penalty.* New York: Basic Books.

Berry, Kate. 2015. *How Judicial Elections Impact Criminal Cases.* New York: Brennan Center for Justice. https://www.brennancenter.org/sites/default/files/2019-08/Report_How_Judicial_Elections_Impact_Criminal_Cases.pdf.

Bianchi, Herman. 1994. *Justice as Sanctuary: Toward a New System of Crime Control.* Bloomington: Indiana University Press.

Binder, Guyora, and Nicholas J. Smith. 2000. "Framed: Utilitarianism and Punishment of the Innocent." *Rutgers Law Journal* 32, no. 1 (Fall): 115–224.

Blackstone, William. 2016. *Commentaries on the Laws of England*, Book 4: *Of Public Wrongs.* Edited by Ruth Paley. Oxford: Oxford University Press.

Bondurant, Samuel R., Jason M. Lindo, and Isaac D. Swensen. 2016. "Substance Abuse Treatment Centers and Local Crime." NBER Working Paper No. 22610, September. https://www.nber.org/papers/w22610.pdf.

Bonner, Raymond, and Ford Fessenden. 2000. "Absence of Executions: A Special Report; States with No Death Penalty Share Lower Homicide Rates." *New York Times*, September 22. www.nytimes.com/2000/09/22/us/absence-executions-special-report-states-with-no-death-penalty-share-lower.html?pagewanted=all.

Bonta, James, and D. A. Andrews. 2007. "Risk-Need-Responsivity Model for Offender Assessment and Rehabilitation." https://www.publicsafety.gc.ca/cnt/rsrcs/pblctns/rsk-nd-rspnsvty/index-en.aspx.

———. 2016. *The Psychology of Criminal Conduct.* 6th ed. New York: Routledge.

Bonta, James, Rebecca Jesseman, Tanya Rugge, and Robert Cormier. 2008. "Restorative Justice and Recidivism: Promises Made, Promises Kept?" In *Handbook of Restorative Justice: A Global Perspective*, edited by Dennis Sullivan and Larry Tifft, 108–20. Abingdon, UK: Routledge.

Bonta, James, Suzanne Wallace-Capretta, and Jennifer Rooney. 1998. *Restorative Justice: An Evaluation of the Restorative Resolutions Project.* Ottawa: Solicitor General Canadian.

Bonta, James, Suzanne Wallace-Capretta, Jennifer Rooney, and Kevin Mcanoy. 2002. "An Outcome Evaluation of a Restorative Justice Alternative to Incarceration." *Contemporary Justice Review* 5, no. 4: 319–38.

Boonin, David. 2008. *The Problem of Punishment.* Cambridge: Cambridge University Press.

Bork, Robert H. 2008. "Oral Argument in *Gregg v. Georgia.*" In *A Time to Speak: Selected Writings and Arguments*, 63–82. Wilmington, DE: ISI.

Bork, Robert H., A. Raymond Randolph Jr., and Frank H. Easterbrook. 2008. "*Gregg v. Georgia*, Amicus Brief for the United States." In *A Time to Speak: Selected Writings and Arguments*, 5–62. Wilmington, DE: ISI.

Bosanquet, Bernard. 1965. *The Philosophical Theory of the State.* 4th ed. London: Macmillan.

Bottoms, A. E., and R. H. Preston. 1980. *The Coming Penal Crisis: A Criminological and Theological Exploration.* Edinburgh: Scottish Academic.

Bovens, Mark. 1998. *The Quest for Responsibility: Accountability and Citizenship in Complex Organisations.* Cambridge: Cambridge University Press.

Bowers, William J., and Glenn L. Pierce. 1975. "The Illusion of Deterrence in Isaac Ehrlich's Research on Capital Punishment." *Yale Law Journal* 85, no. 2 (December): 187–208.

———. 1980. "Deterrence or Brutalization: What Is the Effect of Executions?" *Crime & Delinquency* 26, no. 4 (October): 453–84.

Bowers, William J., Glenn L. Pierce, and John F. McDevitt. 1984. *Legal Homicide: Death as Punishment in America, 1864–1982.* Boston: Northeastern University Press.

Bradley, F. H. 1988. *Ethical Studies.* 2nd ed. Oxford: Clarendon.

Braithwaite, John. 1989. *Crime, Shame and Reintegration.* Cambridge: Cambridge University Press.

———. 2000. "Reintegrative Shaming." johnbraithwaite.com/wp-content/uploads/2016/05/2000_Reintegrative-Shaming.pdf.

———. 2002. *Restorative Justice and Responsive Regulation.* Oxford: Oxford University Press.

Braithwaite, John, Eliza Ahmed, and Valerie Braithwaite. 2006. "Shame, Restorative Justice, and Crime." In *Taking Stock: The Status of Criminological Theory*, edited by Francis T. Cullen, John Paul Wright, and Kristie R. Blevins, 397–417. New Brunswick, NJ: Transaction.

Braithwaite, John, and Philip Pettit. 1990. *Not Just Deserts: A Republican Theory of Criminal Justice.* Oxford: Clarendon.

Braithwaite, John, and Declan Roche. 2001. "Responsibility and Restorative Justice." In *Restorative Community Justice: Repairing Harm and Transforming Communities*, edited by Gordon Bazemore and Mara Schiff, 63–84. Abingdon, UK: Routledge.

Brandt, Richard. 1958. "Determinism and the Justifiability of Moral Blame." In *Determinism and Freedom in the Age of Modern Science*, edited by Sidney Hook, 149–54. New York: Collier.

———. 1963. "Toward a Credible Form of Utilitarianism." In *Morality and the Language of Conduct*, edited by Hector-Neri Castañeda and George Nakhnikian, 107–43. Detroit: Wayne State University Press.

Brison, Susan J. 2002. *Aftermath: Violence and the Remaking of a Self.* Princeton, NJ: Princeton University Press.

Brody, S. R. 1976. *The Effectiveness of Sentencing: A Review of the Literature.* London: HMSO.

Brooks, Thom. 2012. *Punishment.* Abingdon, UK: Routledge.

Brown, Brian, and Greg Jolivette 2005. "A Primer: Three Strikes – The Impact after More than a Decade," October. Sacramento: Legislative Analyst's Office. https://lao.ca.gov/2005/3_strikes/3_strikes_102005.htm.

Brudholm, Thomas. 2010. "Hatred as an Attitude." *Philosophical Papers* 39, no. 3 (November): 289–313.

Brudner, Alan. 2009. *Punishment and Freedom: A Liberal Theory of Penal Justice* Oxford: Oxford University Press.

Bureau of Justice Statistics. 2014. "Capital Punishment, 2013 – Statistical Tables," December 19. https://www.bjs.gov/content/pub/pdf/cp13st.pdf.

———. 2019. "Capital Punishment, 2017: Selected Findings," July. https://www.bjs.gov/content/pub/pdf/cp17sf.pdf.

———. 2020. "Drugs and Crime Facts," February 13. https://www.bjs.gov/content/dcf/enforce.cfm.

Bursik, Robert J., and Harold Grasmik. 1993. *Neighborhoods and Crime: Dimensions of Effective Community Control.* Lanham, MD: Lexington.

Bushway, Shawn D., and Raymond Paternoster. 2009. "The Impact of Prison on Crime." In *Do Prisons Make Us Safer? The Benefits and Costs of the Prison Boom*, edited by Steven Raphael and Michael A. Stoll, 119–50. New York: Russell Sage Foundation.

Butler, Joseph. 2017. "Sermon 8: Upon Resentment." In *Fifteen Sermons Preached at the Rolls Chapel and Other Writings on Ethics*, edited by David McNaughton, 68–74. Oxford: Oxford University Press.

California Commission on the Fair Administration of Justice. 2008. "California Commission on the Fair Administration of Justice Final Report," June 30. Edited by Gerald Uelman. digitalcommons.law.scu.edu/cgi/viewcontent.cgi?article=1000&context=ncippubs.

Canes-Wrone, Brandice, Tom S. Clark, and Jason P. Kelly. 2014. "Judicial Selection and Death Penalty Decisions." *American Political Science Review* 108, no. 1 (February): 23–39.

Carey, Shannon M., Michael Finigan, Dave Crumpton, and Mark Waller. 2006. "California Drug Courts: Outcomes, Costs, and Promising Practices: An Overview of Phase II in a Statewide Study." *Journal of Psychoactive Drugs*, SARC suppl. 3 (November): 345–56.

Carlisle, Madeleine. 2019. "GOP Lawmakers Are Quietly Turning against the Death Penalty." *Atlantic*, June 7. https://www.theatlantic.com/politics/archive/2019/06/new-hampshire-helped-abolish-death-penalty/590803/.

Carlsmith, Kevin M., John M. Darley, and Paul H. Robinson. 2002. "Why Do We Punish? Deterrence and Just Deserts as Motives for Punishment." *Journal of Personality and Social Psychology* 83, no. 2 (September): 284–99.

Carritt, E. F. 1947. *Ethical and Political Thinking*. Oxford: Clarendon.

Carroll, John S. 1978. "A Psychological Approach to Deterrence: The Evaluation of Crime Opportunities." *Journal of Personality and Social Psychology* 36, no. 12 (December): 1512–20.

Caruso, Gregg D. 2019. "Free Will Skepticism and Its Implications: An Argument for Optimism." In *Free Will Skepticism in Law and Society: Challenging Retributive Justice*, edited by Elizabeth Shaw, Derk Pereboom, and Gregg D. Caruso, 43–72. Cambridge: Cambridge University Press.

Cederblom, J. B. 1977. Introduction to *Justice and Punishment*, edited by J. B. Cederblom and William L. Blizek, 1–19. Cambridge, MA: Ballinger.

Chalfin, Aaron, Amelia M. Haviland, and Steven Raphael. 2013. "What Do Panel Studies Tell Us about a Deterrent Effect of Capital Punishment? A Critique of the Literature." *Journal of Quantitative Criminology* 29, no. 1 (March): 5–43.

Chalfin, Aaron, and Justin McCrary. 2013. "The Effect of Police on Crime: New Evidence from U.S. Cities, 1960–2010." NBER Working Paper No. 18815, February. https://www.nber.org/papers/w18815.pdf.

Chalfin, Aaron J., and Sarah Tahamont. 2018. "The Economics of Deterrence: A Review of the Theory and Evidence." In *Deterrence, Choice, and Crime: Contemporary Perspectives*, vol. 23 of *Advances in Criminological Theory*, edited by Daniel S. Nagin, Francis T. Cullen, and Cheryl Lero Jonson, 29–79. New York: Routledge.

Chambliss, William J. 1966. "The Deterrent Influence of Punishment." *Crime & Delinquency* 12, no. 1 (January): 70–75.

———. 1967. "Types of Deviance and the Effectiveness of Legal Sanctions." *Wisconsin Law Review* 1967 (Summer): 703–19.

Charles, Kerwin Kofi, and Steven N. Durlauf. 2013. "Pitfalls in the Use of Time Series Methods to Study Deterrence and Capital Punishment." *Journal of Quantitative Criminology* 29, no. 1 (March): 45–66.

Cheatwood, Derral. 1993. "Capital Punishment and the Deterrence of Violent Crime in Comparable Counties." *Criminal Justice Review* 18, no. 2 (Autumn): 165–81.

Chiang, Harriet. 1996. "Some Jurors Revolt Over 3 Strikes/Penalty Prospects Sway Their Verdicts." *SFGate*, September 24. https://www.sfgate.com/crime/article/PAGE-ONE-Some-Jurors-Revolt-Over-3-Strikes-2965346.php.

Christie, Nils. 1977. "Conflicts as Property." *British Journal of Criminology* 17, no. 1 (January): 1–15.

———. 1981. *Limits to Pain: The Role of Punishment in Penal Policy.* Eugene, OR: Wipf & Stock.

Christopher, Russell L. 2002. "Deterring Retributivism: The Injustice of 'Just' Punishment." *Northwestern University Law Review* 96, no. 3 (Spring): 843–976.

Clark, Richard D. 1988. "Celerity and Specific Deterrence: A Look at the Evidence." *Canadian Journal of Criminology* 30, no. 2 (April): 109–20.

Coates, Robert B., and John Gehm. 1989. "An Empirical Assessment." In *Mediation and Criminal Justice: Victims, Offenders and Community*, edited by Martin Wright and Burt Galaway, 251–63. London: SAGE.

Cochran, John K., and Mitchell B. Chamlin. 2000. "Deterrence and Brutalization: The Dual Effects of Executions." *Justice Quarterly* 17, no. 4 (December): 685–706

Cochran, John K., Mitchell B. Chamlin, and Mark Seth. 1994. "Deterrence or Brutalization? An Impact Assessment of Oklahoma's Return to Capital Punishment." *Criminology* 32, no. 1 (February): 107–34.

Cohen-Cole, Ethan, Steven Durlauf, Jeffrey Fagan, and Daniel Nagin. 2009. "Model Uncertainty and the Deterrent Effect of Capital Punishment." *American Law and Economics Review* 11, no. 2 (Fall): 335–69.

Collins, Peter A., Robert C. Boruchowitz, Matthew J. Hickman, and Mark A. Larrañaga. 2016. "An Analysis of the Economic Costs of Seeking the Death Penalty in Washington State." *Seattle Journal for Social Justice* 14, no. 3 (Spring): 727–79.

Committee on Deterrence and the Death Penalty, National Research Council. 2012. *Deterrence and the Death Penalty.* Edited by Daniel S. Nagin and John V. Pepper. Washington, DC: National Academies Press.

Committee on Pattern Jury Instructions, District Judges Association, Fifth Circuit. 2019. *Pattern Jury Instructions (Criminal Cases).* https://www.lb5.uscourts.gov/viewer/?/juryinstructions/Fifth/crim2019.pdf.

Conrad, Clay S. 2014. *Jury Nullification: The Evolution of a Doctrine.* Washington, DC: Cato Institute.

Corlett, J. Angelo. 2001. "Making Sense of Retributivism." *Philosophy* 76, no. 1 (January): 77–110.

———. 2013. *Responsibility and Punishment.* 4th ed. Dordrecht: Springer.

Corsaro, Nicholas, and David Weisburd. 2018. "Police Interventions." In *Deterrence, Choice, and Crime: Contemporary Perspectives*, vol. 23 of *Advances in Criminological Theory*, edited by Daniel S. Nagin, Francis T. Cullen, and Cheryl Lero Jonson, 239–68. New York: Routledge.

Cottingham, John. 1979. "Varieties of Retribution." *Philosophical Quarterly* 29, no. 116 (July): 238–46.

Cragg, Wesley. 1992. *The Practice of Punishment: Towards a Theory of Restorative Justice*. London: Routledge.

Crew, B. Keith. 1991. "Race Differences in Felony Charging and Sentencing: Toward an Integration of Decision-Making and Negotiation Models." *Journal of Crime and Justice* 14, no. 1: 99–122.

Cullen, Francis T., and Paul Gendreau. 2012. "Assessing Correctional Rehabilitation: Policy, Practice, and Prospects." In *Policies, Processes, and Decisions of the Criminal Justice System*, vol. 3 of *Criminal Justice 2000*, ed. Julie Horney, 109–75. Washington, DC: National Institute of Justice.

Cullen, Francis T., and Cheryl Lero Jonson. 2017. *Correctional Theory: Context and Consequences*. 2nd ed. Thousand Oaks, CA: SAGE.

Daly, Kathleen. 2000. "Revisiting the Relationship between Retributive and Restorative Justice." In *Restorative Justice: Philosophy to Practice*, edited by Heather Strang and John Braithwaite, 33–54. Abingdon, UK: Routledge.

———. 2002. "Restorative Justice: The Real Story." *Punishment & Society* 4, no. 1 (January): 55–79.

———. 2013. "The Punishment Debate in Restorative Justice." In *The SAGE Handbook of Punishment and Society*, edited by Jonathan Simon and Richard Sparks, 356–74. London: SAGE.

Dann, Robert H. 1935. "The Deterrent Effect of Capital Punishment." *Friends Social Service Series* 29: 1–20.

Danziger, Shai, Jonathan Levav, and Liora Avnaim-Pesso. 2011. "Extraneous Factors in Judicial Decisions." *Proceedings of the National Academy of Sciences of the United States of America* 108, no. 17 (April 26): 6889–92.

Darwall, Stephen. 2006. *The Second-Person Standpoint: Morality, Respect, and Accountability*. Cambridge, MA: Harvard University Press.

———. 2007. "Law and the Second-Person Standpoint." *Loyola of Los Angeles Law Review* 40, no. 3 (Spring): 891–910.

Davis, Angela J. 1998. "Prosecution and Race: The Power and Privilege of Discretion." *Fordham Law Review* 67, no. 1 (October): 13–67.

Davis, Kenneth Culp. 1969. *Discretionary Justice: A Preliminary Inquiry*. Baton Rouge: Louisiana State University Press.

———. 1976. *Discretionary Justice in Europe and America*. Urbana: University of Illinois Press.

Davis, Lois M., Robert Bozick, Jennifer L. Steele, Jessica Saunders, and Jeremy N. V. Miles. 2013. *Evaluating the Effectiveness of Correctional Education: A Meta-Analysis of Programs that Provide Education to Incarcerated Adults*. Washington, DC: Rand Corporation. https://www.bja.gov/Publications/RAND_Correctional-Education-Meta-Analysis.pdf.

Davis, Michael. 1992. *To Make the Punishment Fit the Crime: Essays in the Theory of Criminal Justice*. Boulder, CO: Westview.

———. 1996. *Justice in the Shadow of Death: Rethinking Capital and Lesser Punishments*. Lanham, MD: Rowman & Littlefield.

———. 2009. "Punishment Theory's Golden Half Century: A Survey of Developments from (about) 1957 to 2007." *Journal of Ethics* 13, no. 1 (January): 73–100.

Death Penalty Information Center. 1995. "On the Front Line: Law Enforcement Views on the Death Penalty," February 1. www.deathpenaltyinfo.org/front-line-law-enforcement-views-death-penalty.

———. 2020a. "Deterrence: States without the Death Penalty Have Had Consistently Lower Murder Rates." www.deathpenaltyinfo.org/deterrence-states-without-death-penalty-have-had-consistently-lower-murder-rates.

———. 2020b. "Execution List 2018." https://deathpenaltyinfo.org/executions/2018.

———. 2020c. "Executions by State and Region since 1976." Accessed December 31, 2020. https://deathpenaltyinfo.org/executions/executions-overview/number-of-executions-by-state-and-region-since-1976.

———. 2020d. "Policy Issues: Race." https://deathpenaltyinfo.org/policy-issues/race.

———. 2020e. "Time on Death Row." https://deathpenaltyinfo.org/death-row/death-row-time-on-death-row.

Decker, Scott H., and Carol W. Kohfeld. 1990. "Certainty, Severity, and the Probability of Crime: A Logistic Analysis." *Policy Studies Journal* 19, no. 1 (September): 2–21.

de Haan, Willem. 1990. *The Politics of Redress: Crime, Punishment, and Penal Abolition*. London: Unwin Hyman.

Deigh, John. 1984. "On the Right to Be Punished: Some Doubts." *Ethics* 94, no. 2 (January): 191–211.

Delgado, Richard. 2000. "Goodbye to Hammurabi: Analyzing the Atavistic Appeal of Restorative Justice." *Stanford Law Review* 52, no. 4 (April): 751–75.

de Sousa, Ronald. 1987. *The Rationality of Emotion*. Cambridge, MA: MIT Press.

Dezhbakhsh, Hashem, and Paul H. Rubin. 2011. "From the 'Econometrics of Capital Punishment' to the 'Capital Punishment of Econometrics': On the Use and Abuse of Sensitivity Analysis." *Applied Economics* 43, no. 25: 3655–70.

Dezhbakhsh, Hashem, Paul H. Rubin, and Joanna M. Shepherd. 2003. "Does Capital Punishment Have a Deterrent Effect? New Evidence from Postmoratorium Panel Data." *American Law and Economics Review* 5, no. 2 (August): 344–76.

Dezhbakhsh, Hashem, and Joanna M. Shepherd. 2006. "The Deterrent Effect of Capital Punishment: Evidence from a 'Judicial Experiment.'" *Economic Inquiry* 44, no. 3 (July): 512–35.

Diamond, Jared. 2008. "Vengeance Is Ours: What Can Tribal Societies Tell Us about Our Need to Get Even?" *New Yorker*, April 14. https://www.newyorker.com/magazine/2008/04/21/vengeance-is-ours.

Dickey, Walter J. 1996. *The Impact of "Three Strikes and You're Out" Laws: What Have We Learned?* Washington, DC: Campaign for an Effective Crime Policy.

DiIulio, John J., Jr. 1994. "Instant Replay: Three Strikes Was the Right Call." *American Prospect* (Summer). https://prospect.org/article/instant-replay-three-strikes-was-right-call.

Dimock, Susan. 1997. "Retributivism and Trust." *Law and Philosophy* 16, no. 1 (January): 37–62.

Dippel, Christian, and Michael Poyker. 2020. "How Common are Electoral Cycles in Criminal Sentencing?" NBER Working Paper No. 25716, March 2019, rev. March 2020. https://www.nber.org/system/files/working_papers/w25716/w25716.pdf.

Dolinko, David. 1991. "Some Thoughts about Retributivism." *Ethics* 101, no. 3 (April): 537–59.

Donagan, Alan. 1968. "Is There a Credible Form of Utilitarianism?" In *Contemporary Utilitarianism*, edited by Michael D. Bayles, 187–202. Garden City, NY: Doubleday.

Donohue, John J., and Justin Wolfers. 2005. "Uses and Abuses of Empirical Evidence in the Death Penalty Debate." *Stanford Law Review* 58, no. 3 (December): 791–845.

———. 2006. "The Death Penalty: No Evidence for Deterrence." *Economists' Voice* 3, no. 5 (April): 1–6.

———. 2009. "Estimating the Impact of the Death Penalty on Murder." *American Law and Economics Review* 11, no. 2 (Fall): 249–309.

Doob, Anthony N., and Cheryl Marie Webster. 2003. "Sentence Severity and Crime: Accepting the Null Hypothesis." In *Crime and Justice – A Review of Research*, vol. 30, edited by Michael Tonry, 143–95. Chicago: University of Chicago Press.

Drake, Elizabeth K., Steve Aos, and Marna G. Miller. 2009. "Evidence-Based Public Policy Options to Reduce Crime and Criminal Justice Costs: Implications in Washington State." *Victims & Offenders* 4, no. 2: 170–96.

Dressler, Joshua. 2018. *Understanding Criminal Law*. 8th ed. Durham, NC: Carolina Academic Press.

Duff, R. A. 1986. *Trials and Punishments*. Cambridge: Cambridge University Press.

———. 1988. "Punishment and Penance: A Reply to Harrison." *Proceedings of the Aristotelian Society* 62: 153–67.

———. 1992. "Alternatives to Punishment – Or Alternative Punishments?" In *Retributivism and Its Critics*, edited by Wesley Cragg, 43–68. Stuttgart: Steiner.

———. 1996. "Penal Communications: Recent Work in the Philosophy of Punishment." In *Crime and Justice – A Review of Research*, vol. 20, edited by Michael Tonry, 1–97. Chicago: University of Chicago Press.

———. 2001. *Punishment, Communication, and Community*. Oxford: Oxford University Press.

———. 2003. "Restoration and Retribution." In *Restorative Justice and Criminal Justice: Competing or Reconcilable Paradigms?*, edited by Andrew von Hirsch, Julian Roberts, Anthony E. Bottoms, Kent Roach, and Mara Schiff, 43–59. Oxford: Hart.

———. 2011. "Responsibility, Restoration, and Retribution." In *Retributivism Has a Past: Has It a Future?*, edited by Michael Tonry, 63–85. Oxford: Oxford University Press.

Duff, R. A., and D. Garland. 1994. Introduction to *A Reader on Punishment*, edited by R. A. Duff and David Garland, 1–43. Oxford: Oxford University Press.

Durlauf, Steven N., and Daniel S. Nagin. 2011. "Imprisonment and Crime: Can Both Be Reduced?" *Criminology & Public Policy* 10, no. 1 (February): 9–54.

Dworkin, Ronald. 1977. *Taking Rights Seriously*. Cambridge, MA: Harvard University Press.

Egelko, Bob. 2003. "26 to Life for Taking an Exam/Man Took Cousin's Drive Test – Strike 3." *SFGate*, December 30. https://www.sfgate.com/bayarea/article/26-to-life-for-taking-an-exam-Man-took-cousin-s-2524459.php.

Ehrlich, Isaac. 1975. "The Deterrent Effect of Capital Punishment: A Question of Life and Death." *American Economic Review* 65, no. 3 (June): 397–417.

Eide, Erling, Paul H. Rubin, and Joanna M. Shepherd. 2006. *Economics of Crime*. Boston: Now.

Ekelund, Robert B., Jr., John D. Jackson, Rand W. Ressler, and Robert D. Tollison. 2006. "Marginal Deterrence and Multiple Murders." *Southern Economic Journal* 72, no. 3 (January): 521–41.

Ellis, Anthony. 2005. "A Deterrence Theory of Punishment." In *Philosophy and Its Public Role: Essays in Ethics, Politics, Society and Culture*, edited by William Aiken and John Haldane, 210–26. Exeter, UK: Imprint Academic.

Ellis, Mark. 2018. "10 Facts about Crime on the Home Front in the Second World War." *HistoryExtra*, March 12. https://www.historyextra.com/period/second-world-war/10-facts-about-crime-on-the-home-front-in-the-second-world-war/.

Euripides. 2005. *Phoenician Women*. In *The Bacchae and Other Plays*, translated by John Davie, 10–60. New York: Penguin.

European Monitoring Centre for Drugs and Drug Addiction. 2018. *Drug Consumption Rooms: An Overview of Provision and Evidence*, June 7. Lisbon: EMCDDA. www.emcdda.europa.eu/system/files/publications/2734/POD_Drug%20consumption%20rooms.pdf.

Ewing, A. C. 1927. "Punishment as a Moral Agency: An Attempt to Reconcile the Retributive and the Utilitarian View." *Mind* 36, no. 143 (July): 292–305.

———. 1963. "Armstrong on the Retributive Theory." *Mind* 72, no. 285 (January): 121–24.

———. 1970. *The Morality of Punishment, with Some Suggestions for a General Theory of Ethics*. Reprint ed. Montclair, NJ: Patterson Smith.

Fagan, Jeffrey. 2005. "Deterrence and the Death Penalty: A Critical Review of New Evidence." Testimony to the New York State Assembly Standing Committees on Codes, Judiciary, and Correction, January 21. https://files.deathpenaltyinfo.org/legacy/files/pdf/FaganTestimony.pdf.

———. 2006. "Death and Deterrence Redux: Science, Law and Causal Reasoning on Capital Punishment." *Ohio State Journal of Criminal Law* 4, no. 1 (Fall): 255–320.

Farrell, Daniel M. 1985. "The Justification of General Deterrence." *Philosophical Review* 94, no. 3 (July): 367–94.

———. 2004. "Capital Punishment and Societal Self-Defense." In *Philosophy and Its Public Role: Essays in Ethics, Politics, Society and Culture*, edited by William Aiken and John Haldane, 241–56. Exeter, UK: Imprint Academic.

Farrington, David P., Denise C. Gottfredson, Lawrence W. Sherman, and Brandon C. Welsh. 2002. "The Maryland Scientific Methods Scale." In *Evidence-Based Crime Prevention*, rev. ed., edited by Lawrence W. Sherman, David P. Farrington, Brandon C. Welsh, and Doris Layton MacKenzie, 13–21. London: Routledge.

Farrington, David P., Patrick A. Langan, and Per-Olof H. Wikström. 1994. "Changes in Crime and Punishment in America, England and Sweden between the 1980s and the 1990s." *Studies on Crime and Crime Prevention* 3: 104–31.

Farrington, David P., Lloyd E. Ohlin, and James Q. Wilson. 1986. *Understanding and Controlling Crime: Toward a New Research Strategy*. New York: Springer.

Feinberg, Joel. 1970. *Doing & Deserving: Essays in the Theory of Responsibility*. Princeton, NJ: Princeton University Press.

———. 1972. "Justice, Fairness and Rationality." Review of *A Theory of Justice*, by John Rawls. *Yale Law Journal* 81, no. 5 (April): 1004–31.

Ferreira, Susana. 2017. "Portugal's Radical Drugs Policy Is Working. Why Hasn't the World Copied It?" *Guardian*, December 5. https://www.theguardian.com/news/2017/dec/05/portugals-radical-drugs-policy-is-working-why-hasnt-the-world-copied-it.

Feuerbach, Paul Johann Anselm. 1801. *Lehrbuch des gemeinen in Deutschland geltenden Peinlichen Rechts*. Giessen, DE: Heyer.

———. 2014. *Textbook of the Common Penal Law in Force in Germany*. Translated by Raymond Youngs and Markus Dubber. In *Foundational Texts in Modern Criminal Law*, edited by Markus D. Dubber, 373–88. Oxford: Oxford University Press.

Fichte, J. G. 2000. *Foundations of Natural Right, according to the Principles of the Wissenschaftslehre*. Translated by Michael Baur. Edited by Frederick Neuhouser. Cambridge: Cambridge University Press.

Finnis, John. 2011. *Natural Law and Natural Rights*. 2nd ed. Oxford: Oxford University Press.

Fischer, John Martin. 1994. *The Metaphysics of Free Will*. Oxford: Blackwell.

Fischer, John Martin, and Mark Ravizza. 1998. *Responsibility and Control: An Essay on Moral Responsibility*. Cambridge: Cambridge University Press.

Fiss, Owen M. 1984. "Against Settlement." *Yale Law Journal* 93, no. 6 (May): 1073–90.

Flanders, Chad. 2013. "The Case against the Case against the Death Penalty." *New Criminal Law Review* 16, no. 4 (Fall): 595–620.

———. 2019. "Political Philosophy and Punishment." In *The Palgrave Handbook of Applied Ethics and the Criminal Law*, edited by Larry Alexander and Kimberly Kessler Ferzan, 521–45. London: Palgrave Macmillan.

Flew, Antony. 1954. "The Justification of Punishment." *Philosophy* 29, no. 111 (October): 291–307.

Foot, Philippa. 1967. "The Problem of Abortion and the Doctrine of the Double Effect." *Oxford Review* 5: 5–15.

Forde, Robert A. 2018. *Bad Psychology: How Forensic Psychology Left Science Behind*. London: Kingsley.

Fox, Richard, and Arie Freiberg. 1985. *Sentencing: State and Federal Law in Victoria*. Melbourne: Oxford University Press.

"France Arrests People for Flouting Confinement Rules." 2020. *Connexion*, March 20. https://www.connexionfrance.com/French-news/France-arrests-people-for-flouting-confinement-rules-as-Macron-calls-for-confinement-rules-to-be-taken-more-seriously.

Frankfurt, Harry. 1988. "Freedom of the Will and the Concept of a Person." In *The Importance of What We Care About: Philosophical Essays*, 11–25. Cambridge: Cambridge University Press.

Frase, Richard S. 2004. "Limiting Retributivism." In *The Future of Imprisonment*, edited by Michael Tonry, 83–120. Oxford: Oxford University Press.

———. 2005a. "Excessive Prison Sentences, Punishment Goals, and the Eighth Amendment: 'Proportionality' Relative to What?" *Minnesota Law Review* 89, no. 3 (February): 571–651.

———. 2005b. "Punishment Purposes." *Stanford Law Review* 58, no. 1 (October): 67–83.

———. 2013. *Just Sentencing: Principles and Procedures for a Workable System*. Oxford: Oxford University Press.

Fuller, Lon L. 1969. *The Morality of Law*. Rev. ed. New Haven, CT: Yale University Press.

Gabbay, Zvi D. 2005. "Justifying Restorative Justice: A Theoretical Justification for the Use of Restorative Justice Practices." *Journal of Dispute Resolution* 2005, no. 2: 349–97.

Gaes, Gerald G., Timothy J. Flanagan, Laurence L. Motiuk, and Lynn Stewart. 1999. "Adult Correctional Treatment." In *Crime and Justice – A Review of Research*, vol. 26: *Prisons*, edited by Michael Tonry and Joan Petersilia, 361–426. Chicago: University of Chicago Press.

Galaway, Burt, and Joe Hudson, eds. 1996. *Restorative Justice: International Perspectives.* Monsey, NY: Criminal Justice Press.

Galligan, D. J. 1981. "The Return to Retribution in Penal Theory." In *Crime, Proof and Punishment: Essays in Memory of Sir Rupert Cross*, edited by C. F. H. Tapper, 144–71. London: Butterworths.

Gardner, Martin R. 1981. "The Right to Be Punished – A Suggested Constitutional Theory." *Rutgers Law Review* 33: 838–64.

Garland, David. 2010. *Peculiar Institution: America's Death Penalty in an Age of Abolition.* Cambridge, MA: Belknap.

Garner, Bryan A., ed. 2019. *Black's Law Dictionary.* 11th ed. St. Paul, MN: Thomson Reuters.

Garvey, Megan. 2014. "Transcript of the Disturbing Video 'Elliot Rodger's Retribution.'" *Los Angeles Times*, May 24. https://www.latimes.com/local/lanow/la-me-ln-transcript-ucsb-shootings-video-20140524-story.html.

Garvey, Stephen P. 1999. "Punishment as Atonement." *UCLA Law Review* 46, no. 6 (August): 1801–58.

———. 2003. "Restorative Justice, Punishment, and Atonement." *Utah Law Review* 2003, no. 1: 303–17.

Gavison, Ruth. 1991. "Punishment and Theories of Justice: Comments on Sadurski and Hoekema." *Israel Law Review* 25, nos. 3–4 (Summer–Autumn): 351–59.

Geerken, Michael, and Walter R. Gove. 1977. "Deterrence, Overload, and Incapacitation: An Empirical Evaluation." *Social Forces* 56, no. 2 (December): 424–47.

Gendreau, Paul, Paula Smith, and Sheila A. French. 2006. "The Theory of Effective Correctional Intervention: Empirical Status and Future Directions." In *Taking Stock: The Status of Criminological Theory*, edited by Francis T. Cullen, John Paul Wright, and Kristie R. Blevins, 419–46. New Brunswick, NJ: Transaction.

Gentzler, Ryan. 2019. "'Prosecutorial Discretion' Makes Oklahoma's Justice System a Roll of the Dice." *OK Policy Blog*, August 7, 2017, rev. May 2, 2019. Oklahoma Policy Institute. https://okpolicy.org/prosecutorial-discretion-makes-oklahomas-justice-system-roll-dice/.

Gerber, David. 1975. "The Punishment of the Innocent." *American Journal of Jurisprudence* 20: 46–61.

Gibbs, Jack P. 1968. "Crime, Punishment and Deterrence." *Southwestern Social Science Quarterly* 48, no. 4 (March): 515–30.

Gilligan, James. 1996. *Violence: Reflections on a National Epidemic.* New York: Vintage.

Glasgow, Joshua. 2015. "The Expressivist Theory of Punishment Defended." *Law and Philosophy* 34, no. 6 (November): 601–31.

Glover, M. R. 1939. "Mr. Mabbott on Punishment." *Mind* 48, no. 192 (October): 498–501.

Golash, Deirdre. 2005. *The Case against Punishment: Retribution, Crime Prevention, and the Law.* New York: New York University Press.

Golding, Martin P. 1975. *Philosophy of Law.* Englewood Cliffs, NJ: Prentice-Hall.

Goldman, Alan H. 1979. "The Paradox of Punishment." *Philosophy & Public Affairs* 9, no. 1 (Autumn): 42–58.

———. 1981. "Beyond the Deterrence Theory: Comments on van den Haag's 'Punishment as a Device for Controlling the Crime Rate.'" *Rutgers Law Review* 33, no. 3 (Spring): 721–29.

Goode, Erica. 2012. "Stronger Hand for Judges in the 'Bazaar' of Plea Deals." *New York Times*, March 22. https://www.nytimes.com/2012/03/23/us/stronger-hand-for-judges-after-rulings-on-plea-deals.html.

Grasmick, Harold G., and George J. Bryjak. 1980. "The Deterrent Effect of Perceived Severity of Punishment." *Social Forces* 59, no. 2 (December): 471–91.

Grasmick, Harold G., and Robert J. Bursik Jr. 1990. "Conscience, Significant Others, and Rational Choice: Extending the Deterrence Model." *Law and Society Review* 24, no. 3: 837–62.

Grasmick, Harold G., and Donald E. Green. 1980. "Legal Punishment, Social Disapproval and Internalization as Inhibitors of Illegal Behavior." *Journal of Criminal Law and Criminology* 71, no. 3 (Fall): 325–35.

Gray, Louis N., and J. David Martin. 1969. "Punishment and Deterrence: Another Analysis of Gibbs' Data." *Social Science Quarterly* 50, no. 2 (September): 389–95.

Greenawalt, Kent. 1983. "Punishment." *Journal of Criminal Law and Criminology* 74, no. 2 (Summer): 343–62.

Grogger, Jeffrey. 1990. "The Deterrent Effect of Capital Punishment: An Analysis of Daily Homicide Counts." *Journal of the American Statistical Association* 85, no. 410 (June): 295–303.

Gross, Samuel R., and Robert Mauro. 1984. "Patterns of Death: An Analysis of Racial Disparities in Capital Sentencing and Homicide Victimization." *Stanford Law Review* 37, no. 1 (November): 27–153.

Gross, Samuel R., Barbara O'Brien, Chen Hu, and Edward H. Kennedy. 2014. "Rate of False Conviction of Criminal Defendants Who Are Sentenced to Death." *Proceedings of the National Academy of Sciences of the United States of America* 111, no. 20 (May 20): 7230–35.

Guinn, Nathan. 2006. "What Immigrants Deserve" (letter to the editor). *New York Times*, April 30. https://www.nytimes.com/2006/04/30/opinion/what-immigrants-deserve-666440.html.

Hadley, Michael L., ed. 2001. *The Spiritual Roots of Restorative Justice*. Albany: State University of New York Press.

Hall, William J., Mimi V. Chapman, Kent M. Lee, Yesenia M. Merino, Tainayah W. Thomas, B. Keith Payne, Eugenia Eng, Steven H. Day, and Tamera Coyne-Beasley. 2015. "Implicit Racial/Ethnic Bias among Health Care Professionals and Its Influence on Health Care Outcomes: A Systematic Review." *American Journal of Public Health* 105, no. 12 (December): 60–76.

Hamilton, V. Lee, and Steve Rytina. 1980. "Social Consensus on Norms of Justice: Should the Punishment Fit the Crime?" *American Journal of Sociology* 85, no. 5 (March): 1117–44.

Hamilton, Zachary, Christopher M. Campbell, Jacqueline van Wormer, Alex Kigerl, and Brianne Posey. 2016. "Impact of Swift and Certain Sanctions: Evaluation of Washington State's Policy for Offenders on Community Supervision." *Criminology & Public Policy* 15, no. 4 (November): 1009–72.

Hamilton, Zachary, Alex Kigerl, Michael Campagna, Robert Barnoski, Stephen Lee, Jacqueline van Wormer, and Lauren Block. 2016. "Designed to Fit: The Development and Validation of the STRONG-R Recidivism Risk Assessment." *Criminal Justice and Behavior* 43, no. 2 (February): 230–63.

Hamilton, Zachary, Melissa A. Kowalski, Roger Schaefer, and Alex Kigerl. 2020. "Recrafting Youth Risk Assessment: Developing the Modified Positive Achievement Change Tool for Iowa." *Deviant Behavior* 41, no. 10: 1268–89.

Hamilton, Zachary, Jacqueline van Wormer, Alex Kigerl, Christopher Campbell, and Brianne Posey. 2015. *Evaluation of Washington State Department of Corrections (WADOC) Swift and Certain (SAC) Policy: Process, Outcome and Cost-Benefit Evaluation*. Pullman: Washington State University. https://s3.wp.wsu.edu/uploads/sites/436/2015/11/SAC-Final-Report_2015-08-31.pdf.

Hammond, Charles E. 1992. "Waiting for a Thunderbolt." *Asian Folklore Studies* 51, no. 1 (April): 25–49.

Hampton, Jean. 1992a. "Correcting Harms versus Righting Wrongs: The Goal of Retribution." *UCLA Law Review* 39, no. 6 (August): 1659–1702.

———. 1992b. "An Expressive Theory of Retribution." In *Retributivism and Its Critics*, edited by Wesley Cragg, 1–25. Stuttgart: Steiner.

Hanlon, Robert E., Michael Brook, John Stratton, Marie Jensen, and Leah H Rubin. 2013. "Neuropsychological and Intellectual Differences between Types of Murderers: Affective/Impulsive versus Predatory/Instrumental (Premeditated) Homicide." *Criminal Justice and Behavior* 40, no. 8 (August): 933–48.

Hanna, Nathan. 2008. "Say What? A Critique of Expressive Retributivism." *Law and Philosophy* 27, no. 2 (March): 123–50.

———. 2009a. "Liberalism and the General Justifiability of Punishment." *Philosophical Studies* 145, no. 3 (September): 325–49.

———. 2009b. "The Passions of Punishment." *Pacific Philosophical Quarterly* 90, no. 2 (June): 232–50.

———. 2014. "Facing the Consequences." *Criminal Law and Philosophy* 8, no. 3 (October): 589–604.

Hardin, Russell. 1986. "The Utilitarian Logic of Liberalism." *Ethics* 97, no. 1 (October): 47–74.

Hare, R. M. 1981. *Moral Thinking: Its Levels, Method, and Point*. Oxford: Clarendon.

———. 1986. "Punishment and Retributive Justice." *Philosophical Topics* 14, no. 2 (Fall): 211–23.

Harel, Alon. 2005. "Theories of Rights." In *The Blackwell Guide to the Philosophy of Law and Legal Theory*, edited by Martin P. Golding and William A. Edmundson, 191–206. Malden, MA: Blackwell.

Harris, Jo Ann. 1995. "1032. Sentencing Enhancement – 'Three Strikes' Law." Office of the United States Attorneys, U.S. Department of Justice. https://www.justice.gov/jm/criminal-resource-manual-1032-sentencing-enhancement-three-strikes-law.

Harris, Sam. 2012. *Free Will*. New York: Free Press.

Hart, H. L. A. 2008. *Punishment and Responsibility: Essays in the Philosophy of Law*. 2nd ed. Oxford: Oxford University Press.

———. 2012. *The Concept of Law*. 3rd ed. Oxford: Clarendon.

Hawkins, D. J. B. 1944. "Punishment and Moral Responsibility." *Modern Law Review* 7, no. 4 (November): 205–8.

Hegel, Georg Wilhelm Friedrich. 1991. *Elements of the Philosophy of Right*. Translated by H. B. Nisbet. Edited by Allen W. Wood. Cambridge: Cambridge University Press.

———. 2010. *The Science of Logic*. Translated by George di Giovanni. Cambridge: Cambridge University Press.

Heilbrun, A. B., I. J. Knopf, and P. Bruner. 1976. "Criminal Impulsivity and Violence and Subsequent Parole Outcome." *British Journal of Criminology* 16, no. 4 (October): 367–77.

Helland, Eric, and Alexander Tabarrok. 2007. "Does Three Strikes Deter? A Nonparametric Estimation." *Journal of Human Resources* 42, no. 2 (Spring): 309–30.

Hermann, Donald H. J. 2017. "Restorative Justice and Retributive Justice: An Opportunity for Cooperation or an Occasion for Conflict in the Search for Justice." *Seattle Journal for Social Justice* 16, no. 1 (Summer): 71–103.

"The High Price of Killing Killers." 2000. *Palm Beach Post*, January 4. https://deathpenaltyinfo.org/stories/the-high-price-of-killing-killers.

Hobbes, Thomas. 1996. *Leviathan*. Edited by Richard Tuck. Cambridge: Cambridge University Press.

Hoekema, David A. 1980. "The Right to Punish and the Right to Be Punished." In *John Rawls' Theory of Social Justice: An Introduction*, edited by H. Gene Blocker and Elizabeth H. Smith, 239–69. Athens, OH: Ohio University Press.

Holbraad, Carsten. 2017. *Danish Reactions to German Occupation: History and Historiography*. London: UCL.

Holmes, Oliver Wendell, Jr. 2009. *The Common Law*. Cambridge, MA: Belknap.

Holth, Per. 2005. "Two Definitions of Punishment." *Behavior Analyst Today* 6, no. 1 (Winter): 43–47.

Honderich, Ted. 2006. *Punishment: The Supposed Justifications Revisited*. London: Pluto.

Howe, Edmund S., and Cynthia J. Brandau. 1988. "Additive Effects of Certainty, Severity, and Celerity of Punishment on Judgments of Crime Deterrence Scale Value." *Journal of Applied Social Psychology* 18, no. 9 (July): 796–812.

Howe, Edmund S., and Thomas C. Loftus. 1996. "Integration of Certainty, Severity, and Celerity Information in Judged Deterrence Value: Further Evidence and Methodological Equivalence." *Journal of Applied Social Psychology* 26, no. 3 (February): 226–42.

Huber, Gregory A., and Sanford C. Gordon. 2004. "Accountability and Coercion: Is Justice Blind When It Runs for Office?" *American Journal of Political Science* 48, no. 2 (April): 247–63.

Hulsman, Louk. 1991. "The Abolitionist Case: Alternative Crime Policies." *Israel Law Review* 25, nos. 3–4 (Summer–Autumn): 681–709.

Hume, David. 1975. *An Enquiry Concerning Human Understanding*. In *Enquiries concerning Human Understanding and concerning the Principles of Morals*, 3rd ed., edited by L. A. Selby-Bigge, revised by P. H. Nidditch, 5–165. Oxford: Clarendon.

Institute for Defense Analyses. 1967. *Task Force Report: Science and Technology: A Report to the President's Commission on Law Enforcement and Administration of Justice*. Washington, DC: U.S. Government Printing Office.

Jacobs, Bruce A. 2010. "Deterrence and Deterrability." *Criminology* 48, no. 2 (May): 417–41.

Jacoby, Joseph E., and Francis T. Cullens. 1998. "The Structure of Punishment Norms: Applying the Rossi-Berk Model." *Journal of Criminal Law and Criminology* 89, no. 1 (Fall): 245–312.

Johnson, Brian D. 2003. "Racial and Ethnic Disparities in Sentencing Departures across Modes of Conviction." *Criminology* 41, no. 2 (May): 449–90.

Johnstone, Gerry. 2011. *Restorative Justice: Ideas, Values, Debates*. 2nd ed. Abingdon, UK: Routledge.

Kagan, Shelly. 1998. *Normative Ethics*. Boulder, CO: Westview.

Kahneman, Daniel, and Amos Tversky. 1979. "Prospect Theory: An Analysis of Decision under Risk." *Econometrica* 47, no. 2 (March): 263–92.

Kane, Robert. 1996. *The Significance of Free Will*. New York: Oxford University Press.

Kant, Immanuel. 1996a. *Groundwork of the Metaphysics of Morals*. In *Practical Philosophy*, translated and edited by Mary J. Gregor, 41–108. Cambridge: Cambridge University Press.

———. 1996b. *The Metaphysics of Morals*. In *Practical Philosophy*, translated and edited by Mary J. Gregor, 363–602. Cambridge: Cambridge University Press.

———. 1997. *Lectures on Ethics*. Translated by Peter Heath. Edited by Peter Heath and J. B. Schneewind. Cambridge: Cambridge University Press.

———. 1998. *Critique of Pure Reason*. Translated and edited by Paul Guyer and Allen W. Wood. Cambridge: Cambridge University Press.

———. 2007. *Lectures on Pedagogy*. Translated by Robert B. Louden. In *Anthropology, History, and Education*, edited by Günter Zöller and Robert B. Louden, 437–85. Cambridge: Cambridge University Press.

Katz, Lawrence, Steven D. Levitt, and Ellen Shustorovich. 2003. "Prison Conditions, Capital Punishment, and Deterrence." *American Law and Economics Review* 5, no. 2 (August): 318–43.

Kaufman, Whitley. 2008. "The Rise and Fall of the Mixed Theory of Punishment." *International Journal of Applied Philosophy* 22, no. 1 (Spring): 37–57.

———. 2013. *Honor and Revenge: A Theory of Punishment*. Dordrecht: Springer.

Kavka, Gregory S. 1994. "The Costs of Crimes: Coleman Amended." Review of *Risks and Wrongs*, by Jules L. Coleman. *Ethics* 104, no. 3 (April): 582–92.

"Kennedy Discusses Sentencing, Foundations of Freedom." 2003. *The Third Branch* 35, no. 9 (September). https://web.archive.org/web/20100413110928/http://www.uscourts.gov/ttb/sep03ttb/kennedy/index.html.

Kilgore, James. 2015. *Understanding Mass Incarceration: A People's Guide to the Key Civil Rights Struggle of Our Time*. New York: New Press.

King, Ryan S., and Marc Mauer. 2001. *Aging behind Bars: Three Strikes Seven Years Later*. Washington, DC: Sentencing Project. https://www.prisonpolicy.org/scans/sp/inc_aging.pdf.

Kirchgässner, Gebhard. 2011. "Econometric Estimates of Deterrence of the Death Penalty: Facts or Ideology?" CESifo Working Paper No. 3443, May. Munich Center for Economic Studies and Ifo Institute. https://www.econstor.eu/bitstream/10419/46540/1/661596729.pdf.

Kleck, Gary, Brion Sever, Spencer Li, and Marc Gertz. 2005. "The Missing Link in General Deterrence Research." *Criminology* 43, no. 3 (August): 623–60.

Kleiman, Mark A. R. 2009. *When Brute Force Fails: How to Have Less Crime and Less Punishment*. Princeton, NJ: Princeton University Press.

Klein, Lawrence R., Brian Forst, and Victor Filatov. 1978. "The Deterrent Effect of Capital Punishment: An Assessment of the Estimates." In *Deterrence and Incapacitation: Estimating the Effects of Criminal Sanctions on Crime Rates*, edited by Alfred Blumstein, Jacqueline Cohen, and Daniel Nagin, 336–60. Washington, DC: National Academy of Sciences.

Kleinig, John. 1971. "The Concept of Desert." *American Philosophical Quarterly* 8, no. 1 (January): 71–78.

———. 1973. *Punishment and Desert*. The Hague: Nijhoff.

———. 1991. "Punishment and Moral Seriousness." *Israel Law Review* 25, nos. 2–3 (Summer–Autumn): 401–21.

———. 1998. "The Hardness of Hard Treatment." In *Fundamentals of Sentencing Theory: Essays in Honour of Andrew von Hirsch*, edited by Andrew Ashworth and Martin Wasik, 273–98. Oxford: Clarendon Press.

Klepper, Steven, and Daniel Nagin. 1989. "The Deterrent Effect of Perceived Certainty and Severity of Punishment Revisited." *Criminology* 27, no. 4 (November): 721–46.

Kovandzic, Tomislav V. 2001. "The Impact of Florida's Habitual Offender Law on Crime." *Criminology* 39, no. 1 (February): 179–204.

Kovandzic, Tomislav V., John J. Sloan III, and Lynne M. Vieraitis. 2002. "Unintended Consequences of Politically Popular Sentencing Policy: The Homicide Promoting Effects of 'Three Strikes' in U.S. Cities (1980–1999)." *Criminology & Public Policy* 1, no. 3 (July): 399–424.

———. 2004. "'Striking Out' as Crime Reduction Policy: The Impact of 'Three Strikes' Laws on Crime Rates in U.S. Cities." *Justice Quarterly* 21, no. 2 (June): 207–39.

Kovandzic, Tomislav V., Lynne M. Vieraitis, and Denise Paquette Boots. 2009. "Does the Death Penalty Save Lives? New Evidence from State Panel Data, 1977 to 2006." *Criminology & Public Policy* 8, no. 4 (November): 803–43.

Kutateladze, Besiki, Vanessa Lynn, and Edward Liang. 2012. *Do Race and Ethnicity Matter in Prosecution? A Review of Empirical Studies.* New York: Vera Institute of Justice. https://www.vera.org/downloads/Publications/do-race-and-ethnicity-matter-in-prosecution-a-review-of-empirical-studies/legacy_downloads/race-and-ethnicity-in-prosecution-first-edition.pdf.

Lacey, Nicola. 1988. *State Punishment: Political Principles and Community Values.* London: Routledge.

LaFave, Wayne R. 1965. *Arrest: The Decision to Take a Suspect into Custody.* Boston: Little, Brown.

LaFave, Wayne R., David C. Baum, Jerold H. Israel, Nancy J. King, and Orin S. Kerr. 2009. *Criminal Procedure.* 5th ed. St. Paul, MN: West.

Land, Kenneth C., Raymond H. C. Teske Jr., and Hui Zheng. 2009. "The Short-Term Effects of Executions on Homicides: Deterrence, Displacement, or Both?" *Criminology* 47, no. 4 (November): 1009–43.

Lantigua-Williams, Juleyka. 2016. "Are Prosecutors the Key to Justice Reform?" *Atlantic*, May 18. https://www.theatlantic.com/politics/archive/2016/05/are-prosecutors-the-key-to-justice-reform/483252/.

Latimer, Jeff, Craig Dowden, and Danielle Muise. 2005. "The Effectiveness of Restorative Justice Practices: A Meta-Analysis." *Prison Journal* 85, no. 2 (June): 127–44.

Latzer, Barry, and James N. G. Cauthen. 2007. *Justice Delayed? Time Consumption in Capital Appeals: A Multistate Study*, March. https://www.ncjrs.gov/pdffiles1/nij/grants/217555.pdf.

Lawrence, Alison. 2015. *Making Sense of Sentencing: State Systems and Policies.* Washington, DC: National Conference of State Legislatures. https://www.ncsl.org/documents/cj/sentencing.pdf.

Layson, Stephen K. 1985. "Homicide and Deterrence: A Reexamination of the United States Time-Series Evidence." *Southern Economic Journal* 52, no. 1 (July): 68–89.

Leamer, Edward E. 1983. "Let's Take the Con Out of Econometrics." *American Economic Review* 73, no. 1 (March): 31–43.

Lee, Ambrose Y. K. 2019. "Arguing against the Expressive Function of Punishment: Is the Standard Account That Insufficient?" *Law and Philosophy* 38, no. 4 (August): 359–85.

Levinas, Emmanuel. 1997. *Otherwise than Being, or Beyond Essence.* Translated by Alphonso Lingis. Pittsburgh: Duquesne University Press.

———. 1998. "Useless Suffering." In *Entre Nous: On Thinking-of-the-Other*, translated by Michael B. Smith and Barbara Harshav, 91–101. New York: Columbia University Press.

Levitt, Steven D. 1996. "The Effect of Prison Population Size on Crime Rates: Evidence from Prison Overcrowding Litigation." *Quarterly Journal of Economics* 111, no. 2 (May): 319–52.

Levitt, Steven D., and Thomas J. Miles. 2007. "Empirical Study of Criminal Punishment." In *Handbook of Law and Economics*, vol. 1, edited by A. Mitchell Polinsky and Steven Shavell, 455–95. Amsterdam: Elsevier.

Lewis, C. S. 1954. "The Humanitarian Theory of Punishment." *Res Judicatae* 6: 224–30.

Lewis, D. K. 1972. "Utilitarianism and Truthfulness." *Australasian Journal of Philosophy* 50, no. 1 (May): 17–19.

Li, Qi, and Wei Long. 2018. "Do Parole Abolition and Truth-in-Sentencing Deter Violent Crimes in Virginia?" *Empirical Economics* 55, no. 4 (December): 2027–45.

Liddle, Howard A., and Gayle A. Dakof. 1995. "Efficacy of Family Therapy for Drug Abuse: Promising but not Definitive." *Journal of Marital and Family Therapy* 21, no. 4 (October): 511–43.

Liebman, James S., Jeffrey Fagan, and Valerie West. 2000. "A Broken System: Error Rates in Capital Cases, 1973–1995." Columbia Law School Public Law and Legal Theory Working Paper Group, Paper No. 15, June 12. https://scholarship.law.columbia.edu/cgi/viewcontent.cgi?article=2220&context=faculty_scholarship.

Liedka, Raymond V., Anne Morrison Piehl, and Bert Useem. 2006. "The Crime-Control Effect of Incarceration: Does Scale Matter?" *Criminology & Public Policy* 5, no. 2 (May): 245–76.

Lillehammer, Hallvard. 2019. Interview by Richard Marshall. *3:16.* https://316am.site123.me/articles/indifference-cambridge-pragmatists-and-companions-in-guilt?c=end-times-series.

Lippke, Richard L. 2006. "Mixed Theories of Punishment and Mixed Offenders: Some Unresolved Tensions." *Southern Journal of Philosophy* 44, no. 2 (Summer): 273–95.

———. 2007. *Rethinking Imprisonment.* Oxford: Oxford University Press.

———. 2011. *The Ethics of Plea Bargaining.* Oxford: Oxford University Press.

———. 2016. "Reforming Plea Bargaining." In *The New Philosophy of Criminal Law*, edited by Chad Flanders and Zachary Hoskins, 173–91. London: Rowman & Littlefield.

Liptak, Adam. 2007. "Does Death Penalty Save Lives? A New Debate." *New York Times*, November 18. https://www.nytimes.com/2007/11/18/us/18deter.html.

Lipton, Douglas S., Robert Martinson, and Judith Wilks. 1975. *The Effectiveness of Correctional Treatment: A Survey of Treatment Evaluation Studies.* New York: Praeger.

Lloyd, Genevieve. 1993. *The Man of Reason: "Male" and "Female" in Western Philosophy.* 2nd ed. London: Routledge.

Lochner, Lance, and Enrico Moretti. 2004. "The Effect of Education on Crime: Evidence from Prison Inmates, Arrests, and Self-Reports." *American Economic Review* 94, no. 1 (March): 155–89.

"The Lockdown and the Long Haul." 2020. *Economist*, March 21–27, pp. 15–18.

Locke, Don. 1963. "The Many Faces of Punishment." *Mind* 72, no. 288 (October): 568–72.

Locke, John. 1980. *Second Treatise of Government*. Edited by C. B. Macpherson. Indianapolis, IN: Hackett.

Logan, Charles H. 1972. "General Deterrent Effects of Imprisonment." *Social Forces* 51, no. 1 (September): 64–73.

Long, Wei. 2018. "Does Longer Incarceration Deter or Incapacitate Crime? Evidence from Truth-in-Sentencing Reform." *Applied Economics* 50, no. 24: 2664–76.

Lutze, Faith E., Laurie A. Drapela, and Roger L. Schaefer. 2015. *Washington State Correctional Industries: An Outcome Evaluation of Its Effect on Institutional Behavior, Employment, and Recidivism*. Pullman: Washington State University, December 10. https://www.washingtonci.com/skin/frontend/WACI/primary/docs/content/about-ci/wsu-research-report.pdf.

Lynton, Jonathan S. 1995. *Ballentine's Legal Dictionary and Thesaurus*. Albany, NY: Delmar.

Lyons, William. 1974. "Deterrent Theory and Punishment of the Innocent." *Ethics* 84, no. 4 (July): 346–48.

———. 1980. *Emotion*. Cambridge: Cambridge University Press.

Mabbott, J. D. 1939. "Punishment." *Mind* 48, no. 190 (April): 152–67.

———. 1955. "Professor Flew on Punishment." *Philosophy* 30, no. 114 (July): 256–65.

MacCormick, D. N. 1978. "The Obligation of Reparation." *Proceedings of the Aristotelian Society* 78, no. 1 (June): 175–94.

Mackie, J. L. 1982. "Morality and the Retributive Emotions." *Criminal Justice Ethics* 1, no. 1 (Winter): 3–10.

———. 1991. "Retributivism: A Test Case for Ethical Objectivity." In *Philosophy of Law*, 4th ed., edited by Joel Feinberg and Hyman Gross, 677–84. Belmont, CA: Wadsworth.

Magill, M. Elizabeth. 2000. "The Real Separation of Powers in Separation of Powers Law." *Virginia Law Review* 86, no. 6 (September): 1127–98.

Mandinach, Gary M. 2016. "Reported Three Strikes Opinions as of April 5, 2016." https://www.capcentral.org/criminal/sentencing/docs/3x_opinions_as_of04052016.pdf.

Marder, Nancy S. 1999. "The Myth of the Nullifying Jury." *Northwestern University Law Review* 93, no. 3 (Spring): 877–959.

Marshall, S. E., and R. A. Duff. 1998. "Criminalization and Sharing Wrongs." *Canadian Journal of Law & Jurisprudence* 11, no. 1 (January): 7–22.

Marshall, Tony F., and S. E. Merry. 1990. *Crime and Accountability: Victim/Offender Mediation in Practice*. London: HMSO.

Martinson, Robert. 1974. "What Works? – Questions and Answers about Prison Reform." *Public Interest* 35 (Spring): 22–54.

———. 1979. "New Findings, New Views: A Note of Caution Regarding Sentencing Reform." *Hofstra Law Review* 7, no. 2 (Winter): 243–58.

Martinson, Robert, and Judith Wilks. 1977. "Save Parole Supervision." *Federal Probation* 41, no. 3 (September): 23–27.

Marvell, Thomas B., and Carlisle E. Moody. 2001. "The Lethal Effects of Three-Strikes Laws." *Journal of Legal Studies* 30, no. 1 (January): 89–106.

Mathiesen, Thomas. 1974. *The Politics of Abolition*. London: Martin Robertson.

———. 2006. *Prison on Trial*. 3rd ed. Winchester, UK: Waterside.

Matravers, Matt. 2000. *Justice and Punishment: The Rationale of Coercion*. Oxford: Oxford University Press.

Maxwell, Gabrielle M., Allison Morris, and Tracy Anderson. 1999. *Community Panel Adult Pre-Trial Diversion: Supplementary Evaluation*. Wellington, NZ: Crime Prevention Unit Department of Prime Minister & Cabinet and Victoria University Institute of Criminology.

Maxwell, Sheila Royo, and M. Kevin Gray. 2000. "Deterrence: Testing the Effects of Perceived Sanction Certainty on Probation Violations." *Sociological Inquiry* 70, no. 2 (April): 117–36.

McCausland, Phil. 2018. "In Bipartisan Trend, Washington State Advances Bill to Abolish Death Penalty." *NBC News*, February 25. https://www.nbcnews.com/storyline/lethal-injection/bipartisan-trend-washington-state-advances-bill-abolish-death-penalty-n850871.

McCloskey, H. J. 1957. "An Examination of Restricted Utilitarianism." *Philosophical Review* 66, no. 4 (October): 466–85.

———. 1962. "The Complexity of the Concepts of Punishment." *Philosophy* 37, no 142 (October): 307–25.

———. 2015. "A Non-Utilitarian Approach to Punishment." In *Philosophical Perspectives on Punishment*, 2nd ed., edited by Gertrude Ezorsky, 125–40. Albany: State University of New York Press.

McCold, Paul. 2001. "Primary Restorative Justice Practices." In *Restorative Justice for Juveniles: Conferencing, Mediation, and Circles*, edited by Allison Morris and Gabrielle Maxwell, 41–58. Oxford: Hart.

McCold, Paul, and Benjamin Wachtel. 1998. *Restorative Policing Experiment: Bethlehem Pennsylvania Police Family Group Conferencing Project*. Eugene, OR: Wipf & Stock.

McDermott, Daniel. 2001. "The Permissibility of Punishment." *Law and Philosophy* 20, no. 4 (July): 403–32.

McPherson, Thomas. 1967. "Punishment: Definition and Justification." *Analysis* 28, no. 1 (October): 21–27.

Mello, Steven. 2019. "More COPS, Less Crime." *Journal of Public Economics* 172 (April): 174–200.

Melville, Herman. 2016. *Billy Budd*. In *Bartleby, and Other Stories*, 243–328. New York: Penguin.

Mendes, Silvia M. 2004. "Certainty, Severity, and Their Relative Deterrent Effects: Questioning the Implications of the Role of Risk in Criminal Deterrence Policy." *Policy Studies Journal* 32, no. 1 (January): 59–74.

Mendes, Silvia M., and Michael D. McDonald. 2001. "Putting Severity of Punishment Back in the Deterrence Package." *Policy Studies Journal* 29, no. 4 (November): 588–610.

Merryman, John Henry, and Rogelio Pérez-Perdomo. 2018. *The Civil Law Tradition: An Introduction to the Legal Systems of Europe and Latin America*. 4th ed. Stanford, CA: Stanford University Press.

Metz, Thaddeus. 2000. "Censure Theory and Intuitions about Punishment." *Law and Philosophy* 19, no. 4 (July): 491–512.

Miceli, Thomas J. 2019. *The Paradox of Punishment: Reflections on the Economics of Criminal Justice*. London: Palgrave Macmillan.

Miethe, Terance D., and Wendy C. Regoeczi. 2004. *Rethinking Homicide: Exploring the Structure and Process Underlying Deadly Situations.* Cambridge: Cambridge University Press.

Mill, John Stuart. 1978. *On Liberty*. Edited by Elizabeth Rapaport. Indianapolis, IN: Hackett.

———. 2001. *Utilitarianism*. 2nd ed. Edited by George Sher. Indianapolis, IN: Hackett.

Mitchell, Ojmarrh, David B. Wilson, and Doris L. MacKenzie. 2007. "Does Incarceration-Based Drug Treatment Reduce Recidivism? A Meta-Analytic Synthesis of the Research." *Journal of Experimental Criminology* 3, no. 4 (December): 353–75.

Mocan, H. Naci, and R. Kaj Gittings. 2003. "Getting Off Death Row: Commuted Sentences and the Deterrent Effect of Capital Punishment." *Journal of Law and Economics* 46, no. 2 (October): 453–78.

———. 2010. "The Impact of Incentives on Human Behavior: Can We Make It Disappear? The Case of the Death Penalty." In *The Economics of Crime: Lessons for and from Latin America*, edited by Rafael Di Tella, Sebastian Edwards, and Ernesto Schargrodsky, 379–418. Chicago: University of Chicago Press.

Montague, Phillip. 1995. *Punishment as Societal-Defense*. Lanham, MD: Rowman & Littlefield.

Montesquieu, Charles de Secondat baron de. 1989. *The Spirit of the Laws*. Translated by Anne M. Cohler, Basia Carolyn Miller, and Harold Samuel Stone. Cambridge: Cambridge University Press.

Moody, Carlisle E., Thomas B. Marvell, and Robert J. Kaminski. 2002. *Unintended Consequences: Three-Strikes Laws and the Murders of Police Officers*. Rockville, MD: National Institute of Justice/National Criminal Justice Reference Service.

Moore, Michael S. 1987. "The Moral Worth of Retribution." In *Responsibility, Character, and the Emotions: New Essays in Moral Psychology*, edited by Ferdinand Schoeman, 179–219. Cambridge: Cambridge University Press.

———. 1993. "Justifying Retributivism." *Israel Law Review* 27, nos. 1–2 (Winter–Spring): 15–49.

———. 1997. *Placing Blame: A General Theory of the Criminal Law*. Oxford: Oxford University Press.

Morris, Allison. 2002. "Critiquing the Critics: A Brief Response to Critics of Restorative Justice." *British Journal of Criminology* 42, no. 3 (June): 596–615.

Morris, Herbert. 1968. "Persons and Punishment." *Monist* 52, no. 4 (October): 475–501.

Morris, Norval. 1966. "Impediments to Penal Reform." *University of Chicago Law Review* 33, no. 4 (Summer): 627–56.

———. 1974. *The Future of Imprisonment*. Chicago: University of Chicago Press.

———. 1977. "Punishment and Prisons." In *Justice and Punishment*, edited by J. B. Cederblom and William L. Blizek, 157–71. Cambridge, MA: Ballinger.

———. 1981. "Punishment, Desert and Rehabilitation." In *Sentencing*, edited by Hyman Gross and Andrew von Hirsch, 257–71. New York: Oxford.

———. 1982. *Madness and the Criminal Law*. Chicago: University of Chicago Press.

———. 1987. "Alternatives to Imprisonment: Failures and Prospects." *Criminal Justice Research Bulletin* 3, no. 7: 1–6.

Morris, Norval, and Michael Tonry. 1990. *Between Prison and Probation: Intermediate Punishments in a Rational Sentencing System*. New York: Oxford University Press.
Morris, Norval, and Frank Zimring. 1969. "Deterrence and Corrections." *Annals of the American Academy of Political and Social Science* 381, no. 1 (January): 137–46.
Morse, Stephen J. 2006. "Brain Overclaim Syndrome and Criminal Responsibility: A Diagnostic Note." *Ohio State Journal of Criminal Law* 3, no. 2 (Spring): 397–412.
———. 2008. "Determinism and the Death of Folk Psychology: Two Challenges to Responsibility from Neuroscience." *Minnesota Journal of Law, Science & Technology* 9, no. 1: 1–36.
———. 2013. "Common Criminal Law Compatibilism." In *Neuroscience and Legal Reasonsibility*, edited by Nicole A. Vincent, 27–52. Oxford: Oxford University Press.
———. 2014. "Scientific Challenges to Criminal Responsibility." In *Philosophy of Law*, 9th ed., edited by Joel Feinberg, Jules Coleman, and Christopher Kutz, 839–54. Boston: Wadsworth.
———. 2015. "Criminal Law and Common Sense: An Essay on the Perils and Promise of Neuroscience." *Marquette Law Review* 99, no. 1 (Fall): 39–74.
Moss, Andrew. 2013. "Responding to Retributivists: A Restorative Justice Rejoinder to the Big Three Desert Theories." *Contemporary Justice Review* 16, no. 2: 214–27.
"Murder with Impunity." 2020. Unsolved Homicide Database, *Washington Post*. Accessed December 31, 2020. https://www.washingtonpost.com/graphics/2018/investigations/unsolved-homicide-database/.
Murphy, Jeffrie G. 1973. "Marxism and Retribution." *Philosophy & Public Affairs* 2, no. 3 (Spring): 217–43.
———. 1979. "Moral Death: A Kantian Essay on Psychopathology." In *Retribution, Justice, and Therapy: Essays in the Philosophy of Law*, 128–43. Dordrecht: Reidel.
———. 1987. "Does Kant Have a Theory of Punishment?" *Columbia Law Review* 87, no. 3 (April): 509–32.
———. 1988a. "Forgiveness and Resentment." In *Forgiveness and Mercy*, edited by Jeffrie G. Murphy and Jean Hampton, 14–34. Cambridge: Cambridge University Press.
———. 1988b. "Hatred: A Qualified Defense." In *Forgiveness and Mercy*, edited by Jeffrie G. Murphy and Jean Hampton, 88–110. Cambridge: Cambridge University Press.
———. 2003. *Getting Even: Forgiveness and Its Limits*. Oxford: Oxford University Press.
Murray, Joseph, and David P. Farrington. 2005. "Parental Imprisonment: Effects on Boys' Antisocial Behaviour and Delinquency through the Life-Course." *Journal of Child Psychology and Psychiatry* 46, no. 12 (December): 1269–78.
———. 2008. "The Effects of Parental Imprisonment on Children." In *Crime and Justice – A Review of Research*, vol. 37, edited by Michael Tonry, 133–206. Chicago: University of Chicago Press.
Murtagh, Kevin J. 2013. "Free Will Denial and Punishment." *Social Theory and Practice* 39, no. 2 (April): 223–40.
Nagel, Thomas. 1970. *The Possibility of Altruism*. Oxford: Clarendon.
———. 1987. *What Does It All Mean? A Very Short Introduction to Philosophy*. New York: Oxford University Press.
Nagin, Daniel S. 1998. "Criminal Deterrence Research at the Outset of the Twenty-First Century." In *Crime and Justice – A Review of Research*, vol. 23, edited by Michael Tonry, 1–42. Chicago: University of Chicago Press.

———. 2013. "Deterrence in the Twenty-First Century." In *Crime and Justice – A Review of Research*, vol. 42: *Crime and Justice in America: 1975–2025*, edited by Michael Tonry, 199–263. Chicago: University of Chicago Press.

Nagin, Daniel S., Francis T. Cullen, and Cheryl Lero Jonson, eds. 2018. *Deterrence, Choice, and Crime: Contemporary Perspectives.* Vol. 23 of *Advances in Criminological Theory.* New York: Routledge.

Nagin, Daniel S., and Greg Pogarsky. 2001. "Integrating Celerity, Impulsivity and Extralegal Sanction Threats into a Model of General Deterrence: Theory and Evidence." *Criminology* 39, no. 4 (November): 865–92.

Narayan, Uma. 1993. "Appropriate Responses and Preventive Benefits: Justifying Censure and Hard Treatment in Legal Punishment." *Oxford Journal of Legal Studies* 13, no. 2 (Summer): 166–82.

Nathanson, Stephen. 2001. *An Eye for an Eye: The Immorality of Punishing by Death.* 2nd ed. Lanham, MD: Rowman & Littlefield.

National Academies of Sciences, Engineering, and Medicine. 2018. *Proactive Policing: Effects on Crime and Communities.* Washington, DC: National Academies Press.

National Commission on Reform of Federal Criminal Laws. 1971. *Final Report on the National Commission on Reform of Federal Criminal Laws.* Washington, DC: U.S. Government Printing Office. https://researchrepository.wvu.edu/cgi/viewcontent.cgi?article=2844&context=wvlr.

National Research Council. 2004. "The Effectiveness of Police Activity in Reducing Crime, Disorder and Fear." In *Fairness and Effectiveness in Policing: The Evidence*, edited by Wesley Skogan and Kathleen Frydl, 217–51. Washington, DC: National Academies Press.

Neu, Jerome. 2000. *A Tear Is an Intellectual Thing: The Meanings of Emotion.* Oxford: Oxford University Press.

Nielsen, Kai. 1972. "Against Moral Conservatism." *Ethics* 82, no. 3 (April): 219–31.

Nietzsche, Friedrich. 1967. *On the Genealogy of Morals.* Translated by Walter Kaufmann and R. J. Hollingdale. New York: Vintage.

Nozick, Robert. 1974. *Anarchy, State, and Utopia.* New York: Basic.

———. 1981. *Philosophical Explanations.* Cambridge, MA: Belknap.

Nugent, William R., Mona Williams, and Mark S. Umbreit. 2004. "Participation in Victim-Offender Mediation and the Prevalence of Subsequent Delinquent Behavior: A Meta-Analysis." *Research on Social Work Practice* 14, no. 6 (November): 408–16.

Nussbaum, Martha C. 2001. *Upheavals of Thought: The Intelligence of Emotions.* Cambridge: Cambridge University Press.

———. 2015. "Transitional Anger." *Journal of the American Philosophical Association* 1, no. 1 (Spring): 41–56.

O'Connor, Timothy. 2000. *Persons and Causes: The Metaphysics of Free Will.* New York: Oxford University Press.

Packel, Amanda K. 2002. "Juvenile Justice and the Punishment of Recidivists under California's Three Strikes Law." *California Law Review* 90, no. 4 (July): 1157–1202.

Packer, Herbert L. 1968. *The Limits of the Criminal Sanction.* Stanford, CA: Stanford University Press.

Parker, Robert Nash. 2012. "Why California's 'Three Strikes' Fails as Crime and Economic Policy, and What to Do." *California Journal of Politics and Policy* 5, no. 2: 206–31.

Passell, Peter, and John B. Taylor. 1977. "The Deterrent Effect of Capital Punishment: Another View." *American Economic Review* 67, no. 3 (June): 445–51.

Paternoster, Raymond. 1987. "The Deterrent Effect of the Perceived Certainty and Severity of Punishment: A Review of the Evidence and Issues." *Justice Quarterly* 4, no. 2 (June): 173–217.

———. 2010. "How Much Do We Really Know about Criminal Deterrence?" *Journal of Criminal Law and Criminology* 100, no. 3 (Summer): 765–823.

Pereboom, Derk. 2001. *Living without Free Will.* Cambridge: Cambridge University Press.

———. 2019. "Free Will Skepticism and Prevention of Crime." In *Free Will Skepticism in Law and Society: Challenging Retributive Justice*, edited by Elizabeth Shaw, Derk Pereboom, and Gregg D. Caruso, 99–115. Cambridge: Cambridge University Press.

Pereboom, Derk, and Gregg Caruso. 2018. "Hard-Incompatibilist Existentialism: Neuroscience, Punishment, and Meaning in Life." In *Neuroexistentialism: Meaning, Morals, and Purpose in the Age of Neuroscience*, edited by Gregg D. Caruso and Owen Flanagan, 193–222. Oxford: Oxford University Press.

Perlmutter, Martin. 2014. "Desert and Capital Punishment." In *Morality and Moral Controversies: Readings in Moral, Social and Political Philosophy*, 9th ed., edited by Steven Scalet and John Arthur, 184–91. New York: Pearson.

Pestello, H. Frances. 1984. "Deterrence: A Reconceptualization." *Crime & Delinquency* 30, no. 4 (October): 593–609.

Peterson, Ruth D., and William C. Bailey. 1988. "Murder and Capital Punishment in the Evolving Context of the Post-Furman Era." *Social Forces* 66, no. 3 (March): 774–807.

Philips, Michael. 1986. "The Justification of Punishment and the Justification of Political Authority." *Law and Philosophy* 5, no. 3 (December): 393–416.

Pincoffs, Edmund L. 1966. *The Rationale of Legal Punishment.* New York: Humanities.

Piper, Adrian M. S. 1978. "Utility, Publicity, and Manipulation." *Ethics* 88, no. 3 (April): 189–206.

Pizzi, William T. 1993. "Understanding Prosecutorial Discretion in the United States: The Limits of Comparative Criminal Procedure as an Instrument of Reform." *Ohio State Law Journal* 54, no. 5: 1325–73.

Plato. 1961. "Protagoras." In *The Collected Dialogues of Plato*, edited by Edith Hamilton and Huntington Cairns, 308–52. Princeton, NJ: Princeton University Press.

Pogarsky, Greg. 2002. "Identifying 'Deterrable' Offenders: Implications for Research on Deterrence." *Justice Quarterly* 19, no. 3 (September): 431–52.

———. 2007. "Deterrence and Individual Differences among Convicted Offenders." *Journal of Quantitative Criminology* 23, no. 1 (March): 59–74.

Posner, Richard A. 1972. *Economic Analysis of Law.* Boston: Little, Brown.

Poulson, Barton. 2003. "A Third Voice: A Review of Empirical Research on the Psychological Outcomes of Restorative Justice." *Utah Law Review* 2003, no. 1: 167–203.

Pranis, Kay, Barry Stuart, and Mark Wedge. 2003. *Peacemaking Circles: From Crime to Community.* St. Paul, MN: Living Justice.

Pratt, John. 2007. *Penal Populism.* Abingdon, UK: Routledge.

Pratt, Travis C., Francis T. Cullen, Kristie R. Blevins, Leah E. Daigle, and Tamara D. Madensen. 2006. "The Empirical Status of Deterrence Theory: A Meta-Analysis."

In *Taking Stock: The Status of Criminological Theory*, vol. 15 of *Advances in Criminological Theory*, edited by Francis T. Cullen, John Paul Wright, and Kristie R. Blevins, 367–95. New Brunswick, NJ: Transaction.

Pratt, Travis C., and Jillian J. Turanovic. 2018. "Celerity and Deterrence." In *Deterrence, Choice, and Crime: Contemporary Perspectives*, vol. 23 of *Advances in Criminological Theory*, edited by Daniel S. Nagin, Francis T. Cullen, and Cheryl Lero Jonson, 187–210. New York: Routledge.

Primoratz, Igor. 1989. *Justifying Legal Punishment.* Amherst, NY: Humanity.

Przybylski, Roger K. 2009. *Correctional and Sentencing Reform for Drug Offenders: Research Findings on Selected Key Issues*, September. https://www.ccjrc.org/wp-content/uploads/2016/02/Correctional_and_Sentencing_Reform_for_Drug_Offenders.pdf.

Pudlow, Jan. 2010. "Take a Hard Look at the Real Cost of the Death Penalty." *Florida Bar*, March 1. https://www.floridabar.org/the-florida-bar-news/take-a-hard-look-at-the-real-cost-of-the-death-penalty/.

Quinn, Warren. 1985. "The Right to Threaten and the Right to Punish." *Philosophy & Public Affairs* 14, no. 4 (Autumn): 327–73.

Quinton, A. M. 1954. "On Punishment." *Analysis* 14, no. 6 (June): 133–42.

Rachels, James. 1991. "What People Deserve." In *Justice and Economic Distribution*, 2nd ed., edited by John Arthur and William H. Shaw, 136–48. Englewood Cliffs, NJ: Prentice-Hall.

Radelet, Michael L., and Ronald L. Akers. 1996. "Deterrence and the Death Penalty: The Views of the Experts." *Journal of Criminal Law and Criminology* 87, no. 1 (Fall): 1–16.

Radelet, Michael L., and Traci L. Lacock. 2009. "Do Executions Lower Homicide Rates? The Views of Leading Criminologists." *Journal of Criminal Law and Criminology* 99, no. 2 (Winter): 489–508.

Radzinowicz, Leon, and Roger Hood. 1981. "The American Volte-Face in Sentencing Thought and Practice." In *Crime, Proof and Punishment: Essays in Memory of Sir Rupert Cross*, edited C. F. H. Tapper, 127–43. London: Butterworths.

Railton, Peter. 1984. "Alienation, Consequentialism, and the Demands of Morality." *Philosophy & Public Affairs* 13, no. 2 (Spring): 134–71.

Rawls, John. 1955. "Two Concepts of Rules." *Philosophical Review* 64, no. 1 (January): 3–32.

———. 1980. "Kantian Constructivism in Moral Theory." *Journal of Philosophy* 77, no. 9 (September): 515–72.

Raymond, Margaret. 2006. "'No Fellow in American Legislation': *Weems v. United States* and the Doctrine of Proportionality." *Vermont Law Review* 30, no. 2: 251–301.

Reiman, Jeffrey H. 1985. "Justice, Civilization, and the Death Penalty: Answering van den Haag." *Philosophy & Public Affairs* 14, no. 2 (Spring): 115–48.

Reimund, Mary Ellen. 2004. "Confidentiality in Victim Offender Mediation: A False Promise?" *Journal of Dispute Resolution* 2004, no. 2: 401–27.

Relman, John P. 1991. "Overcoming Obstacles to Federal Fair Housing Enforcement in the South: A Case Study in Jury Nullification." *Mississippi Law Journal* 61, no. 3 (Winter): 579–604.

Richards, Kelly M. 2005. "Unlikely Friends? Oprah Winfrey and Restorative Justice." *Australian and New Zealand Journal of Criminology* 38, no. 3 (December): 381–99.

———. 2006. "Rewriting History: Towards a Genealogy of Restorative Justice." Ph.D. thesis, University of Western Sydney. https://researchdirect.westernsydney.edu.au/islandora/object/uws%3A2494/datastream/PDF/view.

"The Right to Nondiscriminatory Enforcement of State Penal Laws." 1961. *Columbia Law Review* 61, no. 6 (June): 1103–41.

Roberts, Robert C. 1988. "What an Emotion Is: A Sketch." *Philosophical Review* 97, no. 2 (April): 183–209.

Robespierre, Maximilien. 2007. "On the Principles of Political Morality that Should Guide the National Convention in the Domestic Administration of the Republic." In *Virtue and Terror*, translated by John Howe, edited by Jean Ducange, 108–25. London: Verso.

Robinson, Paul H. 1987. "Hybrid Principles for the Distribution of Criminal Sanctions." *Northwestern University Law Review* 82, no. 1 (Fall): 19–42.

———. 2000. "Why Does the Criminal Law Care What the Layperson Thinks Is Just? Coercive versus Normative Crime Control." *Virginia Law Review* 86, no. 8 (November): 1839–69.

———. 2003. "The Virtues of Restorative Processes, the Vices of 'Restorative Justice.'" *Utah Law Review* 2003, no. 1: 375–88.

———. 2006. "Restorative Processes and Doing Justice." *University of St. Thomas Law Journal* 3, no. 3 (Spring): 421–29.

———. 2007. "The Role of Moral Philosophers in the Competition between Deontological and Empirical Desert." *William and Mary Law Review* 48, no. 5 (April): 1831–43.

———. 2008a. "Competing Conceptions of Modern Desert: Vengeful, Deontological, and Empirical." *Cambridge Law Journal* 67, no. 1 (March): 145–75.

———. 2008b. *Distributive Principles of Criminal Law: Who Should be Punished How Much?* Oxford: Oxford University Press.

———. 2011. "Empirical Desert." In *Criminal Law Conversations*, edited by Paul H. Robinson, Stephen Garvey, and Kimberly Kessler Ferzan, 29–39. Oxford: Oxford University Press.

Robinson, Paul H., Joshua Samuel Barton, and Matthew Lister. 2014. "Empirical Desert, Individual Prevention, and Limiting Retributivism: A Reply." *New Criminal Law Review* 17, no. 2 (Spring): 312–75.

Robinson, Paul H., and John M. Darley. 1997. "The Utility of Desert." *Northwestern University Law Review* 91, no. 2 (Winter): 453–99.

Robinson, Paul H., and Robert Kurzban. 2007. "Concordance and Conflict in Intuitions of Justice." *Minnesota Law Review* 91, no. 6 (June): 1829–1907.

Roeder, Oliver, Lauren-Brooke Eisen, and Julia Bowling. 2015. *What Caused the Crime Decline?* New York: Brennan Center for Justice. https://www.brennancenter.org/sites/default/files/2019-08/Report_What_Caused_The_Crime_Decline.pdf.

Roettger, Michael E., and Raymond R. Swisher. 2011. "Associations of Fathers' History of Incarceration with Sons' Delinquency and Arrest among Black, White, and Hispanic Males in the United States." *Criminology* 49, no. 4 (November): 1109–47.

Roman, John, Aaron Chalfin, Aaron Sundquist, Carly Knight, and Askar Darmenov. 2008. *The Cost of the Death Penalty in Maryland.* Washington, DC: Urban Institute. https://files.deathpenaltyinfo.org/legacy/files/pdf/CostsDPMaryland.pdf.

Roman, John, Wendy Townsend, and Avinash Singh Bhati. 2003. *Recidivism Rates for Drug Court Graduates: Nationally Based Estimates, Final Report*, July. Washington, DC: Urban Institute. https://www.ncjrs.gov/pdffiles1/201229.pdf.

Rose, Dina R., and Todd R. Clear. 1998. "Incarceration, Social Capital, and Crime: Implications for Social Disorganization Theory." *Criminology* 36, no. 3 (August): 441–80.

Ross, W. D. 2002. *The Right and the Good*. Edited by Philip Stratton-Lake. Oxford: Clarendon.

Rousseau, Jean-Jacques. 1978. *On the Social Contract*. Translated by Judith R. Masters. Edited by Roger D. Masters. New York: St. Martin's.

Rubin, Paul H. 2009. "Don't Scrap the Death Penalty." *Criminology & Public Policy* 8, no. 4 (November): 853–59.

Ryberg, Jesper. 2004. *The Ethics of Proportionate Punishment: A Critical Investigation*. Dordrecht: Kluwer.

Sampson, Robert, Stephen Raudenbush, and Felton Earls. 1997. "Neighborhoods and Violent Crime: A Multilevel Study of Collective Efficacy." *Science* 277 (August 15): 918–24.

Savitz, Leonard D. 1959. "A Study in Capital Punishment." *Journal of Criminal Law and Criminology* 49, no. 4: 338–41.

Scanlon, T. M. 2008. *Moral Dimensions: Permissibility, Meaning, Blame*. Cambridge, MA: Harvard University Press.

Schedler, George. 1977. *Behavior Modification and "Punishment" of the Innocent: Towards a Justification of the Institution of Legal Punishment*. Amsterdam: Grüner.

Scheid, Don E. 1980. "Note on Defining 'Punishment.'" *Canadian Journal of Philosophy* 10, no. 3 (September): 453–62.

———. 1997. "Constructing a Theory of Punishment, Desert, and the Distribution of Punishments." *Canadian Journal of Law & Jurisprudence* 10, no. 2 (July): 441–506.

Schell-Busey, Natalie, Sally S. Simpson, Melissa Rorie, and Mariel Alper. 2016. "What Works? A Systematic Review of Corporate Crime Deterrence." *Criminology & Public Policy* 15, no. 2 (May): 387–416.

Scheman, Naomi. 1993. "Anger and the Politics of Naming." In *Engenderings: Constructions of Knowledge, Authority, and Privilege*, 22–35. New York: Routledge.

Selke, William L. 1983. "Celerity: The Ignored Variable in Deterrence Research." *Journal of Police Science and Administration* 11, no. 1 (March): 31–37.

Sellin, Thorsten. 1959. *The Death Penalty: A Report for the Model Penal Code Project of the American Law Institute*. Philadelphia: American Law Institute.

———. 1980. *The Penalty of Death*. Beverly Hills, CA: SAGE.

Sen, Amartya. 2000. "Consequentialist Evaluation and Practical Reason." *Journal of Philosophy* 97, no. 9 (September): 477–502.

Sentencing Project. 2018. *Report to the United Nations on Racial Disparities in the U.S. Criminal Justice System*, April 19. https://www.sentencingproject.org/publications/un-report-on-racial-disparities/.

Shafer-Landau, Russ. 1996. "The Failure of Retributivism." *Philosophical Studies* 82, no. 3 (June): 289–316.

Shaffer, Michael. 2019. Interview by Richard Marshall. *3:16*. https://316am.site123.me/articles/how-to-idealize?c=end-times-series.

Shapiro, Carol, and Meryl Schwartz. 2001. "Coming Home: Building on Family Connections." *Corrections Management Quarterly* 5, no. 3 (June): 52–60.

Shearing, Clifford. 2001. "Punishment and the Changing Face of Governance." *Punishment & Society* 3, no. 2 (April): 203–20.

Shepherd, Joanna M. 2002. "Police, Prosecutors, Criminals, and Determinate Sentencing: The Truth about Truth-in-Sentencing Laws." *Journal of Law and Economics* 45, no. 2 (October): 509–33.

———. 2004. "Murders of Passion, Execution Delays, and the Deterrence of Capital Punishment." *Journal of Legal Studies* 33, no. 2 (June): 283–321.

———. 2005. "Deterrence versus Brutalization: Capital Punishment's Differing Impacts among States." *Michigan Law Review* 104, no. 2 (November): 203–55.

Sheppard, Stephen Michael, ed. 2012. *The Wolters Kluwer Bouvier Law Dictionary: Desk Edition*. Vol. 2. Frederick, MD: Wolters Kluwer.

Sherman, Lawrence W. 1997. "Thinking about Crime Prevention." In *Preventing Crime: What Works, What Doesn't, What's Promising: A Report to the United States Congress*, edited by Lawrence W. Sherman, Denise Gottfredson, Doris MacKenzie, John Eck, Peter Reuter, and Shawn Bushway, ch. 2 (pp. 2–1 to 2–32). Washington, DC: U.S. Department of Justice.

Sherman, Lawrence W., and Heather Strang. 2007. *Restorative Justice: The Evidence*. London: Smith Institute. www.iirp.edu/pdf/RJ_full_report.pdf.

Sherman, Lawrence W., Heather Strang, and Daniel J. Woods. 2000. *Recidivism Patterns in the Canberra Reintegrative Shaming Experiment (RISE)*. Centre for Restorative Justice, Research School of Social Sciences, Australian National University. Canberra: Australian National University Press.

Sifferd, Katrina L. 2006. "In Defense of the Use of Commonsense Psychology in the Criminal Law." *Law and Philosophy* 25, no. 6 (November): 571–612.

———. 2018. "Non-Eliminative Reductionism: Not the Theory of Mind Some Responsibility Theorists Want, but the One They Need." In *Neurolaw and Responsibility for Action: Concepts, Crimes, and Courts*, edited by Bebhinn Donnelly-Lazarov, Dennis Patterson, and Peter Raynor, 71–103. Cambridge: Cambridge University Press.

Silberman, Matthew. 1976. "Toward a Theory of Criminal Deterrence." *American Sociological Review* 41, no. 3 (June): 442–61.

Slote, Michael. 1985. *Common-Sense Morality and Consequentialism*. Abingdon, UK: Routledge and Kegan Paul.

Smart, J. J. C. 1956. "Extreme and Restricted Utilitarianism." *Philosophical Quarterly* 6, no. 25 (October): 344–54.

———. 1973. "An Outline of a System of Utilitarian Ethics." In *Utilitarianism: For and Against*, by J. J. C. Smart and Bernard Williams, 1–74. Cambridge: Cambridge University Press.

———. 1991. "Utilitarianism and Punishment." *Israel Law Review* 25, nos. 3–4 (Summer–Autumn): 360–75.

Smilansky, Saul. 1990. "Utilitarianism and the 'Punishment' of the Innocent: The General Problem." *Analysis* 50, no. 4 (October): 256–61.

———. 2011. "Hard Determinism and Punishment: A Practical *Reductio*." *Law and Philosophy* 30, no. 3 (May): 353–67.

Smith, Adam. 1976. *The Theory of Moral Sentiments*. Edited by D. D. Raphael and A. L. Macfie. Oxford: Clarendon.

Smith, Robert J., and Justin D. Levinson. 2012. "The Impact of Implicit Racial Bias on the Exercise of Prosecutorial Discretion." *Seattle University Law Review* 35, no. 3 (Spring): 795–826.

Solomon, Robert C. 1976. *The Passions*. Garden City, NY: Anchor.

———. 2003. *Not Passion's Slave: Emotions and Choice*. Oxford: Oxford University Press.

Sophocles. 1984. *Antigone*. In *The Three Theban Plays: Antigone, Oedipus the King, Oedipus at Colonus*, translated by Robert Fagles, 55–128. New York: Penguin.

Sprigge, T. L. S. 2015. "A Utilitarian Reply to Dr. McCloskey." In *Philosophical Perspectives on Punishment*, 2nd ed., edited by Gertrude Ezorsky, 68–81. Albany: State University of New York Press.

Stephen, James Fitzjames. 1883. *A History of the Criminal Law of England*. 2 vols. London: Macmillan.

———. 1967. *Liberty, Equality, Fraternity*. Edited by R. J. White. Cambridge: Cambridge University Press.

———. 2014. *A General View of the Criminal Law of England*. Cambridge: Cambridge University Press.

Stephen, Leslie. 1895. *The Life of Sir James Fitzjames Stephen*. New York: G. P. Putnam's Sons.

Steurer, Stephen J., and Linda G. Smith. 2003. *Education Reduces Crime, Three-State Recidivism Study – Executive Summary*, February. Lanham, MD and Centerville, UT: Correctional Education Association and Management & Training Corporation. https://www.mtctrains.com/wp-content/uploads/2017/06/Education-Reduced-Crime-Three-State-Recidivism-Study.pdf.

St. John, Paige. 2016. "A Revealing Look at California's Death Row." *Los Angeles Times*, January 5. https://www.latimes.com/local/lanow/la-me-ln-death-row-html-20160104-htmlstory.html.

Stolzenberg, Lisa, and Stewart J. D'Alessio. 2004. "Capital Punishment, Execution Publicity and Murder in Houston, Texas." *Journal of Criminal Law and Criminology* 94, no. 2 (Winter): 351–80.

Strang, Heather. 2001. "Justice for Victims of Young Offenders: The Centrality of Emotional Harm and Restoration." In *Restoring Justice for Juveniles: Conference, Mediation and Circles*, edited by Allison Morris and Gabrielle Maxwell, 183–94. Oxford: Hart.

Strang, Heather, and Lawrence W. Sherman. 2003. "Repairing the Harm: Victims and Restorative Justice." *Utah Law Review* 2003, no. 1: 15–42.

Strawson, P. F. 2008. "Freedom and Resentment." In *Freedom and Resentment and Other Essays*, 1–28. Abingdon, UK: Routledge.

Su, Alice, and Ryan Kilpatrick. 2019. "'No National Day, Only National Grief': Police Chief Defends Officer's Close-Range Shooting of Hong Kong Protester." *Los Angeles Times*, October 1. https://www.latimes.com/world-nation/story/2019-09-28/hong-kong-protesters-reject-chinese-nationalism-china-national-day.

Substance Abuse and Mental Health Services Administration. 2017. *Key Substance Use and Mental Health Indicators in the United States: Results from the 2016 National Survey on Drug Use and Health*, September. Rockville, MD: Center for Behavioral Health Statistics and Quality, Substance Abuse and Mental Health Services Administration. https://www.samhsa.gov/data/sites/default/files/NSDUH-FFR1-2016/NSDUH-FFR1-2016.pdf.

Sullivan, Dennis, and Larry Tifft, eds. 2008. *Handbook of Restorative Justice: A Global Perspective*. Abingdon, UK: Routledge.
Sunstein, Cass R., and Adrian Vermeule. 2005. "Is Capital Punishment Morally Required? Acts, Omissions, and Life-Life Tradeoffs." *Stanford Law Review* 58, no. 3 (December): 703–50.
Taibbi, Matt. 2013. "Cruel and Unusual Punishment: The Shame of Three Strikes Laws." *Rolling Stone*, March 27. https://www.rollingstone.com/politics/politics-news/cruel-and-unusual-punishment-the-shame-of-three-strikes-laws-92042/.
Tasioulas, John. 2006. "Punishment and Repentance." *Philosophy* 81, no. 2 (April): 279–322.
Taylor, Ralph B. 1996. "Neighborhood Responses to Disorder and Local Attachments: The Systemic Model of Attachment, Social Disorganization, and Neighborhood Use Value." *Sociological Forum* 11, no. 1 (March): 41–74.
———. 1999. *Crime, Grime, Fear, and Decline: A Longitudinal Look*, July. Washington, DC: U.S. Department of Justice, National Institute of Justice. https://www.ncjrs.gov/pdffiles1/177603.pdf.
Taylor, Ralph B., and Jeanette Covington. 1988. "Neighborhood Changes in Ecology and Violence." *Criminology* 26, no. 4 (November): 553–90.
Ten, C. L. 1987. *Crime, Guilt, and Punishment: A Philosophical Introduction*. Oxford: Clarendon.
Thaxton, Sherod. 2013. "Leveraging Death." *Journal of Criminal Law and Criminology* 103, no. 2 (Spring): 475–552.
Thompson, Karl R. 2014. "The Department of Homeland Security's Authority to Prioritize Removal of Certain Aliens Unlawfully Present in the United States and to Defer Removal of Others," November 19. https://www.courtlistener.com/opinion/4342045/the-department-of-homeland-securitys-authority-to-prioritize-removal-of/.
Thomson, Judith Jarvis. 1985. "The Trolley Problem." *Yale Law Journal* 94, no. 6 (May): 1395–1415.
Tittle, Charles R. 1969. "Crime Rates and Legal Sanctions." *Social Problems* 16, no. 4 (Spring): 409–23.
Tittle, Charles R., and Alan R. Rowe. 1974. "Certainty of Arrest and Crime Rates: A Further Test of the Deterrence Hypothesis." *Social Forces* 52, no. 4 (June): 455–62.
Tonry, Michael H. 1996. *Sentencing Matters*. New York: Oxford University Press.
Tonry, Michael H., and Norval Morris. 1978. "Sentencing Reform in America." In *Reshaping the Criminal Law: Essays in Honour of Glanville Williams*, edited by P. R. Glazebrook, 434–48. London: Stevens & Sons.
Transform Drug Policy Foundation. 2018. "Drug Decriminalisation in Portugal: Setting the Record Straight," November 14. https://transformdrugs.org/drug-decriminalisation-in-portugal-setting-the-record-straight/.
Tso, Tom. 2005. "The Process of Decision Making in Tribal Courts: A Navajo Jurist's Perspective." In *Navajo Nation Peacemaking: Living Traditional Justice*, edited by Marianne O. Nielsen and James W. Zion, 29–41. Tucson: University of Arizona Press.
Tunick, Mark. 2016. "Should We Aim for a Unified and Coherent Theory of Punishment?" Review of *Punishment*, by Thom Brooks. *Criminal Law and Philosophy* 10, no. 3 (September): 611–28.

Tyler, Tom R. 1990. *Why People Obey the Law*. New Haven, CT: Yale University Press.

UCLA School of Law, Juvenile Justice Project. 2010. *The Impact of Prosecuting Youth in the Criminal Justice System: A Review of the Literature*, July. www.antoniocasella.eu/restorative/UCLA_july2010.pdf.

Ulmer, Jeffery T., Megan C. Kurlychek, and John H. Kramer. 2007. "Prosecutorial Discretion and the Imposition of Mandatory Minimum Sentences." *Journal of Research in Crime and Delinquency* 44, no. 4 (November): 427–58.

Umbreit, Mark S. 1989. "Crime Victims Seeking Fairness, Not Revenge: Toward Restorative Justice." *Federal Probation* 53, no. 3 (September): 52–57.

Umbreit, Mark S., William Bradshaw, and Robert B. Coates. 1999. "Victims of Severe Violence Meet the Offender: Restorative Justice through Dialogue." *International Review of Victimology* 6, no. 4 (September): 321–43.

Umbreit, Mark S., and Robert B. Coates. 1993. "Cross-Site Analysis of Victim-Offender Mediation in Four States." *Crime & Delinquency* 39, no. 4 (October): 565–85.

Umbreit, Mark S., Robert B. Coates, and Boris Kalanj. 1994. *When Victim Meets Offender: The Impact of Restorative Justice and Mediation*. Monsey, NY: Criminal Justice Press.

Umbreit, Mark S., Robert B. Coates, and Betty Vos. 2002. "The Impact of Restorative Justice Conferencing: A Review of 63 Empirical Studies in 5 Countries," May 1. Center for Restorative Justice and Peacemaking, University of Minnesota. https://www.prisonlegalnews.org/media/publications/crjp_impact_restorative_justice_conferencing_63_studies_may_2002.pdf.

Umbreit, Mark S., and Jean Greenwood. 2000. *National Survey of Victim-Offender Mediation Programs in the United States*, April. Washington, DC: Office for Victims of Crime. https://www.ncjrs.gov/ovc_archives/reports/restorative_justice/restorative_justice_ascii_pdf/ncj176350.pdf.

United Health Foundation. 2020. *America's Health Rankings Annual Report*. https://www.americashealthrankings.org/explore/annual/measure/Crime/state/TX and https://www.americashealthrankings.org/explore/annual/measure/Crime/state/ME.

United Nations Office on Drugs and Crime. 2006. *Handbook on Restorative Justice Programmes*. New York: United Nations. https://www.unodc.org/pdf/criminal_justice/Handbook_on_Restorative_Justice_Programmes.pdf.

United States Department of Justice. 2013. "Smart on Crime: Reforming the Criminal Justice System for the 21st Century," August. https://www.justice.gov/sites/default/files/ag/legacy/2013/08/12/smart-on-crime.pdf.

———. 2017. "Prison Reform: Reducing Recidivism by Strengthening the Federal Bureau of Prisons," March 6. https://www.justice.gov/archives/prison-reform#_ftn2.

United States Sentencing Commission. 2014. *Recidivism among Offenders Receiving Retroactive Sentence Reductions: The 2007 Crack Cocaine Amendment*, May. https://www.ussc.gov/sites/default/files/pdf/research-and-publications/research-projects-and-surveys/miscellaneous/20140527_Recidivism_2007_Crack_Cocaine_Amendment.pdf.

Vagins, Deborah J., and Jesselyn McCurdy. 2006. *Cracks in the System: Twenty Years of the Unjust Federal Crack Cocaine Law*. Washington, DC: ACLU.

van den Haag, Ernest. 1969. "On Deterrence and the Death Penalty." *Journal of Criminal Law, Criminology, and Police Science* 60, no. 2 (June): 141–47.

———. 1975. *Punishing Criminals: Concerning a Very Old and Painful Question.* New York: Basic Books.

———. 1981. "Punishment as a Device for Controlling the Crime Rate." *Rutgers Law Review* 33, no. 3 (Spring): 706–20.

———. 1982. "The Criminal Law as a Threat System." *Journal of Criminal Law and Criminology* 73, no. 2 (Summer): 769–85.

———. 1983. "The Retributivist's Case against Capital Punishment." In *The Death Penalty: A Debate*, by Ernest van den Haag and John P. Conrad, 17–52. New York: Plenum.

———. 1985a. "The Death Penalty Once More." *UC Davis Law Review* 18, no. 4 (Summer): 957–72.

———. 1985b. "Refuting Reiman and Nathanson." *Philosophy & Public Affairs* 14, no. 2 (Spring): 165–76.

———. 1986. "The Ultimate Punishment: A Defense." *Harvard Law Review* 99, no. 7 (May): 1662–69.

Van Ness, Daniel W. 1993. "New Wine and Old Wineskins: Four Challenges of Restorative Justice." *Criminal Law Forum* 4, no. 2 (June): 251–76.

Van Ness, Daniel W., and Karen Heetderks Strong. 2015. *Restoring Justice: An Introduction to Restorative Justice.* 5th ed. Abingdon, UK: Routledge.

Vitiello, Michael. 1997. "Three Strikes: Can We Return to Rationality?" *Journal of Criminal Law and Criminology* 87, no. 2 (Winter): 395–481.

von Hirsch, Andrew. 1976. *Doing Justice: The Choice of Punishments.* New York: Hill & Wang.

———. 1985. *Past or Future Crimes: Deservedness and Dangerousness in the Sentencing of Criminals.* New Brunswick, NJ: Rutgers University Press.

———. 1993. *Censure and Sanctions.* Oxford: Oxford University Press.

———. 1998. "Proportionate Sentences: A Desert Perspective." In *Principled Sentencing: Readings on Theory and Policy*, 2nd ed., edited by Andrew von Hirsch and Andrew Ashworth, 168–79. Oxford: Hart.

von Hirsch, Andrew, and Andrew Ashworth. 2005. *Proportionate Sentencing: Exploring the Principles.* Oxford: Oxford University Press.

von Hirsch, Andrew, Anthony E. Bottoms, Elizabeth Burney, and P.-O. Wikström. 1999. *Criminal Deterrence and Sentencing Severity.* Oxford: Hart.

Vorenberg, James. 1976. "Narrowing the Discretion of Criminal Justice Officials." *Duke Law Journal* 1976, no. 4 (September): 651–97.

———. 1981. "Decent Restraint of Prosecutorial Power." *Harvard Law Review* 94, no. 7 (May): 1521–73.

Walgrave, Lode. 2008. *Restorative Justice, Self-Interest and Responsible Citizenship.* Abingdon, UK: Routledge.

Walker, Nigel. 1991. *Why Punish?* Oxford: Oxford University Press.

———. 1999. "Even More Varieties of Retribution." *Philosophy* 74, no. 4 (October): 595–605.

Waller, Bruce N. 2018. *The Injustice of Punishment.* New York: Routledge.

———. 2019. "Beyond the Retributive System." In *Free Will Skepticism in Law and Society: Challenging Retributive Justice*, edited by Elizabeth Shaw, Derk Pereboom, and Gregg D. Caruso, 73–95. Cambridge: Cambridge University Press.

Washington State Department of Corrections. 2018. *Swift and Certain Sanctioning: 2018 Report to the Legislature*, January. https://app.leg.wa.gov/ReportsToThe Legislature/Home/GetPDF?fileName=2018%20SAC%20Report%20%28002%29_49eb2d39-061a-4230-b55f-40c7f2cdef85.pdf.

Watson, Gary. 1987. "Responsibility and the Limits of Evil: Variations on a Strawsonian Theme." In *Responsibility, Character, and the Emotions: New Essays in Moral Psychology*, edited by Ferdinand Schoeman, 256–86. Cambridge: Cambridge University Press.

Weitekamp, Elmar G. M. 1999. "The History of Restorative Justice." In *Restorative Juvenile Justice: Repairing the Harm of Youth Crime*, edited by Gordon Bazemore and Lode Walgrave, 75–102. Monsey, NY: Criminal Justice.

Whately, Richard. 1832. *Thoughts on Secondary Punishments, in a Letter to Earl Grey*. London: Fellowes.

Wilcox, Pamela, and Francis T. Cullen. 2018. "Community Members and Deterrence." In *Deterrence, Choice, and Crime: Contemporary Perspectives*, vol. 23 of *Advances in Criminological Theory*, edited by Daniel S. Nagin, Francis T. Cullen, and Cheryl Lero Jonson, 339–62. New York: Routledge.

Wildeman, Christopher. 2010. "Paternal Incarceration and Children's Physically Aggressive Behaviors: Evidence from the Fragile Families and Child Wellbeing Study." *Social Forces* 89, no. 1 (September): 285–309.

Wilks, Judith, and Robert Martinson. 1976. "Is the Treatment of Criminal Offenders Really Necessary?" *Federal Probation* 40, no. 1 (March): 3–9.

Williams, Glanville. 1961. *Criminal Law: The General Part*. 2nd ed. London: Stevens & Sons.

Williams, Kirk R., and Richard Hawkins. 1986. "Perceptual Research on General Deterrence: A Critical Review." *Law and Society Review* 20, no. 4: 545–72.

"Willie Smith Ward, Texas Man, Gets 50 Years in Prison for Stealing Rack of Ribs." 2013. *CBS News*, June 2. https://www.cbsnews.com/news/willie-smith-ward-texas-man-gets-50-years-in-prison-for-stealing-rack-of-ribs/.

Wilson, David B., Catherine A. Gallagher, and Doris L. MacKenzie. 2000. "A Meta-Analysis of Corrections-Based Education, Vocation, and Work Programs for Adult Offenders." *Journal of Research in Crime and Delinquency* 37, no. 4 (November): 347–68.

Wilson, David B., Ajima Olaghere, and Catherine S. Kimbrell. 2017. *Effectiveness of Restorative Justice Principles in Juvenile Justice: A Meta-Analysis*, May 12. Washington, DC: U.S. Department of Justice, Office of Justice Programs, Office of Juvenile Justice and Delinquency Prevention. https://www.ncjrs.gov/pdffiles1/ojjdp/grants/250872.pdf.

Wilson, James Q. 1983. *Thinking about Crime*. Rev. ed. New York: Basic.

Wood, David. 2002. "Retribution, Crime Reduction and the Justification of Punishment." *Oxford Journal of Legal Studies* 22, no. 2 (Summer): 301–21.

Wood, Jennifer D., Amy C. Watson, and Anjali J. Fulambarker. 2017. "The 'Gray Zone' of Police Work during Mental Health Encounters: Findings from an Observational Study in Chicago." *Police Quarterly* 20, no. 1 (March): 81–105.

Woodworth, Michael, and Stephen Porter. 2002. "In Cold Blood: Characteristics of Criminal Homicides as a Function of Psychopathy." *Journal of Abnormal Psychology* 111, no. 3 (August): 436–45.

Wright, Bradley R. E., Avshalom Caspi, Terrie E. Moffitt, and Ray Paternoster. 2004. "Does the Perceived Risk of Punishment Deter Criminally Prone Individuals?

Rational Choice, Self-Control and Crime." *Journal of Research in Crime and Delinquency* 41, no. 2 (May): 180–213.
Wright, Martin. 1996. *Justice for Victims and Offenders: A Restorative Response to Crime*. 2nd ed. Winchester, UK: Waterside.
Wringe, Bill. 2016. *An Expressive Theory of Punishment*. London: Palgrave Macmillan.
Yang, Bijou, and David Lester. 2008. "The Deterrent Effect of Executions: A Meta-Analysis Thirty Years after Ehrlich." *Journal of Criminal Justice* 36, no. 5 (September-October): 453–60.
Yankah, Ekow. 2004. "Good Guys and Bad Guys: Punishing Character, Equality and the Irrelevance of Moral Character to Criminal Punishment." *Cardozo Law Review* 25, no. 3 (February): 1019–67.
Zaibert, Leo. 2006. *Punishment and Retribution*. Aldershot, UK: Ashgate.
Zedner, Lucia. 1994. "Reparation and Retribution: Are They Reconcilable?" *Modern Law Review* 57, no. 2 (March): 228–50.
Zehr, Howard. 2015a. *Changing Lenses: Restorative Justice for Our Times*. Harrisonburg, VA: Herald.
———. 2015b. *The Little Book of Restorative Justice*. Rev. ed. New York: Good Books.
Zettler, Haley R., Robert G. Morris, Alex R. Piquero, and Stephanie M. Cardwell. 2015. "Assessing the Celerity of Arrest on 3-Year Recidivism Patterns in a Sample of Criminal Defendants." *Journal of Criminal Justice* 43, no. 5 (September–October): 428–36.
Zimmerman, Paul R. 2004. "State Executions, Deterrence, and the Incidence of Murder." *Journal of Applied Economics* 7, no. 1 (May): 163–93.
———. 2006. "Estimates of the Deterrent Effect of Alternative Execution Methods in the United States: 1978–2000." *American Journal of Economics and Sociology* 65, no. 4 (October): 909–41.
———. 2009. "Statistical Variability and the Deterrent Effect of the Death Penalty." *American Law and Economics Review* 11, no. 2 (Fall): 370–98.
Zimring, Franklin E., Jeffrey Fagan, and David T. Johnson. 2010. "Executions, Deterrence, and Homicide: A Tale of Two Cities." *Journal of Empirical Legal Studies* 7, no. 1 (March): 1–29.
Zimring, Franklin E., and Gordon J. Hawkins. 1968. "Deterrence and Marginal Groups." *Journal of Research in Crime and Delinquency* 5, no. 2 (July): 100–114.
———. 1973. *Deterrence: The Legal Threat in Crime Control*. Chicago: University of Chicago Press.
Zimring, Franklin E., Gordon Hawkins, and Sam Kamin. 2001. *Punishment and Democracy: Three Strikes and You're Out in California*. Oxford: Oxford University Press.

Index

www.ingramcontent.com/pod-product-compliance
Lightning Source LLC
LaVergne TN
LVHW011115300926
849160LV00008B/395
9780367698164